Information, Accountability, and Cumulative Learning

Throughout the world, voters lack access to information about politicians, government performance, and public services. Efforts to remedy these informational deficits are numerous. Yet do informational campaigns influence voter behavior and increase democratic accountability? Through the first project of the Metaketa Initiative, sponsored by the Evidence in Governance and Politics (EGAP) research network, this book aims to address this substantive question and at the same time introduce a new model for cumulative learning that increases coordination among otherwise independent researcher teams. It presents the overall results (using meta-analysis) from six independently conducted but coordinated field experimental studies, the results from each individual study, and the findings from a related evaluation of whether practitioners utilize this information as expected. It also discusses lessons learned from EGAP's efforts to coordinate field experiments, increase replication of theoretically important studies across contexts, and increase the external validity of field experimental research.

Thad Dunning is Robson Professor of Political Science at the University of California, Berkeley.

Guy Grossman is Associate Professor of Political Science at the University of Pennsylvania.

Macartan Humphreys is Professor of Political Science at Columbia University and a director of the research group "Institutions and Political Inequality" at the WZB, Berlin.

Susan D. Hyde is Professor of Political Science at the University of California, Berkeley.

Craig McIntosh is Professor of Economics at the School of Global Policy and Strategy, University of California, San Diego.

Gareth Nellis is Assistant Professor of Political Science at the University of California, San Diego.

Advance praise: "This is a path-breaking book on multiple levels. It makes a major contribution to our understanding of how ineffective it is to provide voters [with] information and expect improvements in political accountability to result. It also offers a new way to undertake social scientific research that promises greater generalizability of results. Overall, this is one of the most important instances of a multi-project collaborative research initiative in the social sciences to have been conducted in decades."

Miriam Golden, University of California, Los Angeles

Advance praise: "This book offers more than a multisite investigation of governance problems in the developing world. It represents a new model of research collaboration and transparency. Many social scientists adduce evidence selectively in an effort to tell an intriguing theoretical story. The authors of this book put spin aside and guide us through the entire process from theoretical inspiration to site selection to data collection. Their analysis of six parallel experiments is guided by plans set out before the results became known, which makes the findings especially convincing. This book will be remembered not simply as a piece of outstanding original scholarship but as a milestone in the credibility revolution that is unfolding in the social sciences."

Donald P. Green, Burgess Professor of Political Science,
Columbia University, New York

Advance praise: "The Metaketa Initiative represents some of the best of what social science has to offer: rigorous research informed by deep contextual knowledge, focused on urgent questions about how democratic institutions work – and could work better. By employing the highest standards of research transparency and coordinating research across countries, researchers participating in the Metaketa Initiative also directly confronted core methodologic challenges in ways that break new ground. This book is a tremendous contribution to our common search for new and meaningful knowledge in the field of global development and governance."

Ruth Levine, Director, Global Development and
Population Program, The William and Flora Hewlett Foundation

Advance praise: "By coordinating multiple research teams working globally around a much-debated issue, the Metaketa project proves that the old internal validity versus external validity debate presents a false choice – and teaches us important lessons along the way. This ambitious book sets a new standard for research rigor, and in my view it belongs on the shelf of every social scientist."

Edward Andrew Miguel, Oxfam Professor in Environmental and Resource Economics, Department of Economics, and Faculty Director of the Center for Effective Global Action (CEGA), University of California, Berkeley

Advance praise: "This pathbreaking and hugely important book presents and, in a series of illuminating empirical chapters, applies a new method for organizing field experimental research to increase the likelihood of knowledge accumulation from multiple studies. In doing so, it offers the most thoughtful and effective response to date to the challenge of cumulative learning in the field-based social sciences."

Daniel N. Posner, James S. Coleman Professor of International Development, University of California, Los Angeles

Advance praise: "Though social science aspires to the production of generalizable insights, all of the incentives drive scholars toward project differentiation rather than knowledge cumulation. In this important book, Dunning and coauthors illuminate a different path. They introduce a major methodological innovation, the Metaketa, and apply it to one of the oldest questions in political science: the relationship between transparency and accountability. The book demonstrates powerfully how creativity and cumulation can coexist, and offers essential insights into how we can learn best from carefully designed research conducted across different contexts. A must-read for social scientists!"

Jeremy Weinstein, Senior Fellow at the Freeman Spogli Institute for International Studies, and Professor of Political Science, Stanford University

Cambridge Studies in Comparative Politics

General Editors

Kathleen Thelen *Massachusetts Institute of Technology*
Erik Wibbels *Duke University*

Associate Editors

Catherine Boone *London School of Economics*
Thad Dunning *University of California, Berkeley*
Anna Grzymala-Busse *Stanford University*
Torben Iversen *Harvard University*
Stathis Kalyvas *Yale University*
Margaret Levi *Stanford University*
Helen Milner *Princeton University*
Frances Rosenbluth *Yale University*
Susan Stokes *Yale University*
Tariq Thachil *Vanderbilt University*

Series Founder

Peter Lange *Duke University*

Other Books in the Series

Continued after the Index

Information, Accountability, and Cumulative Learning

Lessons from Metaketa I

Edited by

THAD DUNNING
University of California, Berkeley

GUY GROSSMAN
University of Pennsylvania

MACARTAN HUMPHREYS
Columbia University, New York and WZB, Berlin

SUSAN D. HYDE
University of California, Berkeley

CRAIG MCINTOSH
University of California, San Diego

GARETH NELLIS
University of California, San Diego

CAMBRIDGE
UNIVERSITY PRESS

CAMBRIDGE
UNIVERSITY PRESS

University Printing House, Cambridge CB2 8BS, United Kingdom

One Liberty Plaza, 20th Floor, New York, NY 10006, USA

477 Williamstown Road, Port Melbourne, VIC 3207, Australia

314–321, 3rd Floor, Plot 3, Splendor Forum, Jasola District Centre,
New Delhi – 110025, India

79 Anson Road, #06–04/06, Singapore 079906

Cambridge University Press is part of the University of Cambridge.

It furthers the University's mission by disseminating knowledge in the pursuit of
education, learning, and research at the highest international levels of excellence.

www.cambridge.org
Information on this title: www.cambridge.org/9781108422284
DOI: 10.1017/9781108381390

© Cambridge University Press 2019

First published 2019

Printed in the United Kingdom by TJ International Ltd. Padstow Cornwall

A catalogue record for this publication is available from the British Library.

Library of Congress Cataloging-in-Publication Data
NAMES: Dunning, Thad, 1973– author.
TITLE: Information, accountability, and cumulative learning : lessons from
Metaketa I / edited by Thad Dunning, Guy Grossman, Macartan Humphreys,
Susan Hyde, Craig McIntosh, Gareth Nellis.
DESCRIPTION: Cambridge, United Kingdom ; New York, NY : Cambridge University
Press, 2019. | Series: Cambridge studies in comparative politics |
Includes bibliographical references and index.
IDENTIFIERS: LCCN 2019007308 | ISBN 9781108422284 (hardback)
SUBJECTS: LCSH: Government accountability – Developing countries. | Government
information – Developing countries. | Voting research – Developing
countries. | Developing countries – Politics and government – Research. |
BISAC: POLITICAL SCIENCE / General.
CLASSIFICATION: LCC JF60.I54 2019 | DDC 352.3/8091724–dc23
LC record available at https://lccn.loc.gov/2019007308

ISBN 978-1-108-42228-4 Hardback
ISBN 978-1-108-43504-8 Paperback

Contents

vii

IV   CONCLUSION

A further Online Appendix can be accessed at
http://cambridge.org/9781108422284.

Figures

Tables

Contributors

Claire Adida is an associate professor in the Department of Political Science at the University of California, San Diego. She uses quantitative methods to research how countries deal with existing and new forms of diversity. She is the author of two books, *Immigrant Exclusion and Insecurity in Africa* (Cambridge University Press, 2014) and *Why Muslim Integration Fails in Christian-Heritage Societies* (2016, coauthored with David Laitin and Marie-Anne Valfort). Her work is also published in leading political science and economics journals. Her research is supported by the Bill & Melinda Gates Foundation, the National Science Foundation, the Evidence in Governance and Politics Group, and the Hellman Foundation among others.

Eric Arias is an assistant professor in the Government Department at William & Mary. He received his PhD in Politics from New York University in 2017 and was a postdoctoral research fellow at the Niehaus Center for Globalization and Governance at Princeton University. His research combines experimental and observational methods to explore how international capital flows affect development and political accountability, and the role of information in these dynamics. His research has been published or is forthcoming in *American Political Science Review*, *American Journal of Political Science*, and *Journal of Politics*, among others.

Clara Bicalho is a predoctoral research fellow in the Institutions and Political Inequality unit at the WZB Berlin Social Science Center. She received a BA in political science from New York University Abu Dhabi and subsequently joined the NYU Center for Technology and Economic Development as a research assistant. Her recent work focuses on migrant integration and political accountability with an emphasis on experimental methods.

Taylor Boas is an associate professor of political science and Latin American studies at Boston University. His research examines electoral politics and political behavior in Latin America, focusing on topics such as accountability, campaigns, religion, and the mass media. He is the author of *Presidential Campaigns in Latin America: Electoral Strategies and Success Contagion* (Cambridge University Press, 2016) and coauthor of *Open Networks, Closed Regimes: The Impact of the Internet on Authoritarian Rule* (2003). He has published articles in the *American Journal of Political Science*, *Journal of Politics*, and *World Politics*, among other outlets.

Mark Buntaine is an assistant professor at the University of California, Santa Barbara. His research investigates governance and environmental management in developing countries. His book, *Giving Aid Effectively* (2016), received the Don K. Price award for the best book on science, technology, and environmental politics. He has led several field experiments that investigate whether citizen-sourced data improves the governance of urban public services, how transparency encourages citizens to seek accountability from governments, how national-level rating programs affect the actions of local governments, and how citizen monitoring of the environment affects the actions of local governments in authoritarian contexts.

Sarah Bush is an assistant professor of political science at Yale University. Bush obtained a BA with honors from Northwestern University in 2005 and a PhD in politics from Princeton University in 2011. Prior to her arrival at Yale, Bush taught at Temple University and was a research fellow at the Belfer Center for Science and International Affairs at the Harvard Kennedy School. Bush's research examines how international actors try to aid democracy, promote women's representation, and support elections in developing countries. She is the author of a recent book on this topic, *The Taming of Democracy Assistance* (Cambridge University Press, 2015).

Simon Chauchard is a lecturer in discipline in comparative politics at the School of Public and International Affairs, Columbia University. Recent works have appeared in *Political Opinion Quarterly*, the *American Political Science Review*, *Comparative Political Studies* and *Asian Survey*. His book, entitled *Why Representation Matters: The Meaning of*

Ethnic Quotas in Rural India (Cambridge University Press), combines qualitative work and a series of audio surveys to explore the impact of caste-based reservation policies on everyday intergroup relations in India's villages.

Anirvan Chowdhury is a PhD candidate in the Department of Political Science at the University of California, Berkeley and a research associate at the Center on the Politics of Development. His research interests lie in comparative politics, the political economy of development, and gender. He has worked with the International Food Policy Research Institute and the World Bank in Washington DC, USA, and the Centre for Policy Research in New Delhi, India. He has studied public policy and economics at Georgetown University, the Madras School of Economics, and the University of Delhi.

Thad Dunning is the Robson Professor of Political Science at the University of California, Berkeley and directs the Center on the Politics of Development. He is the author of *Crude Democracy: Natural Resource Wealth and Political Regimes* (Cambridge University Press, 2008), which received the Best Book Award from APSA's Comparative Democratization section, and *Natural Experiments in the Social Sciences: A Design-Based Approach* (Cambridge University Press, 2012), which won the Best Book Award of APSA's Experimental Research section. He coauthored *Brokers, Voters, and Clientelism: The Puzzle of Distributive Politics* (Cambridge University Press, 2013), which was awarded the Best Book Award from APSA's Comparative Democratization section and the Luebbert Prize from APSA's Comparative Politics section.

Jessica Gottlieb is an assistant professor at Texas A&M University's policy school. She holds a PhD in political science and an MA in economics from Stanford University. Gottlieb studies democratic accountability in poor countries using field experiments, behavioral games and surveys. Her field work has taken her to Mali, Senegal, Benin, and Liberia. Some of Gottlieb's work has been published in the *American Journal of Political Science*, *World Politics*, and *World Development*, and has been funded by the National Science Foundation, the International Growth Centre, and EGAP's Metaketa program, among others. She is a proud member of EGAP and WGAPE.

Guy Grossman is an associate professor of political science at the University of Pennsylvania. His research interests fall under the broad category of political economy of development, with a regional focus on

Sub-Saharan Africa and Israel–Palestine. In his work, he uses a host of causal inference tools as well as text and social network analysis to address substantive questions regarding political behavior, economic development, and conflict processes. His work has appeared in the *American Political Science Review*, *American Journal of Political Science*, and *Journal of Politics*, among other journals.

F. Daniel Hidalgo is the Cecil and Ida Green Associate Professor of Political Science at the Massachusetts Institute of Technology. He received his doctorate in political science at the University of California, Berkeley and received a BA at Princeton University. Hidalgo is a past recipient of grants from the National Science Foundation, the Fulbright program, and the Experiments in Governance and Politics Network. His research focuses on the political economy of elections, campaigns, and representation in developing democracies, especially in Latin America, as well as quantitative methods in the social sciences. His work has appeared in journals such as the *Journal of Politics*, *Comparative Political Studies*, the *Review of Economic and Statistics*, and the *American Journal of Political Science*.

Marcus Holmlund in an economist in the Development Impact Evaluation (DIME) unit of the World Bank's Research Group. He works in diverse fields including crime and violence prevention, forced displacement, and local governance with a focus on at-risk and under-served populations. Marcus specializes in evidence-based program and policy design and experimentation, and has led large-scale randomized controlled trials in collaboration with governments in several countries including Burkina Faso, Honduras, Jordan, Nigeria, and Senegal. He is currently co-leading a global research initiative on fragility, conflict, and violence and a program on experimental research on local governance in Burkina Faso.

Macartan Humphreys is a professor of political science at Columbia University and a director of the research group "Institutions and Political Inequality" at the WZB, Berlin Social Science Center. He works on the political economy of development and formal political theory. His research focuses on post-conflict development, ethnic politics, democratic development, and political inequality with a current focus on the use of field experiments to study democratic decision-making in post-conflict and developing areas. Macartan's recent work has appeared in the *American Political Science Review*, *World Politics*, and the *Economic Journal*, among other journals. He has written or coauthored books on ethnic politics, natural resource management, and game theory and politics.

Susan D. Hyde is a professor of political science at the University of California, Berkeley. She studies international influences on domestic politics, with a focus on the developing world. She is an expert on international election observation, election fraud, and democracy promotion. Her book, *The Pseudo-Democrat's Dilemma: Why Election Observation Became an International Norm*, won the International Studies Association's 2012 Chadwick Alger Prize for the best book on international organizations and multilateralism, APSA's 2012 Comparative Democratization section best book award, and the 2012 Gustav Ranis International Book Prize for the best book on an international topic by a member of the Yale ladder faculty. Her articles have appeared in the *American Journal of Political Science* and *Comparative Political Studies*, among others.

Ryan Jablonski is an assistant professor of political science at the London School of Economics and Political Science. His research focuses on the politics of development spending, electoral manipulation, and maritime piracy, particularly in Sub-Saharan Africa. His published research appears in *World Politics*, *International Studies Quarterly*, *Journal of Conflict Resolution*, *British Journal of Political Science*, and *World Development*. Dr. Jablonski received his PhD and MA in political science from the University of California, San Diego.

Eric Kramon is an assistant professor of political science and international affairs at George Washington University. His research on clientelism, elections, and distributive politics has been published by Cambridge University Press, the *British Journal of Political Science*, the *Quarterly Journal of Political Science*, *World Politics*, and other journals, and has been supported by the National Science Foundation, the International Growth Centre, Evidence in Governance and Politics (EGAP), and the UK Department for International Development. Kramon received his PhD in political science from UCLA in 2013, and was a pre- and postdoctoral fellow at the Center on Democracy, Development, and the Rule at Stanford University.

Horacio Larreguy is an associate professor of government at Harvard University. He works on clientelism and vote buying, the importance of information for political accountability, and where education fosters political participation. His work is mostly in Latin America and Sub-Saharan Africa and his methodological focus on causal identification using both observational and experimental data. He has conducted large-scale experiments in Liberia, Mexico, Senegal, and Uganda. Horacio has published work in leading economics and political science journals.

Malte Lierl is a research fellow at the German Institute for Global and Area Studies (GIGA). He is a behavioral political economist working on governance issues in developing countries. Lierl investigates how the behavior of public decision-makers depends on the social context in which they operate. For example, are local politicians less willing to embezzle public funds if doing so can affect their social reputations? How do formal institutions, such as democratic elections, affect the social norms and expectations by which citizens evaluate public decision-makers? To shed light on these questions, he has conducted a wide range of experimental studies, from behavioral research in the laboratory and in the field to large-scale policy experiments.

John Marshall is an assistant professor of political science at Columbia University. He studies how news consumption, levels of education, and social networks influence how voters hold politicians to account. Beyond bottom-up voter behavior, he also studies how politicians communicate their platforms, how information shapes campaign strategies, and when media outlets choose to report political news. Among other outlets, his research spanning developing and developed contexts has been published in the *American Journal of Political Science, American Political Science Review, Journal of the European Economic Association, Journal of Politics*, and *Review of Economics and Statistics*. He was a corecipient of the 2015 Kellogg/Notre Dame Award for Best Paper in Comparative Politics at Midwest Political Science Association.

Gwyneth McClendon is an assistant professor in the Department of Politics at New York University. Her research focuses on religious and ethnic politics and political psychology in Sub-Saharan Africa and the United States. She is the author of *Envy in Politics* (2018). She has also published articles in the *American Journal of Political Science*, the *Journal of Politics*, the *Quarterly Journal of Political Science*, *Comparative Political Studies*, the *Journal of Experimental Political Science*, *Public Opinion Quarterly*, and *African Affairs*. Her second book examines the influence of religious ideas on political participation in Africa.

Craig McIntosh is a professor of economics at the School of Global Policy and Strategy at the University of California, San Diego. He is a development economist whose work focuses on program evaluation.

His main research interest is the design of institutions that promote the provision of financial services to micro-entrepreneurs, and he has conducted field evaluations of innovative antipoverty policies in Mexico, Guatemala, Malawi, Rwanda, Uganda, and Tanzania. As codirector of the Policy Design and Evaluation Lab, McIntosh is an expert on issues related to credit, insurance, and savings markets in developing countries, as well as on how to design and conduct randomized controlled trials and the field measurement techniques required to capture outcomes. His work appears in the *American Economic Journal*, the *Review of Economics and Statistics*, and the *Journal of Public Economics*, among others.

Marcus André Melo is currently a professor at the Federal University of Pernambuco. His research interests are corruption, political institutions, and accountability. He was a Fulbright Scholar at MIT, Coca-Cola Company Visiting Professor at Yale, and Fellow of the John Simon Guggenheim and Rockefeller Foundations. His work has appeared in scholarly journals such as *Comparative Political Studies*, *Political Research Quarterly*, *Legislative Studies Quarterly*, and the *Journal of Democracy*. He is the coauthor of *Making Brazil Work: Checking the President in a Multiparty Democracy* (2013) and *Brazil in Transition: Beliefs, Leadership, and Institutional Change* (2016).

Gareth Nellis has a PhD from Yale University and is an assistant professor of political science at the University of California, San Diego. Previously, he was the Evidence in Governance and Politics postdoctoral fellow at the University of California, Berkeley. He specializes in comparative politics and modern South Asia. His research focuses on political parties, in particular on the origins and persistence of weakly institutionalized party systems, and the extent to which parties matter for key development outcomes. A second strand of work addresses the drivers of discrimination against internal migrants in fast-urbanizing settings.

Daniel Nielson is a professor of political science at Brigham Young University. He is a founder and principal investigator of AidData. He received his PhD in international affairs from University of California, San Diego in 1997. His scholarship focuses on international development, foreign aid, international organizations, and international field experiments. He is coauthor of *Global Shell Games: Experiments in Transnational Relations, Crime and Terrorism* and coeditor of *Delegation and Agency in International Organizations*, both published by

Cambridge University Press. He has also authored articles in the *American Journal of Political Science*, *International Organization*, and *World Development*, among other journals.

Paula M. Pickering is an associate professor of government at the College of William & Mary. Her research focuses on the impact of aid for peacebuilding and governance in the Balkans, and the link between information and electoral accountability. Pickering is the author of *Peacebuilding in the Balkans: The View from the Ground Floor* (2007). Recent articles have been published in *Governance*, in *Democratization*, in *East European Politics*, and in *Europe-Asia Studies*. Her research has received support from Evidence in Governance and Politics, the Social Science Research Council, Fulbright-Hays, the US Institute of Peace, and the International Research and Exchanges Board.

Melina R. Platas is an assistant professor of political science at New York University Abu Dhabi. Her research focuses on political accountability, the politics of service delivery, and the role of identity and culture in shaping economic and political outcomes. She is writing a book on the Muslim–Christian education gap in Africa, a region where she has worked and conducted fieldwork in eight countries. She writes for the Washington Post's Monkey Cage blog and is a participant on radio and television media in Uganda, where she previously worked as a reporter. She holds a PhD in political science and BA in human biology from Stanford University.

Pablo Querubín is an associate professor of politics and economics at New York University. Before joining NYU he spent two years at the Harvard Academy for International and Area Studies. His research has centered on the persistence of economic and political elites in different contexts such as Colombia, the Philippines and the US. He has also conducted research on clientelism in Mexico and the Philippines and on state building in Vietnam. His work has appeared in the *American Economic Review*, *American Journal of Political Science*, *American Political Science Review*, *Econometrica*, the *Quarterly Journal of Economics*, and the *Quarterly Journal of Political Science*.

Pia Raffler is an assistant professor in political science at Harvard University. Her work lies at the intersection of comparative politics and political economy. She studies the politics of development, focusing on governance, bureaucracy, and electoral politics in Sub-Saharan Africa. She works closely with government agencies to design and test reforms aimed at improving accountability, often through large-scale field experiments. Prior to joining Harvard, she spent a year at the Niehaus Center and the Center for Study of Democratic Politics at Princeton University. She holds a PhD in political science from Yale University.

Catlan Reardon is a PhD student in political science at UC Berkeley. Her research interests include comparative politics, the political economy of development, and research methods with a particular focus on contexts with weak institutions. She has received grants from JPAL's Governance Initiative and ATAI for research in East Africa. Before coming to Berkeley, Catlan lived in Uganda and Kenya, implementing field experiments with Innovations for Poverty Action. She holds an MA in political science from Leiden University in the Netherlands and a BA in political science from Wake Forest University.

Neelanjan Sircar is an assistant professor of political science at Ashoka University. His recent work has focused on state-level elections in India using data analysis and ethnographic methods He has also been engaged in large-scale survey data collection that explores the role of urbanization in changing social attitudes and behaviors in India. He received a bachelor's degree in applied mathematics and economics from UC Berkeley in 2003 and a PhD in political science from Columbia University in 2014.

Preface and Acknowledgments

This book reports the results of a set of coordinated, large-scale field experiments on the relationship between informational interventions and political accountability. These studies, together with ancillary experiments and analyses reported in these pages, were planned and executed over several years by thirty-one researchers as part of the inaugural set of studies in the Evidence in Governance and Politics (EGAP) network's "Metaketa Initiative." We present in this book the substantive findings from this first group of studies, dubbed Metaketa I. We also introduce the Initiative's novel research model, which aims to foster better cumulative learning through the planned integration of field experiments. Each of the authors of the individual chapters has contributed centrally to the development of this Metaketa approach, as well as to this volume's substantive findings. Despite its appearance with Cambridge University Press as an "edited volume," this book therefore sits uncomfortably in that category.

We have collectively incurred many debts in developing this multiyear project. We would especially like to thank Clara Bicalho at WZB Berlin Social Science Center and Anirvan Chowdhury at the University of California, Berkeley for their crucial and brilliant work on the core meta-analysis reported in Chapter 11. Catlan Reardon, also at the University of California, Berkeley, did outstanding work in helping to bring the policy experiment described in Chapter 12 to fruition. Gareth Nellis was not initially a member of the steering committee, composed of the other coeditors, that launched the Metaketa Initiative. Yet, the other coeditors recognized that his contributions to conceptualization, analysis, and writing have been so fundamental that he should rightly appear as an editor of the volume.

We would like to thank our editor at Cambridge, John Haslam, for his continued interest in this project. We are very grateful to Erik Wibbels for organizing a book workshop at Duke University, where we received invaluable comments from our discussants: John Ahlquist, Pablo Beramendi, Dean Dulay, Scott Demarchi, Germán Feierherd, Zeren Li, Manoj Mohanan, Eddy Malesky, Lucy Martin, Elisa Maffioli, Melanie Manion, Mat McCubbins, Emily Rains, Diego Romero, Victoria Paniagua, Ngoc Phan, Jeremy Spater, Daniel Stegmueller, Kate Vyborny, and Erik Wibbels. We also thank attendees at seminars at Columbia University, the Department for International Development (DFID), EUI (IMBEDS), IBEI Barcelona, Oxford University, Stanford University's CDDRL, University College London, University of Bamberg, University of Barcelona, University of Essex, University of Gothenburg, University of Pennsylvania, University of Washington, Vanderbilt University, and WZB Berlin Social Science Center, as well as participants at an EGAP meeting at Vanderbilt University for their comments. We gratefully acknowledge fantastic support from Abigail Long and Matthew Lisiecki at Columbia University and Jaclyn Leaver at the University of California, Berkeley. Abby Long suggested the name "Metaketa," a Basque (Euskara) word meaning "accumulation," for the Initiative. (She had also proposed Yokuzuza, meaning the same thing in Zulu; however, we are glad to be talking today about Metaketas rather than Yokuzuzas.) We also thank Lily Medina for excellent assistance with Chapter 12. We are grateful to Georgiy Syunyaev and Jorge Mangonnet at Columbia University and Donghyun Danny Choi, Paul Connor, Elizabeth Herman, Nicholas Kuipers, Carlos Schmidt-Padilla, and Alex Stephenson at the University of California, Berkeley for their outstanding work as third-party replicators of the findings reported in Part II.

This first Metaketa was supported by an anonymous funder. That means that we do not know exactly the source of the funding, which we grant has a certain irony for research that focuses substantively and methodologically on transparency. Given our ethical commitments, we did obtain a statement from the funder about what it is not – specifically, that funding did not derive from donations from companies or from directors of companies listed as "Excluded from the Investment Universe" by the Norwegian government's pension fund list. We are deeply grateful to our funder for taking risks to support innovative models of research to improve knowledge, and for providing specific insights, reflections, and wise guidance as we have navigated the many new issues that arose in developing the Metaketa Initiative.

Most of all, we are grateful to the many world-class researchers who comprised seven research teams in six countries and who dedicated their talents to Metaketa I. One of the most rewarding aspects of this experience has been the chance to experience a very open and collaborative way of doing social science. We pay substantial attention in this book to describing the organizational and incentive structures that helped to facilitate the coordination of a large group of researchers, because we think these structures can help to make the Metaketa model a sustainable enterprise; and they also underpin ongoing projects within the Metaketa Initiative. Rather than these incentives, however, it was ultimately the desire to improve cumulative learning from social science research that motivated many researchers to contribute their time and insights generously and often selflessly to this Initiative. We hope that this volume helps to demonstrate the payoff – while also showing the limitations of our work and pointing the way towards future improvements.

Replication files for all analyses reported in this book, as well as the online appendix, are available at https://github.com/egap/metaketa-i. Our meta-preanalysis plan (MPAP) for Chapter 11 is available in the book's appendix, as well as at the EGAP design registry (https://egap .org/registration/736); pre-analysis plans for the individual studies in Part II are linked at http://egap.org/metaketa/metaketa-information-and-accountability. Readers can also assess the sensitivity of our meta-analysis results to various specification choices and to deviations from the pre-analysis plan, using an interactive online interface available at http://egap.org/content/metaketa-i-shiny-app.

PART I

INFORMATION, ACCOUNTABILITY, AND A NEW APPROACH TO CUMULATIVE LEARNING

Do Informational Campaigns Promote Electoral Accountability?

Thad Dunning, Guy Grossman, Macartan
Humphreys, Susan D. Hyde,
Craig McIntosh, and Gareth Nellis

1.1 INFORMATION AND POLITICAL ACCOUNTABILITY

Throughout the world, voters lack access to information about politicians, government performance, and public services. Consider some examples. In Dar es Salaam, Tanzania, a recent survey found that 80 percent of parents with children in primary education were unaware of how their children's school fared in the latest round of national examinations, 39 percent did not know whether teachers at the school came to work, and 25 percent could not say whether the school had toilets.[1] Graft is ubiquitous in India: more than 65 percent of citizens report having paid a bribe to access public services over the past year. Yet dozens of anti-corruption activists have been murdered after legally requesting information under the country's Right to Information Act.[2] Deadly anti-government protests in Caracas in 2014 barely appeared on Venezuelans' television screens. State control of the media ensured that coverage was limited and sanitized. Restrictive laws meant that journalists who reported critically on the government could be fined and thrown in jail.[3] In many areas of the world, voters are in the dark about the state of their nations and the people who rule them.

Such knowledge deficits are problematic on both normative and instrumental grounds. According to classic political theory, an informed

---

[1] Croke (2012).
[2] Vidhi Doshi, "The brutal deaths of anti-corruption activists in India," *The Washington Post*, September 15, 2017.
[3] Fossett (2014).

electorate is vital to a well-functioning democracy.[4] In standard models, voters delegate responsibility for public administration to elected politicians. But representative democracy does not by itself guarantee good governance. For this to come about, voters need to be informed about the backgrounds of candidates running for public office – so that they can select those who are competent, honest, and committed to advancing voters' preferred policies. Incumbents, meanwhile, must be convinced that their actions are open to public scrutiny, and that poor performance and wrongdoing will be punished at the ballot box.[5] It stands to reason that without transparency and a steady flow of reliable information, the corridors of power are likely to be filled with "bad types" of politicians who face few incentives to perform their duties, and they may steal from the citizens they are supposed to serve.[6]

There is plenty of evidence that such misconduct indeed occurs. Legislators in many countries ply voters with side payments rather than better roads, schools, and health services. Corrupt leaders frequently offer no-bid contracts to friends, relatives, or campaign donors. A large literature documents the private returns that accrue to those holding public office, most notably in places where checks and balances are weak or absent.[7] Scholarly work on lobbying suggests that in contexts where access to information is unequally distributed, economic elites are better able to bend regulation and tax policy to their advantage.[8]

Civil society organizations, international donors, and democracy promotion activists have therefore seen transparency as a disinfectant and cure for what ails democracy. They have crafted programs to create more informed electorates.[9] These programs are motivated in part by the idea that political accountability in developing democracies is fundamentally

---

[4] Pitkin (1967); Dahl (1973); Dahl (1989, 338–339); Przeworski, Stokes, and Manin (1999); Brunetti and Weder (2003); Besley and Prat (2006); Malesky, Schuler, and Tran (2012); Bauhr and Grimes (2014).

[5] Amaryta Sen has famously argued that famine has rarely – if ever – occurred under democracy, chiefly because politicians "have to win elections and face public criticism" (Sen, 2001, 3).

[6] For theoretical discussion see, for instance, Fearon (1999); for recent evidence see Humphreys and Weinstein (2013), Grossman and Michelitch (2018).

[7] See, for instance, Fisman, Schulz, and Vig (2014).

[8] Przeworski, Stokes, and Manin (1999), Hollyer, Rosendorff, and Vreeland (2011).

[9] See, for example, the Voting Information Project in the United States (www.votinginfoproject.org), funded by Pew Charitable Trusts and Google, or International IDEA's democratic accountability efforts (Bjuremalm, Fernandez Gibaja, and Valladares Molleda, 2014).

constrained by a lack of information about government performance. Thus, increasing the supply of information should boost accountability and responsiveness.[10] To this end, numerous initiatives have sought to repackage and disseminate information obtained from government audits, publicly available administrative data, official records of politician behavior, and freedom of information requests.[11] For example, the Advocates Coalition for Development and Environment (ACODE), a nonpartisan nongovernmental organization (NGO) operating in Uganda, assembles information about politicians' performance and distributes it to citizens. Google has established online platforms that compile information about candidates and local government quality, increasing voter access to information before elections in countries such as India, Indonesia, the Philippines, and Taiwan.[12] A prominent donor group seeks to "expand the impact and scale of transparency, accountability and participation interventions" through the Transparency and Accountability Initiative.[13] The National Democratic Institute provided technical and financial assistance to more than 15,000 civic groups globally, partly in an effort to encourage "informed, organized, active and peaceful citizen participation."[14] Informational interventions are plentiful, with extensive support from public and private donors.

Despite their prevalence, we have little hard evidence that voter information campaigns work in practice. Moreover, the evidence that does exist paints a mixed picture. The release of audit reports disclosing information about corruption in Brazil significantly impacted voting behavior: incumbents in municipalities in which audits exposed a

---

[10] To be sure, such information is not always widely disseminated or easy to access. See, for example, Lagunes and Pocasangre (2019).

[11] A second group of initiatives has involved training communities to monitor public-sector providers, and/or educating citizens about the importance of legislative process or political parties, and how to mobilize for political change.

[12] See "Google launches 'Know your candidates tool' for Lok Sabha Elections 2014," *Financial Express*, New Delhi, April 8, 2014; "Google, YouTube launch websites for upcoming Taiwan municipality elections," *BBC Monitoring Media*, London, October 17, 2010; Kayleen Hong, "Google Launches Online Tools for India and Indonesia Elections," *The Next Web*, March 26, 2014; "Philippines: Google launches resource page for Philippine elections: Google.com.ph/elections," *Asia News Monitor*, Bangkok, May 3, 2013.

[13] See the Transparency and Accountability Initiative (www.transparency-initiative.org) and the related Transparency 4 Development research project (http://t4d.ash.harvard .edu/); also Kosack and Fung (2014).

[14] NDI Citizen Participation programming (www.ndi.org/what-we-do/citizen-partici pation).

greater-than-median number of infractions experienced a sizable decline in vote share at the next election.[15] In a similar vein, published report cards in India caused voters to punish poorly performing politicians and reward those who performed well.[16] Conversely, other studies from Uganda and Tanzania estimate informational interventions to have no effect on average.[17] An experiment in Mexico even found that disseminating corruption information had unintended negative consequences, depressing voter turnout.[18]

These inconclusive results are not wholly surprising. One can come up with several possible reasons why information might fail to move electorates. Voters may struggle to absorb new information that is delivered to them – perhaps owing to illiteracy, or the simple fact that parsing out the fine details of national accounts or abstruse legal judgments is hard, even for the most "sophisticated" voters.[19] Many citizens may find it irrational to pay attention to information about politics, even when it is made more accessible, particularly if they do not expect a critical mass of other voters to follow suit (a type of collective action failure).[20] Plausibly, too, information about politicians' performance may be overshadowed by other factors, such as copartisanship, a desire to see coethnics hold office, or clientelistic ties that make abandoning incumbents economically risky.[21] There is also the possibility that politicians attempt to offset the effects of transparency with increased persuasion – for example, by claiming credit for policy successes in which they played no part, or by redirecting effort into more visible but potentially less socially beneficial forms of action.[22]

In short, the impact of information on electoral accountability is unclear, giving rise to the empirical questions that animate this book. Do informational campaigns mounted in the lead-up to elections influence voter behavior and increase democratic accountability? Do voters act on information to sanction poor performers and reward politicians

---

[15] Ferraz and Finan (2008).

[16] See Banerjee et al. (2011).

[17] Lieberman, Posner, and Tsai (2014); Grossman and Michelitch (2018); Humphreys and Weinstein (2013).

[18] Chong et al. (2015).

[19] Achen and Bartels (2016: 14) survey a substantial body of literature showing that "most democratic citizens are uninterested in politics, poorly informed, and unwilling or unable to convey coherent policy preferences through 'issue voting'."

[20] Cox (1997); Olson (1965).

[21] Kasara (2007); Stokes et al. (2013).

[22] Voters could thus be better off with less access to information, as long as politicians know what voters know. See, for example, Murphy (2004) or Prat (2005).

who have a positive track record? And if they do, under what conditions are informational interventions more or less likely to be effective?

1.2 THE METAKETA INITIATIVE: A NEW APPROACH TO CUMULATIVE LEARNING

Policymakers, practitioners, and academics have zeroed in on transparency as a key source of political accountability. Yet, research on the impact of informational campaigns suffers from challenges that afflict many – and perhaps most – empirical research agendas in the social sciences. Three obstacles stand out: study sparsity, study heterogeneity, and selective reporting.

Studies on a given topic are usually sparse. Researchers are professionally rewarded for innovative, high-impact studies; by contrast, prizes and promotions rarely go to those who replicate existing findings. This means that second or third evaluations of a specific intervention are rarely proposed and seldom funded. Policymakers and practitioners are often left to rely on a single study in reaching programming decisions.

Even where multiple studies do exist, study heterogeneity can make it hard to draw firm conclusions about the effects of particular interventions. Differences in measurement strategies across studies act as a barrier to systematic meta-analysis – without which it is nearly impossible to evaluate whether disparate results are driven by contextual differences or study-specific distinctions.

A further set of problems springs from selective reporting: above all, failure to publish null findings. This pernicious practice is common to most areas of scientific inquiry. It motivates researchers to go "fishing" for statistically significant results in individual studies; it prevents the comprehensive assessment of evidence; and it jeopardizes our ability to learn about policies that do not work. Taken together, these features of social science threaten the reliability of whole bodies of literature on particular topics.

To address these concerns, we introduce a new model for producing research that seeks to counter several barriers to knowledge accumulation. It does so by increasing coordination among otherwise independent researchers.[23] The findings we present in this book stem from the inaugural project of the Metaketa Initiative, created by the Evidence

---

[23] We are conscious that many of the core components of this model exist already. The contribution of our initiative is to bring together these ideas and best practices under one umbrella.

in Governance and Politics (EGAP) network. "Metaketa" is a Basque word meaning "accumulation." The Initiative is designed to encourage replication, increase harmonization between studies such that meaningful aggregation is possible, and foster commitment to design and reporting standards that guard against selective reporting and publication bias. Its overarching goal is to promote cumulative learning in the social sciences.

The heart of the approach involves commissioning and implementing clusters of coordinated field experiments that are carried out in diverse settings yet center on a single research question – one that should be of interest to academic and practitioner audiences alike. Within a Metaketa round, we collectively select studies that teams design and implement in different locations, but which share a similar, coordinated intervention or treatment arm. This arm is used to test a theory agreed on by all participating researchers in advance. To preserve innovation and researcher incentives, and to compare the common treatment arm to alternatives, studies also include other study-specific treatment arms that focus on complementary interventions or modifications of the common arm. In this manner, each study contributes to both replication (through the common arm) and innovation (through the alternative arm). To protect against publication bias, the Metaketa model emphasizes integrated publication of all study results, regardless of the statistical significance of any individual study or the average effect across all studies. Studies also adhere to best design and reporting standards, including preregistered specification of key tests and third-party replication of data analyses.

Through coordination and harmonization across different teams conducting similar research in diverse contexts, our initiative seeks to fund studies, the data from which are intended to be analyzed jointly in the same theoretical and measurement framework. We use meta-analysis to estimate the average impacts of interventions across these multiple settings. The data also permit systematic assessment of contextual heterogeneity of any effects.

The model is designed to maximize both internal and external validity, as far as practically possible. The fact that all studies are randomized controlled trials (RCTs) helps to bolster the credibility of causal conclusions for each individual study, and thus the aggregated study data. Regarding external validity, we selected studies in this initial application of the model through a competitive process designed to ensure that a sufficient number of high-quality researchers were interested in participating. This means that study sites are not chosen at random. Nevertheless, we feel substantially more confident in the generalizability of conclusions drawn from multiple studies implemented in different settings than we would from any single study carried out in one setting.

The Metaketa Initiative was designed as a general approach to the problem of cumulative learning. In this book, we demonstrate proof of concept by applying it to the substantive issue of information and political accountability. Building on the foundation of Metaketa I, EGAP has begun to employ the model to study other issues as well.[24] We advocate its use and continued refinement in other areas where there is demand for cumulative evidence.

1.3 METAKETA I: APPLICATION

The purpose of this book is both to describe our approach and to present the findings from seven planned field experiments on information and electoral accountability. All experiments assess whether providing citizens with information about politicians affects voting behavior. We carried out the studies in developing democracies – that is, in places where we expect informational problems to be especially acute, and thus where remedial interventions could be especially worthwhile. Jointly, the experiments provide the most systematic and comprehensive evidence to date on the electoral impact of political information campaigns in developing countries.

The type of information administered to voters came in three varieties. In one set of studies, the interventions transmitted information about incumbents' performance in office: their legislative activity (Benin – Adida et al., Chapter 4) and the quality of local public services (Burkina Faso – Lierl and Holmlund, Chapter 8). Another study provided information about candidates' policy positions, as established in "Meet the Candidates" videos (Uganda 1 – Platas and Raffler, Chapter 6). A third cluster of studies informed voters about politicians' malfeasance: spending irregularities (Mexico – Arias et al., Chapter 5, and Uganda 2 – Buntaine et al., Chapter 7), corruption (Brazil – Boas et al., Chapter 9), and criminality (India – Sircar and Chauchard, Chapter 10, although this study was not completed due to implementation challenges). Information was disseminated privately to voters by flyer, text message, or

---

[24] See www.egap.org/metaketa.

video, depending on the study. It was always truthful, nonpartisan, and credibly sourced, with most teams collaborating with a local NGO that took the lead as the implementing partner. In each study, information was delivered no more than a month prior to an election.

Importantly, before the treatments were rolled out, teams measured voters' prior beliefs about the incumbent.[25] This information allows us to assess, for each voter, whether the information they were provided with came as good news – meaning the information was better than their prior beliefs about the politician – or as bad news – meaning the information fell short of their expectations. In endline surveys, teams measured two main outcomes: (a) whether the subject turned out to vote, and (b) whether they cast their vote for the incumbent (about whom the information had been provided). Teams also gathered data on moderators and mediators, allowing us to evaluate hypotheses about heterogeneous effects. Together with experimentally induced variation in the alternative arms in each study, these data allow us to investigate mechanisms that may lie behind the findings.

The intervention, theory, and measurement strategy were conceived and honed in multiple group coordination workshops. All Principal Investigators (PIs) helped to advance both the substantive research described in this book and the Metaketa model as a whole. Our registered meta-analysis pre-analysis plan (MPAP) – coauthored by the five members of the steering committee and all twenty-two of the PIs on the individual studies who participated in this initiative – reflects this shared vision.[26]

1.4 FINDINGS

Our findings are clear and robust. Despite the statistical power gained by pooling the results of the experiments, and despite what we believed to be the timely, relevant, and accessible nature of the information on candidate or party performance, the effects of the common interventions are largely null. Indeed, on average for the incumbent vote choice and turnout outcomes, we find no evidence of impact on the common

---

[25] One exception is the Mexico study which, as explained below, measured priors in a different manner due to budgetary constraints.

[26] See Dunning et al. (2015), reproduced in the book's Appendix. The PIs are the authors of the chapters in Part II of this book. The steering committee was composed of five of the volume's coeditors (Dunning, Grossman, Humphreys, Hyde, and McIntosh).

informational intervention across all studies, and little evidence of measurable impact in the individual study sites. These findings are robust to a wide variety of data construction and analytic choices. They emerge despite the multiplicity of contexts, the variations in the exact nature of information provided, and the heterogeneity in the degree to which voters were already aware of politicians' performance. These null results from the meta-analysis thus provide substantially more credible, robust, and externally valid evidence against the efficacy of simple information interventions than any one study could alone.

What explains these largely null and unexpected results? We find no evidence that copartisan or coethnic attachments between voters and politicians moderate the impact of the informational treatments on vote choice – as we might expect if, say, voters filter information through a "perceptual screen." Further, the effects do not vary according to beliefs about incumbents' likelihood of engaging in vote buying. In fact, the noneffect of the treatment holds remarkably stable across a raft of voter characteristics. In three of the studies, we detect signs that politicians responded strategically to the interventions; that is, they took steps to try to counter the (negative) information being delivered to citizens. (One project, in India, had to be canceled altogether due to politician backlash that prevented implementing teams from fully fielding the intervention.) Based on the pattern of results, though, it seems unlikely that these rearguard actions shaped actual voting behavior.

We find the most likely explanation for the nulls to be that, in hindsight, the treatments were neither strong enough nor salient enough to affect voters' beliefs about politicians. Although the treatment on average caused some voters to absorb the informational treatments, this processing of information about politicians induced no statistically significant changes in perceptions about politicians' honesty or effort. Put simply, voters do not appear to have internalized the information that was placed in front of them in a manner that is politically meaningful, and thus their beliefs about politicians and their propensity to vote for them remained unchanged, even in the face of information that was expected to improve or worsen their judgments.

In light of the null result, it might be tempting to conclude that it was naive or optimistic to expect the interventions to change vote choice and turnout. This is a possibility. Yet, three points are critical to underscore. First, the interventions in this book are modeled on many ongoing programs in the real world, to which donors and NGOs continue to offer high levels of funding and support. Here we establish a comprehensive evidence base suggesting that such widespread interventions may fail to achieve their stated aims. Second, the interventions presented in this book closely mirror several prominent studies in the previous experimental literature.[27] The relative scarcity and heterogeneity of those studies, however, highlights the pressing need for replication to arrive at a firmer set of overall conclusions.

Finally, null results such as those presented in this book are too rarely published in academic venues, and are almost never presented or discussed within the world of practitioners who work on transparency and good governance programs. Yet, they can be extremely important for scientific progress and for policy-relevant learning. The Metaketa approach allows us to present more convincing null results than would be possible in any one study. It aims to safeguard against the tendency for researchers to justify post-hoc decisions that lead them to uncover statistically significant results – and, crucially, ensures the publication of all findings regardless of results. Previous published studies of informational interventions have found significant effects. Given the set of null effects we uncover, however, it seems possible that publication bias could distort our understanding of the efficacy of such interventions as a whole.

The results are likely to come as a disappointment to those hoping to use blanket low-cost informational interventions to improve democratic accountability. Yet, a caveat is also in order. These findings should not be taken to imply that informing voters of politicians' performance can never affect voting behavior. Our common arm evaluated the effect of a particular kind of intervention: information delivered to citizens privately, by video, flier, or SMS, in the immediate run-up to an election. Alternative interventions in several of the individual projects suggest conditions under which information might be more impactful. In the meta-analysis, we evaluate an alternative treatment implemented in three of the studies in the Metaketa, in which information was delivered in public, in the hopes of fostering common knowledge and coordinated action. We find suggestive evidence that such dissemination modes may be more effective in shaping electoral behavior. More experimentation is needed to discover how information about politicians can be communicated effectively – perhaps delivering higher dosages of information, or

---

[27] Specifically, several of the individual studies closely mirror the interventions conducted in high profiles studies, such as Brazil (Ferraz and Finan, 2008), Uganda 1 (Bidwell, Casey, and Glennerster, n.d.), Mexico (Chong et al., 2015).

using different mechanisms to transmit information intensively, interactively, and over a longer timeframe. We hope these hypotheses will be the subject of future systematic investigation.

Does our approach in fact result in better cumulative learning? To assess this question, we also summarize the findings from an additional randomized control trial presented in Chapter 12. A key question regarding the Metaketa Initiative is whether it generates evidence that is more persuasive to practitioners, policymakers, and researchers compared to conventional approaches to research. To test this, we conducted an experiment with nearly sixty policymakers and aid practitioners working in the Washington, DC area. We manipulated the order in which participants were exposed to the individual Metaketa studies, a meta-analysis of multiple Metaketa studies, a non-Metaketa study showing significant results of an informational intervention, and a placebo condition. By taking frequent measurements of participants' beliefs and predictions about the results of an unseen Metaketa study showing a null effect, we find that exposure to the meta-analysis causes significant updating in the expected directions, boosting prediction accuracy. Intriguingly, it has a less marked effect on the financial support that policymakers allocate to voter information campaigns. We also find evidence that exposure to a single statistically significant result from an outside study can move predictions at least as much as the null results from the meta-analysis – but in the wrong direction. In our sample, therefore, policymakers appear to absorb evidence in quite rational but not infallible ways.

Reflecting on the initiative as a whole, we came away even more convinced of the value of registration and third-party replication. In many cases, reasonable disagreements about how to implement analyses were resolved by reference to the pre-analysis plans. In some cases, pre-analysis plans were not sufficiently specific, and analytic judgment calls were needed – yet even then, the existence of the plans makes clear when such researcher degrees of freedom existed. Finally, in some cases, researchers felt that there were good reasons to deviate from pre-analysis plans; again, the existence of these plans makes it possible to identify these ex-post decisions and judge them on their merits. Professional incentives to produce statistically significant and novel results continue to persist within the research community and can be difficult to escape. Our experience suggests that more comprehensive registration – for example, using a design declaration approach (Blair et al., 2019) – would be invaluable.

1.5 ORGANIZATION

This book is not a typical edited volume. Rather, it is an integrated analysis that tightly synthesizes the conclusions from multiple studies. This was made possible through extensive preplanning, coordination, and cooperation among thirty-one scholars, whose contributions we describe in the preface.

Part I of the book describes the challenges to cumulative learning about information and accountability and lays out our collective approach to the accumulation of knowledge. In Chapter 2, we develop in detail the key pillars of the Metaketa approach. We describe the practical challenges that we have faced in getting the incentives right for researchers, and the solutions we have found to ensure replication and harmonization across distinct studies. We also discuss key ingredients of open, collaborative social scientific inquiry. In Chapter 3, we move to information and accountability, describing the theoretical conjectures that motivate our approach, the results of previous empirical research, and the theories of change, hypotheses, and measurement strategies that are common across the studies in Metaketa I.

Part II presents fuller results from the individual studies. Each chapter is written by the corresponding team of PIs. Many chapters also emphasize results from alternative intervention arms of each study, as an exercise in comparative effectiveness and as a way to help explain the results for each study on the common treatment arm. These chapters generate fresh insights about paths forward for scholars and practitioners eager to try new ways to solve information challenges. They may also be of particular interest to regional specialists and to those wishing to understand the variation in context across the set of studies. Researchers wishing to undertake similar field experiments will find in these chapters ample inspiration and ideas, as well as warnings and lessons learned.

Finally, we turn in Part III to "learning about cumulative learning." We first present the results of our meta-analysis, which brings together the studies discussed in Part II and estimates the average effect of informational interventions across the individual studies (Chapter 11). We also use the full sample of cases to probe heterogeneous effects, and assess several potential explanations for our null and unexpected findings. Chapter 12 presents the findings from our policy experiment, in which we put the Metaketa concept itself to the test. Our final chapter, in Part IV, concludes. It digs deeper into the policy implications of our substantive findings. It also sets out future challenges and opportunities for the Metaketa model.

This book makes both substantive and methodological contributions. Substantively, the book contributes to the study of political accountability in developing democracies. We also hope it will prove useful for organizations and governments that work to create more informed electorates – and that want to understand the limitations of efforts to do so. The results from the collective studies here suggest modesty in claims about the likely effects of programs in this area. But they also suggest conditions under which interventions might be more or less effective. Methodologically, the book probes the strengths and limitations of a novel model for social science research. We hope the lessons will be of interest to a wide variety of researchers, some of whom may consider leading or participating in similar initiatives themselves. At a time when many in the scholarly community are considering issues of transparency and reproducibility, as well as the external validity of experiments, we hope that this book can inform future efforts to improve cumulative learning.

2

The Metaketa Initiative

Thad Dunning, Guy Grossman, Macartan Humphreys, Susan D. Hyde, and Craig McIntosh

2.1 THE CHALLENGE OF CUMULATIVE LEARNING

Researchers, practitioners, and policymakers often share an important goal: they want to use research to understand how the world works and to assess what interventions, policies, or programs can make things better. Research, many hope, can guide policy choices in new situations.

Yet, such insights are difficult to acquire from any one research study. In the social and political domain, unlike in some natural science domains, immutable laws that hold across time and place may be the exception rather than the rule. Social scientists often point to the limited "external validity" of particular studies – that is, the extent to which the findings from one study may travel to other interventions, contexts, and study populations.[1] The specifics and vagaries of implementation of particular studies can also make the generalizability of findings uncertain.[2] Therefore, results from a single study may provide an unconvincing basis for asserting generalities, and only a tentative basis for extrapolation. At the same time, some findings may in fact generalize beyond the context of a single research study. The extent of external validity therefore needs to be evaluated with evidence, rather than being left to conjecture.[3] In other words, the common effects of similar interventions need to be

---

[1] Campbell and Stanley (1966) define external validity in terms of "generalizability": To what populations, settings, treatment variables, and measurement variables can [an] effect be generalized?
[2] Berge et al. (2012); Bold et al. (2018).
[3] Campbell and Stanley (1966).

assessed and possibly demonstrated, rather than assumed or rejected a priori.

One sensible solution to the challenge of generalizability is to combine the results of multiple studies on the same topic. Such "meta-analysis" is commonplace in some physical sciences, and it appears from time to time in the social sciences, too.[4] Aggregating evidence from multiple studies may give us greater purchase on whether – and even why – results differ across distinct contexts, or whether, instead, findings point us in the same direction across settings.

Unfortunately, meta-analysis as a solution to the problem of generalizability faces several critical difficulties in the social sciences. Consider in more detail the several obstacles noted in Chapter 1:

Study sparsity. Meta-analyses require as inputs several related studies on a single topic. Yet, one important challenge arises from the practice of social science and the career incentives that many scholars face. Academic research is a decentralized operation; researchers typically pursue questions that are interesting to them, and in consequence may pay less attention to knowledge accumulation over time. Moreover, there is a substantial premium placed on novelty, and relatively fewer rewards for reproducing or validating prior results across time and space. Scholars may benefit more professionally from publishing "groundbreaking" work, compared to the rewards of publishing work that replicates existing findings. Such career incentives to "plant the flag" imply that once a hypothesis or finding is published, too few scholars are willing to invest in corroborating that result. Thus, despite widespread acknowledgment that replication is an essential part of a research agenda, important studies are rarely replicated. This failure, contributing to study sparsity, complicates the goal of combining the results of different studies using meta-analysis.[5]

Study heterogeneity. Formal meta-analyses also typically assume that both the intervention under consideration and the manner in which it is deployed and analyzed is constant across the different studies that they take as inputs.[6] These assumptions are necessary if researchers are to treat different studies as though they are part of the same grand study. This assumption can be a strong one even within a single study. For example, experimental researchers assume that all subjects assigned to

---

[4] See Gerber and Green (2012, chapter 11) for several examples.
[5] Dunning and Hyde (2014).
[6] Gerber and Green (2012): 351.

a treatment condition receive the "same" treatment, but even respondents visited by the same canvassers in a get-out-the-vote experiment might experience a quite different treatment (depending, say, on the canvasser's mood). However, given the varied contexts in which social science studies take place and the incentives to differentiate among studies, this assumption is often especially strong when combining the results of different studies. The difficulty of study heterogeneity can vary across research topics – in testing the effects of, say, financial inducements to purchase malarial beds, or micro-finance schemes to jump-start small businesses, it might be plausible to assume that interventions are sufficiently similar across studies (though, even there, one might ask whether subjects interpret the meaning of a financial inducement differently in different contexts). But for many interventions in the social sciences, especially in the governance space, such homogeneity cannot be assumed.

Selective reporting. Related difficulties arise from the way that research is typically reported. Publication bias – the tendency of academic journals and presses to publish statistically significant (positive or negative) estimated effects, but not null results – poses another genuine threat to the validity of inferences from bodies of research. The evidence of publication bias is now quite extensive and very convincing.[7] This bias can occur not only because referees and editors fail to publish studies reporting null effects, but also because authors sometimes do not write up such results in the first place.[8] This can be a problem for the reliability of individual studies, especially to the extent that authors of individual studies engage in specification searches, data mining or "p-hacking" to turn up and report only significant effects.[9] Yet, publication bias also limits cumulative learning from bodies of research on a particular topic. A null effect is not a null finding; and publishing only non-null effects exaggerates our sense of the causal efficacy of particular policies or interventions.

A final difficulty stems from **private data**. Without publicly available data, third-party researchers cannot reconstruct results to verify that authors used best practices when analyzing their raw unprocessed data,

---

[7] See Gerber, Green, and Nickerson (2001); Gerber, Malhotra et al. (2008); Simonsohn, Nelson, and Simmons (2014).

[8] Franco, Malhotra, and Simonovits (2014).

[9] Humphreys, Sanchez de la Sierra, and van der Windt (2013); Laitin (2013).

nor can they use the data to conduct systematic meta-analyses.[10] The situation has improved since scholars such as Gary King drew attention to the importance of public data in the 1990s.[11] Yet, while several leading journals in political science currently require data posting and even third-party verification of the match between data, code, and reported results, a recent survey of replication policies at 120 peer-reviewed political science journals found that only 19 even had a replication policy.[12] When data are private, third parties cannot readily assess the reliability of conclusions drawn from any particular study. Mistakes are all too easy to make in a long and often complex research process; and when data are available, the record is not encouraging.[13] The inability to access data therefore remains a basic but substantial barrier to open and reliable science, as well as to aggregation.

In sum, study sparsity, study heterogeneity, selective reporting, and private data threaten the feasibility of meta-analysis – and of cumulative learning – in the social sciences. The tendency of social-scientific inferences and policy recommendations to be drawn from a single or small number of high-visibility published studies showing important treatment effects – while less visible studies that suggest null effects are not published, and implementation failures are not reported – leads to a distorted view of the likely effects of interventions. Several scholars may conduct studies on related topics; yet differences in interventions, outcomes, measurement of inputs and outputs and other aspects of study design can limit the comparability of results from such studies. Scholars' incentives to distinguish their work from previous research in the area – reflecting the returns to novelty – further undermines the effort to base conclusions on several studies of a phenomenon, rather than just one.

At issue here is how much and how reliably researchers can learn not just from a single study, but from a collection of studies on a given topic.

---

[10] King (1995). To distinguish such efforts from the effort to replicate results with new data from new study sites, this sort of exercise is variably referred to as "internal replication," "pure replication" (Hamermesh, 2007), or a "reproduction test" (Clemens, 2017).

[11] King (1995).

[12] Gherghina and Katsanidou (2013). The *American Political Science Review* currently requires posting of data and code, while the *American Journal of Political Science* recently began to require third-party verification.

[13] For instance, one attempt at replicating research – in a journal with a policy of mandatory data archiving! – found that data for only 69 of 193 articles were in fact archived; and only 58 had both data and code present. The authors could only reproduce results for 14 of 62 studies (or 23 percent) that they sought to verify (McCullough, McGeary, and Harrison, 2006).

It can be difficult to walk away from a literature on a topic with a clear understanding either of an "average" effect of a policy or program, or a clear sense of the conditions under which a particular effect may hold. These challenges underscore the importance of building strategies that allow us to better validate and aggregate findings as well as to understand heterogeneous results in different contexts.

2.1.1 Internal vs. External Validity? The Rise of RCTs

These difficulties in aggregation have been underscored – and perhaps even exacerbated – by the dramatic recent growth in the use of Randomized Controlled Trials (RCTs) in the social sciences.[14]

Experiments provide a valuable method for understanding which policies and programs may improve socially desirable outcomes. Causal relationships in the real world (outside of controlled laboratory settings) are often obscured by confounding factors. For example, those exposed to a program under consideration may not be comparable to those who are not, in a myriad of ways that are hard to measure or observe. As the mantra goes: correlation is not causation. For this reason, RCTs are sometimes referred to as the "gold standard" of research design. Due to random assignment to intervention (or treatment) conditions, experiments help to avoid the problem of confounding – arguably the most important of threats to the internal validity of studies.[15] Strong research design is often a first, necessary step towards reliable cumulative knowledge about cause and effect.

We therefore welcome this turn towards experiments. Yet our sense, shared with many scholars, is that to realize the full gains of this turn towards randomized designs, this focus must be complemented by other practices and institutions.[16] In particular, the inferential advances brought about by RCTs do not in themselves solve the external validity

---

[14] On the growth of RCTs and related methods, see McDermott (2002), Druckman et al. (2006), De Rooij, Green and Gerber (2009), Humphreys and Weinstein (2009), Hutchings and Jardina (2009), Palfrey (2009), Angrist and Pischke (2010), Dunning (2012), and Hyde (2015).

[15] Internal validity refers to the ability of a study to describe cause and effect relations in a particular setting. Campbell and Stanley (1966) describe internal validity, in the context of experiments, as "the basic minimum without which any experiment is not interpretable: Did in fact the experimental treatments make a difference in this specific experimental instance?" See footnote 1 in this chapter for the contrast with external validity.

[16] Humphreys, Sanchez de la Sierra, and van der Windt (2013), Dunning (2016).

problems noted above. Indeed, because RCTs require intense focus on design details – the implementation of which is often specific to particular contexts – RCTs sometimes lead researchers to drill down into the particularities of distinct study sites. While for many reasons we applaud this close engagement with particular settings, from the standpoint of generalizability, this could risk making matters worse. This concern is therefore sometimes cast as a tension between internal and external validity.[17]

While we note that there is no fundamental reason why a gain on internal validity means a loss on external validity, RCTs alone may do surprisingly little to facilitate cumulative learning. Consider the following reasons for concern:

Excludability. The most obvious is that experiments, by definition, involve intervention, and so claims to external validity rest on an assumption that the intervention itself does not produce effects different to what would be produced by naturalistic variation. This is sometimes referred to as the need to satisfy an exclusion restriction,[18] as well as construct validity.[19] Excludability always poses a risk with experimentation – though plausibly it is less a concern for field experiments than for other forms of experimentation.

Mechanisms. The generalizability of experiments depends on understanding why an intervention is effective; yet experimental designs often ignore or are unable to answer "why" questions of this form.[20] Indeed, very commonly the "estimand" of an experimental research project is the average treatment effect in a population which can be calculated with only a thin model of the way that outcomes are generated.[21] This shift in focus away from models of data generation connects to the external validity of experiments because understanding the underlying mechanism can help answer the question of whether a similar intervention would work in a different context – where different mechanisms may be operative.[22] Experimental design can certainly help shed light on

---

[17] Deaton (2010).
[18] Gerber and Green (2012).
[19] Morton and Williams (2010).
[20] Deaton and Cartwright (2017).
[21] For example, each unit has a potential outcome under treatment and a potential outcome under control, and which outcome is realized depends on the unit's treatment assignment. This is a model of the data-generating process but does not stipulate a theory of any particular unit's response.
[22] See the writings of Nancy Cartwright on this point, e.g., Cartwright and Hardie (2012).

mechanisms.[23] Yet, features of the broader context in which an intervention takes place may not be possible to manipulate, and can clearly condition effects in ways that experiments per se do not necessarily illuminate.

Scale. Experiments are often implemented on a population that differs in scale from the population for which inferences are sought. Scholars such as Daron Acemoglu have emphasized that estimated treatment effects may not provide a reliable guide to what would happen if interventions were taken "to scale." Specifically, experiments tend to evaluate the impact of interventions in partial equilibrium, i.e., without taking account of likely reactions of critical stakeholders. Yet, general equilibrium or feedback effects would be more critical if a treatment were applied everywhere and not just to a small subset of a population.[24]

These concerns are important for producers and users of social science knowledge alike. The goal of much research is not simply to estimate the impact of some intervention, but to understand why the intervention had the effect that it did; to assess what would happen if the intervention were implemented in a different way or in a different context; and to add to basic social science knowledge about where particular causal relationships obtain. To the extent that experimental research falls short of these goals – due to violations of the exclusion restriction, a failure to specify mechanisms, or because results cannot be scaled – it is less illuminating and less useful for both researchers and policymakers.[25]

How, then, can experimental research – with its well-understood internal validity advantages for assessing the causal impact of interventions – address such external validity concerns?

Among proponents of RCTs, one answer has been to argue that experiments should be replicated, in different contexts and at different scales.

---

[23] For a discussion, see Gerber and Green (2012) on "implicit mediation analysis."

[24] See, for instance, Acemoglu (2010). In a small-scale field experiment, Grossman, Humphreys, and Sacramone-Lutz (2019) showed that the use of SMS-based messaging services to communicate with politicians can lead to significant "flattening" of political access; however, they find no evidence for such flattening in a larger-scale national experiment.

[25] These critiques of experiments are valid and important, though we note that they are often unduly generous to observational research – which may not have the advantage sometimes claimed for it on the dimension of external validity. See, for instance, Aronow and Samii (2016). The question of mechanisms in particular turns out to pose more fundamental challenges than causal inference and the challenge in studying mechanisms is no less, and perhaps greater, for observational research (Green, Ha, and Bullock, 2010).

Thus, even if one experiment alone cannot shed light on the external validity of the answer to a research question – so the thinking goes – many such experiments can. For example, Abhijit Banerjee and Esther Duflo note that to address "concerns about generalization, actual replication studies need to be carried out. Additional experiments need to be conducted in different locations, with different teams."[26] In principle, such replication should be especially feasible with experiments: to a much greater extent than is possible for many observational studies, researchers' control over experimental manipulations offers the opportunity to introduce a treatment anew. Modifications and extensions of experimental designs may also offer evidence on operative mechanisms and allow informed discussion of whether those mechanisms are likely to operate in distinct contexts.[27] Replication and carefully scaled-up extensions of experimental designs are thus thought to provide the most reliable route to cumulative learning, and can ultimately inform questions about the conditions under which specific interventions are more likely to work, more likely to be cost effective, or more likely to have unanticipated or unintended consequences.

One can find examples of cumulative learning from replication of experimental research in some domains. These can be categorized into two classes of integrated studies: (a) the same intervention has been implemented in multiple places, and (b) the same intervention has been implemented in different ways, for the direct purpose of comparison across different variants of the same class of intervention. In an interesting example of the first class of studies, which is related to the approach we develop in this book, Abhijit Banerjee and colleagues presented findings from six RCTs that tested the effect of a similar program to support the very poor in obtaining access to assets, life skills coaching, savings accounts, and health information services. This basic program was adapted to the wide variety of geographic and institutional contexts and was implemented with multiple implementing partners.[28] In other contexts, researchers have taken advantage of a set of high-quality RCTs that emerged simultaneously on a similar topic to synthesize evidence.[29] An interesting illustration of the second class of integrated studies comes

---

[26] Banerjee and Duflo (2009).
[27] See Clemens (2017) for a discussion of different forms of replication, verification, and robustness tests.
[28] Banerjee et al. (2015).
[29] See for instance, Banerjee, Karlan, and Zinman (2015).

from Tessa Bold and colleagues, who replicated experiments on the educational impact of hiring additional teachers in Kenya but varied whether the hiring was done by NGOs (as in previous research) or through a government ministry.[30] Their results suggested that hiring through a traditional government ministry did not have the same positive impact on educational attainment as hiring through an NGO. In other words, part of the apparent effect of hiring teachers evident in previous research was due to the fact that this was done through a novel, parallel nongovernmental structure. In the United States, the large body of experimental research on voter mobilization by Alan Gerber and Donald Green suggests a similar program of replication with controlled variation in design that allows research to build on previous experimental findings.[31] Other researchers and organizations have sought to advance the role of systematic meta-analysis; see, for example, recent work by AidGrade.[32] Such examples illustrate how both experimental replication and meta-analysis can provide a valuable tool in the effort to promote generalizable knowledge.

Yet such replication in fact appears quite infrequent, and, for several reasons, rarely offers these benefits. Unplanned replication, to the extent it arises, tends to involve new interventions, distinct outcome measures, and other differences across studies that make it difficult to learn from the comparison of results across studies – the problem we referred to as study heterogeneity. And planned external replication, at least of field-based studies, appears almost as rare in experimental as in observational research.[33] The reasons are likely many, but one key factor may again be strong career incentives that reward innovation, and weak career incentives to replicate. In addition, as we noted, the rise of experiments has increased the deep involvement of researchers with the intricacies of study sites and the requirements for design implementation in a particular context, which while valuable, can further weaken comparability across studies. Moreover, researchers tend to emphasize theoretical innovations – to differentiate themselves from others – such that different papers ostensibly on the same topic focus on distinct aspects of the same problem; and different experiments may not only study distinct

---

[30] Bold et al. (2018).

[31] Green and Gerber (2015). See also the very interesting meta-analysis and planned replication of campaign mobilization studies by Kalla and Broockman (2017).

[32] www.aidgrade.org.

[33] External replication of laboratory studies is easier because the lab, by definition, is devoid of context. See, for example, Henrich et al. (2004).

interventions and theoretical claims but also use different measures and estimation strategies. Indeed, with RCTs (as for observational studies), incentives to innovate extend also to measurement strategies, with professional rewards for novelty. Perhaps for these reasons, as Gerber and Green (2012: 347) put it, "any two experiments differ along an unmanageably large number of dimensions." Uncoordinated replication – itself substantially rare – generates serious challenges to drawing informative conclusions from the aggregation of findings.

The epistemic challenge is therefore how to coordinate RCT research in a manner that doesn't sacrifice internal validity but does meaningfully enhance our understanding of general effectiveness, and of the role played by context, as well as how variations in the implementation of interventions may condition their impacts.

2.2 THE METAKETA APPROACH

The barriers to cumulative learning described in the previous section are substantial. The complexity of the social and political world, the organization of knowledge production in the professional social sciences, and the recent revitalization of RCTs as a mode of strengthening the internal validity of studies collectively pose substantial obstacles.

This book describes our efforts to address these challenges. In particular, we report results of a new initiative of the Evidence in Governance and Politics (EGAP) research network. The inaugural project of the "Metaketa Initiative" that we present integrates seven coordinated studies involving thirty-one contributors from twenty universities.[34] Our motivation stems from the recognition, discussed in the previous section, that individual researchers working independently do not necessarily generate the optimal set of studies for knowledge accumulation: problems of study scarcity, study heterogeneity, selective reporting, and private data can undermine the accumulation of knowledge. Our goal is therefore to generate cumulative evidence by supporting field experimental research across disparate contexts, working with independent project teams to increase coordination among studies that share common research questions and hypotheses. We seek to increase the number and comparability (within constraints discussed below) of studies in a given topic area in order to support cumulative learning from a set of studies as a whole. The

---

[34] It was backed by over $2 million in funding; see our discussion of the funding process in the Preface and below.

data generated by such an effort may be more feasibly integrated in an overall meta-analysis than can the output of individual, uncoordinated studies. Variation in findings both across studies and due to planned experimental variation within studies can, potentially, also contribute to addressing several of the specific challenges to external validity in experimental research, including issues of excludability, mechanisms, and scale. A major portion of this effort involves the construction of research vehicles that incentivize replication as well as innovation. Our wager is thus that greater coordination among experimental researchers can contribute to counteracting several of the difficulties described in the previous section. Our objective in writing this book is partially substantive, in that we lay out answers to questions about information and accountability gleaned from the inaugural Metaketa. But it is also methodological, in that we characterize the rationale for and structure of the initiative, attempt to validate its usefulness as a tool for cumulative learning, and suggest guidance and lessons learned for future initiatives of coordinated studies.

In the rest of this chapter, we describe the Metaketa grant-making model and discuss how this approach may help overcome some of the challenges to cumulative learning described above. In the remainder of the book, we assess and demonstrate the model's utility for addressing important and practically relevant questions surrounding the relationship between informational interventions and political accountability. Beyond that substantive focus, however, we view this inaugural project of the Metaketa Initiative as a replicable model. Indeed, the research reported in this book has motivated three additional EGAP-sponsored Metaketas focused on (a) taxation and accountability, (b) natural resource governance, and (c) community policing, and we hope these will generate additional coordinated experimental research projects that build on this model.[35]

The Metaketa Initiative is based on a number of core pillars, designed to overcome, to the extent possible, challenges both to the reliability of individual studies and, especially, to the credibility of the overall inferences that can be drawn from a set of related studies. We summarize these challenges and the pillars of our approach in Table 2.1. In the

---

[35] As noted in the Preface, Metaketa I was funded by an anonymous donor; the subsequent Metaketas are funded primarily by the United Kingdom's Department For International Development (DfID). Metaketa I was administered by EGAP in conjunction with the Center on the Politics of Development at the University of California, Berkeley.

TABLE 2.1 *The Metaketa Initiative: Extant challenges and pillars*

Extant challenges	Pillars of the Metaketa Initiative
1. Confounding in observational research	1. Randomized controlled trials
2. Limited external validity of single RCTs	2. Multiple studies in diverse contexts
3. Heterogeneous, scattered findings	3. Meta-analysis with overall finding
4. Diversity of interventions	4. "Common arm" intervention
5. Noncomparable measures, impeding aggregation	5. Harmonized measurement of inputs, outcomes, and controls
6. Researcher incentives for innovation over replication	6. "Alternative arm" intervention
7. Private data	7. Open data and replication code
8. Errors in data or code	8. Third-party data analysis
9. Fishing (data mining, specification searching, multiple hypotheses)	9. Pre-analysis plans with limited number of specified hypotheses
10. Publication bias	10. Publication of all registered analyses

next section, we further discuss the rationale for these elements of our approach as well as the steps involved in implementing them.[36]

First, all Metaketa studies employ randomized interventions to identify causal effects (point 1 in Table 2.1). We thus seek a strong basis for causal inference within each study. This, in turn, provides the foundation for valid inferences about overall effects, when aggregating across studies.

Next, and critically, we seek to consolidate evidence on major questions of scholarly and policy relevance – with an emphasis on cumulative learning, rather than primarily on innovation (points 2–6 in Table 2.1). In doing so, we seek to address several related barriers to the accumulation of knowledge in the social sciences, especially the problems of study scarcity and study heterogeneity discussed previously.

Thus, because any single RCT may have limited external validity, we support multiple studies on a single topic across diverse contexts (point 2

---

[36] See also our pre-analysis plan for the meta-analysis in the Appendix, as well as each study's project-specific pre-analysis plan (see http://egap.org/metaketa/metaketa-information-and-accountability).

in Table 2.1). In place of heterogeneous, scattered results, we also aim to produce a meta-analysis, resulting in an overall finding produced from the aggregation of these multiple studies (point 3 in Table 2.1). And to address the diversity of interventions and the proliferation of noncomparable measures in a given area, which can hinder aggregation, research teams strive to coordinate on conceptually similar interventions (point 4 in Table 2.1) and commit to measuring the same variables, including key outcome variables, in a similar way (point 5 in Table 2.1). To be sure, what is meant by "similar" is an important and sometimes difficult question (and one we address in detail for Metaketa I in Chapter 3). The core principle, however, is that, to the extent possible, differences in findings should be attributable primarily to contextual factors – and not to differences in research design or measurement. Overall, notwithstanding some differences that arise naturally from working in different sites, close coordination of interventions and outcomes significantly increases the plausibility and tractability of meta-analysis. At the same time, basic similarities in the interventions imply that differences in treatments across studies can also be considered, and distinct treatment effects in different contexts can be preregistered as hypotheses in light of those differences.

Our emphasis on coordination, replication, and cumulative learning raises an important challenge, however: researcher incentives for innovation over replication. We recognize the importance of innovation for the growth of knowledge. Breakthroughs are rightly prized. Yet, as we outlined above, researchers often have weak incentives to verify previous findings with new studies. This may lead to the privileging of "being first" over "being right." A major question is therefore how to address this issue – recognizing the reality that researchers prize innovation in part because individual studies that are deemed innovative are easier to publish. Our approach, as detailed in the next section, is to coordinate research on a "common arm" intervention among all studies included in the Metaketa round but also build in planned diversity across studies by including at least one "alternative arm" intervention in each study (point 6 in Table 2.1). In this way, research teams generate comparable results that can be integrated through meta-analysis of common interventions – while also allowing for novel individual findings through study-specific interventions.

Additionally, we seek to address several challenges related to selective reporting, as well as private data. Both individual studies and our meta-analysis seek to take advantage of best practices of analytic transparency, including (a) open data and materials (point 7 of Table 2.1); (b) third-party replication of analyses prior to publication (point 8 of

Table 2.1); and (c) preregistration of designs and analysis plans (point 9 of 2.1). Funding for Metaketa I was conditional on researchers' agreement to abide by these and other procedures included in EGAP's statement on research transparency.[37] These practices are designed to limit threats to the validity of individual studies – including fishing expeditions or unintentional errors in data analysis – but also the validity of the meta-analysis. Thus, detailed plans for aggregating results are also preregistered: we seek to bring public and transparent methods to the accumulation of results from the separate field experiments that comprise our project.

Finally, in the Metaketa model, researchers commit to be part of an integrated publication of the results of all of the studies, as a way to avoid publication bias (point 10 in Table 2.1). Thus, regardless of findings, and particularly regardless of whether the estimated effects of individual studies are statistically different from zero, the results of each study would be published in a single prominent outlet.[38] Joint publication of the results – particularly if negotiated with a publisher in advance of analyzing study data, as is the case in this volume – can involve a form of "results-blind" review in which publication decisions are driven by the quality of the research questions, theory, and research designs, but not the statistical significance of the findings.[39] An integrated publication limits publication bias, because null results readily appear. Even the outcome of failed interventions – as in one of the studies in this volume (Chapter 10) – can appear in the final write-up, rather than disappearing in the file drawer of unrealized projects.[40] As we detail later, with our approach it is not possible to sweep study-level attrition under the rug; and knowing about missingness of outcome data within and across studies is informative and useful for the broader social scientific inquiry. This book constitutes the integrated publication for Metaketa I.

A different core set of principles, discussed in the next section, relates to ethics. Given that Metaketa interventions may focus on sensitive and important areas of governance (e.g., democratic elections), ethical concerns – such as "do no harm" principles – constitute a central focus. We discuss ethical concerns in Chapter 3 and elsewhere in the book.

---

[37] See http://egap.org/resources/egap-statement-of-principles/.
[38] In addition, all project teams are writing separate individual articles, often based on the alternative rather than common arms of their experiments; see further discussion below.
[39] On results-blind review, see Findley et al. (2016); Dunning (2016).
[40] Karlan and Appel (2016).

In sum, all studies in this joint initiative aimed to adhere to collective methodological principles, including preregistration and third-party data analysis. By coordinating on interventions and outcomes and adhering to important principles of transparency and reproducibility, the initiative aims to maximize comparability and the accumulation of knowledge across different studies. Research teams in the Metaketa Initiative work on parallel, coordinated research projects. They collaborate on theory, intervention design, and on both measurement and estimation strategies in order to allow for informed comparisons across study contexts. This coordination of design, interventions, and outcome measures across studies also makes our data "meta-analysis ready" to a much greater extent than would be a standard set of disparate experimental studies. And prespecification of the meta-analysis plan limits the scope for data mining at the aggregation stage. In addition, Metaketa I sought to facilitate an exchange that makes for a much more open and collaborative model of science than is sometime practiced in social, political, or economic research, for instance, through the holding of multiple meetings with all of the project teams at multiple research stages – including to workshop research designs, report progress, and present final results. Multiple interactions between teams working in parallel also helped in handling logistical and professional issues, including those around modes of publication of results. At the same time, teams have some incentive both to be innovative and to "check over each other's shoulders" – enabling a degree of informed scrutiny and constructive criticism that is helpful for scientific progress. Finally, researchers also observe common principles for ethical research in the thematic area of research on governance more generally, and information and electoral accountability in the case of Metaketa I.

2.3 MAKING METAKETAS WORK

Operationalizing these principles was perhaps the major challenge of our work. The Metaketa approach is, to our knowledge, unique in the social sciences in its effort to take a large number of independent research teams and forge a collaborative approach that would result in coordinated field experiments in so many countries, with key design and analysis procedures agreed in advance of data collection.[41] Given that, at our

---

[41] See also the Foundations of Human Sociality project that coordinated researchers across 15 sites, all undertaking similar behavioral (laboratory) experiments; Henrich et al. (2004).

first meeting, we did not have an ex-ante consensus on the details of how this coordination was to be achieved, we had to engage with a set of potentially contentious issues. In multiple meetings and workshops held between 2014 and 2016, the seven research teams and the thirty-one coauthors of the chapters in this book therefore collaborated on theory, design, measurement, and estimation strategies in an effort to promote cumulative learning across studies.[42]

It is worth describing several key aspects of this operationalization – i.e., "making the Metaketa work." The goal of the Metaketa Initiative is to facilitate research structures that mitigate the threats to cumulative learning discussed above – in particular, practices and strategies that permit movement away from the status quo and that increase our ability to cumulate reliable knowledge from multiple studies on a single topic. Achieving these goals required new structures as well as practical decisions, and here we describe several of the specific opportunities and challenges we encountered in developing the Metaketa Initiative, the solutions we found, and the advantages we see for this new method for cumulative learning. We emphasize, however, that our approach has limitations; and there are trade-offs to consider with this form of research. Certainly, learning in the social sciences benefits from many approaches, and Metaketas are only one among these. In our concluding Chapter 13, we discuss lessons learned and consider the moments at which and the questions for which a Metaketa may be particularly valuable.

Table 2.2 describes the implementation steps for Metaketa I. In many ways, this looks like any other grant-making initiative: a steering committee issues a call for Expressions of Interest (EOIs) and then a Request for Proposals (RFP); awards are made, and preliminary approvals from university and governmental partners are obtained; baseline data are collected, interventions are fielded, and endline data are gathered; and research results are written up, published, and disseminated to key stakeholders.

Yet, several aspects of the structure of implementation are specific to this initiative, and, in particular, to the challenges we faced in developing coordinated research on a single topic with independent research teams, in the context of an effort to privilege especially the role of replication and the pillars of the Metaketa approach we described above. In the

---

[42] We held such workshops in Princeton (October 19, 2014), Cambridge (December 7, 2014), San Francisco (September 3–4, 2015), and Berkeley (December 8–9, 2016).

TABLE 2.2 *Metaketa I: Steps of implementation*

Preliminaries	Implementation (Preparatory Stage)	Implementation (Study Stage)	Post-Implementation Stage
1. Establish steering committee	1. Coordination meetings	1. Write and register meta-analysis pre-analysis plan (MPAP)	1. Analyze and publish meta-analysis
2. Raise grant	2. Write and register study-specific PAPs	2. Run baseline and interventions	2. Publish individual studies
3. Decide broad focus area	3. Seek IRB approvals and government permissions	3. Endline data	3. Disseminate findings to key stakeholders
4. Solicit Expressions of Interest (EOIs)			
5. Identify research question			
6. Request for Proposals (RFPs) and R&Rs			
7. Final award decisions			

rest of this section, we describe the ways in which we sought to resolve a tension between innovation and replication, with a focus on consolidation of evidence; bolster research transparency; respect key ethical principles; achieve coordination on interventions and outcome measures across projects; and combine the results of the studies in a formal meta-analysis.

2.3.1   Consolidation of Evidence: Innovation vs. Replication

This inaugural Metaketa involved construction of a selection committee – composed of the five coauthors of this chapter and chaired by Dunning – who would work separately from authors of the individual studies and who would take responsibility for several aspects of the overall research strategy.[43]

Our first objective was to identify research questions that (a) fit within a general predefined substantive area; (b) mattered to both researchers and policymakers; and (c) included interventions and outcomes that could feasibly be harmonized across multiple studies. Another central concern was to identify areas in which sufficient numbers of researchers were working, or were interested in working, that a group of similar studies could be pursued. We thus pursued a two-stage proposal process, first distributing a call for EOIs to allow researchers to indicate their potential participation and their ideas for research projects at a relatively low cost in time and effort. For Metaketa I, our EOIs call sought especially to identify potential projects in the areas of both community-based monitoring and informational interventions for political accountability. The latter emerged as the most promising focus, not only because of its substantive interest and importance, but also because of the density of researchers interested in pursuing work in this area. We then released a full RFP that focused on the informational theme and solicited much more detailed descriptions of the proposed projects.[44] We selected projects for funding from among the detailed proposals we received, assessing the quality of the proposed research including the strength of the research designs for causal inference (a pillar mentioned in point 1 in Table 2.1); all of the funded studies proposed randomized field experiments. We also considered especially the substantive fit with the Metaketa I project; and funding decisions were contingent on researchers' agreement to adhere to principles of research transparency, coordination across studies, and other pillars of our approach.

The availability of substantial funding in support of this project certainly eased the task of attracting world-class scholars to participate in it.[45] Yet, it was still nontrivial to ensure sufficient interest in participation. After all, our theory of the problem of knowledge accumulation

---

[43] The ongoing Metaketas II, III, and IV alter this structure somewhat; for example, they allow committee members (but not the chair) to apply to the Metaketa as researchers after the initial definition of core themes through an Expression of Interest round.

[44] This RFP was open to all scholars; it was not limited to current members of the EGAP network, nor to those who had submitted an EOI.

[45] This is perhaps especially true in political science, because money for field experiments is scarcer than in adjacent disciplines such as development economics or public health.

focuses centrally on the incentives of academic researchers to plant the flag, due to strong professional orientation towards novelty discussed in Section 2.1. We cannot (nor would we necessarily want to) globally alter the fact that novelty and innovation are prized in standard publication processes. Yet, we believed that if incentives to do so are improved, enough scholars may be willing to build in additional research time to coordinate across studies, such that their work better contributes to the accumulation and consolidation of evidence.

One major issue, then, was how to promote incentives to engage in replication. This was plausibly further complicated by the fact that most of the researchers on the Metaketa I project teams were tenure-track but untenured researchers or were advanced graduate students at the time the fieldwork was planned and implemented.[46] At the same time, we also sought to recognize the value of innovation and to prioritize the study of comparative effectiveness – that is, learning about what works best to increase political accountability, and where and why it does so.

Our approach to this inherent tension was to develop a structure that fosters coordination and replication but also leaves sufficient leeway for researchers to innovate – as well as to publish independent articles on their project-specific findings. In particular, we called for proposals for research designs with at least two treatment arms:

- One common intervention arm focused on provision of information on the performance of politicians in a way that was as similar as possible across studies (point 4 in Table 2.1); and
- At least one alternative arm that varied across projects, and that allowed for assessment of new hypotheses as well as comparison of the impact of different kinds of treatments (point 6 in Table 2.1).

Studies included in Metaketa I, for example, used their alternative arms to vary inter alia whether information was provided privately or publicly, the density of treated communities within a constituency, the identity of the messenger providing the information, and the presence of alternative

---

[46] Indeed, we also had teams composed of graduate students at the time of application who carried out exceptional execution of their projects (see Platas and Raffler, Chapter 6; also Lierl and Holmlund, Chapter 8). Their participation offered substantial benefits both for the energy and ambition of the project and with respect to the development of younger scholars.

messages that may heighten the perceived salience and relevance of the information (see Chapter 3 and Part II).

We believed that this structure would promote replication and comparability – through the common arm – while preserving room for innovation through the alternative arm. Thus, we would seek to learn about aggregate effects through meta-analysis of results on the common arm, building on the replications of similar interventions across disparate contexts; and we would also seek to learn from variation in effects, both across contexts and through experimental variation that is internal to each study. By differentiating the projects along the alternative arm, we would maximize the chances for independent publication of the results of each study, while still providing a baseline common treatment arm that would be replicated across studies. We felt this model would facilitate researcher participation in a sustainable way and thus could be extended to other initiatives, including future Metaketas. The structure of the call for proposals therefore, we hoped, helped to reconcile the tension between innovation and replication in a way that would allow for the consolidation of evidence on information and accountability.

In the end, to be sure, innovation in research topics and replication of research results remain in some ways in tension with each other. Research funding mechanisms that are open to topic can choose the best projects on a case-by-case basis; and "letting a thousand flowers bloom" may generate very high-quality studies that innovate in new areas of investigation. Yet, they are unlikely to provide a dense body of evidence on a single topic that can cumulate in a manner that is obviously externally valid. Pure replication studies, such as the Banerjee et al. (2015) study analyzing BRAC's Targeting the Ultra-Poor program can be an excellent way of establishing the broad, externally valid impacts of a very specific intervention, but do not allow for innovation in research questions or in project design. The Metaketa approach was designed to strike a balance between these two goals, permitting a kind of crowd-sourcing of topics of interest, using multiple treatment arms to allow researchers to innovate on individual projects, but harmonizing theory, interventions, measurement, and estimation in a manner designed to foster cross-study comparability.

2.3.2 Research Transparency

In structuring this Metaketa and considering the reporting and publication of its results, per Table 2.1, we also sought to combine several features of study registration, pre-analysis plans, and results-blind review. It is useful to describe the extent to which these practices are in fact likely to reduce publication bias and selective reporting – which we identified in Section 2.1 as important barriers to cumulative learning.

Study registration may refer simply to documenting the existence of a study in advance of its execution.[47] In principle, it allows description of a universe of planned studies – which provides a denominator against which one can assess the set of completed or published studies. To date, registration has been somewhat ad hoc, with several different organizations providing third-party registration services.[48] Several political science journals now have a policy of encouraging study registration.[49] However, registration is typically voluntary, and the level of detail about the planned study varies greatly.

Pre-analysis plans, by contrast, typically describe the hypotheses and statistical tests that will be conducted once outcome data are gathered, often in greater detail than study registration alone would require – though there is currently no strong standard for their form and content, and they can involve greater or lesser specificity about the number and kind of tests. Empirically, many pre-analysis plans discuss research hypotheses but are quite vague in terms of the precise operationalization of tests. At the other extreme is Humphreys et al.'s (2011) approach of posting complete analysis code with mock data which allows analysts to simply run the code once the real outcome data are collected (Blair et al. 2019).[50] This arguably represents best practice, since it leaves little guesswork on the part of readers of a pre-analysis plan of exactly what is intended in the analysis.[51] Prespecification of tests promotes credible adjustment for multiple statistical comparisons and limits the scope for data mining.

---

[47] On the benefits of different forms of registration, see Humphreys, Sanchez de la Sierra, and van der Windt (2013) or Monogan III (2013); for a lucid critique and discussion of possible drawbacks, see Laitin (2013).

[48] As of May 2018, the EGAP registry has over 800 designs registered since inception in March 2011 (see http://egap.org/design-registration/registered-designs/). The American Economic Association (AEA) (see www.socialscienceregistry.org), the Open Science Framework, and other entities also host large registries.

[49] See for instance, *Political Analysis*, https://www.cambridge.org/core/journals/political-analysis/information/instructions-contributors

[50] See http://egap.org/registration/602.

[51] An interesting related approach exists for studies with pilots: code can be preregistered after analysis of pilot data, which are likely to have similar characteristics as data collected during scale-up.

Finally, results-blind review – as the name implies – refers to the practice of reviewing a research report blind to the study's findings. Thus, referees evaluate a journal submission on the basis of the interest and importance of the research question, the strength of the theory, and the quality of the empirical design – but not the p-values of the study. Though still quite rare, the practice has been applied in several venues.[52]

These three forms of prespecification likely have different capacities to reduce publication bias. Study registration without pre-analysis plans – although it allows measurement of the phenomenon, by providing a denominator for the number of studies in a given area – seems unlikely to reduce the bias. Indeed, whatever the true source of publication bias, the mere fact of having announced the existence of a study prior to its execution should not affect its chance of publication, conditional on the p-values. Consistent with this conjecture, Fang, Gordon, and Humphreys (2015) find no evidence that the creation in 2005 of mandated study registration in medical journals – which did not, however, require detailed pre-analysis plans or results-blind review – led to a reduction in publication bias.

With pre-analysis plans, the likely impact is subtler and depends on whether the source of publication bias is (a) specification searches or "fishing" on the part of authors; or (b) the preferences of reviewers and editors for statistically significant findings. In principle, prespecifying the set of tests to be performed limits the scope for ex-post specification searches or "fishing" for statistically significant effects; and pre-analysis plans may allow for meaningful adjustment for multiple statistical comparisons – without which the interpretation of nominal p-values may be undermined. A complete pre-analysis plan prespecifies the mode of adjustment for multiple statistical comparisons and thus limits the scope to condition adjustment on realized p-values. However, if journal editors and reviewers simply refuse to publish null estimated effects – perhaps because they find null effects uninformative – prespecifying the tests will not reduce publication bias.

By contrast, results-blind review does appear to offer an effective remedy for publication bias: it is impossible for reviewers and editors to

---

[52] A recent special issue of the journal *Comparative Political Studies* featured only articles reviewed in this results-blind way, though it allowed both planned research, described prospectively, and completed research that was stripped of discussion of results. This practice may encourage a selection bias in the types of articles submitted, since authors of studies with null effects might be more likely to strip their article of results and apply to such a forum.

condition publication decisions on the *p*-values if they do not know what the *p*-values are.

We took several steps to ensure that these dimensions of research transparency were at the heart of Metaketa I. First, the collection of seven studies was registered as part of our research prespecification. This also therefore records the existence of missing studies or data and prompts consideration of the impact of such study-level attrition for our inferences. In fact, one of the seven projects planned for this Metaketa did not occur, as described in Chapter 10. In our meta-analysis in Chapter 11, we consider the implications of this missingness for the robustness of our aggregate conclusions. The critical point here is that without such study registration, no record of this study – nor the fact that it went missing – would exist.

Second, the authors of all the individual studies in this volume registered pre-analysis plans in advance of obtaining outcome data.[53] Even more uncommonly, our meta-analysis reported in Chapter 11 was also preregistered. Critically, the individual project pre-analysis plans were written after several coordination meetings (on measurement and estimation strategies), and after we collectively wrote the meta-analysis pre-analysis plan (MPAP);[54] this helped ensure coordination across studies at the pre-analysis phase and made the meta-analysis much more feasible. In Chapter 11 and the book's Conclusion, we reflect on lessons learned from the execution of the MPAP. Notwithstanding some limitations, we emphasize that the prespecification of the analysis of pooled data made our studies "meta-analysis ready" to a much greater extent than would be the case with a standard set of disparate studies.

Finally, a core principle that was outlined in our RFP is integrated publication of the results of all of the studies. Joint publication of the results – particularly if negotiated with a publisher on the basis of the study designs and in advance of analyzing study data – can involve a form of results-blind review in which publication decisions are driven by the quality of the research question, theory, and empirical design, and not the statistical significance of the findings. Thus, integrated publication can be a tool for limiting publication bias, because null results can readily appear. Even the outcome of failed interventions can be informative for the broader themes of inquiry and is thus useful to the broader social

---

53 In most cases, designs were also registered before interventions were fielded.
54 See Appendix.

scientific inquiry. As mentioned above, this book – for which we obtained approval for an advance contract on the basis of a book prospectus (i.e., not on the basis of the studies' *p*-values) – is published on the basis of such a results-blind review and constitutes a main integrated publication for the initiative.

We also considered different forms that such integrated publication could take; for example, we discussed the possibility of a special issue with the current editor of one leading political science journal, but that route did not appear promising, in part because results-blind review is not yet established as a norm in social science publication, and in part because the editor was hesitant to consider steps necessary for integrated publication – e.g., an up-or-down decision on the entire package of studies. Moreover, the journal format did not provide sufficient space for important details on the structure of this inaugural Metaketa nor to allow for substantial synthesis across studies. We also considered a short, synthetic article with all Metaketa participants as coauthors that would set forth the primary results of our meta-analysis.[55] A book such as this one, however, negotiated with an advance contract, offers several advantages, including the space to pursue the research model and the process of operationalizing it in depth; and the capacity to present in-depth evidence from each study as well as from the overall meta-analysis. We recognize a certain irony that publication of the book may have been eased by the fact that this inaugural Metaketa was intellectually novel and hence involved some "planting the flag" on coordinated research. Nonetheless, we believe volumes on the varied substantive topics of future Metaketas are likely to be appealing to top presses as well.

In addition to this integrated publication, and related to the theme of encouraging participation in the Metaketa Initiative, we encouraged individual project teams to pursue publication of articles, reporting especially on the alternative arms of their studies, in leading journals. We hoped that the distinctions between the projects, especially on the alternative intervention arms, would ease such problems; but again, the promise of integrated publications was critical for addressing such concerns. Yet, there were substantial issues that arose in trying to make this approach work. Because our collaborative project focused on information provided to voters in advance of elections – with voting and turnout measures constituting the main outcome variables – the timing of projects was tightly linked to the timing of elections across studies.

---

55 Such an article is now forthcoming in *Science Advances* (Dunning et al. 2019).

Thus, some projects fielded much earlier than others. For example, the first intervention was fielded in Benin in connection with the March 2015 election, while the last was fielded in Brazil in conjunction with the October 2016 election there. This created some concern among researchers of a "publication advantage" for studies fielded earlier as compared to later studies (reflecting the fact that the research questions and approach would be more novel for the first studies submitting for publication than it would for later studies – again, the returns to novelty provided an important challenge to our collective work). We considered, but ultimately collectively rejected, proposals to ask the "early" studies not to submit for publication before all studies were complete; our emphasis was on offering and coordinating integrated publication on the common interventions, but also facilitating autonomy of researchers to pursue independent publication.

Finally on research transparency, we also committed to public data and replication code, in accordance with EGAP principles of analytic transparency, in order to give third parties the opportunity to replicate findings within each study before publication. Collaboration together with some degree of competition among project teams encouraged third-party verification of analysis. Moreover, each team's analysis was eventually independently replicated by teams of graduate students at UC Berkeley and Columbia University. These internal replications did reveal various minor errors and discrepancies in data and code, which we could correct before compilation of this volume, thus increasing the reliability of reported results. Reproduction of results using publicly available data raised some questions about the meaning and extent of "third-party replication." For example, our preference wherever possible was to work with raw data, and to record all manipulations to the data in replication files so that the path from data to results would be clear – thereby allowing useful checks on data processing errors and other mistakes. Yet, this is feasible only to an extent. Project teams uniformly employed in-country enumerators and survey firms to gather primary data from respondents, and also merged these with official electoral results and other data. Third-party replication unfortunately does not allow checking the quality of the data gathered in the field, which was the responsibility of project teams and the organizations with whom they collaborated. Our approach is to begin third-party replication with the raw data file(s) obtained from survey firms and other sources; yet the inability of third parties to check the quality of the data collection in the field is one limitation that should be kept in mind.

2.3.3 Ethical Principles

We also attempted to codify best practice in terms of the ethical principles to which our studies adhered. We made a shared commitment to the following practices:

First, each of the individual projects was approved by Institutional Review Boards (IRBs) at all of the home institutions of the Principal Investigators working on the respective project. We sought such unanimous approval to avoid incentives for forum shopping (e.g., seeking approval from IRBs thought to be "soft" on appraisal of risks to human subjects). This is a critical baseline requirement. We recognize, however, that IRB approval does not constitute an ethical blank check. Review boards are focused on some kinds of harm – especially, risks to subjects – but they can do so to the neglect of others – for instance, risks to enumerators and other project employees. Moreover, avoiding risk of harm to subjects does not imply that an intervention is necessarily ethical in other ways. Beyond unanimous IRB approval for all projects, we therefore instituted several additional ethical principles, as described in our MPAP.[56]

Second, precisely to overcome the typical IRB blind spot around harm to investigators, we sought to ensure that we would not put enumerators and other project staff in harm's way. This had substantial implications for several of our projects – especially the planned study in India (Chapter 10). In fact, several of the studies involved situations of potential threat to enumerators, and in each situation project teams had to negotiate the best possible way to minimize risks of harm. We have the sense that such risks sometimes arise in field experimental studies yet are rarely discussed in write-ups; the chapters describing individual study results in this book describe these difficulties.

Third, we sought informed consent from all subjects. In most cases, subjects knew that information they received was provided as part of a research project. This commitment goes beyond the usual informed consent, for instance, that researchers use when eliciting participation in a survey. (We recognized the possibility that soliciting informed consent in this way could generate Hawthorne-type effects – i.e., behaviors that are influenced by the simple fact of being studied – and discuss this issue elsewhere.)

---

[56] See Appendix.

Fourth, we sought partnerships wherever possible with local civil society actors (or government bodies, which was the case for the Brazil study) who implemented the experimental interventions. As described in more detail in later chapters, these partners were either already implementing informational interventions similar to those we proposed, or the experimental interventions were consistent with their core missions and activities. Thus, in many cases, these partners, rather than researchers, implemented the interventions (though in collaboration with researchers who designed protocols for randomization and developed other research design details). Also consistent with an idea of country ownership and public transparency, we made core project data publicly available in primary languages, aiding in the effort of communicating the existence and intent of the project to participants as well as others in the study countries.[57] And several of the research teams have conducted public events in their project countries disseminating the results of their studies. We also avoided interventions that could fall afoul of any local laws.

Finally, we elaborated research designs to ensure to the maximum extent possible that our studies would not affect aggregate election outcomes. Our interventions are all designed to be nonpartisan, in that they do not seek to privilege a single party or candidate. Also, researchers sought and received approval from the relevant electoral commission wherever appropriate. We did not require consent from politicians about whom information was provided, even though these may be affected by the interventions; as our pre-analysis plan suggests, "the principle is that any information provided is information that exists in the political system that voters can choose to act upon or not and that this information is provided with consent, in a nonpartisan way, without deception, and in cooperation with local groups, where appropriate." Some of our project teams sought and received consent from high-level political actors, however, as a way of facilitating project implementation.[58] We further discuss specific measures we took to operationalize these ethical principles – and some of the challenges that arose – elsewhere in the book.

2.3.4   Coordination of Interventions and Measures

One of the most difficult issues involved our attempt to harmonize interventions and outcome measures across contexts, to the extent feasible.

---

[57] See http://egap.org/research/metaketa.
[58] See studies in Part II for details.

This was the focus of several meetings, at which all participants collectively debated and planned how coordination would actually take place. In principle, some issues were already settled at that point, as they were spelled out in the RFP and were a condition of funding and participation. Our early coordination meetings dealt with several other issues of design, data collection, and analysis, which bear on the meta-analysis in Chapter 11 as well as the individual studies presented in Part II of the book. We describe a few of these now; in Chapter 3, we lay out more fully the specific hypotheses, analysis, measurement, and estimation strategies that emerged from our workshops.

Perhaps the most fundamental issue for consideration is what it means to coordinate on – and even to "harmonize" – interventions. In what ways are experimental treatments to be considered similar – and, critically, at what level of generality? Here we appeal to Sartori's idea of a "ladder of abstraction."[59] In Sartori's approach, the generality of concepts is heightened by decreasing the number of properties that an empirical observation must satisfy to be considered an instance of the concept – that is, by reducing the intension or connotation of the concept. This more minimal intension in turn increases the number of objects that can be thus classified, that is, it increases the extension or denotation of the concept. These ideas bear centrally on the question of similarity of interventions. At the lowest levels of abstraction, it is clear that any two interventions – particularly those taking place in contexts as distinct as six different countries in Latin America, Africa, and South Asia, as in Metaketa I – must differ on an almost infinite number of dimensions. Thus, as the attributes needed to define a "common" intervention multiply, the number of cases to which the underlying idea can feasibly apply must clearly diminish – illustrating Sartori's tradeoff between intension and extension of a concept. Yet, by focusing on just a few core attributes of commonality and thereby climbing the ladder of abstraction, the generality and extension of the concept can increase. As we discuss in Chapter 3, a central focus in our common study of informational interventions is the distinction between "good" and "bad" news, which we operationalize by studying the relationship between voters' prior beliefs and the information that is provided to them about candidate performance. A concept such as good and bad news about

---

[59] Sartori (1970); see also Teune and Przeworski (1970) on comparative, contextualized measurement.

political candidates is at a middle level of abstraction and can be meaningfully defined across quite disparate contexts, even if the particularities of the interventions differ substantially. If theoretical expectations are defined at this level of abstraction, then empirical aggregation of results can also be feasible and meaningful. Defining a sensible middle level of abstraction was an important outcome of our effort to coordinate interventions in Metaketa I and seems a critical component of the Metaketa approach.

A second challenge in our coordination meetings stemmed from the individual nature of the common treatment arm and the difficulty in measuring individual turnout and vote choice when official outcomes are posted at the polling station level. Several of the participants felt strongly that polling station level data was the gold standard, in the sense that self-reported voter behavior is subject to social desirability bias. We worried that self-reported turnout and vote choice could lead to a spurious treatment effect that would manifest in what voters said they would do, but not in whether and how they actually voted. For projects that inherently take place at the community level, this is not problematic and only required the ability to map the spatial structure of implementation to the corresponding polling stations; however, plausible and meaningful ex-ante hypotheses of nonzero treatment effects require sufficient density of treatment at the cluster level, as was the case with the assignment of polling stations in the Mexico study. For projects such as Uganda 2, that use a delivery channel that is inherently individual (SMS), this was more of a challenge.[60] Even projects such as those in Brazil or Burkina Faso that were unable to tie outcomes to polling station data were encouraged to think in creative ways about how to use individual preference measurement strategies that were as free as possible of social desirability bias, such as their use of blinded "ballots" through which voters recorded their preferences over candidates, although these measures proved difficult to implement in practice for all but two studies. Although we discussed this issue at length, the meta-analysis ultimately relies on self-reported turnout and vote choice, as it was the only measure feasible across all study sites.

---

[60] The implementation of the randomized saturation design undertaken in the Uganda 2 project was the result of an attempt to achieve coordination in this respect, because this generated cluster-level variation in individual treatment intensity that could then conceivably move outcomes at the polling station level. Note, however, that the variation in saturation is among sampled respondents, but they tend to be a small proportion of the communities in which they are nested; see Chapter 7.

Another issue involved the coordination of outcome measures and covariates. In order to permit meta-analysis on any of our hypotheses, and particularly in order to conduct analyses of heterogeneous effects in our pooled study group, we needed to ensure consistency of measurement. Each study had a definition of good and bad news regarding incumbent performance that, while quite distinct across studies, was appropriate to the context and based on objective information about performance (see Chapter 3). Trickier was how to define concepts like "receipt of clientelistic benefits" in a manner that was consistent across contexts. With some types of heterogeneity, such as the role of co-ethnicity in driving the response to politician information, we simply recognized a priori that these concepts would be relevant in some contexts and not others (specifically, in Sub-Saharan Africa and South Asia, but probably not in the Latin American studies). We also prespecified a set of hypotheses that we explicitly recognized would vary across studies due to the heterogeneity in context and implementation.[61] Study teams shared survey instruments freely; the entire group worked to discuss the instruments used by the first team to implement its study in the field (Benin); and this instrument then served as a kind of template for measurement for some of these concepts in the other projects.

We also debated in these workshops many other issues, including the form of eventual publication of the results of the studies, and we held several meetings at which interim and final results were presented. This provided ample opportunity for another aspect of the Metaketa Initiative discussed in Section 2.2, collaboration, as well as some degree of healthy competition. Indeed, these exchanges across numerous researchers before, during, and after the fielding of interventions enabled a degree of informed scrutiny that is helpful for scientific progress, and made for a more open mode of science than is often practiced in social, political, or economic research.

2.3.5 Formal Synthesis

In Metaketa I, we sought to build learning in an area where there is already some evidence base – and even to model interventions on those found in prior research. Teams attempted to build conceptually similar treatments and to measure similar variables, including key outcomes.

---

[61] These are hypotheses H12 through H16; see MPAP in the Appendix.

To the extent possible, we hoped that differences in findings would be attributable primarily to contextual factors – and not to core differences in research design or measurement – and would therefore better contribute to understandings of what works where, why, and when (see Part II). Most importantly, interventions would be conceptually similar in key ways, such that the average effect of informational interventions on political accountability, for the units in our study group, would be a meaningful quantity.

But what do we mean by "the" effect of information, and for which population of units can we characterize such an effect? This was a subject of considerable discussion and even some cordial disagreement among participants in the Metaketa round, and especially members of the steering committee. One important issue was how to conceptualize the study group for the combination of the seven planned studies. Perhaps the simplest approach, and the one that involves the weakest assumptions, is simply to condition inferences on the set of units and respondents that made their way into the study groups for each of the seven studies. Thus, these units/respondents were not usually drawn from a straightforward probability sample of the population of each country (e.g., because particular regions or states were selected purposively, and/or because some types of respondents were screened out in each study prior to random assignment to treatments). And much more obviously, the seven countries included in this Metaketa round are not themselves drawn from the population of countries through some chance procedure but were rather the outcome of the selection process after our RFP was circulated and proposals were submitted. The selection of these countries reflects myriad factors. We certainly hoped for regional diversity, but the quality of the projects and research teams was also paramount in driving funding decisions. Thus, it may strain credulity to suggest that these particular countries, and the effects obtained in each of them, represent some random draw of the possible effects that could be obtained in informational interventions of the sort we consider.

In this view, then, our inferences are drawn to the particular set of units/respondents in our study: we have a large experiment that pools units in the different contexts and assigns them to treatment conditions in a randomized way. As our pre-analysis plan puts it, "The most straightforward way to combine results across the seven studies pools units into one large study group and estimates treatment effects, as one would do in a large experiment in which treatment assignment is blocked. For this analysis we proceed as if blocking is implemented at the country level."[62] This is similar to many social science experiments, in which the study group cannot be conceived of as a meaningful random sample from some larger population, and inferences are drawn to the study group.

An alternative approach seeks to conceive of these cases as part of a larger family of possible cases. The goal here is to use each study to contribute to learning about how things work in the family as a whole in order to be in a better position to learn something about each case from patterns seen in other cases as well as to say something about new cases that have not yet been studied. The ambitions of this approach are clearly much greater, but the assumptions needed to justify it are also much stronger, and too strong for many. Most critical is a willingness to assume that the cases can be treated as if they are a random draw from a well defined population of cases.[63] For skeptics, this kind of analysis might be best thought of as a thought experiment: what kind of general claims could one make if the assumption held? Our pre-analysis plan describes as a supplementary analysis a model for Bayesian hierarchical analysis that provides a way to combine information across the studies in this way. The basic approach assumes a data generating process in which average treatment effects in each case are a draw from a distribution of average treatment effects in a population of cases; the quantity of interest becomes the mean and variance of this distribution; the former provides a best guess for effects in a new case, the latter provides a handle on how much we should expect effects to be similar across cases.[64] Given the different strengths and weaknesses of these two approaches, we opted ultimately to employ both. We provide further details in Chapter 11.[65]

We recognize that our focus on aggregating effects has some costs and involves several tradeoffs. Overall, in thinking through the pros and cons of this type of highly coordinated research activity, we might draw an analogy between centrally planned economies and centrally planned research endeavors. This modality empowered us, as the Metaketa steering committee, to direct research effort and money towards specific

---

[62] MPAP; see Appendix.

[63] In principle one can alternatively incorporate beliefs about sampling probabilities of a case into study and assess robustness of conclusions to this.

[64] MPAP, 12–16; see Appendix.

[65] Several other important considerations arose in the course of our preplanning, for example, about whether or not to adjust for covariates (we prespecified both analyses). We further discuss these issues in Chapter 11 as well as in our Conclusion.

interventions and specific ways of testing hypotheses. While this tightly integrated approach led to a much clearer cumulation of evidence than a looser approach would have, it did not "let a thousand flowers bloom." A more loosely coordinated research endeavor might be a more effective way of discovering the unexpected, and may allow for a higher average quality of project to be funded than endeavors where only projects cohering to a specific project are funded. Hence it is worth recognizing explicitly that this coordination, while worthwhile, came at a cost. The opportunity cost of this approach is the lost creativity of the more varied ideas that would have come out of our project PIs had they not been required to coordinate so closely, and other innovative and impactful research ideas that were not funded because the topic was not sufficiently close to the one we settled on as the subject of this Metaketa round. Moreover, it is clearly the case that not all types of studies lend themselves to coordination, especially when say government agencies are involved in creating and implementing the interventions. We return to these ideas and a discussion of the tradeoffs later in the book, and in Chapter 3, we discuss issues specific to aggregating the effects of informational interventions.

In sum, the challenges of operationalizing our research objectives were considerable. Perhaps the biggest obstacles involved creating a structure that facilitates coordination while also incentivizing innovation, and creating a plan for publication that would sufficiently reward individual teams for their work while also putting central focus on the coordinated effort. Closer to the substance of the research, there were also substantial decisions to be made around the specific hypotheses, research designs, and measurement strategies. In our several meetings with the full group of Metaketa participants, we considered such issues and also presented designs and workshopped pre-analysis plans. These fora also had substantial ancillary benefits, in terms of fostering a sense of commitment to the shared enterprise and also in precommitting teams to research hypotheses and tests in a quite public way. Indeed, one outcome of this public precommitment to research protocols is that deviations would be observable (and would require explanation to the community). Overall, however, perhaps the biggest benefit – and most important departure from usual practice – is the relatively open and collaborative model for social science that the structure helped create. Our approach certainly has drawbacks and limitations, and involves some tradeoffs vis-à-vis other approaches that we discuss later; yet we feel this open and public style of research focused on creating different modalities of replicability has important benefits. And for us as researchers, it involved a refreshing and important change of pace.

The rest of this book reports the results of this collaboration, and also our effort to validate whether this approach improves cumulative learning. In the next chapter, we turn to our substantive focus – the impact of informational interventions on voter behavior and electoral accountability.

3

Informational Interventions: Theory and Measurement

Thad Dunning, Guy Grossman, Macartan Humphreys, Susan D. Hyde, Craig McIntosh, and Gareth Nellis

3.1 INFORMATION DISSEMINATION AND ELECTORAL ACCOUNTABILITY

What are the effects of new information about the performance of politicians on voter behavior and, ultimately, on political accountability? Answering this question is critical for scholars, policymakers, and practitioners. In this chapter, we describe the theoretical underpinnings of this question, summarize some of the previous evidence on the topic, and introduce the empirical operationalizations we pursue in the rest of the book.

3.1.1 Theoretical Motivations

An informed electorate is vital for a well-functioning democracy, or so many political theorists and policy practitioners often believe.

According to liberal theories of democracy, voters delegate representation to politicians who govern and shape policy, ostensibly in the interests of the represented.[1] The goals of politicians and the voters are not always aligned, however. Delegation of governance therefore raises the ubiquitous problem of moral hazard: politicians may wish to take advantage of their position to advance private benefits that come at the expense of voters.[2] Periodic free elections may at least somewhat constrain politicians,

---

[1] Pitkin (1967).

[2] Scholars thus often view the relationship between citizens and their representatives as one instance of a larger class of principal–agent relations, in which the interests of the principals – here, the voters – are not fully congruent with the agent's.

by providing an opportunity for voters to sanction politicians' malfeasance or reward good performers; and letting them screen for the entry of honest and hard-working candidates.[3]

Yet, voters face a problem arising from "asymmetric information": they do not fully observe the motivations and/or the actions of politicians. Indeed, voters may know little about the many hidden activities of their representatives, who are significantly better informed.[4] Citizens may also have little information on the "state of the world" or about governance, making it hard for them to map even politicians' observable behaviors, for instance, policy choices, to welfare outcomes. Informational asymmetries thus provide politicians with opportunities to extract rents, under-deliver services, and otherwise hinder the interests of the voters they purportedly represent.[5]

Good performance can be equally vexing for voters to assess. Politicians exert tremendous effort in claiming credit for actions that are difficult for voters to corroborate.[6] Did incumbents really attempt to promote a particular economic policy reform or target public spending in a valued direction? Were the actions of an individual legislator really responsible for her district's new bridge or school, or did some other process produce that outcome? Recognizing that politicians have incentives to take credit even where no such credit is due, citizens may reasonably discount their representatives' claims to competence, probity, or public spiritedness. Difficulties in claiming credit can thus further weaken incentives for "good" behavior.

Theoretical models thus suggest that better information may bolster democratic accountability, by helping align politicians' preferences – and actions – with voters' preferences.[7] Efforts to improve voter information may have either or both of two distinct motivations, related to the general problem of information asymmetries. First, improved information may ameliorate the moral hazard problem: if politicians learn that voters know more about them, incumbents may improve their performance so as to retain office.[8] Second, better information may reduce "adverse selection": when voters are better able to assess performance, the process

---

[3] Fearon (1999); Besley (2005).

[4] Przeworski, Stokes, and Manin (1999).

[5] Persson and Tabellini (2002).

[6] Cruz and Schneider (2017).

[7] Besley and Prat (2006).

[8] This assumes that politicians anticipate performance information will be compiled and disseminated in an ongoing manner.

of candidate selection is more effective at weeding out underperforming politicians.[9] Ideally, these mechanisms reinforce each other in the
democratic process. Thus, efforts to improve information may enhance
both the initial selection of good politicians and incumbents' incentives
to deliver high-quality performance once elected.

In sum, the link between information and political accountability
rests theoretically on the notion that politicians can exploit their position to underperform or engage in malfeasance because voters are not
willingly ill-informed.[10] Yet, if citizens (a) possess relevant and available information on the actions of their political representatives, (b)
use their vote to reward and sanction politicians based on such informative signals (rather than basing their vote on criteria unrelated to
performance), and if (c) incumbent parties and politicians value reelection, then the accountability of representatives to constituents could be
improved by addressing informational problems.[11] It follows that the
more accurate the informative signal is – that is, the less obscure incumbents' actions to citizens are – the weaker are politicians' incentives
to underperform or to squander public accounts. If a dearth of relevant information about politics is voters' key binding constraint, then
salient information from reliable, independent, impartial third parties –
for example, non-governmental organizations, independent media, or
outside election observers – should help voters exercise control over
incumbents.[12]

This theory of how to improve governance through informational
interventions appears to apply readily to the contexts we study in this
book. While some level of information asymmetry is unavoidable, even in
advanced industrial countries, several structural factors make developing
countries (the focus of our research project) especially low-information
environments. First, government and quasi-statutory agencies that assemble information on government actions and outcomes, such as the auditor
general or statistical bureaus, are often not fully independent of the

---

[9] Fearon (1999).

[10] Naturally, voters may rationally decide to remain ignorant about politics, especially
if they believe that their ability to influence politicians' behavior via participation is
especially low (Achen and Bartels, 2016).

[11] This system of reward and punishment is more effective the more that politicians or their
parties value holding office (due to legal remuneration, opportunities for rent extraction,
or the "warm glow" that incumbency provides) and thus seek reelection.

[12] Humphreys and Weinstein (2013); Guiteras and Mobarak (2016).

incumbent government.[13] Second, even when statutory agencies make politically relevant information publicly available, classic disseminators of information (such as the media, civil society, and opposition parties) are commonly under-resourced, have limited reach, or are outright captured.[14] For these and other reasons, the supply of information to voters is often limited in the settings we study. If the theoretical account sketched above is correct, relaxing impediments to the supply of critical information should boost accountability.

Intuitive and appealing as this simple theory is, however, there are also several reasons to question it. Implicit in this account is a basic theory of change for the ways in which improved information may alter the political process. We summarize the theory in Figure 3.1.[15] In this figure – and the book as a whole – we focus on the impact of informational interventions, that is, efforts by implementers such as civil society organizations to change and improve information available to voters.

Multiple links in the causal chain in Figure 3.1 need to operate for the information–accountability logic to flow. With respect to implementers (boxes 1 and 2 in Figure 3.1), credible information on salient dimensions of politician performance must first exist (box 1). National audit reports, investigative journalism, and reports on attendance and actions of politicians in their day-to-day activities can form the basis of this sort of information. In addition, potential implementers need to have the capacity, reach, and resources to organize, package, and disseminate politically relevant information in a timely manner to as many voters as possible (box 2).

Yet even if information is supplied in this way, it may not be utilized by voters as expected by standard political accountability models – suggesting a second class of constraints on the capacity of information to improve the responsiveness of politicians (boxes 3–5 in Figure 3.1). First, voters must be receptive to politically relevant information and capable of understanding it (box 3). The ability to contextualize political information requires that voters possess some minimal understanding of

---

[13] This may hold especially in electoral authoritarian regimes. Note that in authoritarian systems, transparency interventions may have fundamentally different effects than in democracies; see Malesky, Schuler, and Tran (2012).

[14] Boas and Hidalgo (2011).

[15] For similar efforts to map a causal chain linking information to behavior, see Lieberman, Posner, and Tsai (2014) or Kumar, Post, and Ray (2017).

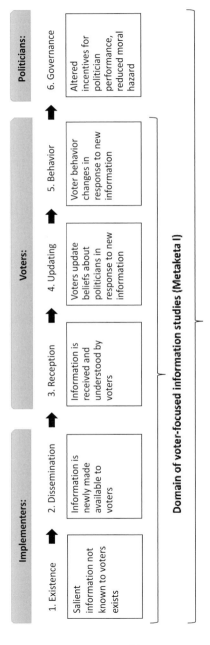

FIGURE 3.1 Information and accountability: a causal chain

politicians' responsibilities and how those translate into government out-comes.[16] Transmitting such understanding could, of course, be one goal of an informational intervention.

Second, while models of political accountability generally focus on the amount of information that voters possess, interventions whose pur-pose is to reduce asymmetric information must also introduce into the electoral process salient, trustworthy information that voters did not previously possess or understand. Voters not only need to be attentive to such information (box 3), but also need to be able and willing to update their perceptions upon receiving it (box 4). In other words, infor-mation is only consequential if and when it changes voter perceptions of the performance or quality of the incumbent (compared to available challengers).

Such updating is not a forgone conclusion, as voters may face limi-tations in information processing. A rich literature in political behavior, for example, suggests that the conceptualization of voters as seekers and neutral utilizers of accurate information on politicians' performance is open to challenge. Scholars of American politics suggest that voters rely on heuristic cues from partisan, political elites but not necessarily third-party information.[17] Much research focuses on motivated reasoning and cognitive bias as key factors in information processing. In the West, a recent rise in populism has engendered disenchantment with experts' con-sensus on policy matters, possibly resulting in voting based on identity rather than performance. Further, novel ways in which voters now con-sume news, including the growth of explicitly partisan media and online social platforms, may have fundamentally altered the ways that they filter the information they do receive. Hence, even in industrial democracies, it is far from assured that making voters more informed will change their perceptions of candidates.

Moreover, even if voters update their priors, this does not guaran-tee that they would change their electoral choices (box 5). Sticky voting behavior may be especially pervasive in the developing country settings that we study. Identity cues related to ethnicity, religion, or region are often prevalent in electoral campaigns. While such ready heuristics could be useful for making political decisions in information-poor environ-ments, they could just as easily be ends in themselves, making voters

---

[16] Grossman and Michelitch (2018).

[17] A seminal source is Zaller (1992); for more recent work, see, for instance, Gerber et al. (2011), Lenz (2012), Broockman and Green (2014), and Kalla and Broockman (2017).

unresponsive to new information. This suggests that voters are more likely to use new salient political information when evaluative criteria unrelated to performance (e.g., candidate identity or partisanship) are not so strong as to make performance information inconsequential. Moreover, in contexts where clientelism is pervasive, voters may be concerned about possible retaliation if they choose to base their vote on performance information. Scholars note, for instance, the way in which clientelism and vote-buying make voters beholden to their political representatives, rather than the other way around – engendering "perverse accountability" in many emerging democracies.[18] Finally, incumbents are not necessarily passive observers: if unflattering information about them is disseminated to constituents, incumbents may seek to offset its effects by undermining the credibility of the information or its source,[19] or engage in vote buying.[20] This also implies a more complicated causal chain than that depicted in our figure, with feedback loops from politician to voter behavior. In short, the link between voter updating (4) and behavior (5) in Figure 3.1 is far from a forgone conclusion.

If boxes and links 1–5 in Figure 3.1 are all operative, then the provision of new information may ultimately improve governance (box 6), by increasing the ability of voters to screen out bad politicians (reducing adverse selection) and giving politicians incentives to perform in voters' interests (minimizing moral hazard). The interventions and effects we study in this book focus on the first outcome – that is, whether informational interventions shape voter behavior and thus impact adverse selection. The connection to moral hazard and to politician behavior is a critical one for information–accountability linkages, but not the link we study centrally here.

To sum up, a rich literature in democratic theory, like many recent political economy models, associates improvements in accountability to the provision to voters of information about the performance of politicians. Yet, any of the links in the theory of change joining informational interventions to better governance may be broken. The connection between information and improved accountability is therefore ultimately an empirical question.

---

[18] Stokes (2005).
[19] Humphreys and Weinstein (2013).
[20] Cruz, Keefer, and Labonne (2016).

3.1.2   Evidence on the Link between Information and Accountability

Policymakers, foundations, and donor organizations throughout the developing world – taking to heart the view that increasing transparency will strengthen accountability – have launched campaigns aimed at promoting a more informed electorate. In countries from Brazil to India, politicians are now required to file affidavits reporting their assets or criminal convictions. Freedom of Information acts allow citizens and civil society organizations to petition for access to other information about the behavior of representatives. However, such information is not always widely disseminated or easy to access.[21] Civil society organizations therefore increasingly conduct informational campaigns and train citizens to access and use data on politician performance.[22] Donor collaboratives seek to "expand the impact and scale of transparency, accountability and participation interventions."[23] Groups such as the National Democratic Institute, a US based international NGO that works to support democratic institutions globally through citizen participation and accountability programming, has funded dozens of citizen watchdog groups. Especially in emerging democracies, such organizations train communities to monitor public service providers, educate them about the importance of legislative process or political parties, and teach them how to advocate and mobilize for political change.[24]

Yet, are these efforts effective? Are transparency initiatives being used to sanction and reward incumbents, and ultimately leading to better incumbent performance? Given the theoretical frameworks discussed in the previous section, it is possible that informational interventions could boost political accountability, but there are also many reasons why they might not. Does a clear picture emerge from the existing empirical literature regarding the sensitivity of voters to newly acquired information? We highlight two points.

---

[21] See for instance, Lagunes and Pocasangre (2019).

[22] A notable example is ACODE, a nonpartisan Ugandan NGO operating in over 30 districts in which it constructed and disseminated politicians' performance information (Grossman and Michelitch, 2018). Another nonprofit organization based in Britain, MySociety, has helped construct innovative websites tracking the legislative activities of Members of Parliament in Zimbabwe (`kuvakazim.com`), Kenya (`mzalendo.com`), and South Africa (*People's Assembly*).

[23] Transparency and Accountability Initiative (www.transparency-initiative.org/about/ definitions). See also the related Transparency 4 Development research project (http:// t4d.ash.harvard.edu), and the review by Kosack and Fung (2014).

[24] See Chapter 1 for additional examples.

First, studies of the effect of information on electoral behavior in low- and middle-income democracies report mixed results.[25] Politician-focused "reduced form" information studies – by which we mean those that simply examine the association between the left-most and right-most links of Figure 3.1 – generally report that a more informed citizenry is positively correlated with better government performance.[26] Yet, empirical accounts focused on whether and how voters process and act on newly acquired politician performance information lead to varied conclusions about the capacity of informational interventions to strengthen political accountability.

Consider first the relationship between media access and voter behavior. In Mexico, Larreguy, Marshall, and Snyder Jr. (2016) find that an additional local media station increased voter sanctioning of incumbent party malfeasance by 1 percentage point. In Brazil, Ferraz and Finan (2008) find that the release of audit information reduced incumbent vote share by 3.2 percentage points, with larger effects in areas with greater radio coverage.[27] In Spain, mayors implicated in a corruption scandal lost 2.8 percentage point votes, for average levels of reporting, but lost greater vote share where media coverage was intensive. Similarly, in Italy, members of parliament charged with corruption hailing from a district of below-median per-capita newspaper circulation have a reelection rate that is 1 percentage point higher than similarly charged incumbents hailing from a district above-median per-capita circulation, but only after 1992, when the media increased dramatically corruption reporting.[28] In the robust media environment of the US, corruption charges have

---

[25] We exclude from our brief review related studies in which information on the positions of candidates were disseminated by their own campaigns, such as the study by Wantchekon (2003) in Benin. Moreover, exploring the relationship between information and voting behavior is far from easy using standard observational data, since there might be unobserved factors that make voters more informed and more likely to vote in a certain way, so we focus here on experimental and natural experimental studies.

[26] For example, Besley and Burgess (2002) show that calamity relief efforts are positively correlated with newspaper circulation in India; Strömberg (2004) finds that New Deal spending in the USA is increasing in radio penetration; Reinikka and Svensson (2011) report that a newspaper campaign in Uganda reduced leakage of public funds leading to a positive effect on education outcomes. But see Keefer and Khemani (2012), who do not find that radio access in Benin is associated with more benefits from government programs.

[27] It is worth noting the asymmetry in both the Mexico and Brazil studies between bad news that reduced slightly incumbents vote share and good news (i.e., no evidence of mayoral malfeasance) that did not translate into more votes for the incumbent.

[28] Chang, Golden, and Hill (2010).

been shown to cost incumbents 6 to 13 percentage points in electoral margins.[29] Prominent studies employing credible research designs also document the impact of long-term exposure to biased television news coverage on voting. One study finds that the introduction of Fox News in the US significantly increased vote shares for Republican presidential candidates – to the tune of 0.4 to 0.7 percentage points.[30] Another demonstrates a similar effect of state television news on electoral support for the incumbent party in Russia.[31] In Brazil, the existence of a licensed radio station with ties to an incumbent raised his vote share by 17 percent and probability of winning by 28 percent.[32]

Other studies find, however, that politicians who have been exposed engaging in corrupt behavior suffer modest electoral penalties, if at all. For example, Eggers (2014) shows that in the high-information environment of the UK, voters were reluctant to punish MPs who were revealed to have improperly used public money when levels of political competition is high and partisan stakes of the local contest were high. Furthermore, Vaishnav (2017) shows that voters maintained support for criminal politicians even when information regarding their wrongdoings became widely available, and Reed (1994) reports that MPs in Japan who are successful at cultivating personal votes do not suffer electoral loss following major scandals involving those MPs.

Moreover, and central to our focus here, the evidence from third-party interventions that have manipulated information directly prior to elections has been even more heterogeneous. Consider the case in which voters receive a positive signal prior to elections with respect to candidates' performance, qualifications, or policy alignment. Positive performance information increased incumbent support by 4 percentage points in mayoral elections in Italy,[33] but had no effect in parliamentary elections in Uganda,[34] nor in municipal councilor elections in India.[35] New information that demonstrated greater alignment between voter and candidates' policy priorities increased (quite dramatically) the vote share of MPs in

---

[29] Peters and Welch (1980); Welch and Hibbing (1997).
[30] DellaVigna and Kaplan (2007).
[31] Enikolopov, Petrova, and Zhuravskaya (2011). The persuasive effects of the media may even extend beyond voting, shaping attitudes about ethnic out-groups too; see Paluck and Green (2009).
[32] Boas and Hidalgo (2011).
[33] Kendall, Nannicini, and Trebbi (2015).
[34] Humphreys and Weinstein (2013).
[35] Banerjee et al. (2011).

Sierra Leone,[36] but had no effect in mayoral elections in either Italy or the Philippines.[37] There is some evidence that positive updating on candidates' qualifications and charisma translated to an increase of between 5 and 6 percentage points in vote share in India and Sierra Leone.[38]

As for negative signals about candidate performance, criminality information in mayoral elections in Brazil reduced the vote share of candidates from right-wing parties by about 2.6 percentage points, on average, but had no discernible effect on vote choice for left-party candidates.[39] A different type of asymmetry in voter behavior has been recorded in Puerto Rico, where audits released prior to elections reduced reelection rates for mayoral incumbents with above median corruption cases, yet had no discernible effect on the reelection probabilities of honest mayors.[40] Interestingly, disseminating information on incumbent malfeasance in Mexico municipal elections caused voters to punish not only incumbents but also challengers. By contrast, disseminating information on the share of the budget allocation for public services unspent by the municipality had no effect on voting behavior.[41] Overall, the evidence on the link between information and accountability is quite varied; and the source of this heterogeneity is not immediately apparent.

A second point about this body of evidence – one that is crucial for our initiative – is that publication bias may distort our understanding of effects. As with many other topics in the social sciences, studies of information dissemination campaigns that find statistically significant effects have tended to be published prominently, while those finding null effects may tend to remain unpublished.[42] The prioritization by journal editors and reviewers of significant findings may encourage selective reporting; alternatively, as in many other research areas, the challenge may be not just that studies with insignificant results are not published but also that they are not even written up as formal working papers.[43] Across the

36 Bidwell, Casey, and Glennerster (n.d.).
37 See Kendall, Nannicini, and Trebbi (2015) and Cruz, Keefer, and Labonne (2016), respectively.
38 Banerjee et al. (2011) and Bidwell, Casey, and Glennerster (n.d.), respectively.
39 De Figueiredo, Hidalgo, and Kasahara (2011).
40 Bobonis, Fuertes, and Schwabe (2016).
41 Chong et al. (2015).
42 Among the published studies, see Banerjee et al. (2011); Chang, Golden, and Hill (2010); Ferraz and Finan (2008) and Bobonis, Fuertes, and Schwabe (2016); among the unpublished, see Banerjee et al. (2011); De Figueiredo, Hidalgo, and Kasahara (2011), and Humphreys and Weinstein (2013).
43 Franco, Malhotra, and Simonovits (2014).

set of studies on this topic, one also finds substantial heterogeneity not only of interventions but also of outcome measures, making the aggregation of findings through formal meta-analysis largely infeasible. Overall, publication bias, along with weak incentives to replicate, may therefore lead to broad conclusions from a few high-impact studies. This makes it more difficult to learn from the whole body of research about the conditions under which informational interventions are more likely to be effective.

These features of the research literature on information and accountability make the topic an excellent candidate for the Metaketa approach outlined in Chapter 2. The previous research does not resolve pressing questions: what can we conclude about the efficacy of third-party information campaigns, such as those supported by many policymakers, donors, and civil society organizations in the developing world? Will voters reward incumbents on the basis of positive information about their performance while in office or punish them for negative performance information? There is some existing evidence base, and thus scope to construct interventions that mirror those in the previous literature. Yet the problems of study scarcity, study heterogeneity, and selective reporting, especially in the guise of publication bias, point to key weaknesses of the literature from the perspective of cumulative learning. This substantive area thus presents useful opportunities to accumulate valuable knowledge.

This book therefore presents a set of coordinated studies aimed at evaluating these questions. Understanding the impact of efforts to improve the democratic process by making voters more informed about politicians' performance is a critical goal. From a theoretical perspective, few issues are as central to the study of political science as clarifying the ways in which voters update beliefs and preferences on the basis of new information. From a policy perspective, efforts to improve and broaden the informational environment in developing democracies has been seen to be both an effective and a legitimate arena for programmatic activity by democracy-promoting civil society groups and international actors.

3.2 CORE HYPOTHESES OF THE METAKETA

In this study of information and accountability, we integrate experimental designs from Benin, Brazil, Burkina Faso, India, Mexico, and Uganda (two studies). All studies feature a common intervention arm, derived from a unified theoretical framework we discuss in this section. In line with our common theoretical framework, each of the studies sought to disseminate publicly available information on performance that is directly attributable to an incumbent candidate or party; to provide this information privately to individuals within a month prior to an election; and to divulge information that is presumed to be relevant to voter welfare, yet not widely known. These interventions echo both previous experimental treatments in the research literature and those promoted by donor organizations that advocate for transparency.

The studies focus on the most basic hypotheses derived from the accountability logics described above; the numbering of hypotheses follows the meta-analysis pre-analysis plan (MPAP):[44]

H1a   Positive information increases voter support for politicians.
H1b   Negative information decreases voter support for politicians.

We define positive and negative information – which we also call "good news" and "bad news" – in more detail below. In brief, the prior beliefs of voters play a key role in our joint theoretical framework, as well as in the operationalization of our approach. All studies were designed to allow measurement of the extent to which voters update their beliefs about the performance of the politicians positively or negatively in light of provided information, and to allow measurement of the difference between prior beliefs and the information. As described in the MPAP, we expected effects to derive from new information rather than any information. Thus, the extent to which updating actually took place should play a key role in comparing the impact of the performance information across contexts.

Note that our emphasis on the importance of priors echoes some, but by no means all, previous work on information and accountability. Ferraz and Finan (2008), for instance, compares municipalities audited for corruption before an election to those audited after, conditional on the number of violations associated with corruption. This comparison "captures the fact that the audits may have had a positive or negative effect depending on the severity of the report and whether voters had over- or underestimated the extent of their mayor's corrupt activities."[45] In many contexts, however, researchers lack information on prior beliefs – leading them to estimate the impact of information without accounting

---

[44] See Appendix.
[45] Ferraz and Finan (2008): 704.

for the likely heterogeneous impact depending on what different voters plausibly learn from the information that is provided. In consequence, they also cannot take into account that certain types of voters, such as those already highly informed about candidates or who already have very positive or negative views of politicians, are less likely to be affected by informational treatments.

Our secondary hypotheses relate to overall participation. Theoretical work suggests that greater information should increase turnout, whether it is good or bad; yet some recent experimental evidence finds that information that highlights corruption may reduce engagement with electoral processes.[46] Prior to data collection, we stated distinct hypotheses on turnout as a function of information content, though we highlighted that our interest is in estimating the relation – whether it is positive, or negative, or context dependent.

H2a   Bad news decreases voter turnout.
H2b   Good news increases voter turnout.

When we present the results of our meta-analysis in Chapter 11, we describe further hypotheses about the impact of our informational interventions on outcomes such as perceptions of candidate integrity and effort; the possibility that politicians would mount campaigns in response to negative information; and the conditional effects of information, depending for example on coethnic and partisan ties between citizens and politicians. These hypotheses allow for the assessment of how information may shape perceptions and behavior in line with the causal chain in Figure 3.1.

3.2.1   Defining Good and Bad News

In thinking through the core issue of the impact of the pooled interventions, we were struck by the inconvenient truth that the main hypotheses of the Metaketa might most naturally be thought of as a triple interaction between treatment, the performance information conveyed, and the priors of the voters in question. Further, neither the quality of the politician nor the priors are randomly assigned. In consequence, even though the informational treatments themselves are randomized, we had the usual problem of heterogeneity analysis in RCTs that it is difficult

---

[46] Chong et al. (2015).

to be sure that the heterogeneous impacts are truly due to the posited mechanism rather than another type of variation that is correlated with political quality or voter priors. The risk of confounding is substantial if causal interpretations are attributed to the non-manipulated variables. This issue can be quite intractable. We felt that registering a core pooled treatment effect in the form of a triple interaction was not desirable: such an approach lacks simplicity and can encourage the interpretation of the conditioning variables as causal quantities.

Consequently, we arrived at an alternative strategy, currently represented by H1a and H1b: rather than pooling good and bad news and running a triple interaction, we would split the respondents into groups for whom information about the politician or party – if delivered – would be positive or negative, based on the measurement of prior beliefs. Whether a voter in one of these groups was actually given good or bad news then depended on her random assignment to the treatment group, i.e., the voters to whom the information was actually disseminated, or to the control group. Random assignment allows us to readily estimate the impact of information for both the good and bad news groups.

This raises the question, however, of how to conceptualize and operationalize good and bad news. To this end, all studies attempted to measure prior perceptions of politician quality on the same scale as the actual information provided. This means, for instance, that voters might be asked at baseline whether the performance of their incumbent politician on some dimension was "much worse," "a little worse," "a little better," or "much better" than other politicians in a comparison group (such as other candidates in the voters' region/department, or the country as a whole); and the provided information would then code the performance of politicians on that dimension on a similar four-point scale. We thereby observe prior beliefs for all study subjects, including those in the treatment and control groups, and we can in each case compare these priors to the provided performance information.[47] Two types of voters are coded as belonging to the good news group: (a) those individuals for whom information about incumbent performance exceeds their expectations, and (b) those for whom it confirms positive expectations. Conversely, in the bad news group, performance information is worse than expectations, or it confirms negative expectations. These

---

[47] One exception to this measurement strategy is discussed below.

quantities can be defined as binary variables (good or bad news); or one can measure standardized information gaps, by dividing the observed gap between priors and information by the standard deviation of this gap in a particular locality or country. These definitions of good and bad news were preregistered in the MPAP, as reproduced in the Appendix.

More formally, let P_{ij} denote the prior beliefs of voter i regarding the performance of politician j; and let Q_j denote the information provided to the treatment group about politician j's actual performance, measured on the same scale. Also, $\hat{Q}_j$ denotes the median value of Q_j in a polity (or the median in the relevant comparison group). Then, we can formally define the set L^+ of individuals who would receive good news if assigned to the treatment group as those subjects for whom $Q_j > P_{ij}$, or $Q_j = P_{ij}$ and $Q_j \geq \hat{Q}_j$. For these individuals, either the information provided exceeds their priors or the information confirms positive priors. Let L^- denote the remaining subjects, who would receive bad news if assigned to the treatment group.

Then, $N_{ij} \equiv Q_j - P_{ij}$ is the gap between information and priors; we denote N_{ij}^+ for the gap in the good news group (i.e., all subjects in L^+) and N_{ij}^- for the gap in the bad news group (subjects in all subjects in L^-). To allow for pooling across studies, we standardize N_{ij}^+ by the mean and standard deviation of $Q_j - P_{ij}$ in the L^+ group in each country (or relevant locality); N_{ij}^+ is therefore a standardized measure of "good news" with mean o and standard deviation of 1. We standardize N_{ij}^- similarly for the bad news group. This formulation also leads to another hypothesis that relates very naturally to our primary hypotheses: information effects – both positive and negative – are stronger when the gap between voters' prior beliefs about candidates and the information provided (i.e., N_{ij}^+) is larger.

In sum, this approach allows us to separate out those voters for whom the performance information exceeded the prior belief about performance, versus those for whom it was less. It also allows us to measure the size of the gap between the information and the priors. Note that even if the response to a given amount of new information is constant across subjects, in the experimental context hypotheses about the effects of good and bad news are subgroup effects (i.e., heterogeneous treatment effects) because they are defined for the strata of voters eligible for exposure to good or bad news – given their prior beliefs and the measured performance of politicians. That is, only a voter whose prior belief about the quality or performance of a politician exceeded the incumbent's actual performance (as measured by our performance information) was capable of receiving bad news. Distinguishing good and bad news strata in this way reflects our theoretical expectation that the impact of information depends on prior knowledge or beliefs; and it allows for transparent estimation of the effect of information in each group.

3.3   INTRODUCING THE METAKETA I STUDIES

In this section, we describe the seven individual studies that make up Metaketa I. In selecting these studies – and in theorizing the level at which their interventions are comparable and may be feasibly aggregated into common analysis – we appeal to Sartori's "ladder of abstraction" discussed in Chapter 2.[48] In particular, we abstract from contextual differences to find commonality in the operationalization of dissemination of good and bad news about politicians in the run-up to an election. From a comparative measurement perspective, all studies therefore focus on the measurement of performance information relative to voters' priors; i.e., what voters already know or believe about their representatives' performance. We believe that the structure of these common arms – in particular, attempts to measure exposure to these interventions in a consistent way and on a common scale – allows for plausible pooling, that is, an estimate of the average effect of good and bad news across studies. At the same time, the interventions in the seven studies differ in several ways, for example, with respect to the specific sector of the public service or the nature of the performance indicator (e.g., the extent to which it can provide an indication of malfeasance or instead of good performance); the specific political office of the candidate (e.g., mayor, district council/chair, or member of parliament) whose performance is reported; and, to some extent, the medium for communicating the information (e.g., leaflets vs. videos). While perfect harmonization of intervention may be possible for some type of social scientific inquiries, it is neither feasible nor desirable for most governance interventions, which must be appropriate for the context in which they are embedded.[49] Moreover, as discussed later, the consequences of some of these distinctions are assessed through experimentally induced variation that is internal to each study (such as the comparison of the effects of common and alternative intervention arms), as well as by comparison of effects across studies.

---

[48] See Sartori (1970).
[49] See Chapter 2.

The common arm interventions included in the Metaketa studies, and described in more detail in Part II of this book, are as follows:

- In **Benin** (Chapter 4), Adida, Gottlieb, Kramon, and McClendon provide information to respondents on the legislative performance of deputies in the National Assembly, using bar graphs in videos to compare the legislator responsible for respondents' commune to other legislators in the department and the country.
- In **Mexico** (Chapter 5), Arias, Larreguy, Marshall, and Querubín disseminate information in advance of municipal elections on unauthorized or misallocated spending, relative to municipalities within the same state that were governed by a different political party.
- In **Uganda 1** (Chapter 6), Platas and Raffler furnish information on the policies and characteristics of general election candidates for Parliament, using screenings of "Meet the Candidates" videos.
- In **Uganda 2** (Chapter 7), Buntaine, Bush, Jablonski, Nielson, and Pickering use text-messaging (SMS) to provide information on budgetary irregularities at the district level, as compared to other districts in the country.
- In **Burkina Faso** (Chapter 8), Lierl and Holmlund supply information on the performance of municipal governments in providing different kinds of services, relative both to national standards and to local (regional) averages.
- In **Brazil** (Chapter 9), Boas, Hidalgo, and Melo distribute information about general government corruption prior to mayoral races, operationalized as the rate of rejection of municipal accounts by an independent audit court.
- In **India** (Chapter 10), Sircar and Chauchard planned to disseminate publicly available information, culled from India's Election Commission, on the criminal backgrounds of candidates in state assembly races.

These informational treatments are summarized in the first column of Table 3.1. The implementation of each intervention was planned to occur in advance of the relevant election in each country, and so the timing of each study was keyed to the schedule of those elections – beginning with Benin's National Assembly elections in April 2015 and ending with Brazil's municipal elections in October 2016. Most study teams partnered with local NGOs or government offices to design or implement the interventions.

TABLE 3.1 *Metaketa experiments: Common and alternative intervention arms*

Study	Focus of Common Informational Treatment	Focus of Alternative Treatment Arm(s)
Benin (Chapter 4)	Legislative performance (relative to department and national averages; high-dosage)	Civics lesson on importance of legislative performance; public provision of info.; low or high dosage
Brazil (Chapter 9)	Accounting irregularities (acceptance or rejection of municipal accounts by auditors)	Municipal education outcomes (ranking of municipalities)
Burkina Faso (Chapter 8)	Quality of municipal services provided by previous incumbent party (relative to other municipalities)	Invitation to participate in municipal government meetings
India (Chapter 10)	Criminal backgrounds of politicians (info. provided by survey enumerators)	Criminal backgrounds of politicians (info. provided by local intermediaries)
Mexico (Chapter 5)	Unauthorized/misallocated spending (relative to opposition municipalities in the same state)	Unauthorized/ misallocated spending, publicly provided via loudspeakers; or not benchmarked
Uganda 1 (Chapter 6)	Voter-candidate policy alignment and candidate characteristics (via videos, in general elections)	Public provision of common-arm information (via videos); in primary and general elections
Uganda 2 (Chapter 7)	Budget irregularities (provided over SMS; high and low density)	Quality of service provision (provided over SMS; high and low density)

The common informational treatments provided information on politician performance privately to individual voters in the month prior to an election; the information was disseminated by flyer, text message, or video, depending on the study. These interventions echo both previous experimental treatments in the research literature and those promoted by donor organizations that advocate for transparency.

In addition to the common intervention arm, and following the Metaketa model described in Chapter 2, each study has at least one complementary, alternative treatment arm, in which distinct information is provided, or core information is provided in a different way (also summarized in Table 3.1). For example, three studies assessed the impact of providing information publicly in group settings, as opposed to privately to individuals, on the theory that group provision would foment common knowledge and help to coordinate voters on electoral action (Benin, Mexico, and Uganda 1). Other studies varied the credibility of the information source (India), embedded the informational treatments in experiments focused on eliciting citizen participation (Burkina Faso), or varied the type of performance information that was provided (Brazil and Uganda 2). For more detail on these alternative arms and the studies' research designs, see the chapters in Part II.

As discussed in Chapter 2, we hoped that the alternative treatment arms would permit researcher innovation within the strictures of the overall Metaketa environment, by allowing assessment of novel means of information provision or novel informational content. They are thus distinguished in purpose from the common arm, where the focus is on replication and consolidation of knowledge. The inclusion of these alternative arms also allows for generation and testing of hypotheses about comparative effectiveness – that is, about the conditions under which information provision would be more effective at shaping voter behavior, and ultimately electoral accountability. However, because treatments in the alternative arms differ across studies by design, we did not plan to conduct pooled analysis or formal comparison of the effects of many of these treatments, with one exception: as described in our MPAP, we report the pooled analysis comparing the effects of private vs. public treatments, for those studies that do provide information publicly in alternative treatment arms (Benin, Mexico, and Uganda 1). This provides a way to assess whether the generation of common knowledge may strengthen the effects of informational interventions (see Chapter 11). Moreover, several of the individual study analyses in Part II of the book also use these alternative arms to probe explanations for the effects they find on their common intervention arm. Thus, although our core analysis in Chapter 11 focuses on the common treatment arm, understanding alternatives is also critical to assessing how, where, and when information affects political accountability. It therefore enters as an important part of our analysis in Parts II and III.

3.4   AGGREGATING GOOD AND BAD NEWS

We discussed the general definition of good and bad news in Section 3.2.1. In this section, we briefly discuss the approach for operationalizing and measuring these concepts in each study. More detailed exposition is left to the chapters that make up Part II of the book, as well as the meta-analysis in Chapter 11; yet this provides a general discussion that may be useful in approaching those chapters. In Chapter 11, we also discuss the core estimating equations that we use to test our hypotheses.

Most teams gathered information on voter priors at baseline (in both treatment and control groups) with respect to the information that would be provided.[50] For example, in Benin, the question on priors in the baseline survey read as follows:

```
Consider [NAME OF REP], does she/he participate in plenary
sessions of the National Assembly much more, a little more, a
little less or much less than other deputies in this Department?
(1) Much more; (2) A little more; (3) A little less; (4) Much less.
```

Information on the performance of the voter's primary legislator was later provided to individuals in the treatment group on this same scale, and also relative to departmental and national averages. In this case, politicians in the 75th–100th percentile of participation were said to participate "much more," those in the 50th–75th percentile participate "a little more," and so forth.[51] In general, prior beliefs were gathered wherever possible using the same scale as the informational intervention itself. Thus, if information about politician performance is provided using a four-category scale, prior assessments are gathered where feasible on that same scale. Then, as described previously, the extent of updating relative to priors is standardized by the within-country and the within-group (good or bad news) mean and variance before combining the information across studies.

Table 3.2 and Figure 3.2 show the definition and distributions of P_{ij} and Q_j in the six fielded studies. As seen in Table 3.2, the measures of

---

[50] The Mexico team did not conduct a baseline survey, due to prohibitive costs. Instead, they gathered aggregate information on priors at the randomization block level, by averaging responses from subjects in control precincts at endline to proxy for priors in treated precincts within the same randomization block (see discussion below and Arias et al., Chapter 5). The Mexico team also proxied for the extent of belief updating in response to the treatment in a given randomization block by showing control respondents the leaflet at the end of the survey. The Burkina Faso (Lierl and Holmlund, Chapter 8) and Brazil (Boas, Hidalgo and Melo, Chapter 9) teams measured priors and then administered treatment as part of the same activity.

[51] For a voter who says his candidate participates "a little more" at baseline and whose candidate is indeed in the 50th–75th percentile, the prior is said to match the information ($P_{ij} = Q_j$). See Adida et al. (Chapter 4) and Adida et al. (2017a) for more details.

TABLE 3.2 *Metaketa: Measuring voters' priors and incumbents' performance*

Study	P_{ij}: Voters' Priors	Q_j: Performance Information
Benin	Legislative productivity, compared to dept. and nation (4-point scale)	Legislative productivity compared to dept. and nation (4-point scale, with bar graphs)
Brazil	Prior beliefs on acceptance of account (0–1)	Account accepted or rejected (0–1)
Burkina Faso	Quantiles of voters' rankings of service quality across municipalities	Quantiles of performance distribution
Mexico	N.A.	Percent misallocated spending, relative to municipalities governed by other parties (continuous measure)
Uganda 1	Opinion of incumbent on six dimensions (and importance of dimensions)	Coding of incumbent's debate performance and policy positions (weighted by importance)
Uganda 2	Budget management relative to other districts (4-point scale)	Budget management relative to other districts (4-point scale, also proportion of problematic spending)

Q_j and P_{ij} are specific to the content of the information provided in each study. For instance, in two studies (Benin and Uganda 2), both priors and performance information were measured on a four-point scale, as in the example in the previous paragraph.[52] In one country (Brazil), the indicators are dichotomous, measuring whether the municipal accounts were accepted or rejected. In Burkina Faso, the measures are nearly continuous – i.e., quantiles of the voters' rankings of service quality across municipalities, and the quantiles of the actual performance distribution – and in Mexico, Q_j is continuous – i.e., percentage differences between misallocated spending in a respondent's own municipality and average misallocation in municipalities governed by opposition parties.[53] Finally,

---

[52] In the Uganda 2 study, however, there is a middle category in P for "don't know," which is not in Q; see Figure 3.2.

[53] As noted, we lack P_{ij} in Mexico.

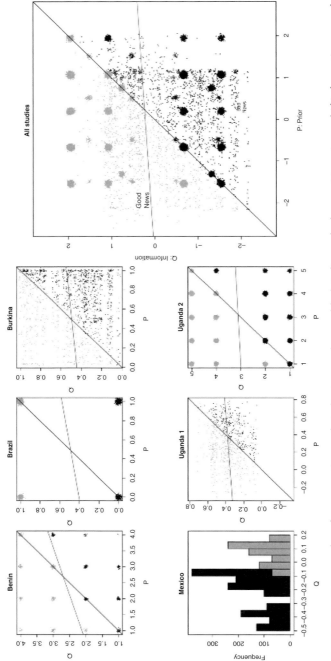

FIGURE 3.2 Priors and performance. Greyscale indicates good news, black indicates bad news. News is good if information exceeds priors, or if it confirms positive priors. No priors data is available for Mexico. Regression line indicates linear fit between priors and information. In the "All studies" plot (right panel), P and Q have a common normalization such that priors are centered at 0 with a standard deviation of 1.

72

in the Uganda 1 study, P_{ij} is measured as voters' perceptions of voter-candidate alignment on policy issues and of candidate characteristics, with each of six dimensions weighted by the perceived importance of the dimension; and Q_j consists of expert coding of these six dimensions of alignment and characteristics. See the chapters in Part II of the book for further details on the measurement of priors and performance information in each study.

The measurement of Q_j and P_{ij} on a common scale within each country allows us to standardize the extent of good and bad news, in a way that is specific to each study, but then combine measures of positive and negative information across studies. There were some exceptions to our general strategy for measuring priors, which lead to distinct strategies in the chapter-specific approaches as compared to the meta-analysis. Most notably, the Mexico study did not field a baseline survey due to feasibility and cost considerations (see Chapter 5). There, assuming that no informational spillovers occurred and that the election itself did not alter beliefs, posteriors in the control group can proxy for the average prior in the treatment group in the same randomization block. This clever approach pursued by the Mexico team in its own analysis is based on the fact that due to randomization and the relatively short time elapsed, the distribution of posteriors in the control group should equal in expectation the distribution of priors in the treatment group. This can then be compared to the posterior in the control group, after that group is exposed to a treatment flyer as part of the endline survey. However, this definition also replaces the MPAP's focus on performance information Q_j with a measure that compares subjective posteriors to prior beliefs. In our meta-analysis, and per the MPAP, we instead use the performance information directly, dividing the good and bad news groups based only on whether Q_j (here, the difference between misspending in the respondent's own municipality and in other municipalities governed by the opposition) exceeded the median value in the sample of municipalities. (This is why the P_{ij} column is missing for the Mexico study in Table 3.2, and $Q_j - P_{ij}$ is undefined for the Mexico study for meta-analysis purposes.) We explore alternative methods of operationalizing good and bad news for this study as well, with similar empirical results (see Chapter 11).

Figure 3.2 gives the distributions of P and Q as used in the combined analyses of Chapter 11, adding a small amount of noise to points to help visualize the density. The differences across studies in the type of scale used for defining good news are apparent. As noted, Mexico has only a measure for Q. Other features are readily observable; for instance, in the Uganda 1 study, the distribution for Q is tighter than the distribution for P.[54] In the Uganda 2 study, there is a middle category in P for "don't know," which is not in Q. In all cases we see that Q and P are positively correlated, as one might expect, but the correlation is, in general, weak (around 6 percent). This means that although subjects have some information about politicians, the ability to provide new information is, in general, very large: as seen from the right-most plot, the scope for learning, in both directions, is clear in the aggregated data.

In sum, then, the study teams sought to develop internally consistent measurement of priors and performance information in each context. For our meta-analysis, we standardize the difference $Q_j - P_{ij}$ within the good and bad news groups and within each country, and combine this information across studies to estimate the aggregate effects of good and bad news.

Given these definitions, the core regression specifications for the meta-analysis partition the data into those who would have received good versus bad news according to the above definitions, and then run separate regressions for the impact of being in the information treatment within these two groups on both vote choice and turnout. This is, of course, consistent with the studies' hypotheses, described above. While the overall effect of information may be ambiguous, theory provides clear predictions of causal effects within each of these two subgroups. In all studies, regressions results are presented controlling only for fixed effects for the blocks within which the randomization was conducted, as well as adjusted estimates that control for a full set of demeaned covariate–treatment interactions. We describe this estimation strategy in detail in Chapter 11.

3.4.1 Issues in Aggregating Our Specific Studies

Chapter 2 discussed general issues involved in aggregating the results of individual studies. We close this chapter by noting some important issues specific to our aggregation in Metaketa I.

In particular, we have emphasized the ways in which we seek commonality across the interventions in our studies at a particular level of

---

[54] For Uganda 1, there are some cases where news is classed as good even though the average priors across dimensions are higher than average information across dimensions since tie-breaking rules were employed dimension by dimension.

abstraction, and in particular through the coordinated conceptualization and measurement of good and bad news across studies.

However, given that the Metaketa approach involved beginning from a set of uncoordinated projects on a similar theme and working to harmonize them subsequent to the initial proposal phase, we did not achieve as tight a coordination as a pure replication study would have done. For this reason, it is important to be very clear about the ways in which the interventions studied here are dissimilar, as are the contexts in which they were implemented; and hence how we might have expected different results across the distinct studies.

Domains of difference that we note are countries' electoral systems, the nature of information and who provided it, and finally, the technology used to disseminate this information.

Electoral systems. The underlying logic of the incentives for voters to punish politicians at the ballot box is driven, in our theoretical account, by the dynamic incentives of incumbency. In countries such as Mexico that do not permit politicians to run twice for the same office, this must be driven entirely by party-based incumbent reputation, and this may serve as a weaker mechanism than systems that permit politicians to run for office multiple times. Our studies also encompass environments that range from being quite uncompetitive at the national party level (Uganda), to those that have featured recent reversals in national-level party dominance (Mexico), and this may drive heterogeneity in impacts. Finally, our studies examine the election of regional representatives in countries that have both parliamentary and presidential systems, as well as proportional representation instead of first-past-the-post systems. Even if, in PR systems with multimember districts such as Benin, parliamentarians are informally understood to take responsibility for particular communes or geographic areas in their constituencies (see Chapter 4), it is nonetheless the case that the connection between regional and national political representation differs across these contexts.

The nature and source of the information provided. Each of our studies provided information about some dimension of performance that could be readily ascribed to the politician or the party in question. The definition of performance, however, varied across studies. At one extreme is the India study in which actual criminality was the focus of the dissemination efforts. Perhaps not coincidentally, this study which was most aggressively calling out underperforming politicians was the one to be shut down by authorities. Some of our studies, such as Mexico and Brazil, publicized performance information that was produced by government entities. Others were directly involved in producing the information disseminated. The Uganda 1 study, by airing political debates that would not otherwise have been seen by rural constituents, broadened the information sets on politician behavior in ways that may be quite subtle and hard to quantify.

The dissemination technology. Voters may respond differently even to the same information depending on the technological channel used to disseminate it. Again, our studies are relatively heterogeneous in this regard. Most of the studies presented information via face-to-face meetings, where an explanation of the performance metrics was given directly in the local language. Uganda 1 showed prerecorded "Meet the Candidates" videos to individual respondents, and Uganda 2 moved the furthest into modern technology by using SMS to distribute information via mobile phone.

Clearly, the information environment, electoral systems, performance metrics and dissemination technologies all varied in important ways across our studies. There are more dimensions of heterogeneity across our settings than we have studies, meaning that had we found strong heterogeneity the question of which dimension was causal to this heterogeneity would have been overdetermined. In the concluding chapter we discuss how future Metaketas that find strong heterogeneity across studies might tackle these issues.

3.4.2   Outcome Measures

To measure individual vote choice – our primary outcome measure – research teams asked individuals to report their vote in ways that sought to maximize the reliability of the measure in each context. Whenever possible, the measurement took place in private, after the election but before official results were announced. While we prespecified that teams asking the question in face-to-face interviews would use a secret ballot approach, where only the researchers had the ability to connect a code on a ballot envelope to the identity of respondents, this approach was used fully only in Burkina Faso.[55] Similar privacy and confidentiality protections were attempted when PIs collected individual-level vote

---

[55] See discussion in Lierl and Holmlund (Chapter 8).

choice remotely via telephone or messaging services (USSD/SMS).[56] The vote choice measure takes a value of 1 if the constituent reported voting for the incumbent (or the incumbent's party when no incumbent is up for reelection) and 0 if she did not (whether or not she actually voted). This outcome measure is denoted as M_1 in our MPAP.[57]

With these common elements and definitions established, in Part II of the book we turn to the project-specific chapters written by the Principal Investigators for each study. These provide rich and nuanced analyses of informational effects in each context, and offer much greater detail on the interventions and research designs. We then move to the aggregate analysis of all studies and to evaluation of the Metaketa model itself in Part III, beginning in Chapter 11.

---

[56] According to our MPAP, data collection should take place before official results were announced; respondents should be contacted by automated voice system or USSD with random question order and random response choice to prevent sample-level reconstruction of the data; and PIs need positive consent in the case where they cannot guarantee encryption of messages/voice response. See discussion of messaging protocols in Buntaine et al. (Chapter 7).

[57] Some teams also collected aggregated vote choice data from official electoral returns; we discuss this later. Objective voting data serves as an important check on the potential social desirability bias that accompanies studies providing normative information on politicians and then asking for self-reported voting behavior.

PART II

FIELD EXPERIMENTS

4

Under What Conditions Does Performance Information Influence Voting Behavior? Lessons from Benin

Claire Adida, Jessica Gottlieb, Eric Kramon,
and Gwyneth McClendon

In line with the motivation for the larger Metaketa, our project set out to better understand the conditions under which information about politician performance affects citizens' electoral behavior. We centered our study around the 2015 National Assembly elections in Benin, a West African democracy that ranks in the bottom quintile of countries on the human development index, but which has consolidated its democratic transition with four peaceful presidential turnovers since 1990. This country of 10 million citizens and approximately 5 million registered voters is divided into twelve departments with two legislative constituencies in each, for a total of twenty-four constituencies. Each of these twenty-four constituencies then comprises, on average, three communes. Arrondissements nest within these communes, and in turn villages (or their urban equivalent, quartiers) nest within these arrondissements and represent the lowest level of administration in the country.

Benin embarked on a decentralization effort in 1998, which culminated in the country's first local elections in 2002 since it transitioned to democracy. Integral to this decentralization plan are two laws that defined the roles and responsibilities of each administrative unit: laws 97-028 (for Benin's departments) and 97-029 (for Benin's communes), both signed on January 15, 1999. According to these laws, departments are a purely administrative division with neither judicial nor financial autonomy. The departmental leader, the *Préfet*, is nominated by the Council of Ministers and represents the state's authority at the departmental level. Communes, by contrast, are endowed with local developmental, planning, and responsibilities (Article 83), namely as they relate to infrastructure and transportation (Section 2), health and the environment

(Section 3), primary education (Section 4), adult literacy (Section 5), health and socio-cultural affairs (Section 6), and commerce and economic investment (Section 7). In other words, the country's seventy-seven communes are the relevant local governing unit created by Benin's 1998 decentralization plan. About 70 percent of their budget comes from revenue they raise from taxes, while only 10 percent are transfers from the central government.[1] Local elections are held every five years (law 2007-28) to determine the composition of communal and municipal councils. The next administrative unit, the arrondissement, is a subdivision of the commune; much like the department, it is primarily an advisory organ. Its council is composed of village/quartier chiefs, and advises the mayor. It also registers births, marriages, and deaths. Finally, the village or quartier is the smallest administrative unit; it, too, plays an advisory role. The village/quartier council, comprising representatives of the village/quartier, advises the arrondissement council.

Benin's is a unicameral legislative system, and National Assembly elections are held every five years. The country's eighty-three legislators are elected directly through a party-list proportional representation system: voters vote for party lists rather than individual legislators. Additionally, Benin's districts are multimember. Yet in spite of this institutional context, voters pay greater attention to individual candidates than to political parties. This occurs for several reasons. First, even though constituencies are multimember districts, in practice, many legislators focus on and "take care of" a particular commune within their constituency, facilitating a one-to-one correspondence of incumbent legislator to commune. Indeed, each constituency comprises an average 3.2 communes; in turn, voters elect an average 3.5 deputies per constituency. Second, experts evaluate the party system in Benin as fragmented and weak.[2] New parties and new coalitions form at almost every electoral cycle, and Benin's last two presidents have both been independent politicians, unaffiliated with existing political parties.[3] In our own study, preexperiment focus groups confirmed that villagers could name and agree on a single legislator as their incumbent representative in at least thirty of the communes in the country. In sum, although the formal institutional

---

[1] Caldeira, Foucault, and Rota-Graziosi (2010).
[2] Banégas (2003), Gazibo (2012).
[3] Benin's former president, Boni Yayi, first ran as an independent. Once he became President, a new coalition – the FCBE – formed in his support. It has since become a political party, and currently holds the most seats in the National Assembly.

context favors party rather than candidate voting, voters in Benin tend to vote for candidates.

Turnout in Benin elections is fairly typical for national elections across the continent, for both presidential and legislative contests. In the last presidential elections in 2016, for example, approximately 66 percent of registered voters turned out to vote in both the first and second round of elections. For comparison, in the 2014–2015 Afrobarometer, approximately 69 percent of respondents from surveyed countries in Sub-Saharan Africa reported voting in their most recent national elections. In Benin, roughly the same proportion turned out to vote in the 2015 legislative elections, a highly salient electoral contest owing to the fact that then-President Boni Yayi was suspected of seeking a change to the Constitution to end presidential term limits in order to seek a third term. And so, in spite of a sparse information environment – particularly with regard to the performance of legislators – Benin voters have stayed engaged and mobilized in part due to the threat of a constitutional crisis.

According to Benin's 1990 Constitution, Article 79, the National Assembly has two responsibilities: to debate and vote on legislation, and to control the actions of the government. Formally, therefore, legislators are expected to discuss and pass laws, and to check the power of the Executive. This differentiates Benin from many other African democracies, where legislators are also expected to provide constituency service.[4] But informally, Beninois voters very much expect their legislators – also called deputies – to provide services to their constituents. Indeed, Benin experts have characterized the country as a clientelistic democracy,[5] where voters expect material favors from their politicians in return for their electoral support.

Finally, Benin's political landscape is characterized by ethnic voting.[6] Three regions, the Southeast, the South-Center, and the North, have competed for political dominance ever since the country's independence,[7] and this competition has come to define the country's national political landscape today. Koter (2013) explains this as a result of the fact that local leaders were either removed (if they resisted) or subdued by French colonizers, weakening existing hierarchies and political organization, and

---

[4] Harris and Posner (2017).
[5] Wantchekon (2003).
[6] Adida (2015), Dowd and Driessen (2008), Koter (2013), Wantchekon (2003).
[7] Decalo (1976), Loko (2007).

leaving the country without local elites to shape the country's electoral mobilization strategies. As a result, "ethnic affiliations have been an important means of political mobilization since independence."[8] Quantitative indicators of ethnic voting corroborate this characterization: according to Koter, relying on Dowd and Driessen (2008)'s index of ethnic politics, more than 40 percent of vote choice in Benin is predicted by ethnicity alone. And 80 percent of Afrobarometer respondents express support for a coethnic presidential candidate.[9]

In sum, Benin is a consolidated clientelistic democracy where ethnic ties shape electoral politics. Benin voters turn out at high rates, even for legislative elections, and their votes are more personalistic than partisan. Finally, the information environment surrounding legislative elections and candidates is sparse, but concerns over presidential term limits have kept voters engaged and mobilized.

4.1 RESEARCH DESIGN

This section details the experimental design that we used to test the effect of the common information treatment. The experiment involved the dissemination of information about incumbent legislative performance, via videos, in advance of Benin's April 26, 2015 National Assembly elections.

4.1.1 The Common Arm: Providing Performance Information

Treated participants in the study were given information about their incumbent legislator's relative performance in the National Assembly. We provided this information in the form of a video in order to hold constant the exact wording and tone of delivery across treatment conditions while making the information accessible to people of all education levels, literate and illiterate. In the video, a male actor read a script in a neutral tone, as a newscaster or radio host might. The video included graphics to illustrate key points. It was recorded in French and then dubbed in local languages as necessary.

[8] Koter (2013): 206.
[9] Koter (2013): 214.

The information provided was drawn from official reports of the Office of the President of the National Assembly.[10] The video provided performance information about an incumbent legislator's: (1) rate of attendance in legislative sessions; (2) rate of posing questions during legislative sessions; (3) rate of attendance in committees; and (4) productivity of committee work (the number of laws considered by the committee). The video provided raw data for each of these four performance indicators and presented two summary indicators. The first, an index of plenary performance on a scale of 1–10, took the average of normalized scores on the first two indicators: attendance and participation during full legislative plenary sessions. The second, an index of committee performance also on a scale of 1–10, took an average of the normalized scores on the second two indicators: attendance at committee meetings and productivity. To further synthesize the performance information, we produced a global performance index that averaged scores from the first two indices.

Figure 4.1 shows two examples of how the information was presented. Bar graphs highlight the performance of the legislator responsible for that commune relative to other legislators in the department (a local average)[11] and the country (a national average). Red bars were used when the incumbent's performance fell below the local average (top bar, Figure 4.1), and green bars were used when the incumbent's performance was above the local average (black bar, Figure 4.1).[12] This intervention thus represents our version of the Metaketa common treatment arm.[13]

---

[10] Reports are supposed to be made publicly available but, in practice, are difficult to obtain. We conducted in-person interviews with radio journalists who confirmed that even they have a difficult time accessing such information. The large share of respondents who at baseline answer "Don't know" to survey questions about legislative performance likely reflects the poor dissemination of this information in practice.

[11] There are two constituencies per department and thus on average six to seven legislators per department.

[12] Pre-intervention focus groups confirmed that the video content was comprehensible to villagers in Benin.

[13] The common treatment arm operationalizes performance information as a relative measure based on individuals' priors ($Q_{ij} - P_{ij}$, where i is the individual and j is the randomization unit, in this case, the village/quartier). In our survey, we code the performance as positive if the information was better than the individual's prior; as negative if the information was worse than the individual's prior; as the individual's prior if the information matches the prior; and as the information itself if the individual has no prior. In our administrative data, performance is positive if it is better than the average performance of other legislators in the department, and negative if it is worse.

Claire Adida et al.

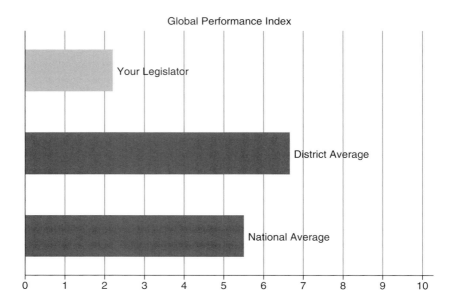

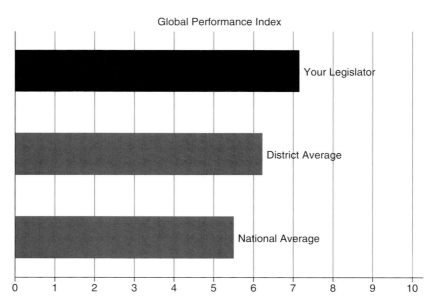

FIGURE 4.1 Benin: Graphical representation of provided information

4.1.2 Randomization

Our full research design included the common arm (Information Only) and two alternative arms. We introduce the alternative arms briefly here to present our randomization strategy, but further elaborate on the intuitions underlying these additional treatment arms in a later section.

The first alternative arm tests whether the salience of the performance information matters: we implement it with a treatment arm that includes a civics message about the importance of legislator performance for everyday citizen wellbeing in Benin (Salience). The second alternative arm tests whether voter coordination matters: we implement this with one treatment arm that varies dosage at the commune level, and one that varies the public nature of the information dissemination at the village level. At the commune level, participants are either told (truthfully) that theirs is the only village (Low dosage) or that theirs is one of twelve villages (High dosage) in the commune receiving the information. At the village level, the performance information is disseminated either privately (face-to-face at the participant's home), or publicly (in a village meeting with approximately fifty other attendees).

Our experimental design followed a two-stage randomization procedure. We began with thirty communes for which we could verify a one-to-one matching of incumbent to commune and in which the incumbent was running for reelection.[14] We then randomly assigned each of those thirty communes to either the low or the high dosage condition, blocking on incumbent legislative performance, which is observed at the commune level, and on north/south, since being in the culturally distinct north or south of the country is an important moderator of political behavior in Benin.[15] Within four blocks (high and low performance in the north and south) of communes, we assigned half to high dosage and half to low dosage treatment.

---

[14] As mentioned above, although Benin's is a PR multimember district system, in practice each legislator focuses on and takes care of a particular commune within his constituency, which facilitates a one-to-one correspondence of incumbent legislator to commune. But in order to be doubly confident of this approach, we restrict our experimental sample to thirty communes in which our local partner organization firmly verified a one-to-one correspondence and in which the incumbent legislator stood for reelection. We further verified the one-to-one correspondence in our baseline survey by asking respondents to identify pretreatment the legislative deputy who is most responsible for their village.

[15] Adida (2015).

Second, we randomly assigned treatment conditions within communes. The unit of randomization was the rural village or its equivalent urban quartier, the lowest level of social and territorial organization. In high dosage communes, we randomly assigned each village/quartier to one of five conditions: (1) Information Only/Private; (2) Information Only/Public; (3) Information + Salience/Private; (4) Information + Salience/Public; or (5) Control. Three villages/quartiers in each of the fifteen high dosage communes were randomly assigned to one of the four treatment conditions, and the remainder villages/quartiers in the commune were assigned to the control group. Thus, in the high dosage communes, we have a 2×2 factorial design with a pure control group. To increase statistical efficiency, we assigned villages to experimental conditions while blocking on urban/rural status and electoral competitiveness of the village in the previous legislative election.[16] We note here that condition (1) Information Only/Private is our version of the Metaketa common treatment arm.

In the low dosage communes, where only one village/quartier received treatment, we randomly assigned units to one of two conditions: (1) Information + Salience/Public, or (2) Control. One village/quartier was assigned to the treatment condition, while the remainder were assigned to control. We use the Information + Salience/Public condition in the low dosage communes because we believed a priori that it would have the strongest effect, thus making it harder for us to detect dosage effects.

Table 4.1 summarizes the experimental design. In low dosage communes, there are fifteen treated units (villages/quartiers) and 643 controls. In high dosage communes, there are forty-five treated units in each of the four treatment conditions (180 treated in total) and 486 controls. As specified in our pre-analysis plan (PAP), we use all nontreated villages/quartiers in our sample communes as controls, which substantially increases our statistical power. A baseline survey was conducted in all treated villages/quartiers (180 in high dosage and fifteen in low dosage), in three control villages in each high dosage commune (forty-five total), and in one control village in each low dosage commune (fifteen total), for a total of 225 units in the survey sample.

In each Private condition village/quartier, forty participants were shown one of the treatment videos. In each Public condition village/quartier, sixty people were recruited and invited to the public

---

[16] In each commune, there are three blocks: urban, rural/electorally competitive, and rural/not electorally competitive.

TABLE 4.1 *Benin: Experimental design*

	Low Dosage (15 communes)				High Dosage (15 communes)		
	Control	Private	Public		Control	Private	Public
Control	643			Control	486		
Info Only				Info Only		45	45
Salience + Info			15	Salience + Info		45	45

Cells represent the number of villages or urban quarters in each experimental condition. In Private condition villages/quarters, forty randomly selected individuals were shown the treatment videos. In Public condition villages/quarters, sixty randomly selected individuals were invited to the public screening of the treatment videos, and on average about fifty individuals attended the screenings.

screening, and on average about fifty participants attended (the standard deviation is thirteen).[17] The average village/quarter in our sample contains about 320 households, meaning that an individual from 12 percent to 15 percent of households was treated.[18] We expected substantial within-household information transmission and we found experimental and qualitative evidence of significant information transmission within communities (results discussed below), which means that many more people in each community were likely exposed to the information in the treatment.

For further clarity on our experimental design, see a CONSORT diagram in Figure 4.2, which outlines the sampling and randomization procedure and shows each of the experimental conditions with the sample size of villages and survey respondents in each condition. Figure 4.3 geographically plots the sampled villages and quarters in each of the thirty sample communes.

4.1.3 Data

To measure the effect of the treatments on aggregate official outcomes at the level of treatment assignment, we collected administrative data

[17] We treated/invited an equal number of men and women.
[18] In urban quarters, the average number of registered voters was about 1,200, which means that at most 3–4 percent of registered voters were treated in urban areas. In rural villages, the average number of registered voters was about 870, and so at most 4.5–6 percent of registered voters were treated.

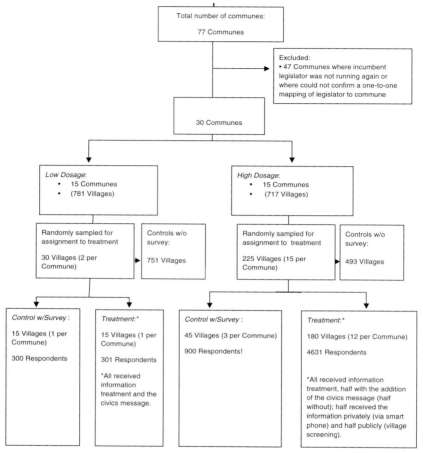

FIGURE 4.2 Benin: CONSORT diagram of research design

on party vote shares at the polling station level and then aggregated to the village level. We were able to match 2015 polling station data to all villages in our experimental sample except for one treated village and two surveyed control villages, which we drop from the analysis.[19] Including control villages that were not surveyed, among all villages and quartiers

---

[19] In one village, enumerators administered both private screenings and a public screening, although in both cases they showed the same video (Info Only). We thus exclude this village from our analyses comparing Public and Private conditions.

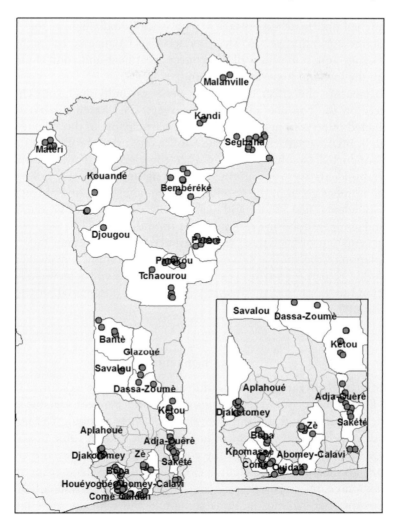

FIGURE 4.3 Benin: Sample of communes and villages/quartiers
Note: The map displays all sample communes (white segments) and sample
villages and urban quartiers (dots).

in our original sample of thirty communes, we were able to match 88 percent to the 2015 outcome data.[20] On most pretreatment characteristics

---

[20] A number of quartiers (the urban administrative equivalent of a village) were split into
two between 2011 and 2015. We were able to match some of these with the help of our
local partner but not all.

unmatched and matched villages are statistically indistinguishable.[21] In the online appendix we also show evidence of balance across high and low dosage communes as well as between treatment and control groups within the low and high dosage communes.

To measure the effect of the treatments on individual vote choice, we rely on the baseline and endline surveys. The baseline survey was conducted in person, just before treating participants in the Private condition or inviting participants in the Public condition. The endline survey was conducted by phone directly after the election. The identities of the respondents were reconfirmed in the endline survey by calling the phone number given in the baseline survey and asking for confirmation of respondents' first names and ages. To discourage attrition, one-third of total compensation per respondent (250 out of 750 CFAs – equivalent to 40 cents out of US $1.20) was transferred as phone credit only after completion of the endline survey. In designing the study, we allowed for a possible 50 percent attrition rate between surveys and achieved a lower attrition rate (44 percent). We discuss patterns of differential attrition in Section 4.3.

4.1.4   Estimation

To estimate the treatment effects of the common arm, we estimate Ordinary Least Squares (OLS) regressions where the dependent variable is one of the measures of incumbent vote share or voter turnout. The models include a dichotomous treatment indicator that takes a value of 1 if the village (or individual) received the common arm treatment, and 0 otherwise. The models also include block fixed effects, which ensures that our experimental estimates are being driven by comparisons of similar villages/quartiers within the same commune and with the same incumbent. In the analysis of the official results, we cluster standard errors by commune-treatment condition. In the analysis of the survey data, we cluster standard errors on village, the level at which treatment was assigned.

As prespecified in our PAP, and in line with the Metaketa meta-analysis pre-analysis plan (MPAP), we evaluate the effects of treatment differently for individuals receiving "good news" – or positive information about their legislator's performance – and individuals receiving "bad news" –

---

[21] See Section A.1 in the online appendix.

or negative information (H1a and H1b in the MPAP). We do this because we expect voters to respond qualitatively differently to information about legislators that is positive versus information that is negative.

In our analysis of the official election results, we leverage the fact that the information provided in the intervention explicitly compares the incumbent legislator's performance to the performance of deputies in the surrounding area (those in the same department) and code positive and negative information relative to this local benchmark. Specifically, we define the information as good news if the incumbent's overall score is better than the average score of other legislators in the department, and bad news if the incumbent's overall legislative score is worse than that of others in this local area.[22]

In our analysis of the survey data, we take advantage of the fact that we have information about individual voters' prior beliefs about the performance of their incumbent. We thus code positive and negative information relative to these prior beliefs.[23] We code the intervention as providing good news if the performance information was better than the respondent's prior, and bad news if it was worse. In instances where the information in the intervention is the same as the respondent's prior, or where the respondent reports that he/she does not know the incumbent's legislative performance, we follow the coding rule used with the official results data. For those whose priors match the information in the intervention, the logic is that the intervention should make them more confident in their assessment. For example, if their prior is that the incumbent is a bad performer and they receive information that validates that prior, they will become more confident in their beliefs. For those who have no priors, the logic is that the intervention provides them with the only information they have and thus they will fully update.

Unlike in Arias et al. (Chapter 5), we find that accounting for priors in our construction of indicators of good and bad news does not affect our interpretation of the results. Indeed, findings using the survey data are robust to employing the same coding rule as the one used with administrative data that does not account for priors. One reason for this is the

---

[22] There are only three communes in which the incumbent performed better than the local average but worse than the national average, or vice versa. Because the graphs shown to treated participants depicted both the local and the national average, we tested whether our results are robust to coding good and bad news relative to the national average instead of relative to the local average. They are.

[23] In our baseline survey, we asked about the incumbent's relative performance, using the same scale that is provided in the intervention.

incredibly weak priors constituents hold about legislative performance of incumbent politicians. Not only is the legislative performance dimension weakly salient among Beninese voters,[24] but a majority (54 percent of baseline participants) had no priors when it came to the legislative performance of their incumbent politician (i.e., they responded "don't know" to our survey questions eliciting priors).

4.2 TREATMENT EFFECTS OF THE COMMON ARM

This section presents our average common arm treatment effects on vote choice, measured attitudinally via individual self-reported survey data (M1), and on vote share, measured behaviorally via aggregate official results (M2).[25] We also present the same results on voter turnout, using the self-reported turnout measure from the survey (M3) and the voter turnout rate in each village using the official results (M4).

Before turning to formal tests, Figures 4.4 and 4.5 present summary means (and 95 percent confidence intervals) of the incumbent vote share measures in the control condition (in villages and for individuals who were given no performance information about their legislator) and in the common arm treatment condition (in villages and for individuals who were given performance information in a private setting). Only observations in the high dosage condition are reported; the common arm treatment condition was not conducted in low dosage communes. As prespecified, the means are broken down by good and bad news.

Figure 4.4 presents the means in treatment and control in the survey data. Among individuals who were treated with good news, the reported vote share for the incumbent was about 46 percent ($n = 214$). Among control individuals – who were not treated but who would have received good news had they been treated – the vote share is about 44 percent ($n = 246$). For those who were treated with bad news, the vote share for

---

[24] Our baseline survey included an experimental vignette describing a hypothetical candidate as either providing transfers, performing legislative duties, or neither (control). Results from this survey experiment indicate that respondents prefer candidates who provide transfers relative to the control candidate; by contrast, respondents were not more likely to prefer strong legislative performers to the control candidate.

[25] We have some reservations about the reliability of our survey data. For example, Table 4.2 indicates much larger incumbent support in the individual self-reported data than in the aggregate official data. This could be due to response bias or to selection bias in the survey data. In Section 4.3, we further discuss possible biases in our survey data.

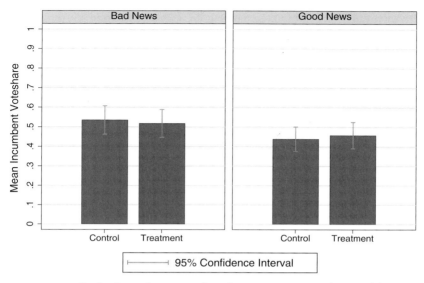

FIGURE 4.4 Benin: Incumbent vote share in common arm and control (survey data), with 95 percent confidence intervals

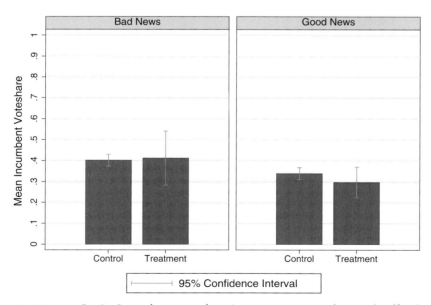

FIGURE 4.5 Benin: Incumbent vote share in common arm and control (official data), with 95 percent confidence intervals

the incumbent was about 52 percent ($n = 195$). Among the bad news control individuals, the vote share was about 54 percent ($n = 187$). This pattern is consistent with the hypothesis that good news should increase support for the incumbent while bad news should reduce it. However, the trend is reversed when we examine the official results data. As shown in Figure 4.5, the vote share for the incumbent is about 30 percent in villages treated with good news ($n = 27$), while the vote share is about 34 percent in control villages that would have received good news had they been treated ($n = 259$). In bad news areas, the vote share of the incumbent in treated villages is 41 percent ($n = 18$), while it is 40 percent in control ($n = 225$). In the official data, the raw means suggest that good news may have lowered the vote share of the incumbent, while bad news might have slightly improved it.

While the survey data and official data tell different stories when we examine the raw means, there is one dimension where they are consistent. In both sets of data, poor performing incumbents, as measured by our index, receive higher vote shares than well performing incumbents. In the survey data, for example, vote share for the incumbent is 53 percent in bad news control, while it is 44 percent in good news control. In the official data, incumbent vote share is 40 percent in bad news control compared to 34 percent in good news control. This suggests that voters may not value the legislative performance that is captured by the performance index. Or, it could be that the types of incumbents who perform poorly on the index are also the types who perform well in other areas that are more effective electorally. For example, poor legislative performers may spend more time or be better at providing constituency service. We return to these ideas when we present the results on the alternative treatment arms that were part of our study in Benin.

Turning to more formal tests, Table 4.2 estimates the effect of the common arm treatment on incumbent vote share. As above, we subset the sample by good and bad news and present results with both the survey and the official results data. All models are estimated using OLS and include block fixed effects. Two results stand out. First, all effects are statistically indistinguishable from zero.[26] This is even more apparent when

---

[26] Our power calculations allowed for identifying a 10 percent change in vote share as this was an effect size previously obtained by a similar information experiment in Benin. In order to increase our statistical power, we also gathered baseline and endline information from a set of control participants living in common arm treatment villages. Because we found evidence of within-community spillover effects from treated individuals to these control individuals, we are unable to use this group of control participants

TABLE 4.2 *Benin: Effects of information in the common arm on voting for the incumbent*

	(1) Good Survey	(2) Good Survey	(3) Good Survey	(4) Good Survey	(5) Good Official	(6) Good Official
Treatment	0.02	−0.02	−0.02	−0.10	−0.02	0.00
	(0.03)	(0.07)	(0.07)	(0.08)	(0.01)	(0.04)
Distance Prior and Performance (good)			0.05			
			(0.06)			
Treatment × Distance (good)			−0.06			
			(0.07)			
Distance Prior and Performance (bad)				−0.07		
				(0.04)		
Treatment × Distance (bad)				0.05		
				(0.06)		
Constant	0.44***	0.54***	0.48***	0.61***	0.34***	0.40***
	(0.02)	(0.05)	(0.05)	(0.05)	(0.00)	(0.00)
Observations	460	382	194	161	286	243
R²	0.21	0.21	0.36	0.29	0.64	0.61
RI p-value	0.99	0.99			0.97	1.00
RI 95% CI	[−0.06, 0.09]	[−0.19, 0.15]			[−0.09, 0.06]	[−0.14, 0.15]

Robust standard errors in parentheses

*** $p < 0.01$, ** $p < 0.05$, * $p < 0.1$

we consider *p*-values generated by randomization inference, reported at the bottom of Table 4.2. Thus, we find no evidence that the common arm treatment had a statistically significant effect on incumbent vote share. Second, as in the raw data, the direction of the effects is reversed in our survey and administrative data: although the survey data show the point estimates we would expect – positive effects of good news (column 1) and negative effects of bad news (column 2) – the behavioral data show just the opposite – in particular, a negative effect of good news (column 5).

In line with the meta-analysis, we also examined whether treatment effects differ depending on the distance between a voter's prior belief and the actual performance information provided (N_{ij}). To do so, we measure the difference between the voter's prior belief and the actual performance information given in treatment, which were both measured and presented on the same four-point scale. For example, a respondent whose prior is that the incumbent is "much worse" than other deputies (score of 1) but finds out that the incumbent was actually "much better" than the other deputies (score of 4), would be scored as a 3 on this distance measure and be included in the good news subset. Similarly, a respondent whose prior is that the incumbent is "better" than other deputies (score of 3) but finds out that the incumbent was actually "much better" than the other deputies (score of 4), would be scored as a 1. We normalize the distance measure (mean 0 and standard deviation of 1) in the good news and bad news subsets.

Columns 3 and 4 of Table 4.2 present the results of analyses in which we interact this normalized distance measure with treatment. In both good and bad news, we find no evidence that treatment effects are conditioned by the distance between priors and actual performance. However, we emphasize an important limitation of the distance measure in our case. Because such a large proportion of respondents reported "don't know" on the baseline survey questions measuring priors, we are unable to construct the distance measure for a large share of the sample. As a result, we are only able to conduct these analyses on the sample of respondents who had priors, which might not be representative. The smaller sample also diminishes our statistical power. Given

---

to estimate the treatment effect of the common arm (because these control individuals were indirectly impacted by treatment).

these limitations, we conducted an additional set of analyses that includes individuals who responded "don't know" when asked about their prior beliefs. In these analyses, we treat these individuals as having a prior of 0, which allows us to calculate the distance measure. For these individuals, the distance measure is identical to the actual performance information. The results from these additional analyses are similar to those reported in Table 4.2.

It is important to note that several of the treatment effect estimates in Table 4.2 are imprecisely estimated, which means that in some cases we should be cautious about interpreting null results as strong evidence of "no effect." This is especially the case in the analysis of the survey data, where we are unable to use the full set of nontreated units in each commune as controls (because we conducted the survey in three control villages per commune). With respect to the administrative data, the effects are more precisely estimated, as indicated by the smaller range of the 95 percent confidence intervals. In the good news communes, most of the 95 percent confidence interval is negative, which suggests that the impact of good news was very unlikely to have been positive. And if the effect was positive, it was likely to have been very small in magnitude. In bad news communes, on the other hand, the coefficient estimate is very close to 0, but less precisely estimated, so this null result should be interpreted with more caution.

In Table 4.3, we present estimates of the effect of the common arm on voter turnout. In each model, we find no evidence that the common arm had an effect on turnout. In both the survey (column 1) and the official results (column 5), good news has a negative effect on voter turnout, although the effects are not statistically significant. By contrast, bad news increases turnout in the survey (column 2) and the official data (column 6), but again the coefficients cannot be statistically distinguished from 0. We also find no evidence that the distance between priors and actual performance conditions the treatment effect (columns 3 and 4). These latter results on distance should be interpreted with caution for the reasons discussed above.

Table 4.4 tests whether the effect of good news in the common arm is conditioned by any of the individual-level covariates that each study in this volume is examining. To do so, we present results of analyses in which we interact each of the covariates with the treatment indicator. In most instances, the interaction coefficients are not statistically significant, indicating that the effect of treatment is not conditioned by the covariate. There are two exceptions. First, the results in column 1 show

TABLE 4.3 *Benin: Effects of information in the common arm on voter turnout*

	(1) Good Survey	(2) Bad Survey	(3) Good Survey	(4) Bad Survey	(5) Good Official	(6) Bad Official
Treatment	−0.03	0.02	−0.03	−0.10	−0.04	0.01
	(0.03)	(0.02)	(0.05)	(0.08)	(0.03)	(0.01)
Distance Prior and Performance (good)			−0.06			
			(0.05)			
Treatment × Distance (good)			0.02			
			(0.06)			
Distance between Prior and Performance (bad)				−0.07		
				(0.04)		
Treatment × Distance (bad)				0.05		
				(0.06)		
Constant	0.89***	0.89***	0.90***	0.61***	0.92***	0.89***
	(0.02)	(0.02)	(0.03)	(0.05)	(0.02)	(0.01)
Observations	524	428	221	161	51	33
R^2	0.19	0.06	0.29	0.29	0.69	0.62

Robust standard errors in parentheses
*** $p < 0.01$, ** $p < 0.05$, * $p < 0.1$

TABLE 4.4 Benin: Heterogeneous effects of good news on vote for the incumbent

	(1)	(2)	(3)	(4)	(5)	(6)	(7)	(8)
Treatment	−0.29** (0.13)	−0.03 (0.05)	0.20* (0.11)	−0.10 (0.09)	0.07 (0.06)	−0.11 (0.10)	0.09 (0.08)	0.23 (0.16)
Treatment × Age	0.01** (0.00)							
Age	0.00 (0.00)							
Treatment × Education		0.01 (0.01)						
Yrs of Education		0.00 (0.00)						
Treatment × Wealth			−0.07* (0.04)					
Wealth (relative)			0.05 (0.04)					
Treatment × Turnout Previous				0.14 (0.10)				
Turnout in Previous Election				−0.07 (0.07)				
Treatment × Incumbent Vote Previous					−0.03 (0.09)			

(continued)

TABLE 4.4 *(continued)*

	(1)	(2)	(3)	(4)	(5)	(6)	(7)	(8)
Vote Incumbent in Previous Election					0.01 (0.08)			
Treatment × Handouts						0.05 (0.05)		
Expect Handout from Incumbent in Future						−0.03 (0.04)		
Treatment × Ballot Secret							−0.06 (0.04)	
Perception of Ballot Secrecy							0.06* (0.04)	
Treatment × Free and Fair								−0.09 (0.06)
Expects Free and Fair Elections								−0.01 (0.05)
Constant	0.55*** (0.09)	0.46*** (0.03)	0.31*** (0.10)	0.49*** (0.07)	0.44*** (0.05)	0.51*** (0.08)	0.36*** (0.07)	0.47*** (0.13)
Observations	450	457	460	460	373	441	435	288
R^2	0.23	0.22	0.22	0.22	0.26	0.24	0.24	0.26

Robust standard errors in parentheses
*** $p < 0.01$, ** $p < 0.05$, * $p < 0.1$

that the effect of good news is negative, statistically significant, and quite large in magnitude among the youngest participants (the youngest in the sample are age 19). The positive and significant coefficient on the interaction between treatment and age indicates that this negative effect moves towards zero as the participant's age increases. Second, column 3 shows that good news improves the incumbent vote share among the poorest participants in the sample, and that this effect moves to zero as relative wealth increases. This result is less precisely estimated, however, especially if corrections for multiple comparisons are made. We did not expect either of these conditional effects to obtain ex ante, but the second result is consistent with the idea that poorer voters may have weaker political views and are thus more subject to be influenced by new information.

Table 4.5 presents the same results among participants in the bad news subgroup. In these analyses, we generally do not find evidence of conditional effects. The interaction between treatment and turnout in the previous election is significant at the $p < 0.1$ level (column 4). The results suggest that while bad news increased the vote share of the incumbent among those who did not vote in the previous elections – this estimate is not statistically significant – the effect of bad news is negative, about −0.05, among those who did (we get this by adding the "treatment" coefficient, which is positive, to the "treatment × turnout" coefficient, which is negative). This marginal effect is not, however, statistically significant.

In summary, we do not find evidence that the common arm impacted voter behavior in our study. Using evidence from self-reported voting behavior and official results aggregated to the village level, we see no evidence that the provision of good news or bad news about incumbent legislative performance alone had an effect on incumbent vote share or voter turnout in the legislative elections.

4.3 INTRODUCING OUR ALTERNATIVE TREATMENT ARMS: SALIENCE AND COORDINATION

In designing the alternative arms for our study, we considered the context in which we delivered legislative performance information to individual voters: a clientelistic democracy where voters seem to care more about the informal activities sometimes undertaken by legislators (providing targeted transfers) than about formal duties (legislating),

TABLE 4.5 *Benin: Heterogeneous effects of bad news on vote for the incumbent*

	(1)	(2)	(3)	(4)	(5)	(6)	(7)	(8)
Treatment	−0.23*	0.04	0.15	0.17	−0.14	−0.22**	−0.06	0.06
	(0.12)	(0.09)	(0.18)	(0.12)	(0.10)	(0.10)	(0.10)	(0.13)
Treatment × Age	0.01							
	(0.00)							
Age	−0.01***							
	(0.00)							
Treatment × Education		−0.01						
		(0.01)						
Yrs of Education		0.00						
		(0.01)						
Treatment × Wealth			−0.07					
			(0.07)					
Wealth (relative)			0.06					
			(0.06)					
Treatment × Turnout Previous				−0.22*				
				(0.13)				
Turnout in Previous Election				0.14				
				(0.12)				
Treatment × Incumbent Vote Previous					0.18			
					(0.11)			
Vote Incumbent in Previous Election					−0.03			
					(0.10)			
Treatment × Handouts						0.08		
						(0.05)		
Expect Handout from Incumbent in Future						−0.05		
						(0.05)		

	(1)	(2)	(3)	(4)	(5)	(6)	(7)	(8)
Treatment × Ballot Secret							0.02	
							(0.04)	
Perception of Ballot Secrecy							0.00	
							(0.03)	
Treatment × Free and Fair								−0.03
								(0.05)
Expects Free and Fair Elections								0.04
								(0.05)
Constant	0.77***	0.52***	0.38***	0.42***	0.56***	0.66***	0.54***	0.49***
	(0.08)	(0.06)	(0.14)	(0.10)	(0.07)	(0.11)	(0.08)	(0.12)
Observations	372	371	382	381	318	381	381	258
R^2	0.21	0.21	0.21	0.21	0.19	0.21	0.21	0.24

Robust standard errors in parentheses
*** $p < 0.01$, ** $p < 0.05$, * $p < 0.1$

and where translating beliefs about legislative performance into vote choice requires coordination. Consequently, we designed two alternative treatment arms that explicitly address two key obstacles to exiting a clientelistic equilibrium where information about legislative performance does not translate into electoral behavior: a salience message, highlighting the ways in which legislative performance can affect voter well-being; and two coordination treatments, saturating a sufficient proportion of the constituency/village with information and letting voters know about it.[27]

To understand the importance of information salience, the experiment varied whether voters heard a civics message emphasizing the importance of the legislative performance dimension to voter welfare. Treated participants were shown a video with either only the information about relative legislator performance (Info Only), or that same information plus the civics message (Salience). The salience message described the main responsibilities of legislative deputies. It then provided three concrete examples of how legislative performance (or lack thereof) can impact voter welfare. A positive example of good legislation was the passage of an anti-graft law requiring public servants to disclose assets. A negative example of a missed opportunity was the failure of the legislature to vote on and pass a health insurance scheme that was proposed in 2008. Finally, a positive example of executive oversight detailed how the legislature opposed changes to the Constitution proposed by the president that would expand his power. The Salience treatment was provided to treated participants immediately before they received the legislative performance information.

To gauge whether coordination between voters was necessary for new performance information to influence voter behavior, we also introduce two treatments meant to encourage coordination at the village level and at the commune level. Scholars have characterized Benin as a clientelistic democracy, where politicians provide voters with targeted transfers in return for electoral support.[28] If so, Beninese voters should care more about transfers from legislators than about legislator performance in parliament (see $H0_a$ in our study's own PAP, linked to the online appendix). Additionally, because collective transfers of this nature motivate bloc voting – where blocs, such as villages or constituencies, are rewarded with a

---

[27] A more complete analysis of these alternative treatment arms is elaborated in Adida et al. (2017a).
[28] Wantchekon (2003).

new clinic, for example[29] – then voters should be unlikely to change their individual vote choices in isolation (see H_{0b} in our study PAP). While low expectations of pivotality may hinder vote changes in any context, isolated vote changes are particularly unlikely in contexts of bloc voting rewards because villages that fail to coordinate high enough levels of support for the winning candidate may face negative repercussions in the next round of private transfer distribution. In other words, voters should want to coordinate both with others in the village to generate a clear enough signal of support and to coordinate with enough other villages in a constituency to ensure that the supported candidate wins. To test our prediction about voter coordination, we varied the method by which the information was disseminated. Because we were unsure whether within-village or across-village coordination problems were more severe in this context, we devised treatments to investigate both.

To overcome within-village coordination constraints, we implemented the information treatment in a public setting. Treated participants received the intervention either privately by watching a video on a smartphone in the respondent's household (Private) or publicly through the screening of the same video via a projector in a public location in the village (Public). The Public condition was designed to facilitate intra-village coordination by making clear to individual participants that others in the village were simultaneously receiving the same type of information that could lead to similar changes in beliefs and thus behavior.

To overcome across-village coordination constraints, we implemented the information treatment in a larger number of villages in the commune – about a quarter – so that these voters would believe in the possibility of coordinating to vote along a new performance dimension. Participants were told during the intervention whether they were the only village or one of twelve villages in their commune receiving legislative performance information. This high dosage treatment was designed to facilitate inter-village coordination by informing individual voters that several other villages were receiving the information such that coordinating on the legislative performance dimension would be more feasible.[30]

---

[29] Rueda (2017).

[30] In designing the experiment, we followed the ethical principles agreed upon by the Metaketa Initiative, as outlined in the MPAP: that the intervention consist of information that existed in the political system, be provided with consent, in a nonpartisan way, without deception, and in cooperation with a local group.

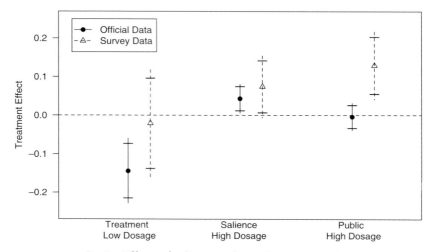

FIGURE 4.6 Benin: Effects of salience and coordination (good news), with 95 percent and 90 percent confidence intervals

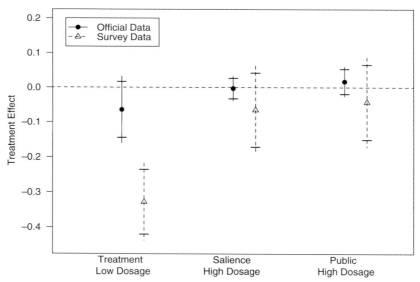

FIGURE 4.7 Benin: Effects of salience and coordination (bad news), with 95 percent and 90 percent confidence intervals

Figures 4.6 and 4.7 below provide results that are consistent with our above hypotheses.[31] As before, we employ block fixed effects and cluster

---

[31] In order to produce visual representations of the confidence intervals around our treatment effects, and to take advantage of our cluster-randomized design in the survey data, we use regression analysis to produce the results displayed in Figures 4.6 and 4.7.

standard errors at the village level in the survey data and at the level of commune × treatment in the administrative data. Only when we provide voters with a civics message that is widely disseminated throughout the constituency do we observe the anticipated positive effect of good news information. For every other treatment arm, the results either contradict what we expected, are statistically indistinguishable from zero, or are fragile to the mode of data collection and model specification. For example, when provided to only one village in a constituency, treatment hurt incumbent performance in both positive and negative information conditions.

While we do not observe our anticipated negative effect of poor performance information on incumbent vote share in the Salience/High dosage treatment, we do detect statistically significant negative effects among those voters receiving the worst information about their legislator's performance. We take advantage of the fact that the verbal information received by voters was divided into four rather than two performance categories: information that the incumbent was "much worse," "worse," "better," or "much better" than other legislators in his department.[32] In Figure 4.8, we find that, in High dosage communes, the Salience treatment had a negative effect on the aggregate vote share of those who performed "much worse" (p = 0.09).[33] Thus, voters do punish the worst performing incumbents, but only when the information is disseminated in combination with the Salience treatment and widely across the commune.

Because we do not see a statistically significant effect of treatment in the Public condition across both data sources (it is positive and significant in the survey data, but a precise zero in the administrative data), we conclude that the coordination constraint faced by voters was at the constituency level (across villages) rather than within villages.[34] This is consistent with the Mexico and Uganda 2 studies (Chapters 5 and 7), which both have null effects of their Public treatment arm. It also highlights what is different about our two coordination arms. In Mexico and Uganda 2 (Chapters 5 and 7), the Public arm was delivered in

---

[32] Categories were defined using quartiles of the performance score in each department.

[33] As in other specifications above, our analysis of the official aggregate data here is not conditional on survey respondents' priors. Recall that our relative measure in the administrative data is relative to the average legislator performance in the department.

[34] Further comparison of our two data sources suggests that respondents may have overreported voting for the incumbent in the survey data (Adida et al., forthcoming), which could explain the difference in effect sizes across survey findings and official data.

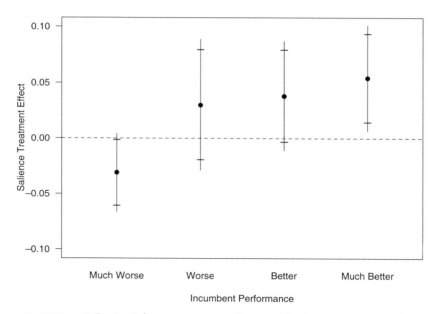

FIGURE 4.8 Benin: Salience treatment effect in high-dosage communes, by incumbent performance, with 95 percent and 90 percent confidence intervals (official data)

such a way that would produce common knowledge within villages or precincts, just as in our Public condition. However, our dosage treatment produces common knowledge across villages and precincts. This suggests that cross-village coordination does pose a constraint to voters acting upon new information while within-village coordination does not pose such a constraint.

This is not surprising when we consider additional evidence collected on Control participants in Privately treated villages. In each Private condition village, we randomly assigned some individuals to receive a survey and no intervention (Control) and some individuals to receive a survey with the intervention (Treatment). When comparing reported support for and views of the incumbent across these Treatment and Control individuals within Private villages, we observe no detectable treatment effects. This provides additional evidence of low barriers to within-village coordination and suggests strong information transmission within the village – so much so that the responses of people who are not directly given treatment are equivalent to the responses of people directly given treatment within the same village. The intra-village coordination problem appears to have already been solved, while our treatment arm helped to facilitate inter-village coordination.

As for the large and significant effect of the Public treatment in the survey data, we have reason to believe these results might be driven by differential attrition across Public, Private, and Control conditions. First, we find that participants in the Public condition are substantively and significantly less likely to attrit relative to the control condition.[35] When we account for this differential attrition in our estimation of treatment effects using inverse probability weights for the predicted likelihood of attrition, the confidence interval of the estimated treatment effect of Public increases even though the coefficient is still significant at conventional levels. However, important individual attributes such as gender (M13) and education are also key predictors of attrition, which suggests that there could be additional unobservables driving this differential attrition that we cannot account for in such an analysis but that are producing a spurious result. For instance, if likely partisans of the incumbent felt more acute social pressure in the Public treatment settings to stay in the sample through the endline survey, then differences in the endline composition of respondents in each experimental condition could produce the illusion of a treatment effect, especially in response to good news.[36]

4.4 CONCLUSION

In sum, we find that the provision of legislative performance information alone had no detectable effect on vote choice, even when that information went against respondents' priors. We find instead that legislative performance information matters to Benin voters when it is disseminated with a salience message emphasizing the salience of performance for voters' wellbeing, as well as with a message highlighting the fact that other villages in the commune are receiving the same information. Our null finding for our common arm treatment, which simply provided performance information to individual participants, is consistent with the meta-analysis results.

---

[35] See Section A.3 in the online appendix.

[36] It is also possible that the differences in the survey between the Public condition and others are driven by social desirability bias. For instance, those in the Public treatment may have been more likely to perceive a social expectation that they at least appear to reward strong performance even if they do not vote that way in the end. For these reasons, we place our confidence in results that are consistent across administrative and survey datasets.

4.4.1 Explaining the Null Results

We propose three possible explanations for the weak effects of legislative performance information on voting behavior. First, Arias et al. (Chapter 5) inform us that treatments such as the one we provided in the common arm might have mobilization effects rather than, or in addition to, persuasion effects (see H2a and H2b of the MPAP). In other words, our intervention could have affected turnout differentially to yield a weak average treatment effect. Second, we expected and prespecified that our treatment might have differential effects on different types of individuals. In other words, weak average treatment effects could mask larger effects within subgroups. Finally, as conveyed by our alternative treatment arms, we expected and integrated into our research design the possibility that our common arm information would not be enough to move voters out of a clientelistic equilibrium. Instead, we expected voters would act on the information only when persuaded that legislative performance affects their welfare and when able to coordinate with others.

Regarding the first potential explanation, our evidence suggests that effects on turnout are unlikely to explain the null results. As presented in Table 4.3 above, treatment does not have a statistically significant effect on voter turnout. If anything, the administrative data suggest that the provision of positive information about the incumbent depressed turnout. For this to be consistent with the masking of a positive impact of strong legislative performance information on incumbent support, positive information would have to simultaneously strengthen voters' preference for the incumbent and keep pro-incumbent voters at home. We do not think this a plausible enough story to call into question the weak treatment effect on aggregate vote share.

Alternatively, it may be that average treatment effects on incumbent vote share mask significant heterogeneous treatment effects based on how different types of individuals respond to our treatment. For instance, in our context it could be that coethnics of the incumbent politician reward good performance, while noncoethnics of the incumbent punish it, yielding a null result in the aggregate. In our pre-analysis plan, we prespecified the following two conditional effects, in addition to several others presented in the online appendix (for which we find no evidence).

First, relying on well-documented research in social psychology, we expected voters to engage in motivated reasoning about their politician when they share with them a salient social identity: in the Benin context where ethnicity is politically salient[37] we expect coethnics to be relatively unresponsive to negative information about the incumbent and more responsive to positive information about the incumbent, and vice versa for noncoethnics.[38] We develop this argument elsewhere,[39] and report our basic findings, which are consistent with ethnically motivated reasoning, below.

Similarly, we expected conditional treatment effects according to whether voters share clientelist linkages with their incumbent. In a clientelistic democracy such as Benin, where many politicians and voters rely on the exchange of private favors and goods for votes,[40] there are two ways in which this clientelistic relationship might moderate our treatment. First, echoing the motivated reasoning logic above, voters with clientelistic linkages to their incumbents might choose to disregard negative performance information and integrate positive performance information about them.[41] Alternatively, if voters care primarily about constituency service and clientelistic transfers, they might be willing to reward good legislative performance only if they have had personal experience with the incumbent's ability to deliver clientelistic goods in the past. Conversely, past experience with clientelism might outweigh the impact of negative performance information, leading to a null effect of bad news among those with a past clientelistic connection to the incumbent. For both reasons, good news might have a positive effect only among those with a past clientelist connection to the incumbent, while bad news might only have a negative effect among those without such a personal history.[42]

To test these hypotheses, we analyze whether treatment effects are conditional on the relevant covariates as measured in our survey. Specifically, we regress the outcome of interest – individual vote choice for the incumbent – on an indicator representing receipt of information

---

[37] Adida (2015).
[38] We prespecified these hypotheses as H19 in our study's own pre-analysis plan, though without much theoretical elaboration. We have further developed the theoretical motivation in Adida et al. (2017b).
[39] Adida et al. (2017b).
[40] Stokes (2005), Wantchekon (2003).
[41] Adida et al. (2017b).
[42] We preregistered this hypothesis as H18 in our study's pre-analysis plan. The MPAP prespecified the expectation that the effects of information (good news increasing support, bad news decreasing support) would be stronger among those who had not received clientelistic benefits from the incumbent (H8 in the MPAP).

in the common arm, the relevant covariate,[43] and the interaction of the two. To reflect our cluster-randomized and stratified design, we include block fixed effects and cluster standard errors at the village level.

Table 4.6 provides results that are consistent with some of the conditional effects hypothesized above but that do not fully account for the null results of the common arm treatment. We find that coethnics and voters with established clientelistic linkages to the incumbent are responsive to positive information about their incumbent.[44] This is consistent with the claim that motivated reasoning and clientelism might condition our treatment effects. However, these explanations for the null results are not fully satisfying, because we find no statistically significant results for negative information in Table 4.6. As we discuss in Adida et al. (2017b), consistent with ethnically motivated reasoning, noncoethnics of the incumbent are more responsive to negative performance information where that negative performance information has been widely disseminated in a welfare-relevant way (i.e., in conjunction with our Salience and High dosage treatment discussed above). But these results only underscore the most plausible explanation for the null results of the common arm treatment, which is that it did not make the performance information salient enough to voters and did not facilitate sufficient levels of voter coordination.

Our common arm treatment did not deliver the information in a way that could easily translate into electoral outcomes in a clientelistic context where transfers matter more to voters than legislation, and where bloc rewards for incumbent support are expected.[45] When voters are informed about the potential for legislation to impact their welfare through a civics intervention, and when voters are additionally informed that a significant proportion of other voters in the constituency are also receiving the information, then positive legislative performance information does lead to enhanced electoral support for the incumbent, and negative legislative performance information does lower incumbent support for the worst performers. We argue that such amendments to the basic intervention overcome the constraint that voters tend not to care

---

[43] See M15 in the MPAP for measures of coethnicity. See Bq28 in our individual pre-analysis plan for the measure of having received a clientelistic benefit from the incumbent.

[44] As shown in the online appendix, the statistical significance of the first conditional effect – with clientelist linkages – survives *p*-value corrections for multiple comparisons while the other result does not.

[45] Rueda (2017).

TABLE 4.6 *Benin: Coethnicity, clientelism, and the impact of information*

	(1) Good News	(2) Bad News	(3) Good News	(4) Bad News
Treatment	−0.07 (0.07)	0.12 (0.16)	−0.01 (0.03)	−0.03 (0.07)
Treatment × Coethnic	0.15* (0.09)	−0.15 (0.16)		
Coethnic with Incumbent	−0.14* (0.08)	−0.03 (0.13)		
Treatment × Personal Assistance in the Past			0.64*** (0.22)	0.10 (0.21)
Personal Assistance in the Past			−0.15 (0.14)	−0.08 (0.12)
Constant	0.52*** (0.05)	0.55*** (0.11)	0.45*** (0.02)	0.54*** (0.05)
Observations	459	381	457	382
R^2	0.22	0.21	0.23	0.21

Robust standard errors in parentheses
*** $p < 0.01$, ** $p < 0.05$, * $p < 0.1$

about legislative policymaking in a context like Benin's, and the fear that voting alone according to legislative performance rather than transfers will incur negative repercussions. We believe this is the most plausible explanation for the null results in the common arm.

4.4.2 Implementation Challenges and Political Reactions

In contrast with Arias et al. (Chapter 5) and Sircar and Chauchard (Chapter 10), we encountered very few issues with implementation, and little political backlash. We designed and conducted the experiment in collaboration with the Centre de Promotion de la Démocratie et du Développement (CEPRODE), an independent, nongovernmental, nonpartisan Benin-based organization. To avoid overlap with the two-week period prior to the election of April 26, 2015, during which political campaigning is prohibited, the experiment and baseline survey were conducted from March 9 to April 9, 2015. In retrospect, we believe that the local expertise of the CEPRODE director was a tremendous asset, from which our project benefited significantly.

Two representatives from CEPRODE implemented the experiment in each treated village/quartier. Upon arrival, they sought permission from the local chief or leader to conduct the study, informing them it was a collaboration between CEPRODE and researchers from American universities.[46] Individuals from the community were then randomly sampled, given information about the project, informed that it was a collaboration between a local NGO and American researchers, and given an opportunity to consent to participate. A subset of consenting participants took the baseline survey.[47] Following the survey (or immediately following consent), participants in the Private condition were shown the video (either Info Only or Info + Salience) on a smartphone. Participants in the Public condition were invited to attend a community-level screening of the videos later in the day (where either Info Only or Info + Salience were shown).

In three instances, CEPRODE encountered some resistance to implementation of the experiment but ultimately the issues were resolved. In Pèrèrè, Kandi, and Bopa communes, local partisans and politicians intervened to stop the dissemination of information. In one commune, the local police were involved and questioned our enumerator team – even though our enumerators all had copies of the National Assembly President's letter of approval. Yet, our CEPRODE director, relying on his local expertise and connections, was able to resolve each issue, and our study was able to proceed. Our enumerator team was unharmed, and the only cost incurred to the project was the time it took to attain resolution.

4.4.3   Implications

Our results intersect in interesting ways with the findings of other studies in this volume. Several other studies find detectable effects of providing information when that information is about non-legislative performance (e.g., Buntaine et al., Chapter 7; Arias et al., Chapter 5). However, in

---

[46] One community leader refused consent. This village was replaced at random by another village from the same commune and block.

[47] For the purposes of power, we required only twenty survey respondents in each village. However, to facilitate intra-village coordination, we aimed for a larger number of attendees at public screenings; at the same time, we wanted to treat the same number of individuals in both Private and Public villages. We thus provided the Private treatment to forty individuals in each Private village even though only half were randomly assigned to complete the longer baseline survey. In Public villages, sixty people received an invitation to attend the public screening, assuming that on average two-thirds of those would attend.

contexts where politics is less programmatic and where voters focus on the delivery of personal benefits or the provision of local public goods rather than on legislative performance, we expect that the provision of legislative performance information alone will have no effect on vote choice absent interventions to make the implications of legislation for voter welfare clear and to facilitate voter coordination.

Furthermore, there may not be constraints to voter coordination at all levels. Just as in Arias et al. (Chapter 5) and in Buntaine et al. (Chapter 7), we find no evidence that providing the information in a more public setting within villages or precincts amplified the effects of the information on voter behavior. However, we find that disseminating information across villages amplified the effects of information on voter behavior when combined with a message making the implications of legislation for voter welfare clear. In other words, coordination mattered but coordination was already happening within villages, and so the treatment that affected voter behavior was the treatment involving cross-village dissemination.

Last, as in other studies in this volume, we find that, where there are treatment effects, positive performance information elicits a stronger response from people than negative performance information does, on average. We do find that people who have received a widely disseminated civics messages punish the worst performing incumbents, but the overall effects of positive performance information are still stronger on average than the effects of negative performance information. One explanation worth considering for this pattern relates to our argument and findings about ethnically motivated reasoning.[48] We find in our study that, where information provision affected voter behavior, coethnics of the incumbent responded to positive (but not to negative) performance information whereas noncoethnics of the incumbent responded to negative (but not to positive) information about him. In the aggregate, we have many more coethnic respondents (and majority coethnic villages) in our experimental sample than noncoethnic respondents (and majority noncoethnic) villages. This distribution could be responsible for the overall pattern of stronger responses to positive performance information than to negative performance information.

[48] Adida et al. (2017b).

5

When Does Information Increase Electoral Accountability? Lessons from a Field Experiment in Mexico

Eric Arias, Horacio Larreguy, John Marshall, and Pablo Querubín

In this chapter we report the results of a randomized intervention conducted during the 2015 Mexican elections. We teamed up with a local, nonpartisan, and transparency-focused nongovernmental organization (NGO) – Borde Político[1] – and conducted a large-scale informational campaign providing citizens with information from official audits revealing the way in which their municipal governments had spent funds intended for infrastructure projects benefiting impoverished localities. While official information on audits of government expenditures is publicly available in Mexico, citizens rarely have access to this information and when they do, the information is often not provided in a way that enables them to evaluate the performance of their politicians.

The material presented in this chapter closely follows Arias et al. (n.d.), where we originally reported our research design and the main results for a larger sample. However, in order to facilitate a comparison between our study and the other Metaketa studies presented in this volume, we focus on the variant of our intervention in which we presented information for the municipality's incumbent party paired with information regarding other municipalities in the state, but governed by a different party.

---

[1] Borde Político is a leading NGO seeking to increase voter knowledge about the actions of their politicians in office, with significant experience in the development of web-based platforms providing politically relevant information to individuals (see http://borde.mx).

5.1 LOCAL ELECTIONS AND ELECTORAL ACCOUNTABILITY IN MEXICO

Mexico's federal system is divided into thirty-one states (and the Federal District of Mexico City) containing around 2,500 municipalities and 67,000 electoral precincts. Following major decentralization reforms in the 1990s,[2] municipal governments – the focus of this chapter – play an important role in delivering basic public services and managing local infrastructure, and account for 20 percent of total government spending. Municipalities are governed by mayors typically elected to three-year nonrenewable terms, although re-election will become possible for incumbents in some states starting in 2018. Traditionally, local political competition in Mexico has been between either the populist Institutional Revolutionary Party (PRI) and the right-wing National Action Party (PAN), or between the PRI and its left-wing offshoot Party of the Democratic Revolution (PRD). Due to regional bases of political support and the often localized nature of municipal politics, municipal elections are typically dominated by one or two main parties. For example, the average Mexican municipality has only 2.5 effective parties.

A key component of a mayor's budget is the Municipal Fund for Social Infrastructure (FISM), which represents 24 percent of the average municipality's budget. According to the 1997 Fiscal Coordination Law (LCF), FISM funds are direct federal transfers reserved exclusively for infrastructure projects that benefit localities containing a significant population living in poverty. Eligible projects include investments in the water supply, drainage, electrification, health infrastructure, education infrastructure, housing, and roads. However, voters are poorly informed about both the resources available to mayors and the mayor's responsibility to provide basic public services.[3]

The use of FISM transfers is subject to independent audits. Responding to high levels of perceived mismanagement of public resources, the Federal Auditor's Office (ASF) was established in 1999 to audit the use of federal funds. Although the ASF reports to Congress, its management autonomy is constitutionally enshrined and it has the power to impose fines, recommend economic sanctions, and file or recommend criminal

---

[2] See Wellenstein, Núñez, and Andrés (2006).
[3] Chong et al. (2015).

cases against public officials.[4] The ASF selects around 150 municipalities for audit each year, based primarily on the relative contribution of FISM transfers to the municipal budget, historical performance and factors that raise the likelihood of mismanagement, and whether the municipality has recently been audited (including concurrent federal audits of other programs).[5] Importantly, the municipalities to be audited in a given year are announced after spending has occurred.

Audits address the spending, accounting, and management of FISM funds from the previous fiscal year. And although the ASF's reports categorize the use of FISM funds in various ways, we focus on two key dimensions of mayoral malfeasance documented in the audit reports (that are not necessarily mutually exclusive): the share of funds spent on projects not directly benefiting the poor, and the share of funds spent on unauthorized projects. Spending not benefiting the poor entails the allocation of FISM funds to social infrastructure projects that do not benefit impoverished localities. Unauthorized spending primarily includes the diversion of resources for nonsocial infrastructure projects (e.g., personal expenses and election campaigns) and funds that are not accounted for. Such spending is akin to the corruption identified by Brazilian audit reports.[6] The results for each audited municipality are reported to Congress in February the year after the audit was conducted. Thus, just as in the Metaketa studies in Benin and Uganda 2, the information reported in our leaflets comes from official government sources. However, the information we distribute is more publicly available since the ASF's reports are made available on its website, www.asf.gob.mx, and traditional media outlets often make reference to them.[7]

According to these metrics, mayoral malfeasance is relatively high. Between 2007 and 2015, 8 percent of audited funds were spent on projects not benefiting the poor, while a further 6 percent were spent on unauthorized projects. Given that the ASF captures only one dimension of malfeasance, it is thus unsurprising that 45 percent of voters do not believe that municipal governments use public resources honestly.[8]

Although economic and criminal punishments for misallocating funds are relatively rare, there are good reasons to believe that voters will hold

[4] See Larreguy, Marshall, and Snyder (2016).
[5] Auditoría Superior de la Federación (2014).
[6] Ferraz and Finan (2008).
[7] Larreguy, Marshall, and Snyder (2016).
[8] Chong et al. (2015).

the incumbent party responsible in Mexico's party-centric electoral context, even without the possibility of reelecting individual mayors. First, voters are considerably better informed about political parties than about individual politicians.[9] Crucially for political accountability, 80 percent of voters in our survey can correctly identify the party of their municipal incumbent. Second, Mexico's main parties have differentiated candidate selection mechanisms that deliver candidates with correlated attributes.[10] For example, 74 percent of voters in the survey we conducted as part of this study believe that if the current mayor is malfeasant, another candidate from within the same party is at least somewhat likely to also be malfeasant. Moreover, the same survey shows that 74 percent and 72 percent of respondents in control precincts respectively regard fighting poverty and honesty as important or very important in deciding which candidate to vote for.

However, existing evidence of electoral sanctions against Mexico's incumbent parties in response to information on malfeasant behavior is mixed. Larreguy, Marshall, and Snyder (2016) observe large electoral penalties among urban voters with access to broadcast media outlets incentivized to report local news. Exploiting plausibly exogenous variation in the release of audit reports prior to elections and access to radio and television stations in urban electoral precincts across the country, they find that each additional local media station decreases the vote share of an incumbent party revealed not to have spent FISM funds on the poor or in an unauthorized manner before the election by around 1 percentage point.[11] This evidence supports the standard electoral accountability model.[12]

Conversely, in a field experiment conducted in twelve municipalities across three states, Chong et al. (2015) find evidence that providing malfeasance information breeds disengagement. That is, while incumbent support declines when the incumbent is revealed as highly malfeasant, challenger support declines at least as much. Further, they find reduced partisan attachment to the incumbent, suggesting an equilibrium where voters disengage because they believe that all politicians are malfeasant.

---

[9] Chong et al. (2015).

[10] Langston (2003).

[11] These results confirm the findings of Ferraz and Finan (2008) in Brazil, who found that the presence of local media is critical for the release of audit reports to affect electoral outcomes.

[12] Barro (1973), Fearon (1999), Ferejohn (1986), Rogoff (1990).

The disjuncture between these accountability and disengagement findings points to the importance of developing theories and interventions to better understand the role of information.

In sum, there are several reasons why Mexico constitutes a valuable case study for the Metaketa. After over seventy years of single-party rule, Mexico has become an increasingly vibrant multiparty democracy since the mid 1990s. Thus, just like in Benin, Brazil, Burkina Faso, and Uganda,[13] we study the effect of information in the context of a new democracy where voters may be particularly uninformed and have relatively less experience with keeping politicians accountable via elections. Nonetheless, in spite of considerable progress (e.g., the creation of an independent federal electoral agency, the reduction of vote fraud, and the creation of a more level playing field for different parties), politics in Mexico – just like in the other Metaketa countries – remains highly clientelistic. The clientelistic nature of political transactions heavily undermines the capacity of voters to keep politicians accountable. Just like in the Uganda 2, Burkina Faso, and Brazil studies in this volume, we provide information on the performance of local politicians, as opposed to national legislators as in the Benin and Uganda 1 studies in this volume. Accountability may operate very differently for local politicians who have executive responsibilities and whose actions are potentially more observable to voters, than for national politicians. Finally, and unlike the other Metaketa studies where the politicians under consideration are allowed to be reelected, we study the accountability of incumbent parties rather than of incumbent individuals, given that Mexico did not allow the reelection of incumbent mayors.

5.2 EXPERIMENTAL DESIGN AND DATA

5.2.1 Experimental Design

We designed a field experiment to test the role of information on electoral accountability, focusing on Mexico's municipal elections held on Sunday, June 7, 2015.[14] Specifically, we seek to identify the effect of providing voters in 678 electoral precincts with the results of audit reports documenting the municipal use of federal transfers designated for

---

[13] See the Metaketa studies in this volume.
[14] Municipal elections reflect state electoral cycles, which are staggered across years. On June 7, 2015, 15 states and the federal district held simultaneous local elections.

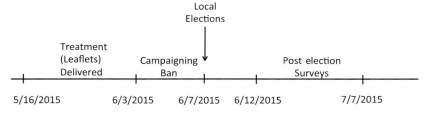

FIGURE 5.1 Mexico: Timeline of the experiment's implementation

infrastructure projects benefiting the poor. We first explain our sample selection, and then describe our information interventions, randomization, and estimation strategy. Figure 5.1 presents the overall timeline of the experiment's implementation.

Sample Selection

Our study focuses on twenty-six municipalities in the central states of Guanajuato (seven municipalities), México (fourteen municipalities), San Luis Potosí (four municipalities), and Querétaro (one municipality), as shown in Figure 5.2.[15] Beyond holding elections in 2015, these four states were chosen for security and logistical reasons and because they contain internal variation in the municipal incumbent party and its performance on the ASF audits.

The twenty-six municipalities were selected from those where an audit was released in 2015 according to three criteria. First, we prioritized the safety of voters and our distribution and survey teams. Nevertheless, just like in the studies in Benin, India, and Uganda 1 (this volume), our field teams faced intimidation and interference in some areas. Immediately after receiving threats upon entering Aquismón and Villa Victoria, the precincts in these municipalities were replaced by Atlacomulco, Temoaya, and additional precincts from Tlalnepantla de Baz in the state of México. Second, we only selected municipalities where at least one of our two measures of reported malfeasance (percentage of misallocated FISM resources) was at least two percentage points lower or, more often, higher than the state average among audited opposition parties. Finally, municipalities were chosen to match the distribution of incumbent parties across audited municipal governments in these four states. Specifically, of our twenty-six municipalities, seventeen were governed by

---

[15] The average municipality contains 259,000 registered voters.

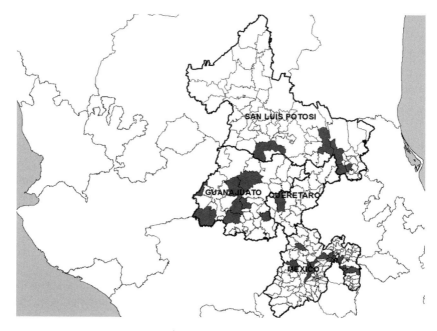

FIGURE 5.2 Mexico: The twenty-six municipalities in our sample

the PRI (including sixteen in coalition with the Teacher's (PANAL) and Green (PVEM) parties), five by the PAN (including two in coalition with PANAL), two by the PRD, and one by the Citizen's Movement (MC).

In order to ensure that our intervention would not affect aggregate electoral outcomes, we selected only up to one-third of the electoral precincts within each municipality.[16] To ensure variation in the information reported in our leaflets, we oversampled precincts from municipalities with particularly high or low levels of incumbent malfeasance, and thus with strong contrasts with respect to opposition parties' malfeasance within the state. Within municipalities, we first prioritized accessible rural precincts, where possible, in order to minimize cross-precinct spillovers and maximize the probability that voters would not

---

[16] Given our focus on rural precincts, effectively this means that fewer than one-third of voters in the municipality were subject to our treatment. In addition, as discussed above, in order to guarantee that our intervention would not unfairly affect any specific party, the distribution of incumbent parties in our sample closely matches the distribution of incumbent parties in the four states.

receive the information through other means.[17] Moreover, to maximize the share of households that we could reach with a fixed number of leaflets, attention was restricted to precincts with fewer registered voters. In urban areas, where we had more precincts to choose from, we restricted our sample to precincts with at most 1,750 registered voters, and designed an algorithm to minimize the number of neighboring urban precincts in our sample.[18] This implies that our estimates are particularly informative for voters in relatively rural and sparsely populated areas.

Information Treatment

In partnership with Borde Político, we distributed to voters leaflets documenting the use of FISM funds in their municipality. For each municipality, the leaflet focused on either the proportion of spending that does not benefit the poor, or unauthorized spending. All treatments were delivered at the electoral precinct level, Mexico's lowest level of electoral aggregation.

Our leaflet was designed to be nonpartisan, accessible, and sufficiently intriguing so that voters would not immediately discard it. The particular design was produced by a local graphic designer based on feedback from multiple focus groups.[19] We also sought legal advice to ensure that our leaflets did not constitute political advertisements, and thus were not subject to distribution restrictions stipulated in Mexican electoral law. To avoid suspicions of political motivation, neither the incumbent mayor nor its party are referred to directly, although as noted above the vast majority of voters can correctly identify the party of their incumbent mayor.

One of the variants of our intervention involved whether the leaflet included information only on the local incumbent party (local treatment) or whether it also reported the average outcome among all audited municipalities within the same state but governed by a different political party (benchmarked treatment). Figure 5.3 provides an example of a

---

[17] Municipalities in Mexico are divided into multiple *localidades* (the equivalent of US Census blocks). Most municipalities consist of both urban and rural *localidades*.

[18] The algorithm started with the set of neighboring precincts surrounding each precinct and identified all neighboring precincts that were eligible for our sample; we then iteratively removed the precinct with most "in-sample" neighbors until we reached the required number of precincts for that municipality. In most municipalities, the algorithm ensured that our sample contained no neighboring precincts.

[19] To avoid any association with any specific political party, the leaflet design was in black and white. We used images to communicate in a simple and friendly way how FISM funds should be spent according to the law.

FIGURE 5.3 Mexico: Example of benchmarked leaflet in Ecatepec de Morelos, México

benchmarked leaflet focusing on a severe case of unauthorized spending in the municipality of Ecatepec de Morelos in the state of México. The front page explains that Borde Político is a nonpartisan organization and that the information contained in the leaflet is based on the ASF's official audit reports available online. The main page first states that FISM funds should only be spent on social infrastructure projects, and provides graphical examples of such projects on the right. The leaflet then informs recipients of the total amount of money their municipality received (146.3 million pesos, in this case), and the percentage of this money spent in an unauthorized way by their government (45 percent). The leaflet also shows the average percentage of unauthorized spending in other municipalities in the state governed by a different party (9 percent).

Block Randomization and Implementation

Our sample of 678 precincts was allocated to treatment conditions according to a factorial design with a pure control, as shown in Table 5.1. The 400 treated precincts were equally divided between the four variants of the information treatment.

Since all of the other Metaketa studies provided benchmarked information, the latter constitutes our common intervention arm and thus, throughout the rest of this chapter, we focus exclusively on the effects of

TABLE 5.1 *Mexico: Factorial design with a pure control*

	Control	Private	Public
Control	278 precincts		
Local		100 precincts	100 precincts
Benchmarked		100 precincts	100 precincts

the benchmarked treatment. For power considerations, and also because we find limited differences between the private and public treatment, in our baseline analysis we pool the private and public benchmarked treatments and use this as our common arm (in Section 5.4 we report separate estimates for the private/public variants). Nonetheless, in the online appendix we also report estimates using only the benchmarked-private treatment as our common arm. As such, the 200 precincts assigned to the local leaflet are dropped from our analysis and thus our effective sample covers 478 precincts. The control group comprising 278 electoral precincts reflects our sampling and block randomization design.

For the randomization, precincts were first stratified into rural or urban blocks of six or seven similar precincts within a given municipality.[20] Precinct similarity was defined by the Mahalanobis distance between twenty-three social, economic, demographic, and political variables provided by Mexico's National Statistical Agency (INEGI) and the National Electoral Institute (INE).[21] Within each block, we then randomly assigned precincts to each of the treatment conditions and, depending on the availability of an additional precinct, either two or three pure control precincts. Our block randomization ensures that different municipalities do not receive different treatment proportions and maximizes the power of the experiment by minimizing differences between treated and control precincts within blocks.

The leaflets were distributed by our implementing partners Data OPM and Qué Funciona para el Desarollo using precinct maps provided by state electoral institutes. Our distribution teams delivered one leaflet to a

[20] Subject to there existing sufficient precincts, and the total treated precincts not exceeding one-third of all precincts, we used blocks of seven precincts.

[21] We used the R package blockTools to assign precincts to blocks. The algorithm is "greedy" in that it creates the most similar group first. Where a surplus of potential precincts were available, we used the most similar blocks to maximize statistical efficiency.

maximum of 200 households in the largest locality (in rural blocks) and in randomly selected city blocks (in urban blocks) within each treated precinct. Within our sample, the median precinct contained 353 households (according to the 2010 Census), 420 private dwellings, and 1,056 voters registered for the 2015 election. Where possible, leaflets were delivered in person with a short message explaining the leaflet's provenance. When no adult was available, leaflets were left in mail boxes or taped to the recipient's front door in a waterproof bag. Leaflet delivery took several hours per precinct, and was implemented over three weeks concluding at the legally designated end of the campaign four days before the election. Our team recorded where leaflets were distributed in order to return to these same places for our follow-up survey.

While compliance with the delivery of our treatments was very good in general, we nevertheless encountered some issues in the field. In a couple of cases, some leaflets were delivered to voters outside the precinct or adverse weather and poor road conditions prevented us from reaching a precinct. To preserve the randomization, we focus on estimating intention to treat (ITT) effects and thus code our treatment dummy according to the original assignment.

Our experimental design, sample, and replacements are illustrated in CONSORT-style Figure 5.4.

5.2.2 Data

Throughout this section we make specific reference to the notation used for different measures in the meta-analysis pre-analysis plan (MPAP).

We collected two sources of data to measure our main outcomes. First, we use official precinct-level electoral returns to measure incumbent party vote share (as a fraction of those who voted) and turnout.[22] These correspond to measures M2 and M4, respectively, in the MPAP.

Second, we conducted a postelection survey interviewing 10 voters from each of the treated precincts and 100 randomly selected control precincts.[23] Despite its success in the administration of the Mexico Panel

---

[22] We had to drop the three precincts in our sample that were merged with another precinct, due to having fewer than 100 registered voters.

[23] For details on the field protocol used for selecting survey respondents see Arias et al. (n.d.).

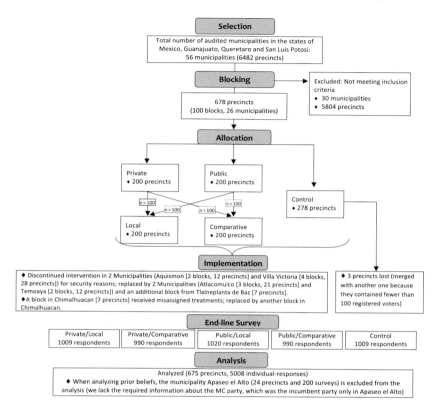

FIGURE 5.4 Mexico: CONSORT diagram of research design

Surveys and Comparative Study of Electoral Systems modules and in the Metaketa study in Burkina Faso, our attempts to gauge individual vote choice by simulating the electoral process with an urn during the survey had little success. Many voters felt uneasy in the aftermath of surprising electoral results, and refused to participate believing that our survey team were working on behalf of a party to identify individual vote choices or to trick voters into casting a different ballot. Furthermore, enumerators reported little confidence that respondents had truly reported the party they voted for. Thus, throughout the baseline analysis we rely only on official precinct-level measures of vote share and turnout, but report results with the self-reported individual-level data in the online appendix.

To measure respondents' evaluations of the incumbent and challenger parties' malfeasance (MPAP measure M6), at the beginning of the survey we asked respondents to rate, on a five-point scale from very low (-2) to very high (2), the level of corruption or the level of interest in supporting the poor of each major party (depending on the measure of malfeasance provided in that municipality). This provides us with a measure of voters' posterior beliefs/evaluations (Q_{ipbm}) where higher values correspond to higher perceptions of malfeasance.[24]

In order to test the hypotheses preregistered in the MPAP, we need to assess how the information provided in the leaflets compares with voters' prior beliefs. This is necessary in order to establish whether the information provided was interpreted as "good news" or "bad news" by voters. However, this is particularly challenging in our context since unlike the other Metaketa studies, due to financial constraints, we were unable to conduct a baseline survey. To address this issue, we use the (postelection) surveys conducted in each block's control precincts to proxy for the average pretreatment beliefs of the treated and control voters within the same block.[25] This provides us with a block-level measure of voters' priors about the malfeasance of the incumbent and challenger parties, P_{pbm} (MPAP measure M9).

Using postelection surveys among the control group to proxy for pretreatment beliefs requires several assumptions. First, control group respondents are similar to treatment group respondents. Second, control group respondent beliefs are consistent across the month between the intervention and the postelection survey. In Arias et al. (n.d.), we show that these assumptions are plausible in the context of this study. First, randomization ensures that treated and control precincts are identical in expectation and relatively similar in realization due to our blocking strategy. Second, we show that municipal-level electoral outcomes do not systematically affect the level or strength of beliefs about incumbent malfeasance among respondents in the control group (indicating that the election outcome itself does not significantly influence voter beliefs). Third, the 2012 Mexican Panel Survey shows that voter assessments of

---

[24] In the MPAP, Q makes reference to the information provided in the leaflet, in our case, the percentage of malfeasant spending. However, we did not ask voters about their expectations of this continuous measure (fraction of resources misspent) as this would have been very hard for our respondents to assess. Thus we define Q as voters' posterior evaluations of each party (after having seen the information in the leaflet) such that we can compare it to our measure of priors on the same five-point scale.

[25] We prespecified that prior beliefs would be defined by control voters at the municipal level. However, we focus on the block-level controls to produce more precise measures. Our results are similar if we define priors using control respondents within municipality (rather than within block).

politicians are relatively persistent.[26] Fourth, we show that there is no compelling evidence of spillovers to neighboring precincts outside our sample. Finally, we also rely on data from the Brazil study in order to test the extent to which our approach of measuring voter priors based on endline responses of control respondents is valid. In the Brazil study, both baseline and endline surveys were conducted, making it possible to directly test the block-level (average) correlation between endline evaluations of control respondents and baseline evaluations of treated respondents. The correlation is close to 0.7, which suggests our approach is indeed valid.

Next, we construct a measure of the gap between the voters' priors (P_{pbm}), and their evaluations (posteriors) after observing the information reported in the leaflet (Q_{pbm}). This allows us to establish whether the treatment caused voters to update favorably or unfavorably about the malfeasance of the different parties. Specifically, at the end of the survey we showed voters the leaflet corresponding to their municipality and again asked them how they perceived the incumbent/challenger party on the same five-point scale. To measure how the information provided compared to their priors, we simply consider the average change in perceptions before and after showing the corresponding leaflets to voters within the block's control precincts. This allows us to compute a block-level measure of the gap between the voters' posterior and prior evaluations of incumbent/challenger malfeasance, namely:

$$G_{pbm} = Q_{pbm} - P_{pbm}$$

Positive (negative) values of this measure imply that the party was more (less) malfeasant than what voters anticipated. We use this continuous measure to generate block-level indicators for whether voters interpreted the information in our treatment as good news or bad news:

$$Good\ News_{pbm} = 1 \text{ if } G_{pbm} < 0 \text{ and zero otherwise.}$$
$$Bad\ News_{pbm} = 1 \text{ if } G_{pbm} \geq 0 \text{ and zero otherwise.}$$

The MPAP hypothesized how good or bad news about the incumbent's party affect the latter's evaluations and vote share. Thus, in our baseline analysis we report the effect of good and bad news (and the gap

---

[26] Voter opinions of the presidential candidates before and after the election – three months apart, in contrast to the three to four weeks apart we examine – exhibit a 0.4 correlation.

between posteriors and priors) for the incumbent party. However, given that our treatment is benchmarked and provides information on both the incumbent and the challenger parties, a natural exercise is to explore how relative good/bad news affect voters' evaluations of the incumbent relative to the challenger (relative posteriors).[27] While we did not preregister hypotheses about relative updating, we present some of these results in the online appendix.

Finally, we construct several measures to analyze the extent to which our information treatment has differential effects depending on context-specific factors. As before, we rely on the postelection survey responses from control precincts in each surveyed block to construct an average pretreatment proxy for our variables of interest. In all cases, for ease of interpretation we standardize all these measures to have a mean of 0 and a standard deviation of 1.

First, we examine the moderating role of partisan identity (MPAP measure M19). Voters with stronger partisan preferences or attachment may be less likely to update their beliefs or voting behavior in response to new information. Here, we define "Incumbent Partisanship" as the block-level fraction of control respondents who identified themselves as sympathizers of the incumbent party.[28] In a similar spirit, we explore the competitiveness of the electoral context (MPAP measure M25). In competitive political environments, newly revealed information on the malfeasance of incumbent and challenger parties is more likely to be pivotal in voters' electoral decision. For this, we create an "Electoral Competitiveness" measure at the precinct level. Using results from the 2012 election, we define competitiveness as 1 minus the margin of victory of the incumbent, where the margin of victory is defined as the vote share of the election winner minus the vote share of the runner up. We also examine the extent to which our treatment effects vary by the

---

[27] More concretely, let G^I_{pbm} measure the gap between posteriors and priors about the incumbent and G^C_{pbm} the corresponding measure for the challenger. This allows us to define the measure *Relative Good News*$_{pbm} = 1$ if $(G^I_{pbm} - G^C_{pbm}) < 0$ and *Relative Bad News*$_{pbm} = 1$ if $(G^I_{pbm} - G^C_{pbm}) > 0$. We can also use as outcome variable a measure of relative evaluation (posterior) of the incumbent's malfeasance defined as $Q^I_{pbm} - Q^C_{pbm}$.

[28] More concretely, the survey question asked: "In general, with which political party do you sympathize?" and coded responses as 1 if the party coincided with the incumbent, and 0 otherwise.

prevalence of clientelistic practices within the community (MPAP measure M22). Clientelism fundamentally undermines the ability of voters to keep politicians accountable[29] and thus informational interventions may be less effective in environments in which the voter-politician relation is mediated by contingent exchange. To measure this, we created a proxy for vote buying as follows: we asked respondents to assess how frequently the municipal incumbent party offered gifts, services, and other favors in exchange for votes, with responses ranging from 'not frequently at all' (1) to 'very frequently' (4), and again estimated the block-level average from control respondents.

Second, we also construct several measures of the informational environment. Our intervention may be particularly effective in places where voters have limited access to other sources of information and thus where our treatment is more likely to provide new information the voters were not already aware of. We create two indexes. First, we construct a political knowledge index. To do so, our survey included three questions evaluating factual questions about local politics, namely (i) how long is the term of the municipal mayor, (ii) which is the party of the outgoing mayor, and (iii) which party won the last municipal elections. We code correct answers with a value of 1 (0 otherwise) and then aggregate the three questions for an individual-level measure ranging between 0 and 3. We then take the average of this measure across control respondents to obtain a block-level proxy of political knowledge. Second, we also create a media consumption index. For this, we asked respondents how often they followed electoral news over TV, radio, newspapers, and internet and social media, respectively, with possible responses ranging from "never" to "daily" (5). We take the mean of these four responses to create an individual-level measure, and once again, take the block-level average across respondents in control precincts.

Finally, related to both the electoral and societal context, we also examine the extent to which our information treatment varies with the level of trust in elections (MPAP measures M26 and M27). If voters are disillusioned and do not believe that elections are an effective mechanism to keep politicians accountable, they may be less likely to change their behavior in response to information on malfeasance. For this, our survey retrieved people's opinions on how clean they perceived the election to

[29] Stokes (2005).

be. More specifically, we asked people to assess how likely it was that the vote count during the June 7 election was free and fair, with possible responses ranging from "not at all likely" (1) to "extremely likely" (5). That is, higher values represent higher beliefs that the electoral process is clean. Again, we take the mean of control respondents to create our block-level proxy.

5.3 ANALYSIS OF TREATMENT EFFECTS ON THE COMMON TREATMENT ARM

We present the main treatment effects of our intervention, focusing on the common treatment arm. We focus on providing estimates for the different hypotheses registered in the MPAP. First, we provide estimates for the effect of our intervention on voters' posterior beliefs on the integrity of candidates from the incumbent party (H3). Next, we report estimates on vote share and turnout (H1 and H2). In all tables, we first report estimates of the average effect of our treatment (i.e., the effect of providing a voter with a leaflet) when we pool all randomization blocks (panel A). We then report separate estimates for blocks in which our information was interpreted by voters as bad news (panel B) and good news (panel C). We explore the effect of different variants of our treatment such as mode of delivery (private vs. public) and the type of audit information reported in the leaflet (unauthorized spending vs. spending on the poor) and finally test for heterogeneous effects on several context-specific factors.

We estimate OLS regressions of the form:

$$Y_{pbm} = \beta T_{pbm} + \eta_{bm} + \epsilon_{pbm}, \tag{5.1}$$

where Y_{pbm} is an outcome variable in precinct p, in randomization block b, in municipality m (individual level outcome variables have an additional subindex i) and T_{pbm} is an indicator for whether precinct p was assigned to treatment.

To estimate differential effects for variants of our intervention or context-specific factors we estimate regressions of the form:

$$Y_{pbm} = \beta T_{pbm} * \mathbf{Z_{bm}} + \eta_{bm} + \epsilon_{pbm}, \tag{5.2}$$

where $\mathbf{Z_{bm}}$ contains different measures on the mode of delivery, type of information of the leaflet and block characteristics.

All our regressions include randomization block fixed effects (η_{bm}) and standard errors are clustered at the municipality-treatment level.[30] Precinct-level observations are weighted by the share of voters to whom we delivered a leaflet (in control precincts, we use the number of leaflets delivered to the average treated precinct). This weighting scheme was not preregistered but permits more precise estimates by de-weighting large precincts where only a small fraction of voters could receive the leaflet. In the online appendix we report similar estimates from unweighted regressions.

5.3.1 Validity Checks

Before reporting the estimates for our main outcome variables, we provide evidence to validate our randomization. In Online Appendix Table B1, we use the basic specification in Equation 5.1 to show that treatment is well-balanced across thirty-seven precinct and survey respondent characteristics, with only a handful of statistically significant differences. However, all of our estimates are robust to controlling for precinct level characteristics (results not reported).

We also conducted some basic manipulation checks reported in Arias et al. (n.d.). Respondents in treated precincts are substantially more likely to report having received a leaflet, remember the content of the leaflet, and say that the leaflet influenced their voting decision. Moreover, respondents assigned to the benchmarked treatment (the focus of this chapter) are more likely to report that information on the opposition parties was also included in the leaflet.

5.3.2 Effects on Beliefs about Party Integrity

First, we examine how our treatment impacted voters' evaluations of the incumbent party's level of malfeasance (Q_{ipbm}). Recall that this variable is measured on a five-point scale and higher values imply higher perceptions of incumbent malfeasance.

The coefficient in column 1 of Table 5.2 suggests that, on average, our intervention improved voters' perceptions about candidate integrity, though it is not statistically significant at conventional levels. However,

---

[30] We cluster at the municipality x treatment rather than the block level since the information reported in the leaflets (i.e., incumbent level of malfeasance) is the same across blocks within a municipality.

Eric Arias et al.

TABLE 5.2 *Mexico: Effect of information treatment on voter posterior beliefs about incumbent party malfeasance*

	Perceived incumbent party malfeasance (very low – very high)			
	(1)	(2)	(3)	(4)
Panel A: Pooled				
Information treatment	−0.030 (0.040)	−0.193*** (0.060)		
Information treatment × Gap between posteriors and priors		0.183*** (0.037)		
Private information treatment			−0.048 (0.048)	
Public information treatment			−0.012 (0.050)	
Unauthorized spending information treatment				−0.039 (0.043)
Not-spending on the poor information treatment				−0.024 (0.060)
Observations	2816	2816	2816	2816
R^2	0.30	0.30	0.30	0.30
Panel B: Bad News				
Information treatment	0.035 (0.048)	−0.285*** (0.092)		
Information treatment × Gap between posteriors and priors		0.237*** (0.050)		
Private information treatment			0.001 (0.055)	
Public information treatment			0.070 (0.057)	
Unauthorized spending information treatment				0.048 (0.070)
Not-spending on the poor information treatment				0.031 (0.059)
Observations	2048	2048	2048	2048
R^2	0.24	0.24	0.24	0.24

TABLE 5.2 *(continued)*

	Perceived incumbent party malfeasance (very low – very high)			
	(1)	(2)	(3)	(4)
Panel C: Good News				
Information treatment	−0.202**	−0.203		
	(0.081)	(0.127)		
Information treatment × Gap between posteriors and priors		−0.006		
		(0.211)		
Private information treatment			−0.179*	
			(0.094)	
Public information treatment			−0.225**	
			(0.100)	
Unauthorized spending information treatment				−0.099
				(0.071)
Not-spending on the poor information treatment				−1.025***
				(0.157)
Observations	768	768	768	768
R^2	0.12	0.12	0.12	0.13

Notes: All specifications include block fixed effects, and are estimated using OLS. Lower-order interaction terms are absorbed by the block fixed effects. Standard errors clustered by municipality × treatment are in parentheses. * denotes $p < 0.1$, ** denotes $p < 0.05$, *** denotes $p < 0.01$.

this average masks substantial variation since the information provided may have represented good news for some voters and bad news for others, relative to their prior beliefs. Consistent with H3, the estimates in column 1 of Panels B and C suggest that good news leads voters to favorably update their beliefs about the incumbent's party integrity, while bad news leads voters to update unfavorably (though the latter coefficient is not statistically significant).

A complementary approach is to explore how our intervention varies with the continuous measure of the gap between voters' prior beliefs and the information reported in the leaflets, G_{pbm}. The coefficient for the interaction term in column 2 of Panel A is positive, which suggests that voters' perceptions of the incumbent party get worse when the information in the leaflet is more unfavorable relative to what voters expected. This is consistent with the different average treatment effects found in the good and bad news samples and provides evidence in support of H12. The estimates in column 2 of Panels B and C, show that once we break down the samples by bad and good news, the gap between posteriors and priors has a statistically significant effect only in the former case. However, the MPAP did not hypothesize about different marginal effects of this or other variables across the bad and good news samples.

Importantly, notice that the different treatment effects across the bad and good news sample as well as the positive interaction with the gap between posteriors and priors, while intuitive, are not mechanical since our block-level measures of priors and posteriors are based on responses from voters in control precincts within the block.

5.3.3   Effect on Incumbent Party's Vote Share and Turnout

Next we look at treatment effects on precinct-level incumbent vote share and turnout. The estimate in column 1 of Table 5.3 is positive, which suggests that on average, our treatment increased the incumbent party's vote share by 2.9 percentage points. This is consistent with the estimate in column 1 of Table 5.2 that, while not statistically significant, suggests that our intervention led voters to update favorably about the incumbent party on average. In our pre-analysis plan we conjectured that our intervention would have, on average, a negative effect on the incumbent's party. However, this was under the assumption that the relatively high levels of malfeasance on average reported in the leaflets would cause the average voter to update unfavorably about the incumbent party.

In Panels B and C we once again break down the effect by whether our treatment was interpreted as bad or good news by voters in the randomization block. Consistent with the estimates in Table 5.2, the electoral reward for the incumbent party is almost 50 percent higher in blocks with good news relative to blocks with bad news. In column 2 we interact our treatment indicator with the continuous measure of the gap between posteriors and priors. The coefficient on the interaction term is negative (consistent with the idea that incumbents are less likely to be rewarded the worse posteriors are relative to priors) though not close to being statistically significant.

The positive and statistically significant coefficient for blocks that interpreted our treatment as bad news for the incumbent may appear somewhat surprising. A first important issue is that the average effect

TABLE 5.3 *Mexico: Effect of information treatment on incumbent party vote share and turnout (weighted estimates)*

| | Incumbent party vote share | | | | Turnout |
	(1)	(2)	(3)	(4)	(5)
Panel A: Pooled					
Information treatment	0.029*** (0.007)	0.027*** (0.007)			−0.002 (0.005)
Information treatment × Gap between posteriors and priors		−0.003 (0.005)			
Private information treatment			0.029** (0.013)		
Public information treatment			0.028*** (0.009)		
Unauthorized spending information treatment				0.025*** (0.008)	
Not-spending on the poor information treatment				0.031*** (0.011)	
Observations	475	459	475	475	475
R²	0.67	0.67	0.67	0.67	0.72
Panel B: Bad News					
Information treatment	0.021** (0.009)	0.016 (0.018)			−0.004 (0.007)
Information treatment × Gap between posteriors and priors		0.004 (0.009)			
Private information treatment			0.019 (0.016)		
Public information treatment			0.022* (0.013)		
Unauthorized spending information treatment				0.006 (0.013)	

TABLE 5.3 *(continued)*

	Incumbent party vote share				Turnout
	(1)	(2)	(3)	(4)	(5)
Not-spending on the poor information treatment				0.026** (0.011)	
Observations	332	332	332	332	332
R^2	0.59	0.59	0.59	0.59	0.75

Panel C: Good News

Information treatment	0.034*** (0.008)	0.019 (0.015)			−0.005 (0.008)
Information treatment × Gap between posteriors and priors		−0.044 (0.034)			
Private information treatment			0.027** (0.012)		
Public information treatment			0.040*** (0.008)		
Unauthorized spending information treatment				0.038*** (0.008)	
Not-spending on the poor information treatment				−0.006 (0.012)	
Observations	127	127	127	127	127
R^2	0.79	0.80	0.79	0.80	0.68

Notes: All specifications include block fixed effects, weighted by the share of the precinct that was treated, and are estimated using OLS. Lower-order interaction terms are absorbed by the block fixed effects. The smaller sample in columns (2), (3), and (5) reflect lack of prior data in Apaseo el Alto. Standard errors clustered by municipality × treatment are in parentheses. * denotes $p < 0.1$, ** denotes $p < 0.05$, *** denotes $p < 0.01$.

for bad and good news is harder to interpret since it may depend on the specific cutoff used to define these categories. It is likely that whenever posteriors and priors are very close to each other (i.e., G_{pbm} very close to zero), voters interpret this as "neutral news" that doesn't change their voting decision. Thus, what is particularly important is the difference (or slope) in the effect between the estimate for good and bad news, which suggests a more positive effect for the former, consistent with a basic model in which voters respond to how they update based on the information received.

In addition, there are several reasons as to why the provision of information may have a positive effect on the incumbent party vote share irrespective of the direction in which voters update. As we show in Arias et al. (n.d.), a basic model of risk-averse voter learning suggests that the provision of information reduces voter uncertainty about the incumbent party's malfeasance, which can in turn increase support for the incumbent. In addition, as we document below, both incumbent and challengers respond strategically to our intervention, which could offset negative effects of unfavorable information on the incumbent's vote share if the incumbent's response were larger or more effective.

Finally, in column 5 of Table 5.3 we report the estimates for the average effect of our intervention on turnout. The coefficients in all panels are very small and statistically insignificant. In this respect, our results do not support MPAP's H2a and H2b that predicted that good news would increase turnout while bad news would decrease it. However, in Arias et al. (n.d.) we present a formal model that predicts that the effect of new information on turnout should be nonlinear. In particular, when voter partisan attachments are bimodally distributed and voters at each mode turn out for different parties,[31] shockingly favorable or unfavorable revelations lead voters at one mode to switch parties and thereby increase turnout, while relatively unsurprising but nevertheless informative favorable (unfavorable) information induces challenger (incumbent) partisans to become relatively indifferent between the parties and instead abstain when faced with a cost of turning out. This logic does not yield clear predictions for the average effect of new information. This specific prediction was preregistered in the preanalysis plan of our study, and the results in Arias et al. (n.d.) support it.

5.3.4 Robustness Checks

The patterns reported in Tables 5.2 and 5.3 are broadly robust to various changes in our empirical specification. In Online Appendix

---

[31] Furthermore, similar results obtain for unimodal distributions when the modal voter initially turns out.

Table B2, we report unweighted estimates for our vote share regressions (recall that the weighting scheme was not registered in our pre-analysis plan). The main patterns in the data remain relatively unchanged though the treatment effect in the good news sample becomes slightly smaller.

The similar treatment effects across the private and public variants of our treatment documented in Section 5.4.1 suggests that our decision to pool both variants of our benchmarked treatment as the common arm is reasonable. Nevertheless, as robustness checks, in Online Appendix Tables B3 and B4, we report our baseline estimates on posteriors and vote share where we use the benchmarked-private treatment as our common arm and compare it against control precincts (i.e., we drop precincts with the benchmarked-public treatment from our sample). While this further decreases the sample size in all regressions, the estimates are similar in magnitude to those in our baseline specification. In fact, the interaction between the treatment and the gap between priors and posteriors is now negative and statistically significant in Panels A and B of the vote share regressions in Online Appendix Table B4, suggesting that the electoral reward for incumbents is smaller in precincts where the information reported in the leaflets is worse than what voters expected.

In Online Appendix Table B5, we report estimates equivalent to those reported in Table 5.3 but where we use individual-level self-reported vote and turnout data (as opposed to official, precinct level aggregates). The results in this case are totally inconsistent with the findings based on official statistics. The average treatment effect in the good news sample (column 1, Panel C) is negative, large and statistically significant suggesting that good news about the incumbent party decreases the likelihood that voters vote for it. Moreover, the interaction of the treatment with the gap between posteriors and priors is positive, on average, and in the bad news sample, suggesting that whenever voters interpret the information as worse than what they expected, they are more likely to vote for the incumbent. However, as discussed in Section 5.2.2, there are several reasons why these self-reported individual-level measures are not reliable (and certainly less reliable than official precinct-level statistics) since many voters refused to report who they voted for, and enumerators expressed little confidence in the veracity of the information provided by those who did fill out the mock ballot.

Finally, in Online Appendix Tables B6 and B7 we report estimates when we focus on relative measures of posteriors and good/bad news.

Results using relative posteriors as the outcome variable in Online Appendix Table B6 show that respondents update more unfavorably about the incumbent, relative to the challenger party, whenever news about the incumbent are worse than about the challenger (Panel B). The coefficient in Panel C for the relative good news sample is negative (as one would expect) though not statistically significant. The interaction with the relative gap between posteriors and priors variable in column 2 is positive and statistically significant in all panels, which is consistent with the idea that voters update more negatively about the incumbent (relative to the challenger) whenever the gap between posteriors and priors is worse (bigger) for the incumbent than for the challenger. On the other hand, the estimates for the vote share regressions in Online Appendix Table B7 show that the effect of the treatment in the relative bad news sample is very close and, if anything, slightly larger, than the effect on the relative good news sample.

5.3.5   Heterogeneous Effects

Finally, we look at heterogeneous effects according to several contextual characteristics specified in MPAP H6–H11.[32] As discussed in Section 5.2.2, given the absence of individual-level voting outcomes, we focus on average precinct or block-level characteristics based on control-group respondents. The results are presented in Table 5.4. All block-level characteristics used in the interaction are normalized to have mean zero and standard deviation equal to one. For reference, in column 1 we report the average treatment effects in each sample.

In column 2 we explore the role of partisanship. Consistent with MPAP H7, we find that, in blocks where voters are more likely to share the partisan affiliation of the incumbent, good news has a weaker effect on the incumbent's vote share. The interaction in the bad news sample is very small and statistically insignificant. These results are consistent with partisan voters having strong ideological attachments to the incumbent, and thus being less likely to update their posteriors or change their voting decisions in response to new information.

---

[32] Because ethnic identity is not particularly salient in Mexico's political context, we did not collect any information about it and do not report any heterogeneous effects on this variable.

TABLE 5.4 *Mexico: Effect of information treatment on incumbent party vote share, by context (weighted estimates)*

| | | | | Incumbent party vote share | | | |
	(1)	(2)	(3)	(4)	(5)	(6)	(7)
Panel A: Pooled							
Information treatment	0.029***	0.029***	0.028***	0.029***	0.029***	0.029***	0.029***
	(0.007)	(0.007)	(0.007)	(0.007)	(0.007)	(0.007)	(0.007)
Information treatment × Inc. Partisanship		−0.017***					
		(0.006)					
Information treatment × Vote Buying			−0.014**				
			(0.007)				
Information treatment × Competitiveness				−0.014**			
				(0.006)			
Information treatment × Political Knowledge					0.002		
					(0.007)		
Information treatment × Media Consumption						−0.000	
						(0.008)	
Information treatment × Trust in Elections							0.000
							(0.007)
Observations	475	475	475	475	475	475	475
R^2	0.67	0.68	0.68	0.68	0.67	0.67	0.67

144

Panel B: Bad News

Information treatment	0.021**	0.021**	0.020**	0.020**	0.021**	0.021**	0.021**
	(0.009)	(0.009)	(0.009)	(0.009)	(0.010)	(0.010)	(0.010)
Information treatment × Inc. Partisanship		−0.007					
		(0.008)					
Information treatment × Vote Buying			−0.012				
			(0.008)				
Information treatment × Competitiveness				−0.018***			
				(0.007)			
Information treatment × Political Knowledge					0.004		
					(0.007)		
Information treatment × Media Consumption						0.008	
						(0.010)	
Information treatment × Trust in Elections							0.003
							(0.009)
Observations	332	332	332	332	332	332	332
R²	0.59	0.59	0.59	0.59	0.59	0.59	0.59

(continued)

TABLE 5.4 (continued)

		Incumbent party vote share					
	(1)	(2)	(3)	(4)	(5)	(6)	(7)
Panel C: Good News							
Information treatment	0.034***	0.038***	0.033***	0.031***	0.033***	0.032***	0.036***
	(0.008)	(0.007)	(0.009)	(0.006)	(0.008)	(0.007)	(0.008)
Information treatment × Inc. Partisanship		−0.027***					
		(0.008)					
Information treatment × Vote Buying			0.005				
			(0.007)				
Information treatment × Competitiveness				0.016			
				(0.010)			
Information treatment × Political Knowledge					−0.022*		
					(0.010)		
Information treatment × Media Consumption						−0.016*	
						(0.008)	
Information treatment × Trust in Elections							−0.018*
							(0.010)
Observations	127	127	127	127	127	127	127
R^2	0.79	0.80	0.79	0.80	0.80	0.80	0.80

Notes: All specifications include block fixed effects, weighted by the share of the precinct that was treated, and are estimated using OLS. Lower-order interaction terms are absorbed by the block fixed effects. Standard errors clustered by municipality × treatment are in parentheses. * denotes $p < 0.1$, ** denotes $p < 0.05$, *** denotes $p < 0.01$.

146

To study the role of clientelism, in column 3 we look at the interaction of our treatment dummy with the block-level measure of vote buying. The interaction coefficient in Panel A is negative (consistent with MPAP H8) and statistically significant. However, the negative effect seems mostly concentrated in the bad news sample (even though the coefficient is not statistically significant). One may have expected incumbents in clientelistic settings of being more effective at counteracting the dissemination of bad news about them in which case we would have expected a positive (or null) interaction term. That said, hypotheses in the MPAP do not make differential predictions for the bad and good news sample. Moreover, since self-reported questions on vote buying are subject to social desirability bias and other problems, these results should be interpreted cautiously.

In column 4 we look at electoral competitiveness. Consistent with H10, we find that the incumbent party was less likely to be rewarded following the dissemination of bad news in more competitive precincts. A one-standard deviation increase in political competition decreases the effect of the treatment by 1.8 percentage points. In other words, a more competitive environment makes bad news more damaging (or less rewarding) for the incumbent. Conversely, the interaction in Panel C for the good news sample is positive (though not statistically significant), which suggests that good news increases the electoral reward of incumbent parties in more competitive environments. Overall our results do suggest that informational interventions may improve accountability (i.e., lead to the electoral sanction of bad behavior and the reward of good behavior) in electorally competitive environments, where it can play a pivotal role.

Finally, in columns 5–7 we explore the moderating effect of political knowledge, media consumption, and trust in elections. The interactions in Panel B for the bad news sample are very small and statistically insignificant. The interactions in Panel C on the other hand, suggest that when our intervention represented good news, it had a smaller effect in places where voters were more knowledgeable about politics or had higher levels of media consumption. This is consistent with MPAP H9, predicting stronger treatment effects in informationally weak environments. This is intuitive since voters may be less likely to update and change their voting behavior if they were already well informed about the incumbent party's performance (through the media or other means). The interaction for our measure of trust in elections is also negative and statistically significant, which goes against MPAP H11.

5.4 TREATMENT VARIANTS

5.4.1 Private vs. Public Treatment

To vary the extent to which the distribution of the leaflets is common knowledge among voters within the precinct, we also introduced a "public treatment" variant where leaflet delivery was accompanied by a loudspeaker informing voters that their neighbors were also receiving the information and encouraging them to share it and discuss it. This feature is also shared by the studies in Benin and Uganda 2, where they increase the public nature of their intervention by, respectively, broadcasting their information in a public location and varying the saturation of treatment. In contrast, we refer to leaflet delivery without the loudspeaker as the "private treatment." The objective of this variant was to make our intervention more public and in this way induce common knowledge and coordination among voters – something that could strengthen the intervention's effect as MPAP H15 suggests.

However, the coefficients in column 3 of Panel A of Tables 5.2 and 5.3 suggest that, on average, the effect of our common treatment arm was similar in places with the private and public treatment. The estimates for the sample of precincts with good news (Panel C) suggest that the improvement in voters' evaluations and vote share of the incumbent were slightly larger for the public than for the private variant of our treatment though the differences are not too large. In sum, these estimates suggest that the use of the loudspeaker did not have a major influence on the effect of our intervention.

There are several reasons why the public variant of our intervention may have had a limited additional effect. First, the use of a loudspeaker may simply be ineffective to generate common knowledge or coordination. Many of the leaflet recipients were not at home during leaflet delivery and thus could not have heard the loudspeaker. The fraction of survey respondents who recall listening to a loudspeaker in control precincts and precincts subject to the private treatment was very small: 3 percent. The same average in those precincts subject to the public treatment was indeed higher and statistically different from zero but still somewhat small; only 10 percent of survey respondents in these households remember the loudspeaker. This suggests that our public treatment was too weak and many respondents in precincts that received this treatment simply did not hear the loudspeaker. It may take stronger dissemination mechanisms in traditional media outlets such as radio or

TV.[33] It is also worth noting that loudspeakers like the ones we used are commonly used by politicians during their campaigns. Thus, one possibility is that the loudspeaker increased the perception that our leaflets were being delivered by a political party and not by an NGO, which may have attenuated its effect on coordination. While plausible, this hypothesis does not receive much support in our data either; respondents in precincts with the public treatment were not more or less likely to believe that the leaflet came from a political party or an NGO.

A complementary explanation is that our private treatment was already sufficiently "public" in the sense that it generated the expectation that all other residents in their community received the leaflet. We asked survey respondents to report the fraction of community members that they believe received the leaflet. The majority of respondents in control and treated precincts believed "a very small number" of community members received the leaflet, though the fraction is lower in treated precincts (78 percent in control precincts vs. 62 percent in treated precincts). However, there is no difference in beliefs regarding the fraction of members who received the leaflet across the public and private treatments. Thus, while our treatment on average did not generate the expectation that everyone received the leaflet (consistent with common knowledge), the public treatment had no effect on this perception relative to the private one. It therefore appears to be more likely that the leaflet reached an insufficient numbers of voters to induce collective action.

5.4.2   Spending on the Poor vs. Unauthorized Spending

Across all treatments we use official information from audits conducted by the ASF. Thus, we cannot explore heterogeneous effects according to the credibility or reliability of the source (MPAP H14). However, recall that for each municipality, the leaflet focused on either the proportion of spending that does not benefit the poor, or unauthorized spending. Both types of spending go against the rules stipulated for FISM funds. But while unauthorized spending should be a valence issue opposed by all voters, it is possible that spending on the poor is interpreted by some voters as reflecting the preferences of the incumbent party for redistribution, rather than malfeasance. In this case, we would expect a stronger effect for leaflets with information on unauthorized spending, a hypothesis closely related to that in MPAP H13.

---

[33] See Larreguy, Marshall, and Snyder (2016).

In column 4, Panel A of Tables 5.2 and 5.3, we show that the coefficients for both types of leaflets are roughly similar, on average. This finding is consistent with the results in Larreguy, Marshall, and Snyder (2016) and suggests that voters interpreted both types of spending as malfeasance. This is not particularly surprising given the relatively high prevalence of poverty in our sample of precincts. In Panels B and C we split the samples between bad and good news, respectively. However, any differential effects of different types of information across these samples must be interpreted cautiously due to power considerations. For example, there are only fifteen precincts in the good news "spending on the poor" cell which may explain the rather large coefficient in column 4 of Table 5.2, Panel C. In the vote share regressions in Table 5.3, the coefficient is larger for the "not spending on the poor" variant in the bad news sample, but larger for the "unauthorized spending" variant in the good news sample. We did not preregister any hypotheses about differences in these treatment variants across the good and bad news samples and thus we prefer not to speculate about these differences, particularly given that some of these coefficients rely on very small samples.

5.5 POLITICAL BACKLASH

In this section we provide both quantitative and qualitative evidence on the reaction of politicians to our intervention. In our survey, we asked respondents whether the incumbent or opposition parties made reference to our leaflets via different (non-mutually exclusive) means such as (a) flyers, (b) campaign rallies, (c) door-to-door visits of campaign operatives, (d) loudspeakers, or (e) traditional media outlets such as radio or TV. We also asked them whether the party was trying to either take attention away from or direct attention towards the audit information reported in the leaflets, apologize for the information reported, or simply claim that all parties are the same.

To explore more systematically whether our intervention triggered a reaction from politicians, we code an individual-level measure for the number of means through which politicians mentioned the leaflet ranging from 0 (none) to 5 (all means). In Table 5.5, we report estimates from OLS regressions to test whether respondents in treated precincts reported more reactions from the incumbent (columns 1 and 2) or opposition (challenger) parties (columns 3 and 4). The estimates in columns 1 and 3 suggest that, on average, our intervention triggered a political response

TABLE 5.5 *Mexico: Effect of information treatment on political party responses*

| | Total party activities | | | |
| | Incumbent reactions | | Challenger reactions | |
	(1)	(2)	(3)	(4)
Information treatment	−0.010	−0.166**	0.074*	−0.038
	(0.043)	(0.078)	(0.039)	(0.052)
Information treatment × Incumbent malfeasant spending		0.727**		0.522**
		(0.272)		(0.205)
Observations	3019	3019	3019	3019
R^2	0.15	0.16	0.13	0.13
Control outcome mean	0.43	0.43	0.40	0.40
Control outcome std. dev.	1.18	1.18	1.17	1.17
Treatment mean	0.62	0.62	0.62	0.62
Treatment std. dev.	0.48	0.48	0.48	0.48
Interaction mean		0.21		0.21
Interaction std. dev.		0.17		0.17

Notes: All specifications include block fixed effects, and are estimated using OLS. Lower-order interaction terms are absorbed by the block fixed effects. Standard errors clustered by municipality × treatment are in parentheses. * denotes $p < 0.1$, ** denotes $p < 0.05$, *** denotes $p < 0.01$.

by opposition but not by incumbent parties (coefficient in column 1 is small and statistically insignificant). However, these average effects once again mask substantial variation in the malfeasance of the incumbent party reported in the leaflet. In columns 2 and 4 we interact our treatment dummy with the level of malfeasance reported in the leaflet. The interaction terms are positive and statistically significant, suggesting that politicians from both incumbent and challenger parties were more likely to react to the leaflets and reach out to voters whenever the leaflets reported high levels of malfeasance. Interestingly, while the average (level) effect is lower for the incumbent than for the challenger, this pattern is reversed for the interaction (slope), which suggests that incumbent parties' decisions to react depends to a large extent on their malfeasance levels.[34] These findings suggest that politicians strategically

---

[34] We also conducted a list experiment in order to assess whether vote buying was higher in treatment precincts. We do not find any evidence of this. However, the list experiment we used for this exercise may not have been effective since it detected overall vote buying rates much lower than those found by previous studies of clientelism in Mexico.

reallocated campaign efforts across precincts, which could – as noted above – explain the positive average treatment effect on the incumbent's vote share, if incumbent responses were more effective than challenger responses.

The quantitative evidence presented in Table 5.5 illustrates the political reactions experienced by voters in treated precincts. However, our staff and implementation teams also faced significant political push-back from municipal incumbents and local political party operatives. From the moment leaflet distribution began, staff from Borde Político started receiving calls with complaints about the content of the leaflet, and inquiring about the possibility of producing additional leaflets disseminating negative information about the opposing party.

While initially our field team was welcomed in most locations, we faced some difficulties early on. On five occasions – Dolores Hidalgo and Juventino Rosas, Guanajuato; Cuatitlán Izcali, Ixtapaluca, and Villa Victoria, Estado de México – several of our team members were taken by the local police under the excuse that people – often local political party operatives – complained that they were disrupting public order, or under false accusations that they were distributing leaflets with political advertisement and that they lacked a commercial permit to do so. In Villa Victoria, residents threatened our team by detaining them until the police arrived and burnt their car. A police unit temporarily detained our team under the accusation of distributing negative information about the municipality. In all cases, our team members were released several hours later since no charges could be pressed. Nonetheless, in all of these places our teams were threatened by the municipal authorities if leaflet distribution continued. We contacted the corresponding State Electoral Institutes. In the state of Guanajuato, officials contacted PRI representatives and the mayor of Dolores Hidalgo with warnings of pressing electoral charges if they continued to prevent the leaflet distribution. Our team was eventually allowed to conclude the delivery of the leaflets. In Juventino Rosas the police intervened after leaflet distribution was completed so this did not interfere with the implementation. However, we could not resume leaflet delivery in Cuatiltlán Izcali, Ixtapaluca, and Villa Victoria since the officials from the State Electoral Institute never replied to requests from Borde Político.[35]

---

[35] In addition, we consulted with our teams in the field and they considered that resuming leaflet delivery would not be advisable for security reasons.

More concerning, in Aquismón, San Luis Potosí, our field staff were intercepted by alleged local police officials in black SUVs with polarized windows, and were told that their safety could not be guaranteed if they continued distributing the leaflets. Following our security protocol, our team members left the municipality immediately but were followed by the SUVs for more than 60 kilometers to the closest city. That same evening, our field staff suffered further intimidation. Leaflet delivery was temporarily suspended in all municipalities in San Luis Potosí and was resumed only after a proper safety assessment by local experts on a municipality-by-municipality basis. Our team, however, never returned to Aquismón.

On other occasions, while local police and party operatives did not directly confront our team, they did take actions towards sabotaging or neutralizing our intervention. In Juventino Rosas, Guanajuato, after our team completed the intervention, PAN representatives removed the leaflets left on the doors of households who were absent during the delivery. Lastly, in Cuatiltlán Izcali, Estado de Mexico, following the detainment of our team, local police also confiscated the leaflets they were distributing. Days later, forged versions of those leaflets, attacking another party (the PAN) were apparently distributed on behalf of Borde Político. Figure 5.5 shows both the original and forged version of the leaflet.

However, the political backlash we experienced in the field provided a unique opportunity to raise attention to this issue. In light of the events in Cuatiltlán Izcali, and in order to prevent a defamation lawsuit from the PAN, Borde Político took immediate actions. First, it reached out to PAN officials to clarify that they were not responsible for the forged leaflets that had been distributed in Cuatiltlán Izcali. Second, it filed protests with the Prosecutor for Electoral Crimes (FEPADE) of the PGR (Attorney General's Office) not only about the situation in Cuatiltlán Izcali, but also about all the other incidents discussed above. Third, Borde Político wrote a press release explaining those incidents which led legislators and senators from various parties to push for a resolution of the Permanent Commission of Mexican Congress.[36] The resolution, which was ultimately approved (http://www.senado.gob.mx/64/gaceta_del_senado/documento/55379), exhorted the FEPADE of the PGR to investigate Borde Político's charges

---

[36] The Permanent Commission is formed by legislators and senators and takes care of urgent matters during recesses.

FIGURE 5.5 Mexico: Original and forged leaflet in Cuatiltlán Izcali, Estado de México

against the municipal authorities that abused their power in order to guarantee Borde Político's right to freedom of expression and our team's safety.

5.6 CONCLUSION

The results of our intervention highlight the importance of considering how information provided to voters compares with their prior beliefs. Contrary to our initial expectations, even moderate levels of malfeasance were often interpreted by voters as good news about the incumbent party. This resulted in higher electoral support, on average, for the incumbent party in treated precincts. Future research should try to understand the determinants of voters' prior beliefs. Interventions aimed at increasing voters' expectations and demands on politicians may also be a prerequisite for other informational interventions to produce the desired effect.

While we focus on the differential effect (slope) of relatively better news, our estimates also suggest that, surprisingly, even information interpreted by voters as bad news had a positive effect on the incumbent's vote share. We conjecture that this result may be partly explained by the decreased uncertainty regarding the parties' malfeasance levels that our intervention generates, and also, potentially, by the responses of politicians to the dissemination of such information.

Our heterogeneous effects also suggest that informational interventions may be particularly effective in electorally competitive environments (where voters are more likely to change their voting decision in response to new information) and in places where voters don't already have access to other media outlets or sources of political information.

Finally, our findings on politician's reactions show that researchers should consider the general equilibrium effects of their interventions.[37] Politicians, who are often the target of many of the interventions conducted, often respond strategically in an attempt to prevent any detrimental effect of the intervention on their political careers. Since this is not always the case,[38] our understanding of equilibrium political behavior may merit further research examining the conditions under which incumbents and challengers engage with informational interventions in different ways. This would be particularly interesting to explore in the context of earlier interventions occurring before candidate and platforms are selected.

[37] Cruz, Keefer, and Labonne (2016).
[38] See, for example, Banerjee et al. (2011).

6

Candidate Videos and Vote Choice in Ugandan Parliamentary Elections

Melina R. Platas and Pia Raffler

"Meet the Candidates" – an intervention where voters watch videos of parliamentary candidates answering questions in a debate-like format – took place during the Ugandan 2016 general elections. Uganda is home to nearly 40 million people and is among the most ethnically diverse countries in the world. The country has been governed by President Yoweri Museveni and his ruling party, the National Resistance Movement (NRM), for over thirty years. After a period of single-party or "no-party" rule, Uganda reinstated multiparty politics in 2005, in the same year that the parliament voted to abolish presidential term limits.

Voters in Uganda today often hold strong preferences with respect to party, and Ugandan political parties are relatively stable over time. Several of the contemporary opposition parties, such as the Democratic Party (DP) and the Uganda People's Congress (UPC) were established around independence. The main opposition party, the Forum for Democratic Change (FDC) has existed as a political party since 2005. While ethnicity is a salient political and social cleavage, the two main presidential candidates for the past four elections are both from the same region, and neither the ruling party nor the main opposition party is dominated by a single ethnic group. Thus, unlike some other African countries, party alignment is not simply a reflection of ethnicity.

While there has not been a peaceful transition at the executive level since independence in 1962, and while the president has been elected on five separate occasions, there is considerable turnover and political competition for most other elected positions, including the highly coveted position of member of parliament. The ruling party dominates at all levels, from local councilor to member of parliament (MP), but competition is often fierce within the NRM.

There are also pockets of inter-party competition, where power at the parliamentary level has oscillated between the ruling party, opposition parties, and independent candidates. While independent candidates are at times truly independent, many of them lose in NRM primaries and then go on to run – and not infrequently win a seat – in the general election. About half of all members of parliament running for reelection between 2006 and 2011 lost their seats, reflecting a high degree of turnover and competition at the parliamentary level.

Parliamentary races in Uganda are frequently very high stakes, with candidates investing their own money, and relying relatively little on party coffers.[1] One estimate puts parliamentary candidates' average spending at US$145,000[2] – a staggering amount in a country with a GDP per capita of just under US$600. Many of these candidates lose both the race and their entire life savings. In this environment, it is perhaps not surprising that parliamentary candidates will do whatever they can to undermine efforts to share information with voters which might affect their electoral chances, as a previous study has shown, information about parliamentarians' performance in office.[3]

The official work of Ugandan members of parliament lies almost entirely in legislative duties. Unlike neighboring Kenya and several other African countries, there is no constituency development fund, and no official constituency service mandated. Nevertheless, MPs report high expectations by their constituents to support community development and personal expenses, such as school fees, health care expenses, and weddings and burials. Candidates for parliament also spend tens or even hundreds of thousands of dollars in campaigns leading up to elections, much of which is used to buy goods such as soap or sugar, or distributed simply as cash handouts.[4]

According to the Afrobarometer survey, Uganda has relatively high levels of political participation from a regional perspective. One-third of Ugandans report being an active member in a voluntary association or community group, about twice as high a percentage as the average for all Sub-Saharan African countries in the most recent round of the Afrobarometer surveys. The same surveys found that more than half of Ugandan respondents reported attending a political rally in the last

---

[1] Collord (2016).
[2] Wilkins (2016).
[3] Humphreys and Weinstein (2013).
[4] Wilkins (2016).

national election compared to 38 percent for the full sample of African countries, 30 percent said they tried to persuade others to vote for a particular candidate compared to 24 percent of all countries, and 21 percent reported working for a candidate or party compared to 15 percent in the full sample.

It is in the context of pockets of inter-party competition, widespread intra-party competition (at least within the ruling party), high levels of interest in politics and political debate, relatively low access to high quality information, and high-stakes electoral campaigns that we designed our intervention: candidate videos in which all the candidates in a given constituency were invited to participate in a recording where they answered a set of questions about their policy positions, background, and experience, in something akin to candidate debates. Video recordings were then viewed by voters who may otherwise have had difficulty acquiring information about the candidates seeking to represent them in office.

During the course of the study, we filmed nearly 100 parliamentary candidates across eleven constituencies, in both the primary elections of the ruling party, held in 2015, and in the multiparty general elections held in 2016. We screened the resulting constituency-specific videos in 265 villages around the country to an estimated 12,000 to 24,000 people. In a subset of villages in four of the constituencies, respondents were randomly assigned to watch the videos privately on tablets or to a control condition in which they did not watch the videos. This chapter focuses on the effect of these privately viewed videos, which we consider the common treatment arm in the Metaketa Initiative. We also briefly discuss the results of the public screenings.[5]

The information we provide is primarily intended to allow voters to compare candidates with respect to stated policy positions, as well as background and experience. This information is therefore different from that provided in the other studies in this volume in that it is not strictly an assessment of incumbents' past performance. We are interested in the process of candidate selection, since voters do not make decisions about the incumbent in isolation of the other candidates. The underlying model of voting, therefore, is more prospective than retrospective. That being said, incumbents had an opportunity to share and justify their performance in office in the previous term, which of course is different from objective performance information.

---

[5] The full results of the public screenings are presented in Platas and Raffler (2017).

6.1 RESEARCH DESIGN

A central goal of this Metaketa round is to better understand how context can condition the treatment effects of political information on voter behavior. Given the powerful nature of party affiliation in Uganda, we sought both to compare the effect of information in an intra- and inter-party environment, but also to focus our work in constituencies with fairly high levels of inter-party competition. We considered several factors in the design of our informational treatment and research design.

First, we specifically sought out an informational treatment that would allow us to provide information on all candidates. Most of the field experiments to date that have provided voters with information about candidate quality and performance have done so for the incumbent politician or party only, and not for challengers. One obvious reason for this is that any information provided about performance in office can, by definition, only be provided about the incumbent. Nevertheless, the expectation for vote choice is not clear in the absence of knowledge about the information available to them about challengers. If a voter receives "good news" about an incumbent, we would expect that she will be more likely to vote for that candidate. If she receives "bad news," however, we would expect that she is less likely to vote for the incumbent, but her choice will likely depend on the quality of the challengers, and what she knows about them. If we find no effect of bad news, it could very well be that her priors on the challengers are much worse than her posteriors on the poorly performing incumbent.

While we do not test the effect of providing information about only the incumbent versus all the candidates, it is nevertheless important to note that the extent of information provided is distinct from many, if not most, other studies examining the effect of information on voter behavior. Despite these differences with other work, the theoretical framework we employ is the same as that in the other Metaketa studies, as are our hypotheses about the effect of good and bad news about candidates on voter behavior. The meta-analysis reported in Chapter 11 (this volume) restricts attention to the impact of our intervention on support for incumbents, for symmetry with the other studies.

Second, among the key lessons learned from earlier work on information and accountability in Uganda is that politicians can and do undermine efforts to promote transparency, including the obfuscation of information provided in a scorecard by the parliamentary incumbents being evaluated.[6] In part because of the backlash by politicians against the Parliamentary Scorecard in Uganda, we sought to design an information treatment that involved the support and buy-in of candidates and political parties. Of course, this was itself a potentially risky strategy, as a lack of cooperation by these parties would have rendered the project infeasible. However, conditional on buy-in, we believed it unlikely that candidates would try to derail the study, for reasons outlined above.

Fortunately, for the most part, candidates and parties saw debates as an opportunity to reach more voters and were generally willing and often enthusiastic about participating. Beyond the feasibility of our study, we sought an intervention with high levels of buy-in by political parties and the Electoral Commission to increase the potential for scale-up. If perceived as useful and beneficial by political parties and the Electoral Commission, such a program is more likely to be scaled-up for future elections, which would likely require both of their participation.

Finally, we were intrigued by the possibility of candidate debates. Presidential debates have been seen across the region, and the 2016 Ugandan presidential debate was the first to feature the sitting president, bringing all eight presidential candidates on stage together – holding hands, no less – just days before the election. The idea of creating a level playing field, quite literally in the case of the presidential debate, was particularly appealing in a context where a single party is overwhelmingly dominant. We were also encouraged by findings from a similar study conducted in Sierra Leone, where Bidwell, Casey, and Glennerster (n.d.) found that watching candidate debates resulted in a greater likelihood in voting for the perceived winner of the debate. While our theory, research design and analysis are distinct from that of Bidwell, Casey, and Glennerster (n.d.), their findings provided us with greater confidence that debates could affect vote choice in the context of Uganda.

6.1.1 The Intervention

Our treatment for the common arm of the Metaketa is viewing videos of candidates answering a set of questions about their policy positions, background, and experience. Voters in the treatment group viewed a video of the parliamentary candidates in their constituency privately on tablets as part of a survey. While for ease of exposition we occasionally

---

[6] Humphreys and Weinstein (2013).

refer to the videos as debates, it is important to note that the candidates did not in fact interact with one another in the videos. The videos were edited such that all candidates were presented together answering questions, but the treatment differs importantly from a true debate in that the candidates did not interact with one another. This decision was made for both logistical reasons and in an effort to control the information environment, giving each candidate the same amount of time for each question without interruption or interference.

In order to produce the videos, we invited all candidates for area MP in a given constituency into a recording studio in Kampala to respond to a set of standardized questions about their policy positions and qualifications.[7] Figure 6.1 shows a candidate in the studio where the videos were recorded. The responses were then edited to produce one video per constituency in which all filmed candidates answer each question in turn. The video also provided a brief introduction with information on the minimum qualifications, roles and responsibilities of members of parliament, as well as the functions of the different branches of government.

The questions centered on two dimensions, which we term "policy" and "image." The three policy questions asked candidates' positions on three separate policy issues, which were salient in the 2016 elections:

FIGURE 6.1 Uganda 1: Candidate during a recording session

---

[7] Area MP refers to the constituency representative and is contrasted with other parliamentary positions reserved for special groups, including women, persons with disabilities, and youth.

(a) their priority sector for the constituency (such as health, education, and security), (b) their position on whether additional administrative districts should be created in Uganda, and (c) their position on the legal consequences for candidates convicted of vote buying. The three image questions included: (a) their qualifications for running for office (education, career history, community experience), (b) the personal characteristic that they believe best prepares them for office, and (c) how their past achievements demonstrate that they will be an effective representative of their constituents in parliament. The exact wording of questions asked of the candidates is provided in the online appendix, subsection C3.

We formulated these questions in collaboration with our implementing partners and shared them with candidates prior to recording. Our goal was to select policy questions in which 1) we would observe variation in responses across candidates, 2) the policy preference was of substantive importance to voters, and 3) the policy issue was unlikely to be brought to the floor of parliament before the election. Achieving these three goals was somewhat difficult, particularly reconciling the second and third consideration. We wanted to avoid issues that were being debated in parliament or where new legislation was likely to pass, since a national discussion might affect the preferences of voters, and we wanted voter preferences to be consistent over time and across the NRM primary elections (October 2015) and the general elections (February 2016). In keeping with the first criteria, we wanted to avoid policy preferences that were associated with party positions, since if this was the case there would have been no variation across candidates in the NRM primaries.

At the studio, trained moderators facilitated the candidate interviews to ensure uniformity of treatment across constituencies and candidates. For example, moderators ensured that each candidate answered every question and received equal time for each question. The videos were filmed in local languages, and candidates' names and party affiliations were included in the video to increase name and face recognition. Figure 6.2 shows an example of how a candidate appeared in the video, together with her name at the bottom and party affiliation (party name and symbol) in the top right corner.

6.1.2 Subjects and Context

In order to be eligible to participate in the study, individuals needed to have registered to vote in the general election and be accessible by phone. Subjects did not necessarily need to own a phone, but needed to be able

FIGURE 6.2 Uganda 1: Candidate as seen in the video

to provide a phone number of a friend, relative, or neighbor through whom they could be reached on election day. Of the sampled voters, 2 percent had to be replaced at the listing stage since they could not be reached by any phone.[8]

The common information treatment was implemented in four parliamentary constituencies located in central and eastern Uganda, shaded with thick black stripes in Figure 6.3. These constituencies were part of a larger set of eleven constituencies included in our broader study. We sought to identify rural constituencies that were competitive both within the ruling party and across parties. In order to identify a set of competitive constituencies, we first selected a set of fifty-eight rural constituencies using the following criteria for competitiveness: (a) different parties won in the previous two general elections (2006 and 2011)[9] and (b) average vote margins across the past two elections were at most 20 percent. We then excluded constituencies where local experts expected electoral violence to take place, as well as constituencies that were difficult to reach, such as islands, and constituencies speaking relatively rare languages where it would be difficult to recruit enumerators.

[8] At the mobilization stage (see subsection 6.1.3), another estimated up to 2 percent of voters had to be excluded because they did not indicate a phone number under which they could be reached. Note that this figure is the upper bound, assuming that all intended respondents for whom mobilizers did not enter a phone number on the tracking sheet did, in fact, not have a number under which they could be reached (rather than not being found and thus not reporting a phone number).
[9] We consider Independents as a party for this exercise. Constituencies where the same MP served for two different parties were excluded from our sample.

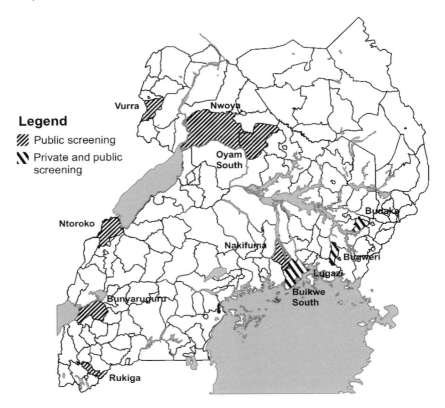

FIGURE 6.3 Uganda 1: Map of selected constituencies

After excluding constituencies for the aforementioned reasons, a total of twenty-seven constituencies remained eligible for inclusion.[10] Of these, we randomly selected eleven for inclusion in the study. The remainder serve as controls, to assess downstream effects of the intervention.[11] In cases where a constituency had to be replaced, this was done following

---

[10] In one constituency, Bugweri, the incumbent had served the previous term, violating criteria (a). However, this constituency was included because the original result tally showed a different party winning the 2011 election. The result was eventually overturned. In any case, this series of events shows the constituency to be highly competitive.

[11] We blocked the sampling of constituencies on (i) region and (ii) whether the incumbent's party was an opposition party or not (defined as NRM or Independent). From the resulting strata, we stick as closely as possible to drawing 1 out of 3. This implies oversampling of the non-opposition strata in the North (2 out of 4) and of the opposition strata in the West (1 out of 2).

the random order, i.e., with the constituency with the next smallest random number within the same strata.[12]

Of the eleven constituencies, four were selected for the individual treatment arm discussed here.[13] For logistical reasons, we selected four constituencies in relatively close geographic proximity. In half of the constituencies the incumbent was a member of the ruling party.

6.1.3 Randomization

To sample polling stations, we selected the three polling stations with the highest overlap between a polling station catchment area and its 'main' village in each parish.[14] We define the main village as the village contributing the highest number of voters to a polling station according to the updated voter register of the national Electoral Commission (2015). Overlap is defined as the percentage of voters in a given polling station that come from its main village. For example, a polling station where 90 percent of voters come from the village contributing the highest number of voters is considered to have higher overlap than a polling station where only a maximum of 20 percent of voters come from one village.

We worked with two units of randomization, polling stations and individuals. First, we randomly assigned sampled polling stations to the public screening, individual arm, or pure control. Randomization was blocked at the constituency level. Second, in polling stations assigned to the individual treatment arm of the study, we randomly assigned individual respondents to one of three treatment conditions: a private video screening (n = 428), exposure to polling results to study bandwagon effects (n = 427), and control (n = 402). (Note that the poll treatment, while prespecified in the pre-analysis plan of the larger project, is not analyzed in this chapter since it is not part of the common arm.) To sample

---

[12] Three constituencies were ultimately replaced with a control constituency from the same strata — One because the constituency was likely to be split, and two others because the NRM data available at the time of final sample selection showed zero or one contestant. In the lead up to the general elections, a number of new constituencies were created. We expect split constituencies to decrease in competitiveness, and therefore exclude any constituency which was listed in the relevant parliamentary committee report. Source: Report by the Sectoral Committee on Public Service and Local Government on the Motion for a Resolution of Parliament to Create New Counties. Office of the Clerk to Parliament, July 2015.

[13] Due to logistical and budget concerns, it was not possible to implement the individual study arms in all eleven constituencies.

[14] To minimize spillover, we excluded polling stations from the sample which: (a) were part of the sample of the Metaketa Uganda 2 team, and/or (b) had a main village where voters are registered in polling stations in two different parishes.

respondents, we first randomly selected 120 names from the official voter registry. Then, an enumerator met with the local village chairperson or other knowledgeable persons if the chairperson was not available, to go through the randomly ordered list and remove from the sample any individual who did not reside in the village and should therefore not have been included in the sample frame in the first place.[15] This process continued until we had a list of eighty-five registered voters who resided in the village or the list was exhausted. This correction process eliminated an average of 26 percent of names from the list randomly drawn from the voter register.[16]

Then, again with the help of the village chairperson, the enumerator drew a map of the village to locate respondent households on a village map. The enumerator(s) then visited each respondent to inform them of the date and time the survey would be taking place. Respondents were replaced if they (a) could not be found, (b) would not be in the village on the day of enumeration, (c) were not in a mental state fit to participate in the survey at the time of mobilization (e.g., intoxication), (d) were unwilling to participate, (e) were ill or busy taking care of someone ill, or (f) could not provide a phone number through which they could be reached on election day. A total of 30 percent of respondents of the corrected sample frame were replaced (7 percent during the meeting with the local council (LC) I chairperson, another 23 percent during household visits). Replacement rates are balanced across treatment and control. 2–4 percent of respondents were replaced because they could not provide a phone number where they could be reached.[17] Figure 6.4 provides further details.

Figures for the mobilization (enrollment) stage are based on scanned listing tools, which are available for nineteen out of twenty-five polling stations. Missing values are imputed by setting them to the polling station mean of the available sample. The remaining figures are based on survey data. The number of respondents who were replaced because they did not have phone access is an upper bound, coded based on the lack of a phone number on the village level mobilization form (which could also be due to inability to find a respondent during mobilization).

---

[15] Specifically, the enumerator read the following script: "I have a list of 120 randomly sampled voters from this village. Our statisticians produced it from the voter register, which the Electoral Commission has shared with us. I will read you each name. Please confirm for each whether they are a resident in this village."

[16] Based on tracking sheets of 44 percent of the sample at time of publication.

[17] Replacement rates are based on scanned tracking sheets of 56 percent of the sample.

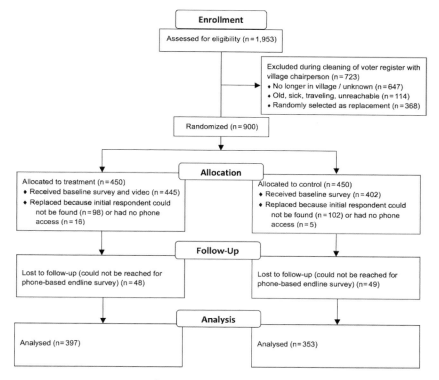

FIGURE 6.4 Uganda 1: CONSORT diagram of research design

6.1.4   Data Collection and Measurement

We conducted two rounds of panel data collection. The first wave of the panel was conducted in person, and for those assigned to the treatment, the treatment was administered in the course of the survey. The second wave was conducted by phone on the day of the election and the days immediately following the election.

In the first survey wave, we collected data on demographics, controls, and moderators as specified by the Metaketa meta-preanalysis plan, political knowledge, and intended vote choice. In addition, we collected data on respondents' priors on a number of dimensions, which we used to construct our measure of good news, discussed in greater detail below. Upon completing this section of the survey, respondents in the treatment group watched the video on tablets with headsets carried by enumerators. After watching the video, they were asked a set of follow up questions about the video and what information they had acquired from it.

In the second, phone-based wave of the survey, we collected data on voting behavior, particularly turnout and vote choice for MPs. We also collected data on political knowledge, perceived likability of the candidates, and information on candidate behavior in the polling station catchment area. Since overreporting of turnout is a concern, respondents were also asked a set of simple factual questions about the voting process in order to verify turnout.

6.1.5 Attrition and Treatment Compliance

Thanks to a detailed tracking protocol, attrition was low. Of the 847 respondents enrolled into the study, 750 (89 percent) completed the endline survey. Attrition is balanced across the treatment and control groups.[18] While attrition is balanced across treatment and control, attrition was negatively correlated with self-reported turnout in 2011 and with wealth. Attrition also varied somewhat across constituencies.

Treatment compliance was high. Of the 445 respondents who were assigned to the treatment group, 91 percent watched the video completely while 7 percent watched most of it, as reported by the enumerator administering the treatment.

6.1.6 Defining Good News

Our intervention necessarily bundled different types of information. Our definition of good and bad news therefore needs to solve the issues of aggregation and appropriate coding. We think of our information treatment as providing information along two different dimensions, candidates' policy platforms and candidates' characteristics, referred to as candidate image in Hacker (2004).[19] In the video, we have three questions related to policy and three questions related to candidate image.[20] We are interested in the degree to which the positions of a given candidate align with the preferences of a given voter, which we assess at baseline. Here, good news is defined as greater than a priori expected congruence

---

[18] The two-sided t-test testing for imbalanced attrition between treatment and control groups yields a p-value of 0.523.

[19] American Politics has a rich literature on voters' perceptions of candidate characteristics and the importance of debates for shaping them (Schill and Kirk, 2014, Brubaker and Hanson, 2009, Benoit, Hansen and Verser, 2003).

[20] Note that information on policy preferences relate to congruence between voters and candidates, while information related to candidate image relates to performance.

between voters' and candidates' policy preferences. Good news can be objectively defined by comparing a respondent's prior on whether a candidate's policy position aligns with her own policy preference with the actual alignment revealed in the video. This approach is applicable to both the treatment and the control group.

With regard to candidate characteristics, we differentiate between three different categories: competence, understanding of policy issues, and eloquence. For each of them, we collect voters' priors, voters' posteriors (in the treatment group) and expert assessments, all measured on the same scale. Good (bad) news on the three dimensions of candidate image is defined as experts' average assessment of a candidate's performance as being better (worse) than a respondent's priors for that candidate.

Policy Dimension

For policy positions, we consider it as good news if a candidate's policy preferences are more aligned with those of the voter than anticipated, or are as aligned as anticipated (thus offering greater certainty), and as bad news otherwise. The distance between the prior and the information provided determines the degree to which news is good or bad.

We consider it "very good news" if a voter had a prior that a candidate's policy position was not aligned, but the position is indeed aligned, as "good news" if a voter didn't have a prior on whether the policy positions were aligned and finds out that they are aligned, and as "weakly good news" if a voter's prior that policy positions are aligned is confirmed, thus reducing uncertainty. Conversely, we consider it "very bad news" if a voter had a prior that policy positions were aligned but the information reveals that they are not, as "bad news" if a voter did not have a prior and the information reveals that they are not aligned, and as "weakly bad news" if a voter's prior that policy positions are not aligned is confirmed.

Image Dimension

We measured the priors about the information content for each of the three image categories for each politician and individual subject during the baseline survey for both treatment and control groups. We then invited Ugandan journalists and civil society members to watch the videos independently, and to answer the identical questions and answer choices as used to measure respondents' priors on the three candidate image categories (competence, understanding of policy issues, and eloquence). Each video was reviewed by four to five experts. An average score based on the expert ratings was calculated for each candidate on each of the three dimensions. Then, we calculated the difference, for each candidate-respondent dyad, between average expert assessment and respondent prior for each of the three dimensions.

We use expert assessments rather than respondents' subjective perception of candidate performance in the videos to define good and bad news for two reasons. The first is conceptual. We care about the information content relative to priors, rather than the direction of updating the information results in, which has been shown in other contexts to be influenced by partisan biases.[21] We deem expert assessments more objective since experts were assessing candidates for whom they were not constituents. The second is practical. By design we cannot ask respondents in the control condition about their perception of a candidate's performance in the video. The alternative method for determining quality of news would be to use predicted updating based on baseline characteristics rather than measured updating, which would introduce a host of assumptions.

Finally, we construct a weighted average of good/bad news across the six different dimensions. The weights for each dimension were collected at baseline for all respondents, asking how they weighted the different categories of information when deciding how to vote.[22] We then used the relative weights[23] to construct a respondent specific average of the type of information each voter received – or would have received, in the case of the control group – on each candidate. As shown in Table 6.1, on average, respondents considered the different dimensions of similar importance. Our results are robust to using equal weighting of the six

---

[21] See the large literature on motivated reasoning, for example, Redlawsk (2002).

[22] The survey question reads: "There are many factors people take into consideration when deciding how to assess a candidate. I'm going to read you a few such factors. For each of them, please tell me how important you consider them in your personal evaluation of candidates for area MP: very important, somewhat important, neither important nor unimportant, somewhat unimportant, or very unimportant. List of criteria: (a) Whether a candidate thinks that the same issues are a priority for your constituency as you do. (b) Whether a candidate has the same policy priority for Uganda as a whole as you. (c) Whether a candidate holds the same position as you on whether or not more districts should be created in Uganda. (d) How well a candidate understands policy issues. (e) How well qualified, considering education, job, and life experience a candidate is to represent your constituency. (f) How well a candidate can express him/herself."

[23] To ensure weights are comparable across respondents, we rescaled Likert responses such that the relative weights assigned to the different categories add up to one for each respondent.

TABLE 6.1 *Uganda 1: Components of information treatment*

Dimension	Category	Weight	Mean weight
Policy	Alignment on constituency policy priority	a	0.178
	Alignment on anti-vote-buying policy	b	0.146
	Alignment on position on district splitting	c	0.143
Candidate image	Competence	d	0.174
	Understanding of policy issues	e	0.181
	Eloquence	f	0.177

Mean weights are based on the baseline survey with n = 750 registered voters.

components. Distributions of these weights are shown in Figure C1 in the online appendix.

All distances between information and prior were rescaled to $[-1, 1]$ and weights applied to construct the aggregate news across the six categories.

6.1.7 Descriptive Statistics

We provide some descriptive statistics on subjects to give a better sense of the context in which the study took place. The four constituencies are relatively ethnically homogeneous, with all but one having an ethnic group constituting a majority of the sample. In Bugweri, 84 percent of the respondents were Basoga, in Budaka 76 percent of respondents were Bagwere, and Buikwe South and Lugazi were 68 percent and 45 percent Baganda, respectively. Given that all but one candidate[24] were also of the majority ethnic group, the majority of respondents were coethnics with all or most of the candidates – 63 percent of the respondent-candidate dyads were coethnics. Table C.2 in the online appendix provides an overview.

---

[24] In one of our four constituencies, one candidate is a Munyarwanda, while the other eight candidates are Baganda.

In terms of political participation and interest in politics, 75 percent of respondents reported voting in the previous general elections in 2011. Of those who reported voting in the 2011 parliamentary elections, 64 percent reported voting for a ruling party candidate, while 92 percent reported voting for the ruling party presidential candidate, Yoweri Museveni, who won that election and the next. Further, 57 percent of respondents reported voting in the primary elections of the ruling party. Thus, the majority of respondents were either NRM leaning or NRM members. However, the difference in reported vote choice for president and parliamentary candidates in the 2011 election suggests that respondents were more willing to vote for non-NRM candidates in the parliamentary than presidential races. 62 percent said that "individual merit" had a more important role to play than party affiliation in the respondent's decision about whom to vote for member of parliament.

The vast majority of respondents knew the party affiliation of their current MP (81 percent) and half knew the name of the speaker of parliament at the time. 34 percent of respondents said they often or very often talked about political issues with neighbors or other members of their community, which was about the same percentage of those who reported such conversations with family members. There was a sizable gender component to discussion about politics, however. While 43 percent of men reported talking often or very often to community members and family about politics, among women, only 25 percent reported talking regularly about politics to family members and only 23 percent to community members. Most respondents reported consuming news frequently ("a few times a week" or "everyday"). Most popular news sources were radios (69 percent), followed by newspapers (13 percent), and by television (12 percent).

6.2 RESULTS

This section summarizes the treatment effects of watching "Meet the Candidates" videos on the two primary outcome variables employed in the meta-analysis: turnout and vote choice. For comparability with other studies in this volume, we first report the effect of good and bad news on turnout and vote choice for the subsample of incumbent candidates. For analyses of vote choice, we also report the effect of good and bad news for the sample of viable candidates (those who received at least 10 percent of the vote share according to official polling results) and all candidates.

Our main specification includes a vector of the demeaned control variables listed in Table C1, as well as the interaction terms between the treatment indicator and the demeaned controls. Results without controls are also presented below. Further, we include a measure of the distance between the prior and the information content, which can be thought of as the amount of news someone received, as well as the interaction between distance and treatment. All else equal, we would expect the treatment effect to be increasing in the amount of news received. We split the sample between respondents eligible to receive good news and those eligible to receive bad news. The estimation equation is included in Section C.2 in the online appendix, further details are included in the pre-registered meta-analysis pre-analysis plan (MPAP) and the pre-analysis plan for this study.[25]

Turnout and vote choice were measured through a phone-based end-line survey, conducted in the evening of election day and the following days. To correct for potential overreporting of turnout, we asked a simple factual question which respondents were likely to answer correctly only if they had in fact voted: which finger had been used to verify their identity in newly introduced biometric machines. 81 percent of respondents said that their right thumb was used. Since the biometric machines were introduced for the first time in this election, it is unlikely respondents could have learned this information from a previous election and it seems an unlikely piece of information to share with family and friends.

We report our results using self-reported voting behavior that has been verified, i.e., only respondents who answered the finger verification question correctly are coded as having voted. Note that in our case vote choice is less subject to social desirability bias than turnout since our treatment never explicitly indicated a best or worst choice of candidate.

Turnout

First we report our findings with respect to turnout. Here, we assess whether receiving good or bad news about the incumbent affected respondents' propensity to vote at all. We find a large and positive treatment effect of good news about the incumbent on turnout, which is statistically significant with and without covariates. There is a nine percentage point increase in turnout among those who received good news about the incumbent in the specification without covariates, compared to the

---

[25] The pre-analysis plan is available here: http://egap.org/registration/1273.

TABLE 6.2 *Uganda 1: Treatment effect on turnout (voter-incumbent dyad)*

	(1) Turnout Good news	(2) Turnout Good news	(3) Turnout Bad news	(4) Turnout Bad news
Treatment	0.078*	0.090**	−0.014	−0.007
	(0.040)	(0.041)	(0.053)	(0.051)
Constant	0.740***	0.725***	0.774***	0.769***
	(0.030)	(0.030)	(0.036)	(0.035)
Controls	Yes	No	Yes	No
N	456	456	294	294
R²	0.141	0.029	0.112	0.029

Notes: The unit of observation is the voter-incumbent dyad. All specifications include constituency fixed effects. Standard errors are clustered at the individual level. *** $p < 0.01$, ** $p < 0.05$, * $p < 0.1$.

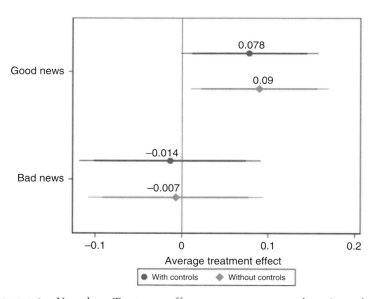

FIGURE 6.5 Uganda 1: Treatment effects on turnout, news about incumbent only

control group. The addition of the prespecified covariates reduces the magnitude of the coefficient on the treatment slightly, to 7.8 percentage points, and remains significant at the 10 percent level. Figure 6.5 illustrates these results. We find no effect on turnout of receiving bad news about the incumbent.

TABLE 6.3 *Uganda 1: Sample sizes by treatment group*

	Incumbents	Viable candidates	All candidates
Good news	456	987	2,328
	61%	49%	53%
Bad news	294	1,034	2,049
	39%	51%	47%
Total	750	2,021	4,377

Notes: The unit of observation is the voter–candidate dyad. Viable candidates are defined as those with a vote share of at least 10 percent.

Vote Choice

Next, we turn to vote choice. Here, the unit of analysis is the voter-candidate dyad. In other words, we ask, did the intervention affect the propensity of voter i to vote for candidate j, conditional on whether the voter received positive news about candidate j during the debate, compared to voters who would have also received positive news, but were not assigned to treatment? Similarly, were voters who received negative news about a given candidate less likely to vote for her, relative to the relevant control group? Those who did not vote at all received a value of 0 for vote choice for all candidate dyads, since they did not vote for any candidate. As noted, for comparability with the other studies in this volume, the main analysis we present here focuses only on the dyads that include the incumbent candidate. However, we also present analyses using the candidate dyads of all viable candidates, defined as all candidates who received at least 10 percent of the votes in their constituency, and then finally all candidates who participated in the election. The sample sizes are shown in Table 6.3.

Interestingly, voters were more likely to receive good news about incumbents than about challengers. 61 percent of voters received good news about the incumbent, compared to 49 percent among viable candidates and 53 percent among the full sample. Since news is defined as the distance between voters' priors on the one hand and actual policy alignment and video performance as assessed by experts on the other, this suggests that voters are overly pessimistic about incumbents' quality in the absence of information interventions. Low priors about incumbent MP quality may partially explain the high levels of turnover at the parliamentary level.

We begin by assessing the effect on an intermediate outcome measure, respondents' expectation of a candidate's future effort levels (Table 6.4).

TABLE 6.4 *Uganda 1: Effect on expected candidate effort if elected*

	(1) Good news	(2) Good news	(3) Bad news	(4) Bad news
Treatment	0.184***	0.161***	0.046	−0.081
	(0.063)	(0.058)	(0.060)	(0.058)
Treat × Distance	0.078*	0.085*	0.015	−0.021
	(0.041)	(0.045)	(0.043)	(0.049)
Distance	−0.172***	−0.210***	−0.108***	−0.204***
	(0.031)	(0.034)	(0.036)	(0.041)
Constant	2.224***	2.253***	2.769***	2.886***
	(0.054)	(0.047)	(0.051)	(0.045)
Controls	Yes	No	Yes	No
N	1,809	1,809	1,639	1,639
R²	0.195	0.050	0.311	0.070

Notes: The unit of observation is the voter-candidate dyad. All models include constituency fixed effects. Standard errors are clustered at the individual level. *** $p < 0.01$, ** $p < 0.05$, * $p < 0.1$.

We find that exposure to good news had a positive treatment effect on respondents' expectations. In particular, respondents who watched videos conveying good news about a candidate were more likely to say that they expected that candidate to exert more effort than other candidates if elected into office, compared to the control group. The effect is of considerable magnitude: 0.18 point increase off a mean of 2.2 points on a four-point scale, and highly statistically significant (sample: all candidates). Receiving bad news did not have a significant treatment effect on expected effort levels.

Next, we examine the effect of good and bad news on our primary outcome variable – vote choice. We find that among incumbent dyads, there is a positive coefficient on the treatment effect for good news but this effect is not significant under any specification, given the considerably smaller sample size. We also do not find an effect of receiving bad news about the incumbent on the likelihood of voting for that candidate.

We also examine the effect of good and bad news about all candidates and all viable candidates in the four constituencies. If voters act strategically, we should not expect them to change their vote choice in favor of a nonviable candidate in response to the treatment: Even the most positive news is unlikely to bring such candidate into the realm of winning office, thus rendering any ballot cast in favor of such candidate a wasted vote. To take this into account, we create a sample that includes viable

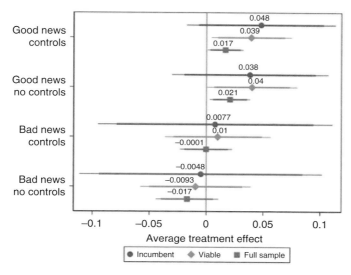

FIGURE 6.6 Uganda 1: Treatment effects on vote choice

candidates, which we define as those with at least 10 percent of the vote share.[26] To account for the fact that observations are voter-candidate dyads, and therefore not independent at the voter level for those analyses including multiple dyads per respondent, we cluster standard errors by voter.

The treatment effects of receiving good and bad news for the three samples, incumbents only, viable candidates, and all candidates, are shown in Figure 6.6. As expected, treatment effects of good news are stronger among viable candidates than among the full sample: the probability of voting for a viable candidate increases by 3.9 percentage points if exposed to good news, compared to 1.7 percentage points in the full sample. Like the analysis of incumbent dyads, bad news does not seem to shift vote choice away from viable candidates more so than candidates in the full sample. It could be that voters more readily, positively rather than negatively, update their beliefs about viable candidates. Robustness tests with self-reported vote choice taken at face value are presented in Table C5 in the online appendix. The findings are consistent with those presented here.

---

[26] Vote share is necessarily a posttreatment measure. Since we treated only a small share of voters in any constituency, it is highly unlikely that vote shares were affected by the intervention. Note that we did not prespecify this analysis.

TABLE 6.5 *Uganda 1: Treatment effect of good news on vote choice*

	(1) Incumbent	(2) Viable	(3) All	(4) Incumbent	(5) Viable	(6) All
Treatment	0.048	0.039**	0.017**	0.038	0.040**	0.021**
	(0.033)	(0.018)	(0.008)	(0.035)	(0.020)	(0.009)
Treat × Distance	0.006	0.009	0.010	0.025	0.003	0.002
	(0.027)	(0.016)	(0.009)	(0.027)	(0.017)	(0.009)
Distance	−0.020	−0.018*	−0.009	−0.040**	−0.039***	−0.014**
	(0.019)	(0.011)	(0.005)	(0.019)	(0.011)	(0.006)
Constant	0.144***	0.144***	0.067***	0.150***	0.147***	0.065***
	(0.025)	(0.013)	(0.006)	(0.026)	(0.014)	(0.006)
Controls	Yes	Yes	Yes	No	No	No
N	456	987	2,328	456	987	2,328
R^2	0.262	0.254	0.258	0.082	0.073	0.027

Notes: Sample restricted to voters who were eligible to receive good news about a given candidate, i.e., their priors were equal or lower than the expert assessment of candidate performance and revealed policy alignment. The unit of observation is voter–candidate dyad. All specifications include constituency fixed effects. Standard errors are clustered at the individual level. *** $p < 0.01$, ** $p < 0.05$, * $p < 0.1$.

Together, these results suggest a consistent effect of good news on vote choice, but no effect of bad news. The fact that the coefficient for the incumbent only is almost identical to that of viable candidates, only in the case of the former the treatment effect is not significant, suggests that we are underpowered when examining an analysis of only the incumbents.

One may ask what type of candidate our treatment "helped" the most. That is, what were the drivers of good and bad news about candidates? The lowest average share of respondents who (would have) received good news about a candidate was 24 percent, the highest share was 71 percent; both for candidates who turned out to win their constituency races. Were there any predictors of the average good news score for candidates?

Figure 6.7 shows the relationship between five potentially relevant variables and average good news scores. Each coefficient was estimated in a separate regression model with only one predictor, where the unit of analysis was the candidate ($n = 24$). Candidate popularity, as measured by intended vote choice, was negatively correlated with good news, as was being a candidate from the ruling party. This could reflect a tendency of voters to be overly optimistic about the quality of those who they plan to vote for, and about ruling party candidates. It could also suggest that in the absence of an information campaign voters hold very

TABLE 6.6 *Uganda 1: Treatment effect of bad news on vote choice*

	(1) Incumbent	(2) Viable	(3) All	(4) Incumbent	(5) Viable	(6) All
Treatment	0.009	0.010	0.000	−0.005	−0.009	−0.017
	(0.052)	(0.024)	(0.012)	(0.054)	(0.025)	(0.014)
Treat × Distance	−0.020	0.025	0.010	−0.002	0.027	0.007
	(0.047)	(0.026)	(0.016)	(0.048)	(0.026)	(0.018)
Distance	−0.013	−0.036*	−0.024*	−0.037	−0.092***	−0.087***
	(0.033)	(0.020)	(0.013)	(0.034)	(0.019)	(0.014)
Constant	0.337***	0.318***	0.178***	0.337***	0.312***	0.182***
	(0.035)	(0.016)	(0.008)	(0.037)	(0.017)	(0.010)
Controls	Yes	Yes	Yes	No	No	No
N	294	1,034	2,049	294	1,034	2,049
R^2	0.310	0.290	0.387	0.128	0.071	0.065

Notes: The unit of observation is voter–candidate dyad. Sample restricted to voters who were eligible to receive bad news about a given candidate, i.e., their priors were higher than the expert assessment of candidate performance and revealed policy alignment. All specifications include constituency fixed effects. Standard errors are clustered at the individual level. *** $p < 0.01$, ** $p < 0.05$, * $p < 0.1$.

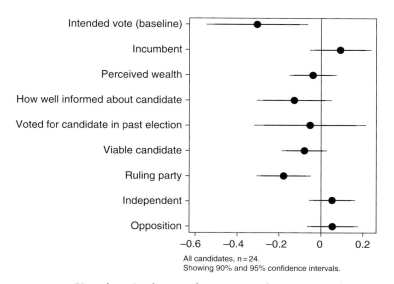

All candidates, n = 24.
Showing 90% and 95% confidence intervals.

FIGURE 6.7 Uganda 1: Predictors of average good news rating (bivariate relationships)

low opinions of those whom they do not plan to vote and those about whom they know little.

This analysis may shed some light on why our findings on good news are more robust than on bad news. Voters are most likely to receive bad news about the person they are most likely to vote for. It is perhaps not surprising then, that the effect of bad news is weak or even nonexistent.

6.2.1   Heterogeneous Treatment Effects

We do not find evidence for the existence of any of the heterogeneous treatment effects specified in the MPAP, with two notable exceptions. First, the positive treatment effect of good news on vote choice cancels out for candidates from whom voters did not expect to receive any personal favors if elected (significant in the specification with controls only, but signs are consistent). Second, as one might expect, we find that the positive treatment effect of good news on vote choice is entirely driven by respondents who reported at baseline that they considered a video about candidates to be a credible source of information. Tables C3 and C4 in the online appendix summarize these results. Unfortunately due to a programming error we did not measure expected corruption, which was a prespecified heterogeneous treatment effect in the MPAP.

6.3   ALTERNATIVE ARM: PUBLIC SCREENING OF CANDIDATE VIDEOS

The alternative arm of our study included the same intervention as described above, but altered the way in which information was delivered, and also varied the political context in which the information was shared. Specifically, we conducted public rather than private viewings of "Meet the Candidates" videos in eleven constituencies, inclusive of the four in which we conducted private screenings. We compiled and screened these videos in two types of electoral environments: the primary elections of the ruling party, the NRM, and the multiparty general elections.

Given the powerful nature of party affiliation in Uganda, we sought both to compare the effect of information in an intra and inter-party environment, focusing our work in constituencies with fairly high levels of inter-party competition. In party strongholds, whether ruling party or opposition, we expected information effects would be weaker or even nonexistent during the general election. That is, in areas that strongly support a particular party, and where the candidate from that party will almost surely win, news about the likely winner or the challengers – whether good or bad – is less likely to matter than where the race is more competitive. In the event of bad news about the likely winner, voters are less likely to change their vote unless they believe many others will as well, else their vote is likely to be wasted. In a closer race, voters would need a relatively smaller number of voters to change their vote from the likely winner in order for their vote not to be wasted. While we do not test whether this feature of the context conditioned treatment effects, we note that our intervention took place in the context of constituencies that were expected to be competitive, and not party strongholds.[27] As noted, about half of incumbents running for reelection lose their seats each election cycle. In fact, incumbent disadvantage has been documented in several similar contexts.[28] In our context, party strongholds are not necessarily equivalent to incumbent politician strongholds. That is, turnover among party members is relatively high also within party strongholds. We therefore expect stronger effects of information in primary elections, but less so in the general elections when the party flagbearer has already been chosen. In order to test our theoretical expectations about information effects in primary versus general election settings, we selected constituencies which we expected would be competitive in both races. Because of the strength of party identification, we believed voters would be more likely to change their vote in response to new information in an intra rather than inter-party setting.

Just as in the common arm of the study, we filmed all candidates willing to participate in each of the eleven constituencies, once during the primary elections of the ruling party, and once during the general election. We randomly assigned polling station catchment areas to either treatment or control, where the treatment comprised a public screening of the video, like that shown in Figure 6.8. As in the common arm, we conducted a baseline survey, a posterior survey of those who had watched the video, and an endline survey on election day and the subsequent days. Altogether we filmed 80 percent of the candidates participating in the

[27] Our theoretical expectations are in line with respect to strongholds versus competitive constituencies, along with those of Grossman and Michelitch (2018), who also work in the context of Uganda, but they diverge from those of Cruz, Keefer, and Labonne (2016), who find larger information effects in party strongholds. Unlike the Philippines, our context is not one in which incumbent politicians have a strong electoral advantage.

[28] Klašnja (2015).

FIGURE 6.8 Uganda 1: "Meet the Candidates" public screening
(alternative arm)

primary election and 91 percent of those participating in the general election, for a total of nearly 100 candidates. The full results of the study can be found in Platas and Raffler (2017) and are noted in brief below.

First, we find that watching the videos increased political knowledge, measured as an index of the roles and responsibilities of Members of Parliament, share of candidates known, and knowledge of candidates' priority sector for the voter's constituency. We do not find that watching the videos had an effect on turnout in the aggregate. We also do not find effects on vote choice of either good or bad news about candidates.

Second, as anticipated, we find that while there is an effect on self-reported, verified vote choice of watching the videos in both the primary and general election, the way in which the treatment affects vote choice differs. Specifically, we find that watching the videos in the primary election results in greater switching from intended vote choice to the best performer in the video, both as defined by ratings provided by the sample of all viewers as well as by the panel of experts. In the general election, voters are not more likely to switch to the best performer after watching the video. Rather, we find that voters are more likely to switch away from the ruling party candidate and towards opposition candidates. Note that we cannot detect these effects in official polling station data.

We are able to rule out the possibility that vote switching is due to response bias – it is not the case that those who watched the videos were less likely to believe the research team was sent by government and therefore more likely to report their true vote choice, for example, for an opposition candidate. We can also rule out the possibility that flag-bearers of the ruling party performed badly, or worse than the average candidate. On the contrary, ten of the eleven candidates of the ruling party were rated above the median in terms of debate performance. Rather, the evidence suggests that watching the videos encouraged some NRM-leaning voters to reconsider other options. Together, the results suggest that public debates in party primaries and general elections may result in the election of popular candidates and also potentially level the playing field where one party dominates others in the electoral space.

6.4 CONCLUSION

The results of "Meet the Candidates" offer a somewhat more promising outlook for the role of information in shaping voter behavior than other studies in this volume. We find that voters are more likely to vote for those candidates about whom they receive good news, and more likely to turnout to vote after receiving good news about the incumbent. We do not find a significant effect of good news on voting for the incumbent, but the magnitude of the treatment coefficient is very similar to that of the sample of viable candidates. We find no effect of bad news on voter behavior. While we do not find an effect of good news on vote choice in the alternative treatment arm in which debates were publicly screened, we find that voters switched to the debate winner in the primary elections and from the ruling to the opposition party in the general elections. How and why do our findings differ from the other studies, and the meta-analysis, which finds no overall effect of good or bad information on voting behavior? In what ways are our findings similar to others in this volume and beyond? Why is it that we find an effect of good news but no effect of bad news?

While we cannot answer these questions definitively, we discuss some possible explanations. First, the type of information with which we provided voters was somewhat different than that of the other studies in that it did not include an external assessment of past incumbent performance. Our measure of good news was not so much about past performance in office – as is the case for the other studies – as degree of alignment on policy positions, demonstration of understanding policy issues, ability to express oneself, and perceived competence. Of course, we can by no means definitively say whether this type of information is more or less relevant to voters than, say, the percentage of plenary sessions or committee meetings an incumbent attends, since we did not directly compare the two. We can say, however, that voters responded to the type of information we provided by voting for those candidates – incumbents and others – about whom they received good news.

Additionally, respondents heard directly from candidates themselves. It is possible that hearing information from candidates made the content of the information more salient, or perceived as more credible. One can imagine even in the context of a developed democracy, voters may place greater import on campaign promises than prior legislative performance (or even experience in politics), especially when it is difficult to assess how legislative performance relates to candidates' ability to benefit their constituents. A voter may not care how often her representative shows up to parliament as long as her policy preferences are realized. It is possible that campaign promises delivered by candidates and aimed at constituents are easier to comprehend than statistics about legislative performance, and therefore may require relatively less cognitive effort to incorporate into voters' decision-making processes.

Second, we sought to provide information about all candidates, rather than the incumbent alone. The goal of providing information across the studies in this volume is the same – to help voters make a more informed decision about whom to vote for – but the information we provided encouraged comparison between candidates rather than purely retrospective assessment of incumbent performance in office. Again, we cannot say whether the treatment effects we detect suggest voters are more likely to assess candidates prospectively rather than retrospectively, but this possibility is something to consider.

That said, our results are not entirely inconsistent with others. For example, with respect to vote choice, our results are similar to those found by Buntaine et al. (Chapter 7), and to some extent, to Arias et al. (Chapter 5) in Mexico. In other words, as predicted, we find that good news has a positive effect on vote choice. It is worth recalling that both Buntaine et al. (Chapter 7) and our study took place in Uganda, and both on the sample of the population that had access to mobile phones. Also similar to most other studies, we do not find an effect of bad news on voter behavior. Why? Evidence from Mexico suggests that providing information about corruption depressed turnout,[29] and we might have imagined turnout and vote share similarly effected in our study. However, the "bad" news in our information treatment was nowhere near as negative as reports of corruption – voters may have been disappointed

---

[29] Chong et al. (2015).

by candidates' performance or policy positions, but it is unlikely they would have been disgusted in the way they might have if provided with corruption reports.

Next we assess implementation issues, and particularly politician responses, in comparative perspective. By far the most problematic interference by politicians in this round of studies took place in the study by Sircar and Chauchard (Chapter 10), which was forced to stop in the middle of implementation due to interference and threats by affiliates of a single politician. As Sircar and Chauchard (Chapter 10) note, they do not believe there would have been widespread opposition to the information treatment, as there appeared to have been in Humphreys and Weinstein (2013), but also show that even one incident of interference can derail a field experiment. One of the measures they suggest for future researchers is to "Better informing candidates mentioned in the treatments, including small candidates from small parties (Sircar and Chauchard, Chapter 10, pp. 309)."

Our own experience underscores this suggestion. We held meetings with the leadership of almost all of political parties participating, and reached out to all candidates, informing them of the study and the treatment. In the end, a handful chose not to participate, but there is no evidence that they interfered with the information dissemination in any way. Perhaps more illustratively, we encountered one case where a candidate was, for part of the primary campaign period, prevented by his own party from standing, and the video for that constituency therefore did not include him. He was informed of the project however, and when he was later allowed to join the race – but too late to join the video – instructed his agents not to interfere with the screenings. Another candidate reported "bumping into" a public screening and leaving immediately, explaining, "I couldn't stay as it might be misinterpreted."[30]

Surely, part of the lack of politician interference in our study was also due to the particular nature of our treatment, which allowed candidates to shape the content of the information. We recognize that there is important information for voters that candidates would be unwilling to provide about themselves, for example, poor attendance of legislative sessions, misallocation of funds, or even criminal behavior. As our findings suggest, in contexts with very low levels of information about candidates

---

[30] Qualitative surveys with MPs conducted after the election.

to begin with, it is also worth considering informational interventions that share candidates' policy preferences and other professional information that may be relevant to a voter's decision but also information the candidate willingly provides.

Finally, we turn briefly to a discussion of the second arm of our study – namely, holding public screenings of "Meet the Candidates" videos. Here we find that watching these videos increases political knowledge and affects vote choice, but also that the way in which candidate videos affect vote choice varies across intra- and inter-party electoral contests. How generalizable are these results? First, it is worth noting that a similar study in Sierra Leone also found an increase in political knowledge and an increase in vote share for the best performers in candidate debates.[31] Thus, we now have two data points from two different political contexts suggesting that candidate debates can shape voters' knowledge and behavior. More studies on the effects of debates are currently underway. However, much less is known about how voter behavior and response to information varies in intra- versus inter-party contests. Further, we specifically sought out competitive constituencies as we expected that the effect of information would be largest in these areas, for reasons outlined previously. Whether or not information can sway voters away from an incumbent party in the party stronghold is unclear.

It is also somewhat surprising that treatment effects for good news on vote choice and turnout were stronger for the individual than the public treatment arm. If anything, we had expected, in line with some other studies in this volume, that the treatment would be stronger with public screenings, where respondents have the opportunity to discuss with others and potentially coordinate on vote choice.

There are at least two possible explanations why we observed stronger effects of good news in the private arm. First, it could be that respondents paid greater attention to the video when watching it alone. In a public setting, they could have been sitting far from the screen, showed up late, or chatted with friends during part of the video. In the private screening, they watched the entirety of the video on a tablet with earphones. There were few opportunities for distractions.

Another possibility is that the quality of the news received relative to one's priors becomes "muddied" in the presence of other viewers for whom watching the same video resulted in different assessments of

---

[31] Bidwell, Casey, and Glennerster (n.d.).

candidates. The same video, as we have shown, can provide good news about a candidate to some people and bad news about that same candidate to others. Perhaps discussing candidate quality and performance with a diverse crowd results in further updating by respondents, thus making their final assessment after watching the video and discussing with friends noisier than if they had watched the video alone and only had their own assessment to consider.

Together, the common arm of the study, where voters watch candidate videos privately, and the alternative arm, where voters watch videos in a public setting, suggest that these videos, and perhaps candidate debates more generally, are a promising means of sharing information with voters. The evidence suggests both that voters learn about candidates through these videos and that this learning affects their vote choice. We take these findings as evidence that Ugandan voters care about more than just handouts around election time or the ethnicity of the candidate, two factors often emphasized in studies of African voters.

7

Budgets, SMS Texts, and Votes in Uganda

Mark T. Buntaine, Sarah S. Bush, Ryan Jablonski,
Daniel L. Nielson, and Paula M. Pickering

This study examined the effects of information about government performance on voters' choices in the February 2016 district and March 2016 sub-county elections in Uganda. It was designed to understand how new information promotes accountability when it is disseminated in ways that are difficult for politicians to control and counter. As discussed previously in this volume, although political information has been theorized to enable voters to make choices in line with their interests, the empirical evidence in support of this proposition is decidedly mixed. The mixed evidence is particularly apparent in electoral autocracies, where incumbent politicians can use a variety of tactics to counter the information that might threaten their hold on power, including repression and alternative messaging.[1]

Contemporary Uganda was a fitting research site to deepen our understanding of the effects of political information since it is a low-income electoral authoritarian regime rated as "not free" by Freedom House at the time of our study.[2] Uganda holds elections for president, parliament, and local offices. However, the government of President Yoweri Museveni and his long-ruling party, the National Resistance Movement (NRM), have taken many steps to hamper opposition candidates and civil society. The elections held in 2016 – including the general elections for president and national parliament in February and the local elections that began six days later – were no exception. The repressive steps taken by the government around these contests included changes to electoral and

---

[1] Humphreys and Weinstein (2013), Driscoll and Hidalgo (2014), Ferree et al. (2015).
[2] Freedom House, "Uganda Country Report 2016." Available at https://freedomhouse .org/report/freedom-world/2016/Uganda. See also Tripp (2010).

civil society laws, restrictions on media freedom, and voter intimidation. As such, at the time of our study, Uganda fit the definition of an electoral authoritarian regime provided by Steven Levitsky and Lucan Way: a country in which "formal democratic institutions exist... [but] incumbents' abuse of the state places them in a significant advantage vis-à-vis their opponents."[3]

The common treatment arm in our study focused on elections for Uganda's 111 district councils, which represent the highest tier of local government in the country and are equivalent to states or provinces elsewhere. Due to a decentralization process that began in 1992, Uganda has several tiers of local government, including districts (known locally as LC Vs), subcounties (LC IIIs), and villages (LC Is).[4] Each district council is led by a chairperson, who is elected by the district's voters and leads the council, and a group of councilors, who are elected by the constituencies of the smaller subcounties that comprise each district. Elections are held for the different levels of local councils sequentially over several weeks.

District elections provided a worthwhile case for studying information and voting since they are substantively important for Ugandans. Local governments are responsible for between 15 and 18 percent of the Ugandan national budget, and district-level politicians play an important role in the management of local public works, health, and education.[5]

The primary responsibilities of LC V chairs and councilors include writing district legislation and development plans, supervising district staff, overseeing public programs and contracts, and executing budgets. In other words, the issues at stake in district elections matter for Ugandan voters' well-beings. In addition, voter decisions at the local level are likely less tied to the partisan and identity politics that shape national elections in Uganda.[6] As such, district elections may be considered a more-likely case to identify significant effects of new information on Ugandan voters' choices than national elections, such as for parliament or president, which have been explored by some previous studies that did not find positive evidence of information affecting voters' choices.[7] Finally, district

---

[3] Levitsky and Way (2010): 5.

[4] Grossman and Lewis (2014).

[5] Although appointed local bureaucrats are also key actors in local public service provision, LC V politicians must approve of bureaucrats' budgets and work plans (Raffler, 2017, Green, 2015). A large proportion of subjects in our baseline survey indicated that good budget management was important in deciding how to vote for district officials.

[6] For example, Carlson (2015).

[7] Humphreys and Weinstein (2013).

elections are sufficiently localized as to make it difficult for local politicians to muzzle information sent privately by mobile phones, which facilitated our study.

We cooperated with Twaweza, a Ugandan nongovernmental organization (NGO) that seeks to convey politically relevant information to citizens for both local elections and more generally. The overall goal of Twaweza throughout the region is to improve governance by making more information available to the public and by improving the ability of citizens to engage in public life. By focusing on local as opposed to national elections, it was possible to conduct an information campaign without threatening the ruling NRM party in a way that might be dangerous for our partner (or participants), since it leveraged outreach efforts that they were already conducting.

Though local elections in Uganda are dominated by NRM candidates, they legally permit—and in practice involve—multiparty competition. In our sample (described in detail below), more than four-fifths of the elections for district chairs and councilors were contested and involved candidates from multiple parties.[8] However, NRM candidates won most district elections, prevailing in 77 percent of the elections for chair and doing so with an average margin of victory of 28 percent. But the electoral dominance of NRM should not be mistaken for widespread satisfaction with its local officials. Indeed, citizens tend to level broad criticisms at local governments, expressing especially serious concerns about the effective provision of public services and the prevalence of corruption within district councils.[9] For example, 54 percent of Ugandans reported that they thought their district councils were doing a bad job at maintaining local roads in the 2015 Afrobarometer survey.[10]

Yet there is ample evidence that Ugandan citizens do not have much credible and specific information about politicians' performance at the district level, beyond the general sense that district and sub-county governments are corrupt and ineffective.[11] As such, informational interventions around the district elections might enable voters to hold politicians accountable at the polls for specific problems.

Several factors contribute to the public's lack of understanding of local government. One factor is the restricted media environment, where

---

[8] In addition, the elections involved three candidates for district chair on average.
[9] Stohl, Stohl, and Leonardi (2008).
[10] Afrobarometer (2015): questions 67a and 67b.
[11] Natamba et al. (2010).

opposition speech in radio and newspaper is restricted.[12] Another factor is that it is difficult for the public to gain specific and accurate information about the performance of district and subcounty councils. When it comes to budget performance, information is available in principle to citizens, but it is not accessible to them. Although the Ugandan Auditor General provides annual information on budget discrepancies involving local governments, this information is presented in highly technical language and lengthy reports that are not easily digested or accessed by the public. In this way, the electoral authoritarian government in Uganda is obfuscating local government performance partly via information overload, in which voluminous data is released to the public in thousand-page reports containing difficult-to-decipher tables and graphs surrounded by jargon-filled text. Although politicians and the media might help make the information accessible to citizens, the reports are not debated in the national parliament or covered by the media.

In some ways, it is easier for citizens to observe local government performance in the area of public services, since they can monitor the quality of road, health clinics, water facilities, and schools that they encounter in their daily lives. However, understanding how those public services compare to other locations is more difficult for citizens. The lack of information on local governments' relative performance on public services thus also limits the potential for accountability.

We thus tested whether two kinds of information treatments impact whether voters turned out and who they chose at the polls. First, we sent a series of messages about irregularities in district budgets to voters in LC V elections (common arm). By making information that is otherwise obfuscated in technical volumes accessible to voters and in a way that is almost impossible for local politicians to counter, we hypothesized that we could enable voters to hold district politicians accountable for their oversight of district budgets. Second, prior to beginning our experiment, we asked each subject to tell us the kind of public service that was most important for them when voting: roads, primary schools, water access, or health facilities. One reason why previous scorecard experiments around elections may not have had much of an effect on vote choice was that the information presented to voters was not salient. In a second experimental arm (alternative arm), we allowed voters to opt into the kind of public

---

[12] Tripp (2010): 96–101.

service that they receive information about, seeking to use new communication technologies to personalize information and boost its salience.

7.1 RESEARCH DESIGN

Our study involved a field experiment in which information about district budget management and local public services were transmitted to citizens via SMS text messages as part of two separate experimental arms. We also varied the density of the treatment for the arm with budget information to explore whether the attempt to create common knowledge about politicians' performance led to different treatment effects. The overall flow of the experiment for the budget information arm is provided in Figure 7.1.

7.1.1 Common Arm and Mode of Dissemination

We expected that information about local officials' management of budgets, which directly affects the quality of everyday services that citizens use, would be salient to citizens. That expectation was supported in our baseline survey, where more than 80 percent of subjects indicated that good budget management was important in deciding how to vote for district officials. We compiled information on the management of district budgets from the most recent annual public reports of audits conducted on local government authorities and released by the Office of the Auditor General.[13] This little-known audit tracks and validates whether the district council followed procurement rules, completed projects as specified, and accounted for expenditures.[14] Our treatment sought to make the detailed audit information compiled by this internationally respected government office more accessible and meaningful.[15] We did so by simplifying it, adding brief comparative information, and delivering it directly to voters via SMS text messages in the week before district elections. Specifically, we provided information about how the percentage of unaccounted-for funds in a citizen's district

---

[13] Office of the Auditor General (2014).

[14] Note that the Office of the Auditor General is organizationally independent, even though its findings often lack follow-up by authorities and are limited in their public impacts in various other ways (World Bank, 2010).

[15] In our study, 51 percent of respondents trusted information from the Auditor General, whereas 19 percent did not trust it and 31 percent did not know.

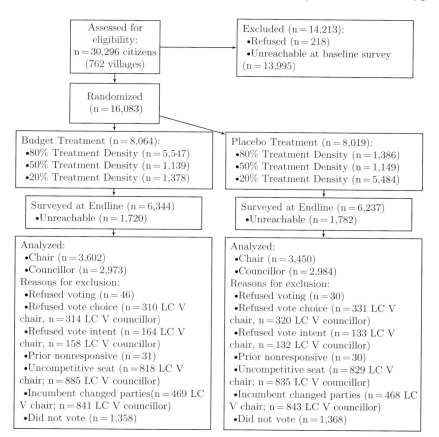

FIGURE 7.1 Uganda 2: CONSORT diagram of research design. Though we originally sampled 870 villages, we were refused permission to work in 30 villages and rain made 78 villages inaccessible during subject recruitment.

compared with unaccounted-for funds elsewhere.[16] We also included several concrete examples of unaccounted-for funds when the district ranked below the median on budget management as part of treatment. When district budgets had fewer irregularities than the median district, messages contained examples of public projects that were managed well.

[16] This percentage was obtained by calculating the total sum of "funds not accounted for," "procurement issues," and "payroll anomalies." This amount was divided by each district council's budget to compare financial irregularities across districts. For further examples of treatment and placebo messages, see the online appendix.

For example, an individual living in a village where the district council performed much worse than expected could have received the following sequence of SMS messages:

- "The Auditor General conducts yearly audits to record instances where LC Vs could not satisfactorily explain how its money has been spent."
- "Unexplained spending is often an indicator of mismanagement, fraud or poor quality services."
- "Your LC V did much worse than most other LC Vs in the recent audit."
- "In your LC V, the auditor found issues with 120 million UGX from its budget of 19 billion UGX. This is much worse than in other districts."
- "This means that 6.3 out of 1000 UGX in your LC V budget had issues. In most LC Vs, 2.2 out of 1000 UGX had issues. Your LC V did much worse than average."
- "One reason your LC V did much worse than average is that payments of 98 million UGX were made without proper documentation."
- "Another reason your LC V did much worse than average is that a bid for borehole construction included unexplained expenditures."

To isolate the effect of new information on voting behavior from the increased salience that subjects might have attached to an issue when prompted to think about it, we also sent messages to subjects in a placebo group. These individuals received public service messages about good personal financial management without any information about the performance of their politicians at managing budgets.[17] We sent a total of twelve SMS text messages about budgets to treatment group respondents and five to placebo group respondents. We sent a total of 207,940 messages across all subjects and treatment arms. Messages were translated into one of Uganda's eleven primary languages, depending upon subjects' preferences.[18]

Despite our best efforts to convey information from the Auditor General in a clear and salient way, it is possible that respondents did not

---

[17] Our treatment and placebo subjects were well balanced across pretreatment covariates. See online appendix.

[18] Messages were sent using a bulk SMS delivery service developed by SMSOne, a communications technology company based in Kampala.

interpret the "good news" or "bad news" in the treatment messages as we intended, or that some ambiguity about which elected officials were responsible for budget management remained. As such, our estimates below might be viewed in some ways as "intention to treat" analyses. However, we do have a measure of whether the treatment messages were received, as our endline survey asked respondents whether they recalled seeing our messages in the alternative arm. This measure provides an indicator of treatment compliance. We refer to respondents who responded that they did receive our messages in the analyses below as "verified recipients."[19]

Our main outcome variable (M1) captured whether the subject voted for the incumbent or a politician from the incumbent's party if the incumbent did not run for reelection.[20] Our secondary outcome variable was turnout (M3), which captured whether a subject reported voting in the district elections. In other words, as was done in other Metaketa studies, we use self-reported data from the endline survey for these measures. As we discussed below, we use official returns only for validation, since we did not treat at a high-enough density to have any reasonable ability to detect treatment effects in official returns. We made this choice for ethical and practical reasons, to which we return below.

7.1.2 Site Selection and Sampling

Our study took place in villages in twenty-seven districts that comprised a nationally representative sample assembled by Twaweza. Specifically, we used the sampling frame associated with Twaweza's Uwezo education initiative. This enabled Twaweza to expand its capacity to disseminate its original information about primary education outcomes to citizens through SMS messages. Figure 7.2 shows the sampled villages within the district boundaries of Uganda.

Within the sampled villages, local enumerators recruited 31,310 individuals to participate using both collective gatherings and door-to-door

---

[19] 80 percent of respondents remembered receiving our messages, and only 12 percent said it was "difficult" or "very difficult" to distinguish them from other messages. Given that Ugandans receive many other SMS messages around elections, this finding is important since it might have been difficult to distinguish our nonpartisan factual messages from those that have a more political purpose.

[20] This is a variation of the measurement of our outcome variable registered in our study's pre-analysis plan. In that pre-analysis plan, we used the pretreatment outcome to directly rescale the post-treatment outcome measure.

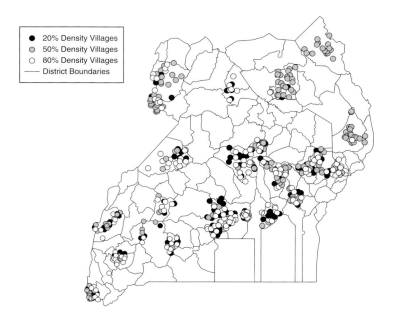

FIGURE 7.2 Uganda 2: Map of sampled villages in Uganda

visits between November 29 and December 19, 2015. To participate, individuals had to be Ugandan citizens, aged eighteen years or older, own a mobile phone, and be willing to sign a consent form. Of those interested volunteers, 16,083 individuals completed the baseline telephone survey between January 11 and 16, 2016.[21] We refer to this group as our experimental sample. We conducted a postelection endline survey between February 25 and 29, 2016. To encourage subjects in the experimental sample to participate in the entire study, we provided UGX 1,000 (roughly USD $0.30) of telephone airtime for each completed survey. Our efforts to encourage completion were fairly successful, as 12,581 individuals completed the endline survey.[22]

[21] The vast majority of the attrition from intake to study recruitment was due to call center staff being unable to successfully contact subjects who provided their contact information in the field, for example because the provided number was invalid or because no one answered the phone after three attempts. 218 individuals were contacted and refused to participate in the survey and were dropped from the effective sample prior to randomization.

[22] Tests outlined in the meta-analysis pre-analysis plan (MPAP) found no evidence of differential rates of attrition between the treatment and placebo conditions.

To compare the experimental sample to the general population, we looked to the 2015 Afrobarometer survey.[23] In terms of age, our sample was representative; similar to the Afrobarometer, our median age was thirty-three. Our subjects also had similar levels of NRM party affiliation (76 percent) to those in the Afrobarometer (78 percent). However, our use of mobile technology as a screen for eligibility skewed the sample in favor of men and better-educated respondents. For example, 67 percent of our respondents were men, which is consistent with the gender imbalance in mobile phone ownership in Africa.[24] Moreover, whereas only 4 percent of our subjects had no formal schooling and 42 percent had completed some or all of secondary school, these figures were 14 percent and 30 percent, respectively, in data from the Afrobarometer.

We note that the composition of our experimental sample could have important implications for the interpretation of our findings. It is possible that our relatively well-educated subjects were more politically sophisticated than average Ugandans, making it more difficult to change their minds and suggesting that any average treatment effects identified by our study could be lower bounds on the true population effects. At the same time, better-educated subjects might have found it easier to understand and process the new information, implying that treatment effects might not be significant with a more representative national sample. However, since we are interested in the effects of information disseminated by personal communication technologies, our sample is likely to be representative of the population that can be reached with information in this way.

7.1.3 Randomization Strategy

Within sampled villages, we used complete randomization at the level of individual, with each subject receiving either treatment or placebo messages. We randomly assigned the treatment density between villages, which contained an average of 240 households. Within each district, sampled villages were partitioned by participation levels. In villages with fewer than fifteen subjects, half were assigned to the treatment and half to the placebo. For villages with at least fifteen subjects, we created paired blocks based on an ordered sorting of the number of participating subjects. Within each pair, we assigned one village to have 80 percent of subjects treated and the other village to have 20 percent of subjects treated. In villages where 80 percent of subjects were treated, the SMS

[23] Afrobarometer (2015).
[24] Pew Research Center (2015).

message was modified to inform voters that "we are going to be sending you and many of your neighbors information.[25] We did this in order to encourage coordination among recipients in high density villages.[26] This operationalization of "common information," which still used a private mode of information dissemination, sought to avoid allowing politicians the opportunity to spin budget management information and potentially undermine the main treatment. However, this choice means that we did not disseminate information in a way most likely to achieve "common knowledge" – i.e., in a public setting.[27] Nonetheless, because information can spread quickly in village networks, we expected that seeding some villages with a density of information would be more likely to achieve common knowledge on average.[28]

For ethical reasons, our design was purposefully crafted to have a very low probability of affecting aggregate election results. We sent messages to approximately 20 subjects per village on average, when villages typically have more than 1,000 eligible voters. Moreover, our sample only included 750 villages out of approximately 25,000 nationally. We sampled villages at a low enough density that even affecting aggregate results in local elections was highly improbable.

7.1.4 Estimation

Estimation of vote choice in relation to priors generally conforms with the meta-analysis pre-analysis plan (MPAP), with a few key exceptions documented in our individual pre-analysis plan. To begin, we asked for voters' priors about candidate quality along a scale – "much worse," "a little worse," "better," or "much better" – since we did not believe that voters would have well-formed priors about the percentages of unaccounted-for funds. To determine the actual candidate quality Q_j, we divided the range of budget discrepancies at the district level into quartiles to roughly match the categories in the priors we elicited from subjects. We considered it ill-advised to map the strength of news onto a continuous, normalized scale as in the MPAP. Thus, we use a modified approach, maintaining the MPAP notation to the extent possible.

---

[25] As discussed, messages differed slightly between high and low density villages. The null effects in Figure 7.5 suggest this difference was not meaningful for the treatment response.

[26] See Chwe (1998).

[27] Arias (2018). Thanks also to Etienne Poliquin.

[28] Larson and Lewis (2017).

To estimate the effect of good news, we collapse all types of good news into a single treatment indicator T_i^+, which equals one when the subject i is treated and is part of the subset of people receiving good news, L^+. Thus, the good news subgroup included subjects who thought budget discrepancies were "much worse" than average at baseline and were eligible to receive information that they were only "a little worse." We use the same procedure for bad news.

Our primary estimating equation is given by Equation 7.1, which is notated for the good news subgroup. In it $y_{ij,t=1}$ indicates whether the subject voted for the incumbent party for the political office j, $y_{ij,t=0}$, indicates whether the subject intended to vote for the incumbent party, β is a vector of estimated coefficients, Z_i is a matrix of prespecified, pretreatment covariates, v_j is a village fixed effect, and ϵ_{jh} is the error term clustered by politician (j) and district (h). As specified in our pre-analysis plan, we test our hypotheses on vote choice with and without pretreatment covariates: perception of living conditions (M18); gender (M13); level of education (M17); age (M14); trust in information provided by our NGO partner (M24); perceptions that powerful people will learn about vote choice (M26); perceptions about the fairness of elections (M27); whether the subject voted for the incumbent in 2011 (M21); and intent to vote. Unlike the MPAP estimating equation, we do not interact our treatment indicator with the covariates in the main specification.

$$y_{ij,t=1} = \alpha + \tau_1 T_{ik}^+ + \varphi y_{ij,t=0} + \beta Z_i + v_j + \epsilon_{jh} \qquad (7.1)$$

All p-values for our main treatment effects (τ) are computed by randomization inference on the relevant parameter of the estimating equation. We assume a sharp null hypothesis and create a sampling distribution of the estimate under 10,000 iterations of our exact randomization process described above. Our reported standard errors are the standard deviation of the resulting sampling distribution and our p-values derive from comparing the estimated parameter value to the sampling distribution under the sharp null assumption.[29] Thus, our characterizations of uncertainty derive from our design, rather than the particular model that we use to estimate treatment effects.

---

[29] We recognize that these estimate the standard deviation of the distribution of estimated effects only insofar as this is the same as the standard deviation under the null.

7.2 RESULTS ON THE COMMON ARM (BUDGET INFORMATION)

7.2.1 Vote Choice

First, we evaluate the effect of good and bad news on vote choice. Figure 7.3 presents our main estimates of the treatment effects, derived from Equation 7.1. As preregistered and because our hypotheses are directional, we use one-tailed tests. Since we consider chair and

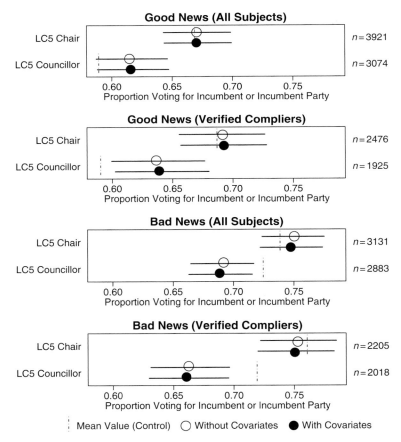

FIGURE 7.3 Uganda 2: Treatment effect of budget disclosures on vote choice. Bars show 90 percent confidence intervals, equivalent to one-tailed test at $\alpha = 0.05$. Figure displays treatment effects scaled to the control group mean, rather than levels directly.

councillor elections to provide two distinct tests of the hypothesis about vote choice, we apply the Benjamini–Hochberg correction for false discovery in the tests described in the main text.

We do not find that good news affected votes for district chairs, with subjects no more likely to vote for incumbents in the treatment condition compared to the placebo condition. However, good news caused an increase of 3 percentage points in reported votes for district councillor incumbents ($p = 0.12$), with a swing of 6 percentage points among verified recipients of the treatment messages ($p = 0.02$). The pattern repeats in the bad news condition. The bad news treatment caused no significant change in votes for district chairs, but bad news resulted in a 3 percentage point decrease in votes for district councilors compared to placebo ($p = 0.03$) and a 6 percentage point drop among verified recipients ($p = 0.01$).

We take a number of steps to rule out systematic bias in terms of reported vote choice. For example, in the online appendix, we compare reported vote choice to official results. The patterns are consistent with accurate reporting. In other words, the rate of self-reported voting for the incumbent party is correlated with the official election results, although people in low vote areas may have been somewhat more likely to report voting for the incumbent party than the official data suggest. This difference may be due to the fact that we over-sampled NRM voters relative to the population, and NRM was the incumbent party in all but six chair elections.

Moreover, in Online Appendix Table D2, we explore whether our results hold for the subset of respondents who accurately recalled the basin color in their polling station. We find that none of the effect sizes change in magnitude in ways that are inconsistent with the main model, but that the effect of good news on vote choice is no longer inconsistent with random chance, whereas the effect of bad news remains statistically significant at approximately $p = 0.03$ in specifications both with and without covariates.

Another potential reason for misreporting is social desirability. If respondents believed that our enumerators or NGO partner desired a particular response, then they might have overreported voting for well-performing incumbents and underreported voting for badly performing incumbents. This dynamic is difficult to rule out, though we view it as unlikely. To evaluate it, we examined whether treatment effects were stronger among respondents who stated that they trusted Twaweza in the baseline survey. If respondents are trying to tell Twaweza what they think it wants to hear, then we would expect stronger effects among this subgroup. As Table 7.3 shows, we do not.

A different form of reporting bias would arise if respondents over-reported voting for the official winner out of a desire to fit in or to avoid punishment from the government. However, under the reasonable assumption that the treatment and placebo groups were equally likely to overreport for the winner, this dynamic would not have affected the treatment estimates. To evaluate whether such overreporting exists, we compared self-reported votes for the incumbent in surveys conducted prior to the release of the official results and surveys conducted after the release. As the Online Appendix's Figure D2 shows, we see no systematic difference.

A final concern is that our results are idiosyncratic to particular parties, or biased in favor of one party. For instance, if only NRM voters were eligible for good news and only opposition voters were eligible for bad news, one might be skeptical about the generalizability of the effects. In Online Appendix Tables D8 and D9, we show the distribution of good and bad news by party. The results illustrate that these effects were not driven by voters or incumbents of a particular party, suggesting the broad applicability of using information technologies to decrease the information advantage of incumbents in electoral autocracies, particularly when it comes to functions of government that are directly attributable to politicians like overseeing public budgets.

7.2.2 Turnout

Contrary to our expectations, subjects treated with good news were not more likely to turn out for the district elections. Similarly, subjects treated with bad news were not less likely to turn out. Figure 7.4 presents these results. In addition, and as Table 7.2 shows, we do not find evidence to support our expectation that the effect of information on turnout would be moderated by voters' alignments with the incumbent party.

As previously acknowledged, an important concern is that respondents might not have accurately reported turnout. As shown in Figure 7.4, more than three-quarters of the experimental sample reported voting. This figure is quite a bit higher than the officially reported turnout in the districts sampled in this study, which averages around 45 percent. This difference could be due to people in our study saying that they voted when they did not because voting was seen as socially desirable. It could also be due to the ways that our experimental sample was not representative of Uganda as a whole (as discussed above), and

TABLE 7.1 *Uganda 2: Conditional effect of budget treatment on turnout based on alignment with incumbents*

	DV: Turnout for LC V Election	
	Good News (1)	Bad News (2)
Budget Treatment	−0.018	0.021
	(0.026)	(0.028)
LC V Chair Alignment	0.019	0.0004
	(0.019)	(0.017)
LC V Councillor Alignment	0.024	0.021
	(0.027)	(0.018)
Budget Treatment × LC V Chair Alignment	−0.002	−0.014
	(0.020)	(0.021)
Budget Treatment × LC V Councillor Alignment	0.025	−0.024
	(0.033)	(0.026)
Polling station fixed effects	Yes	Yes
Covariates	Yes	Yes
Observations	5,200	5,404
Adjusted R^2	0.091	0.143

Note: SEs clustered by politician; one-tailed tests; contested elections only.

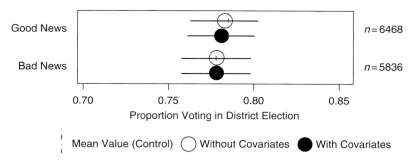

FIGURE 7.4 Uganda 2: The unconditional treatment effect of good and bad news on voter turnout. Bars show 90 percent confidence intervals, equivalent to one-tailed test at $\alpha = 0.05$.

may have over-represented voters by relying on mobile technology or recruiting subjects who were interested in local governments and public services.

As noted above, to assess whether respondents accurately reported turnout, we asked respondents to name the color of the water basin at their polling stations. Most respondents were able to answer this question

TABLE 7.2 *Uganda 2: Effects of budget treatment on evaluations of candidate integrity and effort*

	Dependent Variable:							
	Chair Integrity				Councillor Effort			
	Good News		Bad News		Good News		Bad News	
	(1)	(2)	(3)	(4)	(5)	(6)	(7)	(8)
Budget	−0.012	−0.010	−0.002	−0.005	−0.014	−0.015	0.025	0.021
Treatment	(0.029)	(0.032)	(0.025)	(0.023)	(0.022)	(0.022)	(0.017)	(0.018)
Covariates	No	Yes	No	Yes	No	Yes	No	Yes
Village FEs	Yes	Yes	Yes	Yes	Yes	Yes	Yes	Yes
Observations	6,175	6,039	5,557	5,433	5,897	5,776	5,507	5,386
Adjusted R²	0.162	0.176	0.180	0.189	0.148	0.154	0.170	0.176

Note: SEs clustered by politician; one-tailed tests; contested elections only.

in internally consistent ways, which suggests that they were accurately reporting their turnout. 91 percent of respondents who voted recalled a basin or basin color in their polling station, and among those individuals, 77 percent were able to name the color in an internally consistent manner.[30] This provides greater confidence in the self-reported turnout data.

7.2.3 Attitudes about Politicians' Integrity and Effort

Although we consider vote choice and turnout to be our primary outcomes, we prespecified that we would test for the effect of the treatment on a number of other outcomes, which are also reflected in the Chapter 11 meta-analysis. In particular, we hypothesized that the treatment would change voters' evaluations of candidate integrity and effort. Specifically, we asked voters how surprised they would be to hear about corruption involving the district chair and whether their district councillor put in more or less effort to get things done compared to other councilors in the district. We do not find evidence that the treatment affected voters' attitudes about their district officials, as shown in Table 7.2. The null result of the integrity measure for the chair tracks the null result for the main vote choice outcome reported above.

7.2.4 Heterogeneous Treatment Effects

We preregistered a number of conditions under which we expected information to be more likely to shape vote choice, as reflected also in the Chapter 11 meta-analysis. Similar to the meta-analysis, we fail to find evidence that the following factors lead to larger effects for the information treatment (see Table 7.3):

1. Gap between voters' prior beliefs about candidates and the information provided;
2. Less certainty of priors about politician performance;
3. Copartisanship;
4. Importance of information about budget management for voting;
5. Weaker partisan attachment;
6. Trust in the Auditor General (source of information treatment);
7. Trust in Twaweza (implementing partner sending information); and
8. Lower expectation of clientelist benefits.

---

[30] For more details on this analysis, see the online appendix.

TABLE 7.3 Uganda 2: Moderation of information effects on vote choice

	Dependent variable:			
Moderation Effect	Chair (Good)	Councillor (Good)	Chair (Bad)	Councillor (Bad)
Baseline Category: Accurate Prior				
Actual One Better	−0.016 (0.044)	0.018 (0.053)		0.066* (0.034)
Actual Two Better	−0.113** (0.044)	0.063 (0.060)		0.027 (0.041)
Actual Three Better	−0.022 (0.045)	0.062 (0.059)		0.047 (0.052)
Actual Four Better	−0.086* (0.045)	0.043 (0.077)		−0.160 (0.173)
Baseline Category: Accurate Prior				
Actual One Worse			0.011 (0.029)	0.066* (0.034)
Actual Two Worse			0.059* (0.033)	0.027 (0.041)
Actual Three Worse			0.023 (0.059)	0.047 (0.052)
Actual Four Worse			0.034 (0.164)	−0.160 (0.173)
Baseline Category: Very Certain Priors				
Certain Priors	0.011 (0.022)	0.047 (0.039)	−0.060* (0.034)	−0.008 (0.042)
Not Certain Priors	0.068 (0.056)	0.019 (0.049)	−0.067 (0.050)	−0.024 (0.044)
Very Uncertain Priors	0.008 (0.116)	0.009 (0.125)	−0.028 (0.060)	−0.044 (0.089)
Missing Certainty Priors	0.181 (0.169)	−0.171 (0.294)	−0.354 (0.234)	0.747** (0.339)
Baseline Category: Budget Management Not Important				
Budget Not Very Important	−0.085 (0.087)	−0.060 (0.086)	−0.134 (0.085)	0.013 (0.069)
Budget Somewhat Important	−0.064 (0.085)	−0.055 (0.086)	−0.058 (0.074)	−0.030 (0.070)
Budget Very Important	−0.048 (0.089)	−0.010 (0.078)	−0.078 (0.062)	0.017 (0.055)
Missing Budget Importance	−0.514** (0.260)	−0.401 (0.315)	−0.068 (0.303)	−0.408 (0.257)

Baseline Category: Not Aligned LC V Chair			
Aligned LC V Chair	−0.014 (0.040)	−0.031 (0.049)	
Missing LC V Chair Alignment	−0.020 (0.061)	−0.054 (0.068)	
Baseline Category: Not Aligned LC V Councillor			
Aligned LC V Councillor		0.044 (0.040)	0.009 (0.041)
Missing LC V Councillor Alignment		−0.083 (0.077)	−0.045 (0.079)
Baseline Category: Not Same Tribe LC V Councillor			
Same Tribe LC V Councillor		0.016 (0.035)	0.009 (0.041)
Missing Same Tribe LC V Councillor		—	0.914*** (0.168)
Baseline Category: Do Not Trust Auditor General			
Don't Know Trust Auditor General	0.059** (0.027)	0.100* (0.056)	0.028 (0.045)
Trust A Little Auditor General	0.062 (0.042)	0.104** (0.052)	0.012 (0.044)
Trust A Lot Auditor General	0.070 (0.048)	0.092 (0.068)	−0.015 (0.046)
Missing Trust Auditor General	0.011 (0.198)	0.126 (0.225)	0.032 (0.083)
Baseline Category: Do Not Trust Twaweza			
Don't Know Trust Twaweza	−0.135* (0.074)	−0.136 (0.093)	−0.147* (0.085)
Trust A Little Twaweza	−0.083 (0.082)	−0.178* (0.098)	−0.107 (0.073)
Trust A Lot Twaweza	−0.091 (0.085)	−0.165* (0.094)	−0.152* (0.077)
Missing Trust Twaweza	0.715*** (0.176)	−0.158 (0.279)	−0.137 (0.148)

(continued)

TABLE 7.3 (continued)

	Dependent variable:			
Moderation Effect	Chair (Good)	Councillor (Good)	Chair (Bad)	Councillor (Bad)
Baseline Category: Vote Buying Very Likely				
Vote Buying Somewhat Likely	0.003 (0.060)	0.053 (0.064)	0.001 (0.044)	−0.009 (0.062)
Vote Buying Somewhat Unlikely	−0.065 (0.072)	−0.001 (0.079)	0.036 (0.066)	0.043 (0.062)
Vote Buying Very Unlikely	−0.012 (0.045)	0.029 (0.061)	−0.014 (0.051)	0.086 (0.060)
Vote Buying Don't Know	0.008 (0.057)	0.078 (0.082)	0.060* (0.035)	0.066 (0.073)
Missing Vote Buyings	−0.088 (0.143)	−0.271 (0.192)	0.024 (0.297)	−0.032 (0.191)
Baseline Category: Very Strong Party Attachment				
Party Attachment Strong (6)	0.019 (0.049)	−0.117** (0.049)	0.063 (0.048)	−0.009 (0.043)
Party Attachment (5)	0.012 (0.037)	−0.042 (0.052)	0.016 (0.044)	0.013 (0.045)
Party Attachment (4)	0.047 (0.048)	−0.108 (0.085)	−0.054 (0.058)	0.022 (0.058)
Party Attachment (3)	0.031 (0.092)	−0.077 (0.102)	0.132 (0.096)	−0.091 (0.091)
Party Attachment (2)	−0.191 (0.174)	−0.057 (0.152)	−0.010 (0.108)	−0.097 (0.093)
Party Attachment Very Little (1)	−0.048 (0.092)	−0.128 (0.116)	0.038 (0.063)	0.034 (0.057)
Party Attachment Not Applicable	−0.020 (0.040)	−0.095* (0.057)	−0.036 (0.071)	−0.062 (0.046)
Missing Party Attachment	0.026 (0.039)	0.086 (0.096)	0.157** (0.072)	0.062 (0.097)
Observations	3,921	3,074	3,131	2,883
Adjusted R^2	0.214	0.330	0.347	0.399

$* p < 0.1; ** p < 0.05; *** p < 0.01$

7.2.5 Treatment Density

Finally, we varied treatment density to allow us to evaluate whether common knowledge reinforced information effects. This choice also allowed us to assess the extent to which voters shared messages with their neighbors. If subjects shared messages with each other, then we expected control subjects in high-density villages to be more likely to vote according to treatment information than control subjects in low-density villages.[31]

To estimate the conditional effect of the good news and bad news treatments based on treatment density, we use the modified estimating equation given by Equation 7.2, which includes a density treatment indicator D_j assigned at the village level. Because the density treatment is assigned at the level of the village, we use a paired-village fixed effect b_j to mirror our assignment strategy.[32] For analysis of the density treatment, we only consider the subset of subjects from villages with at least fifteen subjects:

$$y_{ij,t=1} = \alpha + \tau_1 T_{ik}^+ + \tau_2 D_j + \tau_3 T_{ik}^+ D_j + \varphi y_{ij,t=0} + \boldsymbol{\beta Z_i} + b_j + \epsilon_{jh} \quad (7.2)$$

Figure 7.5 displays results for the density condition among treated subjects. They are null, suggesting that treating 80 percent of subjects at a polling station did not significantly alter votes for district chairs or councilors compared to the control condition with 20 percent of subjects treated. Although we varied the density of treatment among subjects, the individuals who volunteered to participate were often a relatively small subset of the local population, so even 80 percent treated may have failed to induce common knowledge. Moreover, given the generally unfree political environment, Ugandans reported taking great care when discussing politics, so they may have failed to pass along the budget information regardless of the local size of the experimental sample.

Table 7.4 displays the results of the village-level density treatment combined with the subject-level budget information treatment. This specification combines the two binary treatment conditions into the four possibilities with the comparison condition being subjects receiving placebo information in a low-density treatment village. The coefficients

---

[31] Based on a post-experiment survey of 103 randomly selected participants in the treatment group, 43 percent of respondents who recall receiving the message shared it with another person.

[32] We mistakenly omitted the notation for paired block fixed effects in our study's pre-analysis plan.

Mark T. Buntaine et al.

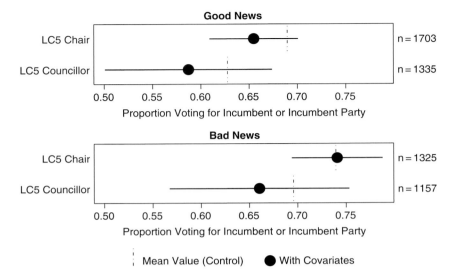

FIGURE 7.5 Uganda 2: The treatment effect of higher treatment density among treated subjects. Bars show 90 percent confidence intervals, equivalent to one-tailed test at $\alpha = 0.05$.

show the effects of the combination of the density and information treatments on vote choice when compared to the placebo and low-density conditions at the baseline. We include fixed effects for the paired villages.

We find that control subjects in high-density villages were less likely to vote for incumbent chairs in the bad news condition, possibly indicating that they were affected by spillover. Note that the effect of the budget treatment remains significant in both the low-density ($p = 0.03$) and high-density ($p = 0.04$) subgroups. In the bad news condition, all treated subjects for both elections were less likely to vote for the incumbent than their counterpart placebo subjects in the low-density villages. This finding provides some potential insight into the divergent results between chair and councillor elections in the bad news subgroup, since negative spillover to control subjects may be muting the treatment effect when using village fixed-effects in our estimating equation. However, the average effect of the high-density treatment across treated and control subjects is not inconsistent with random chance for either chair ($p = 0.18$) or councillor ($p = 0.13$) elections. In contrast, the good news subgroup does not yield any results on the budget treatment or treatment density that are inconsistent with the null hypotheses.

TABLE 7.4 *Uganda 2: Effect of budget treatment density on vote choice for district (LC V) incumbents. Data subset excludes constituencies that were redistricted or where incumbents switched parties.*

	DV: Vote Choice for the Incumbent			
	LC V Chair	LC V Councillor	LC V Chair	LC V Councillor
	Good News		Bad News	
	(1)	(2)	(3)	(4)
Control, High Density (RI)	0.004	−0.028	−0.034	−0.044
	(0.029)	(0.050)	(0.029)	(0.055)
Budget Treatment, Low Density (RI)	0.023	0.0012	−0.027	−0.054**
	(0.026)	(0.030)	(0.025)	(0.028)
Budget Treatment, High Density (RI)	−0.010	−0.020	−0.028*	−0.091**
	(0.021)	(0.045)	(0.021)	(0.050)
Control, High Density	0.004	−0.028	−0.034*	−0.044
	(0.032)	(0.036)	(0.024)	(0.040)
Budget Treatment, Low Density	0.023	0.012	−0.027*	−0.054**
	(0.043)	(0.028)	(0.019)	(0.025)
Budget Treatment, High Density	−0.010	−0.020	−0.028*	−0.091***
	(0.022)	(0.031)	(0.019)	(0.034)
LC V Chair Intent	0.081***		0.023	
	(0.025)		(0.029)	
LC V Councillor Intent		0.049**		0.006
		(0.016)		(0.021)
Paired village fixed effects	Yes	Yes	Yes	Yes
Covariates	Yes	Yes	Yes	Yes
Observations	3,281	2,585	2,633	2,391
Adjusted R²	0.211	0.244	0.286	0.264

Note: SEs clustered by politician; one-tailed tests; contested elections only. $^*p < 0.10$; $^{**}p < 0.05$; $^{***}p < 0.01$

7.3 ALTERNATIVE ARM: PUBLIC SERVICES INFORMATION

The management of budgets is an important issue in Uganda, as explained above. Yet it remains a fairly distant issue for many voters. In contrast, the quality of public services is directly relevant to their well-being and often the most tangible interaction that they have with their local governments.

At the local level, politics often turns on the ability of politicians to deliver public services effectively, especially given the decentralized political system in Uganda. Although recent legislation has made local governments more dependent on the central government both administratively and financially, local governments by law have substantial responsibility to provide a variety of essential public services as part of the country's "radical and early decentralization."[33] Furthermore, surveys indicate that Ugandan citizens hold subcounty officials partly responsible for providing public services such as water access – although not as much as the central government.[34] In light of the potential salience of local public services to voter behavior, our study also included an alternative arm that involved collecting and disseminating novel information about the relative quality of local public services within districts.

More generally, we designed our alternative arm to address issues of low salience that may have led to null results in related scorecard experiments on "legislative performance" both previously and as part of this volume.[35] We do so in a way that takes advantage of the ability of new mass communication tools to personalize information flows by allowing the voters in our sample to select into hearing about the public service they care most about in the context of local elections. This process ensures both that the information is tailored and salient, largely ruling out a failure of treatment design in driving choices.

7.3.1   Research Design

Concurrent to the subject recruitment activities described above, we conducted independent audits of three public services that are managed locally and that pre-study focus groups indicated would be especially salient to voters in local elections in Uganda. Specifically, we audited access to improved water sources, road conditions, and the conditions of local health facilities. For the water audit, we recorded the round-trip walking time to the nearest improved water source from a central location at each village, tallied the wait time to access the water source, and recorded whether fees were charged for access. For the road audits,

---

[33]   Ndegwa and Levy (2004), Green (2015).

[34]   Given that many Ugandans blame the central government first for poor public services, we note that it may be difficult to identify a significant effect of new information on vote choice within the context of local elections.

[35]   Humphreys and Weinstein (2013)

we used the tablet application "RoadLab" to record the roughness encountered by vehicles that attempted to traverse a local county road leading to the closest major trading center. For the health audit, we recorded the cleanliness and availability of medicines in district and subcounty-operated health clinics.

We also utilized the results of the Twaweza Uwezo education audits. Twaweza independently tested school children for scholastic achievement outside of the school environment to avoid manipulation. Thus, we have independent data on a total of four public services that are likely to be especially important to voters. All of these services fall under the combined responsibilities of district and subcounty governments.

For each audit, we created an index of "service quality" and then normalized that value within the district. The process produced our treatment, which indicates whether services in the village where each of the subjects live were "much better," "better," "a little worse," or "much worse" than other villages in the same district. These categories were similar to those used in the budget information treatment. The intent of the public-services treatment was to provide subjects with some perspective about whether politicians were doing a good job or bad job as compared to other areas of the district, which was likely to make the information more meaningful than if it simply contained the raw observations already available to voters. Normalizing the treatment information within districts also helped us avoid problems in analysis that would arise from differences in district-level attributes that are relevant for public-service provision, such as MP effectiveness and revenue transferred from national government ministries.

Prior to assigning the treatment, we used the same baseline survey described above to determine the public service (i.e., roads, water, education, and health) that each individual considered most important when deciding how to vote in local elections. During this survey, we asked each person what kind of information he or she would like to hear about prior to the upcoming district and subcounty elections. With our partner Twaweza, we deployed the same informational treatments related to public services prior to both the district and subcounty elections, which were held in February and March 2016 approximately three weeks apart.[36] In other words, subjects in our experimental sample received messages

---

[36] To the extent that we did not have data on the public service that an individual indicated was most important to them when voting, we gave them information on the public service they indicated was the second most important. For the small subset of subjects

prior to the district elections about both budget irregularities and public services, and they received further messages prior to the subcounty elections about only public services. For district elections, the public-services treatment was assigned independently of the budget treatment. For subcounty elections, only the public service treatment was deployed since the management of district budgets was not relevant for LC III voting.

We randomly assigned half of the subjects within each village to receive information about public services. The subjects not assigned to receive the public services information treatment instead received placebo messages about the importance of the four public services that we audited. These placebo messages contained information about the welfare of Ugandans without any information about the actual state of public services as revealed in the audits that we conducted. The placebo messages were sent to ensure that any treatment effects that we detected were not just a reflection of priming effects.

7.3.2 Finding for the "Salient Public Service" Treatment

The overall result for the alternative arm is that we fail to reject the null hypothesis for any of the prespecified hypotheses on main effects, including vote choice, turnout, and evaluations of candidate quality. This finding is consistent across all offices and all elections, as reported in Table 7.5. These results contrast with the findings for the budget arm and are very surprising given the design of this arm's intention to enhance the salience and personalization of information.

7.4 DISCUSSION

7.4.1 Common Arm

Our findings for the common arm present a mixed picture with respect to the effect of budget information on accountability. On the one hand, and as expected, we found that bad news about budget discrepancies led to fewer votes for incumbent district councilors. Similarly, we found that good news about budget discrepancies led to increased votes for the incumbent district councilors. These findings support the overall Metaketa project's theoretical framework about the ways that

---

for whom we did not have audit data for either the first or second choice, we provided information randomly on a public service for which we do have data.

TABLE 7.5 *Uganda 2: Main effects of salient public services treatment. Data subset excludes constituencies that were redistricted or where incumbents switched parties. Table shows estimated treatment effect (clustered standard errors, one-tailed p-value). None of the treatment effects displayed have adjustments for covariates or standard errors via randomization inference.*

Office	Treatment Effect (Good News)	Treatment Effect (Bad News)
DV: Vote Choice for the Incumbent		
LC V Chair	−0.014	0.017
	(0.014)	(0.020)
	[0.85]	[0.81]
LC V Councillor	−0.046	−0.007
	(0.017)	(0.020)
	[0.99]	[0.37]
LC III Chair	−0.001	0.005
	(0.017)	(0.019)
	[0.51]	[0.60]
LC III Councillor	0.007	0.009
	(0.023)	(0.029)
	[0.37]	[0.63]
DV: Turnout		
LC V Election	0.010	0.029
	(0.010)	(0.014)
	[0.16]	[0.98]
LC III Election	0.003	0.012
	(0.013)	(0.018)
	[0.40]	[0.75]
DV: Evaluation of Chair Integrity		
LC V Chair	0.031	−0.027
	(0.027)	(0.034)
	[0.13]	[0.21]
LC III Chair	0.019	0.027
	(0.035)	(0.038)
	[0.30]	[0.76]
DV: Evaluation of Councillor Effort		
LC V Councillor	0.019	−0.018
	(0.027)	(0.032)
	[0.25]	[0.29]
LC III Councillor	0.006	−0.039
	(0.027)	(0.031)
	[0.41]	[0.10]

Note: SEs clustered by politician; one-tailed tests; contested elections only.

new information can improve political accountability. They also support one of the intuitions motivating our specific intervention: salient political information disseminated via mobile phones can significantly affect voter behavior even in the context of an electoral authoritarian regime (Uganda) where previous studies have not always found the expected effects of information. Because the treatment messages were disseminated privately immediately prior to elections, politicians did not have opportunities to directly counter the information in the messages.

On the other hand, our study also had some unexpected null findings that are in keeping with the Metaketa project's overall null results. In our view, most important among the unexpected null findings from our study was the limited influence of the informational treatments on voter behavior for district chairs. Whether presented with good news or bad news, our treatments did not affect voter behavior. If we had found more consistent results for chairs and councilors, then we could draw conclusions with more confidence about the significant role of information in shaping voter choice and the applicability of using mobile technology to make information available to voters in settings like Uganda.

Developing and testing a full explanation for our mixed findings is beyond the scope of this chapter. As with any study involving null results, the findings may be the result of specific design choices or the research context – or they may reflect a "true null," i.e., in our case, they could suggest that information does not affect accountability at all on average.[37] In our chapter's earlier section on research design, we reflected on some of the factors (e.g., the design of the treatment and the sample) that may have led to a null result in terms of the chairs. Below, we suggest several broader explanations related to the overall research context that could account for the null result for chairs but not councilors.

First, it is possible that voters do not understand which level of government or which officials are most responsible for budget management, especially when responsibilities are shared. Governance is complex and citizens in many settings, including Uganda, do not have a good understanding of who is ultimately responsible for delivering public goods and services.[38] In general, voters are less able to sanction incumbents when lines of responsibility for outcomes are not clear, as we suspect may be the case in post-decentralization Uganda.[39] There is evidence that

---

[37] Bush et al. (2016): 1731.
[38] Hobolt and Tilley (2014), Hobolt, Tilley, and Wittrock (2015), Grossman and Michelitch (2018).
[39] Tavits (2007).

information about responsibility for governance conditions how citizens react to government performance.[40] It is possible that the voters in our sample underestimated the responsibility of chairs and overestimated the responsibility of councilors in managing district budgets. Adding a civic education component to the intervention, similar to the civics message used in Benin,[41] might have been a useful design modification.

Second, it is possible that higher-level elections take place within a more saturated information environment. Indeed, NGO audits of district level officials in 26 districts scored chairs as better than councilors, on average, in contacting their electorates.[42] Furthermore, races for district chair positions are more professional affairs that involve a larger amount of campaigning through both traditional and social media outlets. In contrast, races for district councillor positions involve lower budgets and less traditional campaigning in ways that might get information into the hands of voters. Consequently, voters for councillor may have been more receptive to new information about budget performance. This logic not only might explain the difference between our findings about chairs and councilors but might also offer insight as to why we uncovered some significant effects of new information in a local election in Uganda but studies focusing on national elections have not found similar evidence.[43]

Third, and relatedly, it is possible that higher-level elections are decided further in advance and as a consequence of a longer-term accumulation of knowledge and information. In higher-level elections, voters who have already made up their minds might engage in more motivated reasoning about their choices when presented with new information towards the end of a political contest. As such, future studies could investigate not only the content and mode of information treatments, but also the timing. Most existing studies of this type have been carried out using survey experiments rather than deploying treatments in field settings, yet timing is a crucial variable facing organizations who seek to empower voters.[44]

The limited influence of informational treatments on voter behavior for district chairs was not our only unexpected finding. Although we hypothesized that new information would drive turnout, we did not find positive evidence for that in any case. This null effect was surprising

---

[40] Gottlieb (2016).
[41] Adida et al., Chapter 4.
[42] Bainomugisha (2015).
[43] E.g., Humphreys and Weinstein (2013).
[44] Chong and Druckman (2010).

because most canonical models of voter behavior highlight how informed voters should be more likely to turn out because they face less uncertainty in their choices.[45] Being able to identify whether a politician is managing a budget better or worse than expected should provide more information about politician type and thus increase the utility that voters derive from participating, since conditional on participating they will be able to make a choice more effectively. We also hypothesized that the effect would depend on the alignment of the voter: a voter that received good news about an incumbent with which they align would be more likely to turn out, whereas a voter that received good news about that same incumbent when they align with the challenger would be less likely to turn out.

One reason why we may not have detected the effect that we expected is that voters were deciding on how to participate in multiple races during the district elections. It is possible that moving voters' estimates of candidate quality on only the lowest office being contested was not strong enough in the context of an election where the contest for district chair brings people to the polls. Indeed, in many other contexts up-ballot races drive turnout, and it may be these up-ballot races that are most immune to having information treatment change voter choices.

7.4.2   Alternative Arm

The results on the alternative arm of our study are perhaps the most surprising. That voters did not respond to information that they personally stated was most important to them when they go to the polls suggests a number of possibilities. First, this result may simply echo the results of the meta-analysis (Chapter 11) that suggest information is not likely to be used by voters on average. For public services in particular, it is possible that it was difficult to attribute the information in our treatments to any particular politician or that voters did not link public services to local politicians in the way that we hypothesized they would. If we were to run this experiment again, we would have collected more information from voters about who they held responsible for performance as it related to budget management and the provision of public services.

Nonetheless, by personalizing the information, we had expected to overcome problems with interpretation that arise from informational treatment with limited salience. Because we are confident that we provided salient information, this result leaves us more skeptical about the

---

45 Lassen (2015).

ability of information to affect vote choice. More broadly, it speaks to the limits of elections as informational signals to officials about the delivery of public services. It may be the case that other kinds of information signals, such as petitions for direct responses to failings in the delivery of public services, will be more effective at promoting effective and accountable governance. Indeed, Cleary (2007) finds that voters' contact with officials and participation between electoral cycles is more important than the threat of electoral sanctioning for shaping the delivery of public goods. The broader implications of these findings for governance is that the communication technologies that we used to deploy the treatments might be better suited to promoting ongoing and two-way flows of information between voters and officials.[46]

7.4.3 Conclusion

Information presented to voters privately, as in our study, is likely to be considerably harder for politicians to uncover and counter. Information presented publicly – such as through the media, fliers, community meetings or public screenings – is subject to constant spin or downright falsification by politicians. Other projects in the Metaketa Initiative reveal these dynamics; in Mexico, politicians actively developed strategies to falsify information;[47] in India, politicians shut down the unwanted information completely;[48] and in the Uganda 1 study, politicians attempted to distort how citizens process information.[49] Of course, politicians may still use other strategies to counter mobile messages, such as overloading voters with irrelevant or fake information via SMS or even shutting down mobile networks. For an NGO-initiated information campaign about accountability to impact citizens' actions, organizations must take steps to protect their own credibility and the credibility of the information they provide in the eyes of the citizens against potential efforts to discredit them. However, on average it should be harder for politicians to prevent voters from accessing the information they need to vote when information is conveyed through text blasting and quickly evolving encryption techniques.

[46] Grossman and Michelitch (2018).
[47] Arias et al. (Chapter 5).
[48] Sircar and Chauchard (Chapter 10).
[49] Platas and Raffler (Chapter 6).

Text messages have other advantages as well. Targeted information can be deployed via SMS messages during the final days of elections or in response to critical events. New technologies allow NGOs to get information to voters during debates, after campaign appearances, and following candidate statements, which may help voters make choices according to their interests. One constraint of SMS delivery is the challenge of condensing credible, new, and salient information into a short message that fits within the 160-character limit. Future research will be needed to offer guidance on how and when a similar organization might effectively disseminate information with mobile technology. We suspect the form of the most effective messages could be highly contextual.

Widespread and growing mobile phone ownership, nationwide network coverage, and the relatively low cost of SMS technology makes our approach to providing information feasible for many NGOs and citizens' groups to use to spread the information they are already gathering. Our study has demonstrated the feasibility and potential impact of using cheap, SMS text messaging to empower citizens with credible information to use to hold accountable local elected officials for the quality of their budget management. This approach holds some promise even in an electoral authoritarian regime. Yet, that the same information on budget management did not affect citizens' votes for incumbent district chairs, who are on paper those officials most accountable, strongly suggests that development experts and donors need to give more attention to educating citizens in decentralized systems about political responsibilities for budget management and different public services.

8

Performance Information and Voting Behavior in Burkina Faso's Municipal Elections: Separating the Effects of Information Content and Information Delivery

Malte Lierl and Marcus Holmlund

In this chapter, we report a field experiment in Burkina Faso, which aimed to isolate the effects of information content from other channels of influence through which an information intervention could affect voting behavior. The experiment was carried out in thirty-eight rural municipalities, prior to the 2016 municipal elections. These thirty-eight municipalities had been controlled by the same party for the past two electoral cycles, since the first nationwide municipal elections in 2006. In our experiment, we presented 741 randomly selected study participants with detailed information about their previous municipal government's performance along nine indicators of municipal service quality in the areas of health, primary education, water access, and civil services. These indicators reflected national standards for municipal services, i.e., widely accepted service delivery targets. Simultaneously, a control group of 752 study participants was presented merely with information about the indicators of municipal government performance, without any information on the actual performance of their previous municipal government. Thus, our experiment varied study participants' access to information about municipal government performance, but it held their knowledge of service delivery targets, as well as the method of information delivery, constant across the treatment and control conditions.

Our research design allows us to make several unique contributions to the Metaketa Initiative on information and accountability. First, we complement the other studies in the volume by focusing specifically on the effects of information content, in isolation from other aspects of information interventions. Often, political information interventions do much more than just provide voters with information. For example, they prime or educate voters about specific aspects of incumbent performance,[1] convey normative messages about what constitutes good performance,[2] suggest metrics by which voters can compare different candidates,[3] and involve media consumption or direct social interaction with the individuals who provide the information.[4] In most information interventions, these treatments are bundled together. We aim to disentangle the effects of information content from how the information is delivered, by comparing two experimental conditions that only differed with respect to the availability of factual information about the performance of the incumbent government, holding the method of information delivery constant. In this respect, our experiment resembles Gottlieb (2016), which varies whether or not a civic education course included information about local government performance. It differs from Gottlieb (2016) in that our study is carried out at the individual level, focusing on individual-level heterogeneity in the effect of information access on pro-incumbent voting.

A second unique aspect of this study is its results-blind approach to data analysis. In addition to elaborating our original motivations for the study in a pre-analysis plan, we carried out a first pass of data analysis on a blinded data set. In the blinded data set, any variables that would have allowed us to infer the experimental condition an individual was assigned to were obscured. However, the total number of treated and control units and the unconditional distribution of outcome variables and covariates was preserved, by randomly permuting the treatment assignment variable in the data set. Blind analysis prevents researchers' knowledge of experimental results from consciously or unconsciously influencing their choice of analytical methods, which can cause them to over-interpret results. While blind analysis has become a standard procedure in experimental physics,[5] its adoption in the social sciences is limited.[6] Compared to a pre-analysis plan (a practice that has been criticized for being error-prone and leading to "robotic" data analysis[7]), a results-blind analysis allows for methodological choices in data processing and data analysis that are informed by the actual data and by descriptive inferences about

[1] Banerjee et al. (2011), Lieberman, Posner, and Tsai (2014).
[2] Chong et al. (2015).
[3] Humphreys and Weinstein (2013).
[4] Reinikka and Svensson (2005), Aker, Collier, and Vicente (2017).
[5] Klein and Roodman (2005).
[6] See Humphreys and Weinstein (2013) for a notable exception.
[7] Gelman (2013).

the study population. We documented this blinded analysis by submitting a full, results-blind report to the Evidence in Governance and Politics (EGAP) network experimental design registry,[8] and then replicating this results-blind analysis with the final, non-blind dataset.[9]

This chapter draws on material from Lierl and Holmlund (2017), which reports our study in greater detail.

8.1 LOCAL GOVERNMENT PERFORMANCE AND ELECTORAL ACCOUNTABILITY IN BURKINA FASO

Burkina Faso is a low-income, land-locked, multiethnic West African country of about 18 million inhabitants, covering three climate zones, from the hot, arid Sahel zone in the north, to a tropical savanna climate in the country's south. Like many other low-income countries, Burkina Faso adopted a decentralized system of local governance in the early 2000s. Since the first nationwide municipal elections in 2006, elected municipal governments have played an important role in the provision of local-level public services in Burkina Faso. Municipal governments provide inputs and services that are critical for the ability of primary schools and health centers to serve the population. Additionally, they are responsible for the maintenance of water points, which are one of the most important local infrastructures in Burkina Faso's hot and semi-arid climate. Municipal governments also provide important administrative services, such as the civil registry.

Even though municipalities have only partial responsibility for the performance of certain public services, such as schools and health centers, their failure to provide the necessary inputs and authorizations to service providers is more often than not a limiting constraint on the overall quality of these services. For example, municipal governments in Burkina Faso are responsible for procuring gas bottles for health clinics, which are needed to operate their refrigerators. If municipalities fail to replenish the gas stock on time, vaccines and medications will spoil and health centers are unable to treat their patients. Gas stockouts and similar service failures are widespread and can have devastating externalities for local health, education, and development outcomes. The

---

[8] http://egap.org/file/2154/download?token=Feoo2HOiBjiUTz5HUR6IxZJSu9epzo
RMNV18-IeSoGo

[9] http://egap.org/file/2388/download?token=hzbpFKTGCTjreLgFnttdrSQh9-8
jPWU6PcMl3ijLTDA

frequency of such failures is indicative of a fundamental problem in local government accountability: municipal administrators usually have few consequences to fear if they do not live up to their stated responsibilities.[10] This is suggestive of inherent limitations of electoral and bureaucratic accountability at the local level.

8.1.1   Local-Level Electoral Accountability

In the past, one of the major obstacles to electoral accountability was a lack of political competition. During the first two municipal elections in 2006 and 2012, the national party in power, the Congrès pour le développement et le progrès (CDP), won the vast majority of municipal council seats. In 2006, the CDP commanded 12,854 out of 17,786 municipal council seats. In 2012, it commanded 12,340 out of 18,552 council seats. Municipal councils elect the mayors, who in turn head the municipal governments. Mayors are elected without term limits. Municipal councils, in turn, are elected by the residents of the municipality in the municipal elections. On the municipal council, every village of the municipality is represented by two delegates. In communes with fewer than ten villages, the number of council delegates is adjusted upwards in proportion to population size, for a minimum council size of twenty. Municipal councilors are elected by party lists. This means that voters choose between parties, not between individual candidates. Ballots are unique by municipality, but not by village. Mayors are typically from the party that wins the most municipal council seats.

In 2014, the CDP's stronghold on power crumbled. On October 31, 2014, former president Blaise Compaoré was ousted in a popular uprising, reacting to his attempt to circumvent his term limit by manipulating the constitution. The CDP government was replaced by a military government that eventually agreed to form a joint military-civilian transition government under a civilian interim president, but with military control over key cabinet positions. The transition government adopted a roadmap towards democratic multiparty elections. However, the plan to hold elections was put in jeopardy by a violent coup d'état by the presidential guard in September 2015, an elite special force loyal to the former president Blaise Compaoré. The junta encountered massive resistance from civil society. After one week, the national army intervened

---

[10] Mahieu and Yilmaz (2010).

against the presidential guard, forcing the junta to surrender. The transitional government was reinstalled and peaceful national elections were held in November 2015, the results of which were recognized by all parties. Under the new national government, led by the majority-winning Mouvement pour le progrès (MPP), transitional municipal elections were announced for May 2016. The May 2016 municipal elections marked the end of Burkina Faso's political transition. Figure 8.1 visualizes this timeline.

In the wake of the popular uprising, the civil-military transition government dismissed all elected municipal governments in December 2014 and replaced them by nonpartisan, externally appointed special delegations. These special delegations were mandated to carry out the institutional responsibilities of the previous elected municipal councils and mayors, operating within the same legal and institutional frameworks. However, members of the special delegations were not eligible for candidacy in the 2016 municipal elections. The special delegations merely acted as interim caretakers, to fill the void created by the dismissal of the incumbent municipal governments. Thus, in the 2016 municipal elections, the previous incumbent parties competed with the newly strengthened opposition parties, giving most voters greater freedom of choice than ever before.

8.1.2 Distinctive Features of the Burkina Faso Case

The municipal elections in Burkina Faso differ in several respects from other cases in this volume. First, voters' access to information is particularly limited. Burkina Faso has one of the lowest levels of formal education in the world. While adult literacy rates have been increasing steadily in recent years, they remain extremely low at 38 percent.[11] In our study sample, only 15 percent of respondents report knowing how to read and only 14 percent report having completed any kind of formal education. The low levels of literacy and formal education create a context in which citizens' access to political information is naturally restricted. This means that written media have only marginal importance as sources of political information, whereas face-to-face communication and radio programs are potentially more important than in other contexts.

---

[11] Database query at http://data.worldbank.org, accessed February 19, 2017.

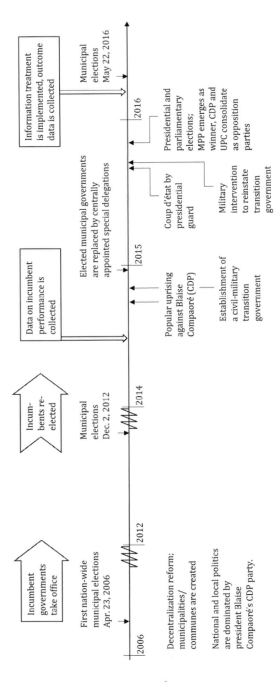

FIGURE 8.1 Burkina Faso: Timeline

Second, conducting a political information experiment in a multiethnic population with very limited access to formal education involved particular challenges. Perhaps the greatest challenge was to present information in a way that was accessible to illiterate citizens with different linguistic backgrounds. Additionally, the information had to be accompanied by an explanation of its relevance, in terms of its implications for the lives of ordinary citizens. Therefore, any form of information provision had to be accompanied by substantial additional explanation and interaction. This created a particular research design challenge: should the experiment evaluate the impact of a bundled treatment (an information campaign that includes elements of civic education, interpersonal interaction, etc.), or should it try to isolate the causal effect of the information content, while holding all other elements of the information intervention constant?

Several other studies in this volume pursue the first-mentioned approach, evaluating the aggregate electoral impact of a bundled information intervention, for example of the public video screening of candidate statements (Platas and Raffler, Chapter 6), or the distribution of print media by an advocacy nongovernmental organization (NGO) (Arias et al., Chapter 5). These approaches have the advantage of generating evidence about a realistic social intervention (especially if implemented in collaboration with local NGOs or other potential scale-up partners). In contrast to these other studies, we opted for the second approach, pursuing a highly controlled individual-level information experiment on a relatively small sample of voters. We hold all explanations and interactive procedures constant between the treatment and control groups and only vary the availability of actual information content about the performance of the incumbent municipal government. This approach has the advantage of isolating the effects of information access from other mechanisms, making causal attribution unambiguous and hence making it possible to test theoretical hypotheses at a higher level of abstraction. In part, this decision was due to the specific challenges, including ethical questions, of carrying out a large-scale voter information campaign in Burkina Faso's fragile political environment – a research context that substantially differed from the other studies in this volume. Additionally, however, our highly controlled experiment complements this book's research agenda by shedding light on the most crucial element of the causal chain that links information interventions to changes in electoral behavior: the information content itself.

There are several additional respects in which our experiment contrasts with the other studies in this volume. First, our information

treatment was targeted at the individual level and was therefore relatively limited in scope, covering merely 758 individuals across thirty-eight
municipalities. We had no reason to expect that local politicians would
react to the provision of information to voters, nor did we observe any
such reactions. In contrast to interventions with much broader coverage, such as Chauchard and Sircar (Chapter 10) and Arias et al.
(Chapter 5), there was no indication that "[p]oliticians mount[ed]
campaigns to respond to negative information" spread through our information treatment (Hypothesis H5 in the meta-analysis pre-analysis plan
(MPAP)), or that they reacted to positive information in any way.[12]
We also did not expect any measurable impact on aggregate election
outcomes. For this reason, we focus our analysis on individual voting
behavior.

Second, our study concerns the electoral accountability of political
parties in a closed-list proportional representation system, rather than of
individual politicians in single-member districts. In a closed-list system,
voters cannot hold individual candidates accountable, but have to choose
between party lists. Mayors are indirectly elected by municipal council majority, and there are no officially designated mayoral candidates
prior to the constitutive session of the newly elected municipal councils
(although, in case of the incumbent party, it is usually obvious to voters
that the incumbent mayor or her/his chosen successor will seek reelection by the council if the incumbent party wins the election). For these
reasons, information about individual list candidates is potentially less
relevant for voters than information about the overall performance of
the incumbent government.

Since information about municipal government performance is not
easily attributable to individual candidates, but rather to incumbent
parties as a whole, we do not analyze the impacts of performance
information on perceptions of candidate integrity and candidate effort
(Hypotheses H3 and H4 in the MPAP). These outcomes are politician-
specific and cannot easily be generalized to parties as a whole. Furthermore, political parties in Burkina Faso are cross-ethnic and do not usually
campaign on platforms that emphasize special interests of particular
ethnic groups. Therefore, it is not directly possible to identify whether
a party is "coethnic" or "non-coethnic" from a voter's perspective.
This limits our ability to evaluate Hypothesis H6 in the MPAP, that
"[i]nformation effects are more positive for voters that do not share
ethnic identities."

---

[12] See MPAP in the Appendix.

8.2 EXPERIMENTAL DESIGN AND DATA

8.2.1 Treatment and Control Conditions

Our experiment was designed to hold all aspects of the information intervention constant between the treatment and control conditions, except for the availability of actual information content. To achieve this, we provided study participants in both the treatment and control groups with identical and detailed explanations of a municipal governments' most essential inputs to local public services in the areas of primary education, health care, water, sanitation, and civil services, as well as their relevance for citizens' everyday lives. We also provided study participants with information about national standards for municipal service delivery in these areas. For most study participants, these benchmarks were new information. Additionally, we confronted study participants in the treatment and control groups with an identical set of survey questions to measure their prior beliefs about their municipal government's performance, their assessment of different electoral candidates, and their electoral participation. We therefore consider our control condition a "placebo" or "baseline" treatment that is equally applied to members of the treatment and control groups.

Relative to this control condition, our study evaluates the effect of individual-level access to factual information content regarding the performance study participants' previous (and temporarily suspended) incumbent municipal government. These previously elected incumbent governments were competing for reelection in the May 2016 municipal elections. Since the special delegations that temporarily replaced them between January 2015 and May 2016 were nonpartisan, technocratic, and barred from candidacy in the municipal elections, we consider the party that had won the previous municipal elections in 2012 to be the incumbent.

It is important to emphasize that the performance information we presented to study participants in the treatment group is unambiguously attributable to the previous incumbent municipal government, rather than to the performance of the interim special delegation. It is based on data we collected in 2014, prior to the popular uprising and prior to the dismissal of the elected municipal governments. Moreover, the incumbent parties in our study had been in power for an uninterrupted period of eight years. Given that elected municipal governments were only created in 2006, this means that an incumbent government's performance record cannot have been influenced by a predecessor government.

Assignment to the treatment and control conditions was block-randomized at the individual level with equal numbers of treatment and control units per village. To eliminate spillover effects within villages, the performance information in the treatment condition, as well as the information about performance benchmarks in both the treatment and control conditions, was provided to study participants in a one-on-one setting, through a flashcard presentation by our surveyors. Our outcomes of interest, including intended vote choice and propensity to turn out to vote, were measured immediately afterwards through a polling station simulation and a set of survey questions.

In what follows, we describe in greater detail the type of information study participants in the treatment and control conditions were given, as well as the procedure for delivering this information.

8.2.2 Information Content

Our information about the performance of the previous incumbent municipal governments is based on a municipal government performance survey we carried out in 2014. Based on the survey data, we calculated nine indicators of municipal service delivery performance in the areas of primary education, primary health care, water, sanitation, and administrative services:

1. The difference between primary school completion rates in the municipality and the national average;
2. The average delay in the provision of school supplies at the beginning of the school year;
3. The proportion of births taking place at a health facility;
4. The proportion of newborns having received the full set of recommended vaccines;
5. The proportion of primary healthcare facilities receiving a sufficient supply of natural gas each month (for refrigeration);
6. The proportion of residents with access to a functioning source of clean water, defined according to the national norm (a source located within a distance of 1,000 m or closer that is shared by no more than 300 people);
7. The proportion of primary schools with a functioning source of clean water;

8.	The proportion of primary schools with functioning latrines; and
9.	The proportion of newborns for whom a birth certificate was issued.

This combination of performance indicators was selected to satisfy seven criteria. Each individual indicator is (1) tied to activities within the legal and practical purview of municipal governments; (2) substantively significant for citizens' quality of life; (3) measurable in quantitative and objective terms; (4) based on information that is already available or can be collected at low cost; (5) comparable across municipalities and over time; (6) consistently relevant across Burkina Faso's socially and ecologically diverse regions; and (7) low-dimensional and understandable without technical training.

The selection and validation of the performance indicators was a year-long iterative process that involved close exchange with our government partner, the Territorial Collectivities Support Program (*Programme d'appui aux collectivités territoriales*, or PACT) of the Ministry of Territorial Administration and Decentralization (MATD), the review of primary documents, field visits of municipal administrations and service providers in the Sahel and Plateau Central regions, and consultations with approximately forty mayors as well as with technical and administrative staff at the municipality levels. Additional comments were received from the Ministry of Health, Ministry of Education, the Ministry of Water, several national NGOs, as well as the National Land Management Program (PNGT). The relevant statistical directorates were consulted at the national, regional, and district levels on the availability and quality of data, and site visits were carried out to understand the availability and quality of primary records at health facilities, health districts, school districts, and municipal administrations. The end result is a set of indicators for which clearly defined national performance standards exist and that are readily acknowledged by municipal officials to be within their scope of responsibility.

### 8.2.3	Information Delivery

Study participants in both conditions were provided with information about widely accepted benchmarks for municipal service quality. Study participants were informed that:

For the different responsibilities of municipal governments, for example with respect to primary education, health, water supply and sanitation and administrative services, there are certain national standards every municipal government should fulfill. But not all municipal governments perform equally well at attaining these standards. I am now going to show you some images that depict several important responsibilities of municipal governments. I will also explain to you why these responsibilities of municipal governments are important. At the end, I am going to ask you how well, in your opinion, the previous elected municipal government in your commune performed at fulfilling those responsibilities.

Subsequently, study participants received an interactive presentation of each of the nine performance indicators, using illustrated flashcards. These illustrations were produced by an experienced Burkinabé illustrator who had previously visualized information for illiterate populations. The illustrations were repeatedly pilot-tested on both illiterate and literate citizens and refined until they were fully and easily understood. The flashcards contained two contrasting images that illustrated the respective norm and its importance. The two images differed only with respect to the presence or absence of a municipal government input. For example, one image would show a child using a latrine on the school yard, whereas in the other image the latrine was lacking and the same child would defecate in the open in the same place of the school yard (Figure 8.2). Respondents were asked to identify the difference between the two pictures.

After being asked to explain the message of each flashcard to the surveyor, study participants were read a brief description of the importance of this particular aspect of municipal performance for citizens' lives. For example, in the case of school latrines, the following explanation was given:

Municipal governments have to ensure that all primary schools have a functioning latrine for each class. A functioning latrine provides a safe place for schoolchildren to urinate and defecate. Access to a functioning latrine is important, because otherwise the schoolchildren lack a safe place where they can keep good hygiene and preserve their dignity. If the children do not have access to functional latrines at school, this could increase the spread of epidemic diseases and discourage young girls from attending school. Certain diseases, such as diarrhea or cholera, can spread easily if children do not use proper sanitation.

In the case of functioning water points, it was explained that:

Municipal governments have to ensure that all people have access to a functioning source of potable water that is at most 1 km away and for no more than 300

FIGURE 8.2 Burkina Faso: Flashcard illustrations of municipal performance indicators. Top: Provision of school latrines. Bottom: Provision/maintenance of water points.

people. A borehole provides potable water from the ground. Access to potable water is important, because otherwise people will get sick. Also, if people do not have access to clean water close to their homes, they will spend a lot time fetching water, instead of using this time for income-generating activities or to send young girls to school.

Analogous descriptions were provided for each of the nine indicators, with the full process (flashcards, interactive questions, and explanations) taking approximately ten minutes. The original French scripts were repeatedly translated into six vernacular languages and back-translated into French, until we arrived at a version that was equally well understood in each of the six languages. While the English translation above appears slightly awkward and wordy, this is owed to the fact that it closely follows the version that worked best in Mooré and the other vernacular languages.

During the presentation of the flashcard illustrations, the surveyors recorded, without the respondents' knowledge, whether or not the respondent had correctly understood the meaning of the indicator just by

TABLE 8.1 *Burkina Faso: Intuitive comprehension of graphic illustrations of performance indicators (left) and correct recall of performance information (right)*

Indicator	Proportion of study participants	
	correctly interpreting illustrations without verbal explanation	correctly recalling performance information at first attempt
School Water Sources	0.74	0.61
School Latrines	0.84	0.63
School Supplies	0.53	0.59
CEP Admission	0.76	0.58
Functioning Water Points	0.9	0.58
CSPS Gas Stockouts	0.73	0.6
Infant Vaccination Rates	0.87	0.6
Assisted Deliveries	0.76	0.62
Birth Certificates	0.76	0.62
Observations	1493	741

comparing the two illustrations, prior to the explanation of the indicator. The data show that over 70 percent of respondents correctly understood the illustrations of at least eight of the nine performance indicators. The primary source of comprehension problems was the indicator concerning the average delay in the delivery of school supplies. This was arguably the most complex indicator (involving averages across schools) and also the most challenging indicator to illustrate (because delay is not the same as absence). It was understood by only 53 percent of respondents (Table 8.1).

Following the presentation of the nine indicators, surveyors recorded study participants' beliefs about the performance of their previous incumbent municipal government (before the regime change in October 2014) along these dimensions of service delivery. Study participants were asked about their beliefs in two ways: first, in terms of five broad descriptive categories, and second, in terms of their municipality's rank within their region (the total number of municipalities in the region was provided in the question prompt). Study participants were also asked about their certainty with respect to each of these assessments, and about their assessment of the level of effort of their previous elected mayor compared to that of most other mayors in the region. This concluded the "control" condition.

Experimental Variation: Information on Municipal Service Delivery Norms With and Without Performance Information

In addition to the presentation of the performance indicators, participants assigned to the treatment group received information about their previous incumbent municipal government's actual performance along these indicators. This information was again delivered through flash cards, which contained the municipality's name, written information (that was read aloud by the surveyor), as well as a simple bar chart illustrating the indicator value (Figure 8.3).

The information flashcards were accompanied by a brief explanation, read aloud by the surveyor:

Now, I would like to tell you about the availability of latrines at primary school in the municipality of [MUNICIPALITY] in 2013, under the previous elected municipal government that was controlled by the [INCUMBENT PARTY]. In this graphic, the LENGTH of the green bar indicates the proportion of schools

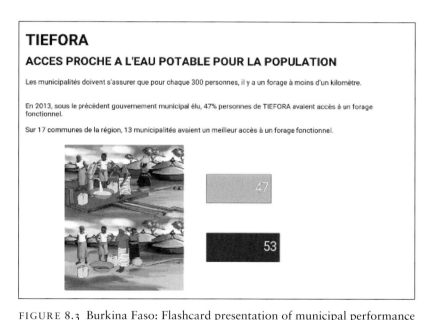

FIGURE 8.3 Burkina Faso: Flashcard presentation of municipal performance information (municipality of Tiefora). The text reads: "Municipalities must ensure that for every 300 people, there is a borehole available within 1 kilometer. In 2013, under the previous elected municipal government, 47 percent of persons in Tiefora had access to a functioning borehole. Out of 17 municipalities in the region, 13 municipalities had better access to functioning boreholes."

that have functional latrines for each class and the length of the red bar indicates the proportion of schools without functional latrines for each class. In 2013, [x] out of every 100 primary schools in [MUNICIPALITY] had access to functional latrines for each class. This means that in [1 − x] percent of the schools, the previous elected municipal government had not provided functional latrines for each class.

The flashcards and explanations were given for all nine indicators as well as for the overall performance rating of the municipality. This process took approximately ten minutes. Following the information treatment, surveyors and study participants were asked a series of questions to measure attentiveness to, interest in, and comprehension of the information treatment.

8.2.4   Understanding of the Information Content

We asked the interviewers administering the information treatment to subjectively evaluate each study participant's attention to the information treatment, on a scale from 1 (completely bored) to 10 (extremely attentive). On 844 data points (including five additional municipalities in which the incumbent party was no longer running for reelection), the average score was 6.79, with standard deviation 2.19, and 4 missing values. This is consistent with study participants' self-reported interest in the information treatment. After being informed about the information source, study participants were asked how credible they found the information. 83.5 percent of respondents described the information as "credible," another 13.2 percent as "probably credible." Moreover, study participants were asked about the pertinence of the information ("If you wanted to explain to your friends how well the previous elected municipal government performed at fulfilling its responsibilities, how useful would this information be?"). 83.8 percent claimed to find the information "very useful; more useful than any other information," another 12.9 percent described it as "useful, but other information would have been more useful." Finally, study participants were asked if, in all honesty, they found the information interesting or boring. 74.5 percent described the information treatment as "very interesting," another 22.4 percent as "somewhat interesting," and only 1.2 percent described it as "somewhat boring" or "very boring." Thus, at least according to study participants' self-reports, the information treatment was widely perceived as credible, pertinent and interesting.

Furthermore, despite the complexity of the performance information, a majority of study participants found it understandable. 51.7 percent found it "easy to understand," 27.5 percent found it "understandable, but complicated," while 20.8 percent found it "very difficult to understand." Study participants' initial understanding of the performance information was verified through comprehension checks that were conducted after information treatment. For example, study participants were asked: "How well did your previous elected municipal government perform with respect to the proportion of schools with a functioning water source, in comparison to other municipal governments in your region? Better, about the same, or worse?" Depending on their response, study participants were then told if their answer was correct or incorrect. If study participants answered incorrectly or indicated that they did not know the answer, they were given the correct answer to ensure that they subsequently internalized the information. Table 8.1 summarizes the initial comprehension checks. Depending on the indicator, between 59 and 63 percent of respondents were able to correctly recall the information.

8.2.5   Study Population

The population of interest for our study are voting-age adults, i.e., residents of a municipality who are eligible to vote (i.e., aged eighteen and above) and unlikely to suffer from mobility constraints that might impede them from voting or otherwise exercising their rights to participate in local governance processes. This was proxied by sampling individuals who were between eighteen and seventy years old in a census of adult village residents that was carried out in 2014. Table 8.2 describes this study population.

8.2.6   Study Sites and Sampling Procedure

We carried out our research in six of Burkina Faso's thirteen regions, covering each of the country's main cultural and geographic zones, from North to South: Sahel, Centre-Nord, Plateau Central, Centre-Est, Centre-Sud, and Cascades (Figure 8.4). Within these six regions, our study covered a total of thirty-nine municipalities that satisfied the following inclusion criteria: (1) they were part of a random sample of fifty-eight rural municipalities in which we carried out an experimental "citizen observer" intervention where randomly sampled voting-age citizens were

TABLE 8.2 *Burkina Faso: Demographics of the study population and tests of balance between treatment and control group*

	Treatment Mean	Control Mean	*p*-value Difference
Age (years)	39.43	39	0.55
Female	0.5604	0.57	0.71
Years of education	0.68	0.86	0.11
Literate	0.133	0.15	0.34
Voted in 2012	0.63087	0.63	0.97
Voted for incumbent in 2012	0.5456	0.54	0.83
Relative living conditions [−2, 2]	−0.0283	0.0037	0.53

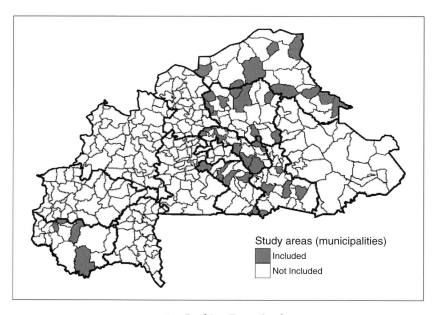

Study areas (municipalities)
Included
Not Included

FIGURE 8.4 Burkina Faso: Study areas

invited to observe meetings of the special delegations;[13] and (2) they were governed by the same incumbent party since the first municipal elections in 2006, i.e., the incumbent party was reelected in 2012. Out of the forty-four municipalities that satisfied these inclusion criteria, forty were

[13] Lierl and Holmlund (2016).

controlled by the CDP, three by the CFD-B, and one by the ADF/RDA. In thirty-one of these forty-four municipalities, the incumbent party was running again in the 2016 municipal elections. In eight additional municipalities, the incumbent party had dissolved or merged into a different party, and the incumbent mayor was running for reelection using that party's name.[14] In those cases, we treat the incumbent mayor's party in the 2016 elections as the incumbent party. In one of these cases, the incumbent CDP government was running unopposed under the MPP's name. We exclude this municipality from the study and limit our analysis to the thirty-eight municipalities in which the incumbent municipal government was seeking reelection in 2016.

Within these thirty-eight municipalities, our study was carried out in a total of 146 villages, sampled at random from within the villages in each municipality. In each of these villages, we sampled up to twelve individuals from a census of village residents aged 18–70 in 2014. Per village, half of the sampled individuals were assigned to the control condition and half to the treatment condition. The treatment assignment was blocked by treatment assignment in our cross-cutting experiment, in which randomly sampled individuals were invited to volunteer as "citizen observers" during a meeting of the municipal special delegation. Since treatment assignment in this cross-cutting experiment was randomized with equal assignment probabilities among the voting-age residents of a village, we can treat the treatment assignment in the cross-cutting experiment as ignorable and analyze the data as if our experimental treatment had been block-randomized at the village level. The selection of study sites and the treatment assignment are illustrated in Figure 8.5 below.

8.2.7 Defining "Good News" and "Bad News"

Using the common notation of the studies in this volume, we define the information content Q as the quantile of the distribution of municipal service delivery performance scores within a region to which the incumbent municipal government's performance corresponds, i.e., $Q = 1$ if the incumbent government was the top-performer in the region and $Q = 0.5$ if the incumbent was the median performer. To elicit study participants' prior beliefs P, study participants were given the total number

---

[14] Of the three CFD-B mayors in the sample, two were now running for the UPC and one for the NTD. In four municipalities where the CDP had dissolved locally, two mayors were running for the NAFA, one for the NTD, and one for PAREN.

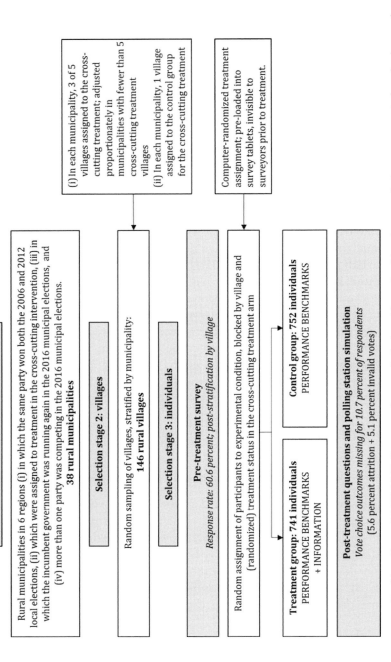

FIGURE 8.5 Burkina Faso: CONSORT diagram of research design. *Note:* Attrition in vote choice outcomes is largely due to the chemical decomposition of ballot identifiers that were printed in UV-visible ink and accidentally exposed to sunlight.

of municipalities in their region and were asked to guess their municipal government's rank among those M municipalities, which was then divided by M to yield quantiles. So both P and Q are greater than zero and less than or equal to one.

We define the good news subgroup as the subset of study participants for whom either $P - Q < 0$ or both $P - Q = 0$ and $Q \geq 0.5$, i.e., the study participants who underestimated their municipal government's performance rank, plus the study participants who correctly estimated their municipal government's performance rank and their municipal government's performance was greater than or equal to the median in their region. Analogously, we define the bad news subgroup as those study participants for whom either $P - Q > 0$ or both $P - Q = 0$ and $Q < 0.5$. By this definition, the information treatment was good news for study participants who previously underestimated their incumbent municipal government's relative performance (in comparison to other municipalities of their region) and bad news for those who previously overestimated it.

8.3 EFFECTS OF PERFORMANCE INFORMATION

Like the other studies in this volume, we estimate the effects of our experimental treatment – access to performance information – separately for two subgroups: those study participants who had underestimated incumbent performance at baseline (the good news subgroup) and those who had overestimated incumbent performance (the bad news subgroup). Our analyses focus on two outcomes of interest: vote choice and turnout intent. We first explain how data on these individual-level outcomes was collected. We then report average treatment effects for each of the two subgroups, before presenting results on treatment effect heterogeneity.

8.3.1 Data and Measurement

Data on intended vote choice and intent to vote was collected immediately following the information treatment, by our implementation partner Innovations for Poverty Action in April and May 2016, prior to the May 22 municipal elections. The outcome data was collected by the same surveyors who carried out the baseline survey and administered the treatment and control conditions.

Intended Vote Choice

Study participants' intended vote choice was measured through a polling station simulation, immediately following the information treatment. This approach was chosen in order to minimize respondent-related measurement biases. Since vote choice is a potentially sensitive question, respondents may be reluctant to reveal information if they are asked directly, even if they are told that their responses will be kept confidential. Also, self-reported vote choice may be subject to social desirability bias. Respondents' answers could be influenced, consciously or subconsciously, by what they perceive to be the most socially accepted choice or the surveyor's preference. This makes it necessary to measure vote choice under conditions of complete anonymity and in a situation that resembles the actual elections as much as possible.

We asked study participants to participate in a preelection poll, where they would cast a vote in a mock polling station, complete with voting booths and sealed ballot boxes. The layout of the ballots in the polling station simulation was identical to those that were subsequently used in the actual elections. Study participants were informed this was not the real election, and that our objective was to estimate the number of votes different parties will get in the actual elections on May 22. They were also informed that aggregate results of the mock election would eventually be publicly accessible on the internet, so that people could compare them with the official election results. Respondents were furthermore informed that their vote would be completely confidential and that no one, including no government authority, would be able to infer from our data who the respondent voted for in the mock election.

To ensure anonymity of the votes cast in the mock election, each ballot contained two unique ID codes. One was printed on a detachable receipt at the top of the ballot. Prior to handing the ballot to the respondent, the surveyors detached this portion of the ballot and explained to respondents that they are sending it back to their organization as proof of the number of votes cast, which would be cross-checked against the number of unused ballots that were returned. This procedure closely mirrors the use of unique, detachable ballot receipts in the actual municipal elections. The second ID was printed in invisible ultraviolet ink directly on the main part of the ballot. The two ID codes were linked through a concordance list that was locked in advance of data collection. The surveyors recorded only the visible ID from the detached receipts together with the survey data. The surveyors were not aware of the invisible ink identifiers that were printed on the ballots.

Ballots that were submitted in the mock election were handled strictly separately from the survey data. Vote choices were manually entered by a separate vote count team, along with the invisible ballot identifier codes that were inspected under ultraviolet light. Our data collection partner did not have access to the concordance list that would have allowed them to match ballot data to individual survey responses. Instead, our data collection partner provided us with anonymized survey data that contained the visible ballot identifiers, as well as with the voting data that contained the invisible identifiers. Using the concordance list, we matched the identifiers from the ballots to the identifiers in the survey data after anonymization of the survey data. That way, we were able to ensure full anonymity of study participants' vote choices, because we had no access to personal identifying information in the survey, whereas our data collection partner, who had access to respondents' identifying information, did not have access to the concordance list by which it could be matched to individuals' vote choices.

Turnout Intent

We use a self-reported measure of turnout intent, based on the following survey question: "Considering that in the real elections citizens have a choice whether to vote or abstain, how likely is it that you will actually vote in the municipal elections on May 22nd?" Response options for this question are: (1) I definitely plan to vote and will make every reasonable effort to do so; (2) I will probably vote, but am not completely sure yet; (3) I am not sure yet, but I tend towards voting; (4) I am not sure yet, but I tend towards not voting; (5) I probably won't vote, but am not completely sure yet; and (6) I am determined not to vote, and I will try hard to avoid it. For ease of analysis, we assume that the six response categories approximately map into turnout probabilities of 0, 0.2, 0.4, 0.6, 0.8, and 1.

8.3.2 Effects on Vote Choice and Intent to Vote

The average added effect of access to performance information on pro-incumbent voting in the polling station simulation is statistically indistinguishable from zero. In the overall sample, the estimated 95 percent confidence interval ranges from -1.7 percentage points to $+8.0$ percentage points.

In the good news subgroup, i.e., among voters who underestimate incumbent performance, our population-weighted estimate is that 34.1 percent intended to vote for the incumbent party, based on the vote choices in the control group. Performance information changed the pro-incumbent voting intent between −11.5 and +7.6 percentage points (95 percent confidence interval). We find no evidence that study participants who had underestimated the incumbent's performance more severely reacted more strongly to the information treatment.

In the bad news subgroup, i.e., among voters who overestimated incumbent performance, our population-weighted estimate is that 29.4 percent intended to vote for the incumbent party, while the information treatment changed pro-incumbent voting intent between −0.3 and +11.5 percentage points (95 percent confidence interval). Again, we find no evidence that study participants who had overestimated the incumbent's performance more severely reacted more strongly to the information treatment.

With respect to self-reported turnout propensity, access to performance information has no substantially significant effect in either subgroup. We find no evidence that receiving better-than-expected news about incumbent performance increases voter turnout among those who had underestimated the incumbent's performance or that worse-than-expected information would suppress voter turnout among those who had overestimated the incumbent's performance.

If we combine voting intent and self-reported turnout propensity to calculate expected effects on the incumbent's ultimate vote share, access to performance information increased the incumbent's vote share in the bad news subgroup, by an estimated 5.8 percentage points (with a standard error of 3.0 percentage points). In the good news subgroup, it is more likely that information access decreased, rather than increased, the incumbent vote share (with a point estimate of −4.4 percentage points, and a standard error of 4.9 percentage points).

In interpreting these results, it is important to keep in mind that they reflect only the added causal impact of truthful information content, after providing voters with a detailed explanation of municipal government responsibilities and benchmarks for their performance. In the eventual municipal elections, 29.4 percent of voters from the same set of villages voted for the local incumbent, whereas the corresponding estimate from the polling station simulation is 30.8 percent (±3.5 percentage points) in the control group. The difference is minimal and insignificant. That being said, it remains possible that an effect of information about the

TABLE 8.3 *Burkina Faso: Average treatment effects and interaction with the gap between prior beliefs and performance information (P − Q). The table shows OLS coefficients. All specifications include village fixed effects. Standard errors in parentheses.* (s) *Mean-centered/ standardized within subgroup.* $^{*}p < 0.1$, $^{**}p < 0.05$, $^{***}p < 0.01$.

	(1) Pro-incumbent voting intent	(2) Turnout Propensity	(3) Extrapolated incumbent vote share
Panel A: Pooled			
Information treatment	0.035	0.019	0.029
	(0.024)	(0.013)	(0.025)
× Gap between priors and information(s)	0.027	0.0069	0.03
	(0.025)	(0.013)	(0.025)
Observations	1333	1487	1316
Panel B: Good News Subgroup			
Information treatment	−0.018	0.0045	−0.041
	(0.049)	(0.025)	(0.05)
× Gap between priors and information(s)	0.025	−0.0062	0.029
	(0.05)	(0.025)	(0.05)
Observations	421	477	417
Panel C: Bad News Subgroup			
Information treatment	0.051*	0.023	0.055*
	(0.03)	(0.016)	(0.03)
× Gap between priors and information(s)	0.0091	0.011	−0.0045
	(0.031)	(0.016)	(0.032)
Observations	912	1010	899

municipal service delivery indicators and performance benchmarks on pro-incumbent voting was obscured by the time gap of up to a few weeks between our survey and the actual elections.

8.3.3 Heterogeneous Treatment Effects

In line with the MPAP, we further examined if the effects of performance information on vote choice and voter turnout varied with relevant individual- and village-level covariates. In Tables 8.4 and 8.5, we report the estimated linear interaction coefficients between the information treatment and (1) whether a respondent reported to have voted for the incumbent in 2012; (2) whether he/she expects to receive a campaign gift (by any party); (3) perceived electoral competitiveness at the village level, measured by voters' expectations about the incumbent's vote margin over the strongest local opposition party (averaged among the respondents in the control group in a given village); and (4) respondents' perceptions of electoral integrity, specifically of the chance that the counting of votes will be fair and free of the risk that ballots are not secret.

Of these, only perceived local competitiveness shows a significant interaction effect with the information treatment, and only in the good news subgroup, where its effect on pro-incumbent voting is particularly negative in villages where the incumbent ties with the opposition.

8.4 CROSS-CUTTING EXPERIMENT: PERSONAL EXPOSURE TO MUNICIPAL GOVERNANCE PROCESSES

In addition to the common treatment arm – providing voters with information about incumbent performance – we carried out a cross-cutting experimental treatment with a random subset of our study participants, prior to the information experiment. This cross-cutting treatment consisted of personalized invitations to volunteer as "citizen observers" at a meeting of the municipality's special delegation. With the support of our government partner and six regional NGOs, we convinced the presidents of the special delegations (the interim mayors) to personally invite randomly sampled voting-age residents of the municipality to a special delegation meeting. The invited citizens received a formal invitation letter (addressed by name and hand-signed by the president of the special delegation) that encouraged them to attend a specific special delegation meeting as "citizen observer" and to share their views in a question and answer session that would follow the meeting. Records collected at the meetings show that more than 60 percent of the invited citizens actually attended.

Our goal in evaluating this cross-cutting treatment is to test if personal experience with municipal decision processes influences voters' interest in and response to performance information. The fact that the elected municipal councils were temporarily suspended and replaced by

TABLE 8.4 *Burkina Faso: Heterogeneous treatment effects. The dependent variable is pro-incumbent voting in the polling station simulation. The table reports OLS coefficients. All specifications except (4) include village fixed effects. Standard errors in parentheses.* [c] *Adjusted for clustering at the village level.* [s] *Mean-centered/standardized within subgroup.*
$*p < 0.1, **p < 0.05, ***p < 0.01.$

	(1)	(2)	(3)	(4)	(5)	(6)
				Pro-Incumbent Voting Intent		
Panel A: Pooled						
Information treatment	0.035	0.061*	0.02	0.015	0.016*	0.035*
	(0.024)	(0.037)	(0.027)	(0.037)	(0.028)	(0.024)
× Incumbent supporter		−0.047				
		(0.051)				
× Expects campaign gift			0.083			
			(0.065)			
× abs(Expected vote margin)				0.11		
				0.12 [c]		
× Fair vote count [s]					−0.0028	
					(0.029)	
× Ballot secrecy [s]						−0.011
						(0.025)
Observations	1333	1333	1333	1333	1056	1315
Panel B: Good News Subgroup						
Information treatment	−0.019	−0.0097	−0.049	−0.12	−0.033	−0.019
	(0.049)	(0.072)	(0.054)	(0.068)	(0.061)	(0.05)
× Incumbent supporter		−0.014				
		(0.1)				

(Continued)

247

TABLE 8.4 (continued)

			Pro-Incumbent Voting Intent			
	(1)	(2)	(3)	(4)	(5)	(6)
× Expects campaign gift			0.15 (0.12)			
× abs(Expected vote margin)				0.46* (0.24)[c]		
× Fair vote count[s]					−0.048 (0.063)	
× Ballot secrecy[s]						−0.061 (0.049)
Observations	421	421	421	421	310	419
Panel C: Bad News Subgroup						
Information treatment	0.052* (0.03)	0.069 (0.046)	0.031 (0.034)	0.081* (0.046)	0.023 (0.034)	0.051* (0.031)
× Incumbent supporter		−0.028 (0.063)				
× Expects campaign gift			0.12 (0.082)			
× abs(Expected vote margin)				−0.069 (0.17)[c]		
× Fair vote count[s]					0.029 (0.036)	
× Ballot secrecy[s]						−0.003 (0.033)
Observations	912	912	912	912	746	896

248

TABLE 8.5 *Burkina Faso: Heterogeneous treatment effects. The dependent variable is pro-incumbent voting, adjusted for self-reported turnout intent. The table reports OLS coefficients. All specifications except (4) include village fixed effects. Standard errors in parentheses.* [c] *Adjusted for clustering at the village level.* [s] *Mean-centered/standardized within subgroup.*
$*p < 0.1, **p < 0.05, ***p < 0.01.$

	(1)	(2)	Extrapolated Incumbent Vote Share (3)	(4)	(5)	(6)
Panel A: Pooled						
Information treatment	0.029	0.042	0.013	0.0092	0.0092	0.029
	(0.025)	(0.039)	(0.028)	(0.037)	(0.028)	(0.025)
× Incumbent supporter		−0.021				
		(0.052)				
× Expects campaign gift			0.086			
			(0.066)			
× abs(Expected vote margin)				0.12		
				$(0.12^{(c)})$		
× Fair vote count[s]					−0.0073	
					(0.03)	
× Ballot secrecy[s]						0.0032
						(0.026)
Observations	1316	1316	1316	1333	1040	1298

(Continued)

TABLE 8.5 (continued)

	(1)	(2)	(3)	Extrapolated Incumbent Vote Share (4)	(5)	(6)
Panel B: Good News Subgroup						
Information treatment	−0.044	−0.071	−0.081	−0.14**	−0.056	−0.044
	(0.049)	(0.076)	(0.055)	(0.068)	(0.061)	(0.049)
× Incumbent supporter		0.052				
		(0.1)				
Panel A: Pooled						
× Expects campaign gift			0.18			
			(0.12)			
× abs(Expected vote margin)				0.5**		
				$(0.24^{(c)})$		
× Fair vote count[s]					−0.081	
					(0.065)	
× Ballot secrecy[s]						−0.031
						(0.049)
Observations	417	417	417	421	306	415

TABLE 8.5 *(continued)*

Panel C: Bad News Subgroup

Information treatment	0.055*	0.063	0.036	0.078*	0.026*	0.054*
	(0.03)	(0.048)	(0.034)	(0.047)	(0.034)	(0.031)
× Incumbent supporter		−0.0084				
		(0.064)				
× Expects campaign gift			0.11			
			(0.083)			
× abs(Expected vote margin)				−0.081		
				$(0.17)^{(c)}$		
× Fair vote count$^{(s)}$					0.032	
					(0.036)	
× Ballot secrecy$^{(s)}$						0.0045
						(0.033)
Observations	899	899	899	912	734	883

externally appointed special delegations created a unique opportunity to shed light on this question. It means that we could expose voters to the municipal governance process without simultaneously exposing them to the incumbent and thus inevitably affecting their level of information about incumbent performance.

In addition to evaluating the effects of the "citizen observer" intervention on civic participation more generally (in a larger field experiment in 118 rural municipalities,[15] of which the thirty-eight municipalities covered by this study are a subset), we also prespecified three hypotheses about its interaction with the information treatment.[16] Specifically, we intend to test if having been selected as a "citizen observer"

1.   increases citizens' interest in performance information and the attention they pay to it,
2.   causes voters to place greater weight on expected performance in evaluating electoral candidates, and
3.   as a result of the two aforementioned mechanisms, reinforces the effect of performance information on vote choice.

In other words, we are interested in whether personal experiences with municipal governance processes make voting in municipal elections more "performance based" as opposed to "affinity based" (i.e., driven by sources of political affinity that are unrelated to a party's expected performance in governing the municipality, such as clientelism, ideology, identity politics, or national-level politics). Receiving an invitation to serve as citizen observer and subsequently attending a special delegation meeting could cause citizens to reflect about the importance of municipal government performance for their own lives, but also cause them to associate questions of municipal governance with a positive, memorable experience. Therefore, we expect that individuals in the cross-cutting treatment arm will show increased interest in performance information and greater concern for municipal government performance, relative to the control group. However, since our experiment shows that a positive reception of the information treatment and strong self-reported concern for municipal service delivery performance did not translate into the expected results, we are forced to reconsider whether we expect that the cross-cutting treatment reinforces the impact of performance information on vote choice, or rather attenuates or reverses it.

[15]   Lierl and Holmlund (2016).
[16]   Hypotheses 3.1, 3.2a, and 3.2b in our pre-analysis plan.

8.5 CONCLUSION

In examining the effects of performance information about incumbent municipal governments in Burkina Faso, our experiment focused on isolating the effects of information content from other aspects of political information interventions. The results were unexpected, at least in light of the theoretical expectations that were articulated in the MPAP. Rather than shifting voters' support for the incumbent in the direction of the information signal, information access appeared to do the opposite. Voters who had previously overestimated incumbent performance were approximately six percentage points more likely to support the incumbent after receiving bad news about the incumbent government. This was not the case among voters who had previously underestimated incumbent performance, where we find that good news had no significant effect (and our point estimates are negative). Overall, we observe that information access seemed to benefit the electoral prospects of poorly performing incumbents without helping high-performing incumbents. At first glance, this pattern of results, although estimated with considerable noise, seems at odds with conventional thinking about retrospective electoral accountability.

However, amidst the other experiments in this volume, our results are not an outlier. The signs of subgroup-specific treatment effects in our experiment are the same as in Arias et al. (Chapter 5) and Adida et al. (Chapter 4; in the case of actual election results, rather than self-reported vote choice). They contrast with the "Meet the Candidates" experiment in Uganda, where those voters who received better-than-expected information about a candidate where more likely to vote for that candidate (Platas and Raffler, Chapter 6), and Buntaine et al. (Chapter 7), where voters who received worse-than-expected information about local budget discrepancies were less likely to vote for the incumbent district councilors.

What might explain the counterintuitive effects we observe? In our first attempt at understanding this result we relied on a detailed analysis strategy we had developed without prior knowledge of the results: a full results-blind report that focused on seven important questions along the causal chain that connects study participants' processing of performance information with their ultimate voting behavior.

A first important observation was that the distribution of prior beliefs cannot explain why low-performing incumbents gained from information dissemination. Unlike Arias et al. (2018) who conjecture that incumbents gained from information about fiscal malfeasance, because voters had originally expected even greater malfeasance, our results-blind analysis revealed that voters in rural Burkina Faso were biased towards overestimating incumbent performance. In fact, low-performing incumbents were particularly likely to be overestimated, but disclosing performance information did not reduce their electoral support.

We next turned to how voters who overestimated incumbent performance might differ from those who underestimated incumbent performance. For example, Adida et al. (2017b) hypothesize that motivated reasoning explains why negative performance information failed to reduce politicians' electoral support among coethnic voters. If some voters selectively ignore negative information about the incumbent, they are likely to be biased towards overestimating incumbent performance. Those voters are more likely to be in the bad news subgroup, whereas voters who process information more rationally would be equally likely to be in the bad news or good news subgroup, provided that they had prior access to unbiased information. As we argued in our results-blind report, these selection effects could lead to the counterintuitive outcome that information which is bad news for most voters leads to a more positive average assessment of the incumbent, simply because the beliefs of voters who underestimated incumbent performance are corrected more easily than the beliefs of voters who overestimated incumbent performance.

However, we find no support for this motivated reasoning mechanism in our data. Instead, it appears that information about the incumbent government's past performance had generally no significant impact on expectations about future performance, in either subgroup. Interestingly though, receiving good news about the incumbent government appeared to have negative externalities on study participants' expectations about the electoral challengers. Such externalities, however, cannot explain why performance information failed to increase incumbent support in the good news subgroup. Moreover, if information about past performance failed to significantly change expectations about future performance, why did the information treatment nevertheless increase incumbent support in the bad news subgroup?

Having found no support for either of these potential mechanisms, we turned our attention to a new explanation that had hitherto been neglected in the literature on information and voting behavior: the fact that voters might be ambiguity averse and therefore prefer those candidates about whom they have the most information. In Lierl and

TABLE 8.6 *Burkina Faso: Heterogeneous effects of performance information by uncertainty about prior beliefs. Uncertainty is measured on a five-point scale (0...completely certain to 1...no idea). The table reports OLS coefficients. Standard errors in parentheses. Individual controls in column (3) are gender, age, years of education.* (s)*Standardized.*
$^*p < 0.1$ $^{**}p < 0.05$ $^{***}p < 0.01$.

	Pro-incumbent vote choice		
	(1)	(2)	(3)
Information treatment	−0.037	−0.037	−0.042
	(0.035)	(0.035)	(0.035)
Uncertainty about priors	−0.035	−0.0043	−0.048
	(0.058)	(0.059)	(0.059)
Information treatment × Uncertainty	0.22***	0.22***	0.23***
	(0.078)	(0.077)	(0.077)
Incumbent performance(s)		−0.45	−0.5
		(1.2)	(1.2)
Prior beliefs(s)		−0.0015	0.00027
		(0.014)	(0.014)
Voted for Incumbent in 2012		0.11	0.092
		(0.026)	(0.027)
Individual controls			Yes
Village & municipality fixed effects	Yes	Yes	Yes
Observations	1333	1333	1333

Holmlund (2017), we argue that one-sided performance information about the incumbent reduces ambiguity about that candidate, turning unknown risks about incumbent performance into known risks. If voters have a strong preference for known risks over unknown risks, even bad news about incumbent performance could make the incumbent the more attractive choice.

Our data strongly support this interpretation (Table 8.6), suggesting that the impact of performance information is moderated by voters' uncertainty about their prior beliefs. The more uncertain voters were about the incumbent's performance, the more the information treatment caused them to support the incumbent, conditional on the incumbent's actual incumbent performance. As it happened, voters who overestimated incumbent performance were much more uncertain about their assessment than voters who underestimated incumbent performance (Figure 8.6). If voters are ambiguity averse, this correlation between prior beliefs and uncertainty, whatever may be the cause of it, can plausibly

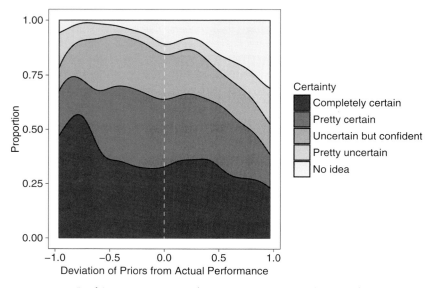

FIGURE 8.6 Burkina Faso: Voters who overestimate incumbent performance are less certain about their beliefs

explain why voters who received bad news about the incumbent were more likely to vote for the incumbent. Given voters' uncertainty, the ambiguity-reducing effect of information access may have been strong enough to outweigh the fact that receiving bad news about incumbent performance reduces the attractiveness of the incumbent party.

9

Horizontal But Not Vertical: Accountability Institutions and Electoral Sanctioning in Northeast Brazil

Taylor C. Boas, F. Daniel Hidalgo, and Marcus André Melo

Institutions of horizontal accountability often aim to sanction malfeasant or corrupt officeholders before they have an opportunity to seek reelection. In Italy, Silvio Berlusconi was expelled from the Senate and barred from public office under an anti-corruption law after being convicted of tax fraud in 2013. In Peru's 2016 election, electoral authorities disqualified Cesar Acuña as a candidate in the presidential race for vote buying activities when he was mayor of Trujillo. Though decisions to bar candidates are sometimes controversial and seen as politically motivated – as in the case of Caracas mayor Leopoldo López, a leading opponent of Venezuelan president Hugo Chávez – they can often further the cause of good governance by preventing dishonest politicians from perpetuating their hold on power.

Yet horizontal accountability institutions do not always succeed in their efforts to block malfeasant officeholders from seeking reelection. In Brazil, the 2010 Clean Slate Law (*Ficha Limpa*) allowed candidates to be disqualified if a government auditing agency had charged them with corruption or financial irregularities during prior terms in office. However, a 2016 Supreme Court ruling held that, in the case of malfeasance by executives, disqualification required that the charge be confirmed by the corresponding legislature – which, at the state and municipal levels, typically does the bidding of the governor or mayor.

When horizontal accountability is stymied by legal obstructions or candidates' political connections, citizens have the potential to step in and exercise vertical accountability, voting against incumbents who have been charged with corruption or malfeasance but managed to remain on the ballot. Electoral sanctioning requires, first and foremost, that voters be made aware of incumbents' transgressions while in office. Towards this end, auditing agencies often seek to disseminate their decisions as part of a broad public education mission. Yet it also requires that voters condemn malfeasance by elected officials, and that they be willing to act upon this norm when they go to the polls.

Our Metaketa project aimed to test whether horizontal accountability institutions could induce vertical accountability by informing citizens of significant wrongdoing, or lack thereof, by incumbent politicians running for reelection. Partnering with the State Accounts Court of Pernambuco, a government auditing agency in Brazil, our intervention told voters whether the Court's annual audit of municipal accounts had found substantial evidence of malfeasance attributable to the mayor. We examine the effect of this treatment on self-reported vote for the mayor, measured via a secret ballot question in a postelectoral wave of the panel study.

Our study found that informing voters of the approval or rejection of their mayor's accounts has no significant effect on the decision to vote for his or her reelection. This null effect also applies to evaluations of the mayor's performance and to levels of certainty regarding this evaluation. We argue that the divergence between norms and action explains these null effects. While Brazilians strongly condemn corruption in the abstract, their behavior in the real world is constrained by factors such as loyalty to local political dynasties and the greater salience of more pressing concerns like employment and health services.

9.1   THE POLITICS OF HORIZONTAL ACCOUNTABILITY IN PERNAMBUCO

A key feature of our study is that we collaborated with one of Brazil's State Accounts Courts (*Tribunais de Contas dos Estados*, or TCEs), the main institutions of horizontal accountability charged with monitoring state and municipal governments' compliance with the law.[1] Brazilian TCEs are key actors in state politics and policymaking because their decisions provide the primary legal and political basis for sanctioning local and state governments. Relying on a large and highly trained staff, the courts engage in routine annual audits of all government bodies, as well as conducting ad hoc audits of specific programs and governments. The process culminates in an overall recommendation that audited accounts

---

[1] Most TCEs are charged with auditing both municipal governments and the state government. In a few states, there is a separate Municipal Accounts Court that handles only the municipal audits.

be "approved," "approved with reservations," or "rejected." In the case of executive audits, the recommendation is then sent to the corresponding legislature for a final decision. At the municipal level, the court's recommendation regarding a mayor's accounts can only be overturned by a two-thirds vote of the city council.

Municipalities and the mayors that lead them are central political actors in Brazil. Akin to a US county, municipalities are largely responsible for the provision of basic social services such as primary education and health care, in addition to local services like garbage collection, housing, and water provision. Comparative analyses of inter-governmental relations classify Brazil as among the most decentralized polities in the world, with very high levels of fiscal and political decentralization, although taxation capacity at the municipal level remains generally low.[2] Directly elected mayors are the most important local political actors because they control the local municipal apparatus and also function as important intermediaries between citizens and the state and federal governments. Political competition is largely nonideological, and parties tend to be weak,[3] especially in smaller municipalities. While many voters may have persistent loyalties to political families or other groups within the municipality (discussed further below), swing voters tend to vote on more personalistic or clientelistic grounds.

We chose the state of Pernambuco as the location for our study largely because of the professionalism and efficiency of its TCE. As discussed below, Brazilian auditing agencies vary in the degree to which they are considered independent, professional organizations free from overt political meddling; the reputation of Pernambuco's court, the TCE-PE, is among the best.[4] In addition to the likely effect of boosting citizen confidence in the court's judgments and their potential influence on voting behavior, the TCE-PE's professionalism meant that it was more open to a partnership with academics than a more politicized agency would have been. Brazilian TCEs also vary widely in their efficiency. Some routinely take five or more years to review municipal accounts, meaning that information on a mayor's first four-year term is not available until after he/she has stood for reelection. In Pernambuco, the TCE typically completes its review in three years or less, meaning that for the vast majority of mayors, a judgment of their first year's accounts is issued prior to the

---

[2] Falleti (2010): 150.
[3] Novaes (2018).
[4] Melo, Pereira, and Figueiredo (2009).

next election and is available to communicate to voters. By the time our intervention began, the TCE-PE had reviewed the accounts from 2013, the first year of the current mayoral term, in 95 percent of the state's municipalities.

Rejection of a municipality's accounts occurs when the TCE finds that the municipal government failed to comply with regulations and laws that govern local government expenditures, such as procurement legislation, constitutionally mandated spending, and hiring procedures. The court issues a report (*parecer prévio*) that describes any violations, recommendations for remediation, and recommended punishments. Not every violation is sufficient basis for the rejection of accounts, as the court has the option of recommending "Approval with Reservations" when improprieties are less serious. In the municipalities included in our study, the rejection of a mayor's accounts occurred for a variety of reasons. In the municipality of Flores, the court cited excessive personnel expenditures, municipal debt that far surpassed legal limits, and the failure to properly report details about government spending. In Santa Filomena, the court highlighted failure to spend required amounts on education and to transfer employees' pension contributions to the state pension fund, among other violations. In Bom Conselho, the court charged that the mayor had incurred substantial debt without approval from the local legislature, among other infractions. Reports for other municipalities with rejected accounts described similar violations.

Reassuringly, the decisions of the TCE-PE are correlated with other, independent measures of government irregularities. The most well-known auditing agency in Brazil, the Comptroller General of the Union (*Controladoria-Geral da União* or CGU) performs regular audits of federal transfers to municipalities – an area outside the purview of the TCE – and publicizes the names of public servants responsible for irregularities. Using these data, we computed the number of public servants named in CGU audits in all municipalities in the state, normalized by the total number of municipal bureaucrats employed in 2008.[5] To assess the extent to which the TCE-PE's overall judgment correlates with the CGU's audit findings, Figure 9.1 plots the distribution of CGU irregularities by the TCE-PE's approval or rejection of the mayor's 2013 accounts. On average, municipalities whose accounts had been rejected by TCE-PE

---

[5] Specifically, we used the list of public servants whose accounts were judged "irregular" by the CGU between 2008 and 2016. The number of municipal bureaucrats was obtained from IBGE's *Perfil dos Municípios Brasileiros*.

FIGURE 9.1 Brazil: Number of federal transfer irregularities by accounts status. These irregularities are reported by the federal government auditing agency CGU. Total number of irregularities has been normalized by number of bureaucrats employed in 2008.

had many more public servants found to have misspent federal funds. This finding suggests that the TCE-PE's judgments do reflect broader differences in governance among Brazilian municipalities.

Decisions taken by Brazilian TCEs have potentially severe consequences for politicians, yet in practice these institutions are often quite hampered in their ability to exercise horizontal accountability. A 1990 law allowed politicians to be barred from running for office for eight years if their accounts had been rejected, the legislature had upheld the decision (in the case of executive officeholders), and all possibilities for appeal had been exhausted. However, the long, draw-out appeals process meant that incumbents with rejected accounts were typically able to run again – and even finish a second term – before a final decision on their case could be rendered.[6] In 2010, the new Clean Slate Law sought to close the judicial appeals loophole, allowing candidates to be barred based solely on the rejection of their accounts by the TCE. However, a Supreme Court decision in August 2016 significantly weakened the law

---

[6] Speck (2011): 145.

by ruling that, in the case of executive accounts rejection, candidates could only be disqualified if the rejection had been upheld by the corresponding legislature. City councils often incur substantial delays in voting on the TCE-PE's recommendation, during which time the mayor may have run for reelection. Moreover, since city councils are usually dominated by the mayor's allies, they routinely overturn recommendations that accounts be rejected. From 1994 to 2013, 50 percent of rejection recommendations were overturned by the city council, versus only 5 percent of approval recommendations.

In addition to their efforts to exercise horizontal accountability, TCEs seek to induce vertical accountability by publicizing their auditing decisions and educating the public about their general mission. In Pernambuco, the TCE-PE employs a dedicated public outreach staff and publishes a column in a major newspaper that reports on its activities, including decisions on accounts. More generally, it seeks to directly inform the public about various aspects of municipal governance in Pernambuco. For example, its website *Tome Conta* (roughly translated as "Supervise" or "Take Notice") conveys indicators of government performance in a variety of areas, including health and education. The TCE-PE also has an outreach program, *TCEndo Cidadania* (a play on "weaving citizenship"), that involves holding public forums in municipalities around the state in order to educate citizens about local governance and help them hold elected officials accountable.

Although Brazil's TCEs project themselves as impartial arbiters and investigators, they are political institutions by design. TCEs are led by a panel of seven councilors (*conselheiros*), three of whom are appointed by the governor and four by the state legislature. The governor is fairly constrained in two of his three choices – one must be an Accounts Court career auditor, the other must be a career public prosecutor, and both have to be chosen from a list of three candidates compiled by either the Accounts Court or the Public Prosecutor's Office. However, the governor's third choice, and all four of the legislature's choices, are essentially unrestricted, meaning that political criteria often factor into their decisions. Councilors selected by the legislature are typically former state deputies belonging to the dominant coalition and have a clearly political, rather than technical, profile. All councilors have protected tenure until a mandatory age of retirement.

The TCEs' institutional structure means that audit decisions are at least partly responsive to political factors, especially in the annual review of accounts, their most visible and legally consequential function. Many courts are dominated by councilors with partisan or family ties to politicians. In Pernambuco, the court had five members with political ties: three were former state deputies, one was the former cabinet chief of the governor, and another was a cousin of the governor who appointed him.[7] An emerging literature on horizontal accountability in Brazil has documented the implications of these political ties. TCEs tend to punish governments more readily when the councilors are politically diverse,[8] whereas councilors tend to treat copartisan politicians more leniently.[9] The degree to which political factors influence decision-making varies substantially, and Pernambuco's court is considered one of the most professional and least politicized.[10] However, decisions by its councilors with political careers do show some evidence of favoritism towards copartisan mayors.[11]

In addition to sometimes treating copartisans more leniently, there is clear evidence that the bar for rejection of everyone's accounts is raised or lowered depending on the political sensitivity of the period in which they are being judged. The top panel of Figure 9.2 shows the percentage of municipalities with rejected accounts over time. The first year of each mayoral term – the only one for which accounts are likely to be adjudicated before the next election, and hence, the most politically consequential judgment – always has the lowest rejection rate. Indeed, our contacts within the court confirm that first-year accounts are judged more leniently because of election-year sensitivities.[12]

This electoral accountability cycle has direct implications for the types of municipalities that are approved or rejected in particular years. In the bottom panel of Figure 9.2, we plot the normalized number of CGU irregularities – as noted above, an independent measure of municipal malfeasance – in the median municipality with approved accounts. In electorally sensitive years, the number of irregularities found by federal auditors is unusually high in municipalities declared to be law-abiding by the TCE-PE.

---

[7] Paiva and Sakai (2014).

[8] Melo, Pereira, and Figueiredo (2009).

[9] Hidalgo, Canello, and de Oliveira (2016).

[10] Melo, Pereira, and Figueiredo (2009).

[11] Hidalgo, Canello, and de Oliveira (2016).

[12] An alternative explanation is that mayors are simply too inexperienced in their first year to engage in serious malfeasance. This hypothesis is belied by the fact that we see similar patterns among mayors in their second term.

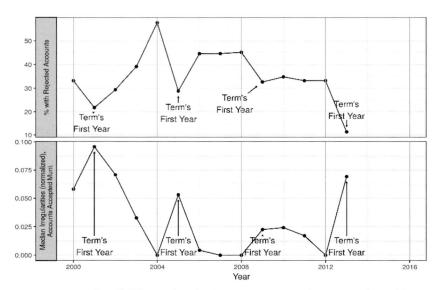

FIGURE 9.2 Brazil: Electoral cycles in accounts court decision-making. Top panel shows the proportion of municipalities with rejected accounts by year. Bottom panel shows the normalized median number of irregularities reported by federal auditors in municipalities with accepted accounts by year.

The TCE-PE's hesitation when rejecting accounts was likely exacerbated by the 2010 passage of the Clean Slate Law, which, as discussed above, made the court's decision itself grounds for barring a candidacy. Starting in 2006 – the accounts for which would have been judged in 2009, while the Clean Slate Law was being debated – we see a steady decline in rejection rates. Likely due to a combination of these two dynamics, the rejection rate in 2013 was the lowest since our data series began, at only 12 percent of municipalities in the state. This drop was accompanied by a large increase in the number of audited irregularities among municipalities with approved accounts.

The TCE-PE's unusually lenient approach to judging mayors' accounts in 2013 has several implications for our research design. At the time of the 2016 election, the 2013 accounts were the most recent ones that had been judged for nearly all municipalities in the state and the only ones corresponding to the first year of the incumbent mayor's term. The fact that the rejection rate in 2013 was unusually low, and that only a subset of mayors with rejected accounts ran for reelection, meant that we would have to sample every eligible municipality with rejected accounts, and a larger proportion of voters within these municipalities, in order for equal numbers of respondents to receive "good news" and "bad news" about their mayor's performance in office. Moreover, the set of municipalities with both approved and rejected accounts in 2013 was unusual compared to other years. As the federal auditing data indicates, municipal governments with approved accounts were more likely to be "bad types" than in previous years, possibly rendering court's decisions less informative about the overall quality of municipal governance. Meanwhile, the small set of municipalities that cleared the bar for rejection were likely to be especially egregious violators.

9.2 EXPERIMENTAL DESIGN

9.2.1 Treatment

Our common treatment arm informed voters as to whether the mayor's accounts were approved or rejected by the TCE-PE in 2013, the first year of the current mayoral term. Information was delivered to voters in the form of a flyer handed out by enumerators during the baseline wave of the survey; examples for each type of municipality are contained in Figures 9.3a and 9.3b. Enumerators also summarized the information orally to maximize information retention and facilitate comprehension among illiterate voters. The flyer design was refined based on feedback from two rounds of focus groups conducted with voters from three municipalities as well as review by our government partner, the TCE-PE. The front of the flyer bore the logos of the TCE-PE and its affiliated academic institution, the Public Accounts School, and it briefly explained the court's auditing responsibilities. The reverse side conveyed municipality-specific details, including a pie chart with comparative metrics.[13]

The implementation of the field experiment involved sampling municipalities, census tracts, and individuals, who were then individually randomized to three different treatment conditions. The overall structure of our research design is summarized in Figure 9.4. Below we describe in detail each stage of the process and their implications for interpretation of our findings. The timing of the pilot, baseline, and endline is shown in Figure 9.5.

---

[13] We initially designed the flyers to mimic vivid advertising common in campaigns, but our focus groups indicated that recipients would likely believe that the flyers were distributed by politicians and not by the TCE. As a result, we adopted a more neutral and staid design.

**GESTÃO
FINANCEIRA**

Em 2013, as contas do prefeito de **ABREU E LIMA** foram **APROVADAS**, como aconteceu em **88%** dos municípios de Pernambuco.

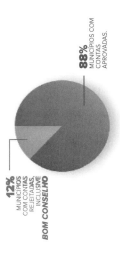

12%
MUNICÍPIOS
COM CONTAS
REJEITADAS

88%
MUNICÍPIOS COM
CONTAS
APROVADAS,
INCLUSIVE
ABREU E LIMA

Estas informações estão sendo fornecidas no contexto de uma pesquisa acadêmica conduzida por professores da **Universidade Federal de Pernambuco**, o **Instituto Tecnológico de Massachusetts** e a **Universidade de Boston**, em parceria com a **Escola de Contas Públicas Barreto Guimarães do TCE-PE**.

PARA MAIS DETALHES, VISITE **WWW.MBTAKETA.ORG/TCE**

(a) Accounts Approved Flyer.

**GESTÃO
FINANCEIRA**

Em 2013, as contas do prefeito de **BOM CONSELHO** foram **REJEITADAS**, algo que aconteceu só em **12%** dos municípios de Pernambuco.

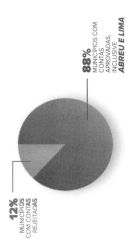

12%
MUNICÍPIOS
COM CONTAS
REJEITADAS,
INCLUSIVE
BOM CONSELHO

88%
MUNICÍPIOS COM
CONTAS
APROVADAS.

Estas informações estão sendo fornecidas no contexto de uma pesquisa acadêmica conduzida por professores da **Universidade Federal de Pernambuco**, o **Instituto Tecnológico de Massachusetts** e a **Universidade de Boston**, em parceria com a **Escola de Contas Públicas Barreto Guimarães do TCE-PE**.

PARA MAIS DETALHES, VISITE **WWW.MBTAKETA.ORG/TCE**

(b) Accounts Rejected Flyer

FIGURE 9.3 Brazil: Flyers distributed to voters

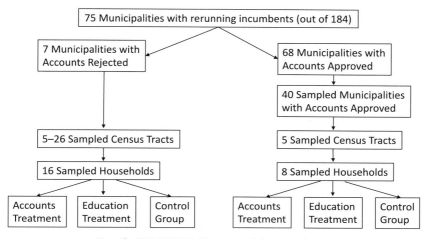

FIGURE 9.4 Brazil: CONSORT diagram of the sampling and treatment assignment process

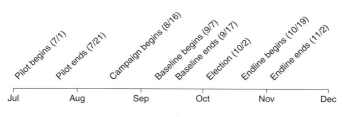

FIGURE 9.5 Brazil: Project timeline

9.2.2 Subjects and Contexts

Sampling Municipalities

The primary criterion for sampling municipalities was achieving a balanced sample, such that an equal number of respondents would receive positive and negative information about the incumbent government. Because there were only seven municipalities where incumbents with rejected accounts ran for reelection, we included all of them in the study. To construct the sampling frame of municipalities with approved accounts, we eliminated the smallest municipalities (where it might be difficult to sample the requisite number of voters) as well as the state capital, Recife. We then grouped the remaining seventy-five municipalities into two strata based on information to be conveyed in our alternative arm – performance on the National Literacy Exam (*Avaliação Nacional da Alfabetização*, or ANA), a standardized test given in elementary

FIGURE 9.6 Brazil: Sampled municipalities in Pernambuco State, Brazil

schools – and sampled an equal number of municipalities from each stratum with inclusion probabilities proportional to the 2010 population. Our sample of municipalities is depicted in Figure 9.6, which shows the geographic distribution of sampled communities as well as accounts status. As shown by the map, the accounts-rejected municipalities are geographically distributed across the state, though six out of the seven municipalities are located in the poor, semi-arid region known as the *sertão*, whose politics is often characterized as relatively traditional and clientelistic.

On basic socio-demographic variables, our sample is poorer and more rural than Brazil or Pernambuco as a whole. As indicated in Table 9.1, municipalities with both approved and rejected accounts have higher levels of extreme poverty, lower rates of access to running water, lower average monthly incomes, and worse educational performance. The poorer socioeconomic profile of our sample is not surprising, given the Northeast's persistent underdevelopment and our exclusion of Recife, the wealthiest city in the state. Within our sample, however, the accounts-rejected municipalities are substantially poorer and more rural than their accounts-approved counterparts. For example, the average monthly income in accounts-rejected municipalities is less than half of the Brazilian average and 20 percent smaller than the accounts-approved average. Similarly, the agriculture sector's share of the workforce is about 13 percentage points higher in the accounts-rejected municipalities.

With respect to electoral participation and competition, our sample is quite representative of Pernambuco and Brazil as a whole. Turnout and average vote share for the incumbent in the last election (2012) are broadly comparable to national and state averages. Elections are quite competitive, with incumbents only garnering around 52–53 percent of valid votes. Due to compulsory voting, turnout is high, with average rates of 78–83 percent. On these basic political indicators, accounts-approved and accounts-rejected municipalities are broadly comparable.

TABLE 9.1 *Brazil: Socio-demographics and political characteristics of sampled municipalities. Source: 2010 Census and Superior Electoral Court.*

Variable	Brazil	Pernambuco	Sampled Accounts Accepted	Sampled Accounts Rejected
Socio-Demographic Variables				
% in Extreme Poverty	6.6	12.3	15.1	22.9
% with Running Water	92.7	83.7	76.6	65.2
% Students Held Back	38.2	43.6	45.2	52.0
% Working in Agriculture	13.6	18.9	29.3	44.7
Average Income (BRL)	794	525	347	279
Human Development Index	0.73	0.67	0.62	0.57
Electoral Variables				
2012 Winner Vote %	54.4	55.6	53.0	52.2
2012 Turnout (% of registered)	83.5	83.7	83.3	78.2
Baseline Survey Variables				
Muni. Government Evaluation (five-point scale)	–	–	3.0	3.1
Confidence in Muni. Government (seven-point scale)	–	–	4.2	4.1
Confidence in Accounts Court (seven-point scale)	–	–	4.3	4.5
Vote Buying Offer is Somewhat or Very Probable (%)	–	–	33.0	30.1
Vote Monitoring is Somewhat or Very Probable (%)	–	–	29.3	31.0

Attitudes towards the government and perceptions of the electoral process were also quite similar across the two types of municipalities. In the bottom rows of Table 9.1, we present data from our baseline survey on evaluations of the municipal government and the TCE, as well as perceptions about the prevalence of vote buying and the secrecy of the ballot. Across all five variables, we see quite similar responses in both accounts-rejected and accounts-approved municipalities.

Sampling Respondents

Within each municipality, we used a two-stage sampling procedure that involved choosing census tracts and then respondents. Census tracts were sampled with probability proportional to the number of households in the 2010 census, excluding the least populous and most rural tracts where, based on pretesting, we anticipated logistical problems during fieldwork. In accounts-approved municipalities, we sampled five census tracts, while in accounts-rejected municipalities, we sampled between five and twenty-six census tracts, varying with municipality size. Within each tract, enumerators sampled sixteen households in accounts-rejected municipalities and eight households in accounts-approved municipalities. To ensure that interviews were geographically distributed throughout the tract – thus reducing the risk of spillover among neighbors assigned to different treatment conditions – we calculated a tract-specific number of houses to skip after a successful interview by dividing the total number of households in the tract by twice the number of interviews to be conducted. To avoid large imbalances in basic demographics, we used census data to construct sex-specific age quotas that interviewers were required to meet in each census tract.

9.2.3   Threats to Validity

Attrition

Because we measure our outcome using a postelection survey, it was important to minimize attrition, both to preserve statistical power and to reduce the possibility of posttreatment bias. Our survey enumerators returned multiple times to interviewed households and often tracked missing respondents to their workplace or other locations to complete the endline interview. Recontact was more difficult, and attrition was noticeably higher, in more urban municipalities where respondents tended to work further from home. Overall, we achieved a recontact rate of 81 percent.

Figure 9.2 shows how basic demographic and political variables vary by attrition status. As expected, men and higher income individuals were more difficult to reinterview as they were more likely to be employed and away from home during second-round visits. With respect to political variables, the two groups are broadly comparable: 2012 voting behavior as well as evaluation of the incumbent were very similar. Finally, the attrition rate in the treatment group was 3 percentage points higher than in the control group. While this difference is not large, it is statistically

TABLE 9.2 *Brazil: Comparison of attrited and reinterviewed respondents*

Variable	Attritted	Reinterviewed
Age	38.1	41.2
Male (%)	58%	48%
Income < R$880.00 (%)	44%	51%
Evaluation of Incumbent (five-point scale)	3.0	3.1
2012 Vote for Incumbent (%)	55%	52%
2012 Turnout (%)	84%	85%
Accounts Treatment	36%	33%

significant with a *p*-value of 0.03.[14] While the significant difference in attrition is a potential threat to inference, the fact that attrition is weakly correlated with political variables suggest that any bias would likely be small.

Measurement Error

A second important threat to the validity of our estimates is the fact that our main dependent variables are self-reported. In Brazil, electoral precincts (*seções*) do not correspond to specific, mutually exclusive geographical units in which voters reside, so we did not have the option of randomizing and measuring outcomes at the precinct level, as some other projects did. Self-reported outcomes are, of course, subject to recall, demand, and pro-winner biases. Of these three potential sources of error, demand effects are most likely to induce a correlation between measurement error and the treatment, as voters who received flyers may seek to pander to survey enumerators and falsify their vote choice. Recall effects, even if correlated with treatment, are unlikely to be correlated with the outcome of interest – vote for the incumbent mayor – so they should not affect our estimates. Likewise, the well-known propensity to overreport vote for the winning candidate is also unlikely to induce differential measurement error because our block randomization design ensures that we compare voters within municipalities, who would all presumably experience the same pro-winner effect.[15]

---

[14] This *p*-value was estimated using permutation inference, testing the null of no effect on any individual's propensity to attrit. We employed the *t*-statistic from the specification listed in Section 3 as the test-statistic and performed 10,000 simulated randomizations.

[15] If the treatment causes a pro-winner bias (as opposed to pro-incumbent bias), this source of measurement error could lead to erroneous inferences. It is difficult to conceive of a scenario in which this would be the case.

PARA PREFEITO DE ABREU E LIMA

FIGURE 9.7 Brazil: Simulated ballot used to measure vote choice

To reduce all three forms of bias, we used a secret ballot vote choice question. Respondents were given municipality-specific printed ballots (see Figure 9.7 for an example) and asked to privately check off their vote choice, fold the ballot, and deposit it into a sealed "ballot box" carried by the enumerator. To facilitate recall, our ballots included the same candidate photographs that are displayed on the confirmation screen of the electronic voting machine. Respondents also had the option of marking a blank or null vote, as is possible with electronic voting.

To assess the extent to which we successfully minimized measurement error, it is informative to benchmark our survey against actual election outcomes. This exercise has limitations, as our sampling frame omitted sixteen- and seventeen-year-olds (enfranchised in Brazil) as well as residents of the most rural census tracts. Furthermore, our target population excludes voters who do not reside in the municipality where they are registered to vote, a common occurrence in areas, such as rural Pernambuco, that have experienced substantial out-migration. Nonresident registered

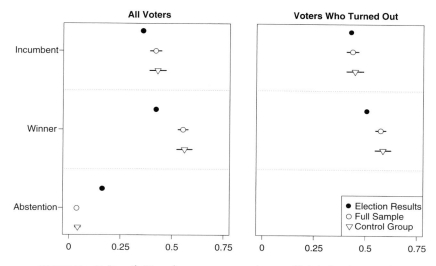

FIGURE 9.8 Brazil: Vote for mayor: sample vs. official election results

voters tend to inflate official abstention rates, which would not be captured in our survey. Despite these caveats, benchmarking our sample can be informative, in that substantial deviations from electoral outcomes could be indicative of measurement error.

To construct a benchmark for comparison, we weighted each municipality's electoral results in proportion to its share of respondents in the endline sample. Results are displayed in Figure 9.8. The largest discrepancy is with respect to turnout, which could be driven by social desirability bias but probably also reflects our inability to sample non-residents. As is common in post-election surveys, we also find that voters somewhat overreport vote for the winning candidate. When we exclude abstainers, however, our estimate of the incumbent vote share is statistically indistinguishable from the official electoral results. Furthermore, the difference between the official vote returns and self-reported vote for the winning candidate diminishes – but does not disappear – after conditioning on turnout.

Candidate Self-Selection
A final potential concern is that, among mayors with rejected accounts, politically weak incumbents may have expected to lose and chosen not to run again. The remaining incumbents with rejected accounts might have a strong record of achievement or attractive personal qualities,

making it less likely that supporters would change their vote when presented with negative information. If so, our sample would exclude those places where effects might be larger, creating a bias in favor of a null finding.

Evidence from our pilot argues against this interpretation. About a month prior to the candidate registration deadline, we conducted a large-scale ($n = 2,000$) pilot study in all municipalities where the incumbent was eligible to run for reelection, providing the same treatment information and inquiring about intended vote if the incumbent were to rerun. We obtained similar results to those from the field experiment, suggesting that the findings reported below are not an artifact of self-selection into the sample of candidates.

9.2.4 Implementation Challenges

In the vast majority of municipalities, our project encountered no implementation difficulties, but in four municipalities where the mayor's accounts had been rejected, our survey prompted reactions from local politicians or their allies. While the negative valence of our treatment information may partially account for these reactions, it is also important to remember that we sampled a much larger fraction of the electorate in these municipalities, making the intervention more noticeable to local political actors. According to enumerators, reactions from local politicians were most often triggered not by the content of the flyers but rather by questions in the baseline survey about the likelihood of vote buying – an activity that is illegal in Brazil and severely punished by electoral authorities.

Political reactions to our survey fell into two categories: inquiries or complaints through official channels, and harassment of enumerators in the field. In two municipalities, public servants sent an email to our official project account or complained to the Brazilian IRB and State Accounts Court. The complaint to the Accounts Court generated some concern, and they asked us to cease the intervention in the corresponding municipality, but fieldwork had already been completed so our results were unaffected. In three municipalities, enumerators were harassed by allies of local politicians, and in some cases, they were followed and observed during fieldwork. As a result, they were unable to finish a handful of interviews (seven during the first round and forty-eight during the second) in two municipalities. In both cases, incidents were confined to one or two census tracts in peripheral communities where there was little or no police presence. Fieldwork was unaffected in more centrally located parts of these municipalities, from which the majority of respondents had been sampled.

9.2.5   Ethical Considerations

In concert with the overall objectives of the Metaketa Initiative, we sought to ensure that our study adhered to ethical principles. First, one of the Principal Investigators is Brazilian and a resident of the state of Pernambuco, so our study is not an instance of a strictly foreign team of academics intervening in an election abroad. Second, we obtained approval from the Institutional Review Boards of each of our universities.[16] This includes the *Comitê de Ética em Pesquisa* (Ethics in Research Committee) of the Federal University of Pernambuco, which, like all Brazilian IRBs, generally reviews only medical studies.[17] Thus, we went much further in obtaining approval than is typically done for studies of Brazil, especially those done by Brazilian social scientists.

Third, we partnered with the Brazilian government agency that produces the auditing decisions that we conveyed to voters in the common arm. The TCE-PE gave us formal permission to use its name and logo in the study, and it reviewed, requested modifications to, and ultimately approved the final version of the flyers. While we cannot claim that the intervention would have happened anyway without our participation, the design of the study is entirely consistent with the public education mission of the TCE-PE. We presented our research proposal to the TCE-PE as evaluating a method of direct outreach to individual citizens that they might consider adopting in the future.

Fourth, prior to the experiment we had very little basis for believing that our intervention could change the outcome of the election. In no municipality did our treatments reach more than 1 percent of the electorate. To estimate the number of votes moved in each municipality prior to launching the study, we relied on a full-scale ($n = 2,000$) pilot conducted in July 2016, administering the same treatments in many of the same municipalities. Based on the average treatment effects on intended

---

[16] Boston University, protocol 4094X; MIT, protocol 1604551604; *Universidade Federal de Pernambuco, número de parecer 1571592.*

[17] IRB review in Brazil is similar to the situation in the United States, in that university-based committees review research protocols according to a set of regulations that are defined at the federal level and apply nationwide.

vote for mayor in our pilot study, we estimated that our interventions could shift the votes of 8 percent of the number of treated voters in each municipality. In most places, this amounts to a mere two votes; in the most heavily sampled municipality, it constitutes twenty-two votes. As shown in our pre-analysis plan, our treatment effect would have had to be 3.25 times larger than estimated in the pilot study to have had a chance of changing the outcome of the closest prior election in these forty-seven municipalities over the past sixteen years. In fact, our treatment effect was much smaller than estimated in the pilot, so it is even more unlikely that our intervention made the difference between any candidate winning and losing.

9.3   RESULTS

To examine the overall impact of our treatment, we estimate the average treatment effect using the following estimating equation:

$$Y_{im} = \beta_0 + \beta_1 T_{im} + \sum_{j=1}^{k} \left(\mu_j X_{im}^j + \gamma_j X_{im}^j \cdot T_{im} \right) + \epsilon_{im} \qquad (9.1)$$

Y_{im} is the outcome variable for individual i in municipality m, T_{im} is the treatment indicator, X_{im}^j is the jth pretreatment covariate (demeaned using the sample average) and ϵ_{im} is the disturbance term. In the results presented here, X_{im}^j only include census tract dummies, which are our blocking variable; in the online appendix, we present all relevant specifications prespecified in the meta-analysis pre-analysis plan (MPAP), including those with covariate adjustment. Because we demean the covariates and include their interaction with treatment, β_1 is a consistent estimator for the average treatment effect.[18] For the standard error of our estimates, we employ the "HC2" heteroskedastic consistent estimator. In addition to conventional inference, we also test the sharp null of no treatment effect using permutation inference in each of our specifications. Our test statistic is the t-statistic of our experimental estimate. Our prespecified hypotheses are directional, so reported p-values are one-sided.

While the effect on vote choice is of primary interest, we first show the effect of our intervention on intermediate knowledge and attitudinal variables that should be affected if the information were to change behavior.

---

[18] Lin (2013).

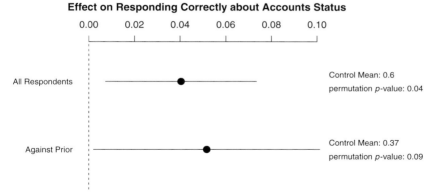

FIGURE 9.9 Brazil: Effect of treatment on learning. Dependent variable is a variable measuring if the respondent answered correctly about whether municipality accounts had been rejected by the TCE. The "Against Prior" sample consists of respondents who were incorrect about accounts status at baseline. Lines are 95 percent confidence intervals. *P*-values in the right margin are from one-tailed tests computed using permutation inference.

Specifically, we examine whether or not respondents learn as a result of the treatment, change their evaluation of the mayor in the specific domain of management of accounts, decrease self-reported uncertainty over their evaluations, and change their overall evaluation of the mayor's record.

First, we show that our intervention increased citizens' knowledge about whether their mayor's accounts had indeed been rejected or approved in 2013. In Figure 9.9, we present the estimated effect of treatment on respondents' knowledge of the TCE's decision on their mayor's accounts, both for the full sample and for as those who had been incorrect about the mayor's accounts at baseline. About 65 percent and 60 percent of respondents provided the correct answer in the treatment and control groups, respectively; the difference is statistically significant. While statistically detectable, the intervention did not dramatically increase the number of respondents giving correct answers. This suggests that many respondents either forgot the information or did not believe it. Among the group of respondents who answered incorrectly at baseline, about 37 percent of control group respondents provided the correct answer at endline, possibly indicating that some learning occurred over the course of the campaign.

Upon learning the information, did respondents change their assessment of the incumbent's handling of the municipality's accounts? As

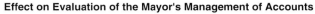

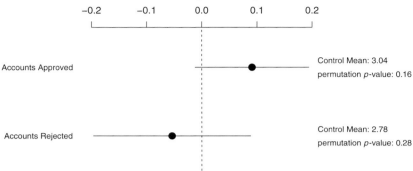

FIGURE 9.10 Brazil: Effect of treatment on evaluation of mayor's management of accounts. Dependent variable is the respondent's assessment of the mayor's management of the municipality's accounts on a five-point scale (higher values indicating a more positive evaluation). Lines are 95 percent confidence intervals; *p*-values in the right margin are from one-tailed tests computed using permutation inference.

evident in Figure 9.10, we find some evidence that respondents changed their views of the incumbent's performance on this dimension in the expected directions, as measured on a five-point scale. In both groups, however, the effect is imprecisely estimated. If we combine both groups and change the polarity of dependent variable to match the valence of the information (not shown), then the effect estimate is statistically significant with a point estimate of about .07. This latter specification is not prespecified, however.

We find inconsistent evidence that respondents' uncertainty over their assessment of the mayor's management of the municipal accounts diminishes as a result of treatment (Figure 9.11). Among respondents in accounts-approved municipalities, the average effect of the treatment is to diminish uncertainty by .05 on a five-point scale. In accounts-rejected municipalities, however, we find a small positive (and insignificant) effect. Overall, the effect is negligible.

Finally, we find null effects with respect to our main dependent variable, vote for the incumbent, as well as evaluation of the incumbent's record in office. As shown in Figures 9.12 and 9.13 the point estimates are in the expected direction but small and statistically insignificant. For vote choice, the point estimate for respondents in both types of municipality is no greater than .02. Accounting for sampling uncertainty, we

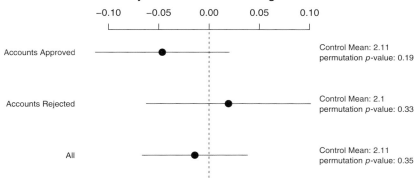

FIGURE 9.11 Brazil: Effect of treatment on uncertainty over evaluation of mayor's management of accounts. Dependent variable is the respondent's uncertainty over the their own assessment of the mayor's management of the municipality's accounts on a five-point scale (higher values indicating more uncertainty). Lines are 95 percent confidence intervals. *P*-values in the right margin are from one-tailed tests computed using permutation inference.

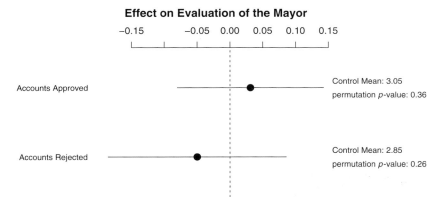

FIGURE 9.12 Brazil: Effect of treatment on evaluation of mayor's record. Dependent variable is the respondent's assessment of the mayor's record on a five-point scale (higher values indicating a more positive evaluation). Lines are 95 percent confidence intervals. *P*-values in the right margin are from one-tailed tests computed using permutation inference.

can rule out effect sizes greater than about .06 with 95 percent confidence. Overall, these results indicate that the respondents' vote choices are not sensitive to the information we distributed. We turn to possible explanations of this result in the next section.

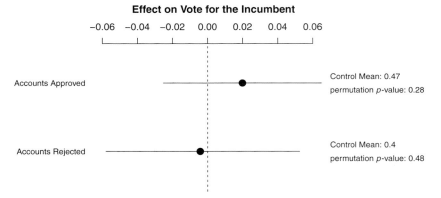

FIGURE 9.13 Brazil: Effect of treatment on vote for the incumbent. Dependent variable is the respondent's self-reported vote. Lines are 95 percent confidence intervals. *P*-values in the right margin are from one-tailed tests computed using permutation inference.

9.4   EXPLANATION OF EFFECTS

Why might our intervention have failed to exert any significant effects on the decision to vote for or against mayors running for reelection? One obvious answer might be that Brazilians fail to condemn corruption or malfeasance by elected officials. Yet numerous empirical studies and public opinion surveys suggest that, to the contrary, Brazilians are some of the most intolerant of official corruption in the world. In the most recent wave of the World Values Survey, Brazil ranked eighth out of sixty countries in the percentage who said that accepting a bribe is "never justifiable." In the AmericasBarometer surveys from 2004 to 2017, Brazilians have the highest levels of popular concern with corruption in the region, judged by an open-ended question about the most serious problem facing the country.[19]

In the context of Brazilians' staunch opposition to corruption, survey experiments presenting voters with hypothetical vignettes about a corrupt mayor running for reelection have found large and statistically significant electoral punishment effects, of much greater magnitude than similar studies in Colombia, Moldova, Peru, and Sweden.[20] In our own

[19] Boas, Hidalgo, and Melo (2019).
[20] Avenburg (2016); Botero et al. (2015); Klašnja and Tucker (2013); Vera Rojas (2017); Weitz-Shapiro and Winters (2017); Winters and Weitz-Shapiro (2013); Winters and Weitz-Shapiro (2016).

survey, we were able to replicate these large negative effects when presenting our treatment information about the rejection of accounts in the context of a hypothetical vignette.[21] The strong negative response in the vignette experiment shows that voters consider a rejection of accounts to be worthy of punishment; hence, the null effects of our field experiment should not be attributable to miscomprehension of the delivered information.

Our survey also underscores that Brazilians strongly support the horizontal accountability mission of the TCE-PE, especially under the original sanctions regime of the Clean Slate Law. In the second wave of our survey, we asked respondents whether mayors who had had their accounts rejected by the TCE should have the right to run for reelection. In the full sample of respondents, 91 percent answered "no." Even among respondents who reported voting for the incumbent mayor and had been informed of the rejection of his or her accounts, 84 percent said that such mayors should not have the right to run again – effectively claiming that the candidate they supported should not have been on the ballot.

Another explanation for the null finding might be pervasive cynicism about incumbents and challengers. If voters do not perceive the other candidates in the race as better alternatives with respect to corruption or malfeasance, negative information might not affect their voting behavior. The problem with this explanation is the lack of any effect of positive information. If voters' ex-ante opinions about all candidates were highly negative, the provision of positive information should induce some citizens to vote for incumbents with approved accounts since this new information would counter their priors. The absence of both positive and negative effects suggests that low expectations is an unlikely reason for our null findings.

Rather than suggesting that Brazilians do not care about corruption or malfeasance or that their expectations are already too low, we argue that they fail to act upon a strong anti-corruption norm due to a variety of factors that constrain voting behavior.[22] Here, we highlight two particularly important constraints: the greater salience of more tangible aspects of incumbent performance, such as job creation and the quality of health services, as well as voter loyalty to political dynasties, which serves as a functional equivalent to strong party identification in many

---

[21] Boas, Hidalgo, and Melo (2019).
[22] Boas, Hidalgo, and Melo (2019).

municipalities. In addition to our survey, this section draws upon several sources of qualitative data: background reports on fourteen municipalities prepared by Brazilian research assistants and postelectoral focus groups in three municipalities.

Our research makes it clear that corruption in general, and the judgment of a mayor's accounts by the TCE-PE in particular, are relatively low-salience concerns for voters in Pernambuco.[23] In the baseline survey we asked respondents to name the biggest problem in their municipality, and in the endline survey we asked what issue candidates had most discussed during the campaign. At the top of both lists are health (mentioned by 33 percent as the biggest problem, and 46 percent as the biggest campaign issue), crime (15 percent and 8 percent), employment (15 percent and 10 percent), and dealing with a severe drought affecting much of the state (15 percent and 7 percent). Only 2 percent mentioned corruption or municipal accounts as the biggest campaign issue, and fewer than 1 percent considered it the biggest problem.

Evidence from the focus groups underscored these findings from the survey. Asked about problems in their municipality, participants most often mentioned poor employment prospects, an issue exacerbated by the region's severe drought, which has made it difficult to earn a living in agriculture. Issues related to corruption and municipal accounts never arose spontaneously. When asked about the quality of the municipal government's "financial management," a term used in the survey to refer to the status of the mayor's accounts, participants talked instead about whether the municipal government paid public servants on time.

A second factor that likely constrains voters' responses to information about malfeasance concerns their loyalty or opposition to traditional political dynasties. Mass partisanship is relatively weak in Brazil, so it is unlikely to play the role that it is often thought to play in advanced democracies – limiting the effect on voting behavior of information gleaned during the campaign. Yet dynastic politics is likely to serve as a functional equivalent in many small towns. In the majority of our fourteen case study municipalities, one or more of the principal

---

[23] One possible factor behind the divergence between our findings and those of Ferraz and Finan (2008), who find large effects of releasing audit information, is that actors such as the media are essential for making audit results salient, as well as facilitating coordination among citizens who wish to act on the information.

candidates for mayor in 2016 was a close relative – parent, child, grand-child, sibling, niece/nephew, or current or former spouse – of a former mayor in that municipality. In some instances, candidates' families had dominated municipal politics for decades. Their campaign strategies often made these family ties explicit, such as featuring photos and names of ex-mayor relatives in their advertising materials.

Evidence from the focus groups underscores that loyalty to political dynasties may serve a similar function as traditional partisan attach-ments in more established democracies. While members of local political dynasties often switch formal party affiliations from one election to the next, participants often used the term "party" to refer to these groups. According to one participant in Flores, "all my life it's been two parties, either one of them has 5,000 votes guaranteed, and there are 2,000–3,000 votes left for them to dispute... the candidate can be Joe Nobody, he enters and gets 5000 votes." In Tabira, another participant said that "whoever votes for that party never ceases to be [loyal]... it's a real tra-dition. They are people that put on the shirt of their team and never take it off."

In sum, while Brazilian voters strongly condemn corruption and malfeasance in the abstract, it simply ranks too low on their priority lists to have much chance of influencing voting behavior in real elec-tions. Some residents of small towns may support the candidate of a local political dynasty out of longstanding loyalty to that particular clan. For voters such as these, any aspect of incumbent performance may have little influence over their decisions. Where local dynasties are weaker, residents may be more inclined to reward good performers and punish bad ones. Yet those voting based on performance criteria may be largely swayed by a mayor's record on tangible and highly salient issues such as job creation and local health services, leaving little room for additional information about the judgment of an auditing agency to influence their decisions.

9.5 RESULTS FROM THE PILOT AND SECOND ARM

Consistent with the idea that issue salience matters for the effectiveness of informational interventions, results from our pilot study and second arm show that certain types of information about incumbent performance can change voting behavior, but only for those citizens with a personal stake in the issue. In our large-scale pilot study, we provided information on municipal efforts at combating mosquito-borne illnesses such as Zika, dengue, and chikungunya, and in our second arm of the field experiment, we provided information on standardized test scores in municipality-run elementary schools. Mosquito-borne illnesses were a potentially salient issue at the time of our fieldwork because Pernambuco was the epicenter of an outbreak of congenital Zika syndrome, the series of severe birth defects, including microcephaly, associated with the Zika virus. For its part, school performance is potentially salient for parents of children enrolled in local schools, thus providing meaningful heterogeneity in the degree to which respondents had a personal stake in the policy.

With respect to the information on combatting mosquito-borne illnesses, our pilot study provided voters in the treatment condition with information about the municipality's hiring of Anti-Endemic Disease Agents (*Agentes de Combate às Endemias*, or ACE), specialized public health workers who visit homes to combat mosquitos and to teach residents about disease prevention. Municipalities are in charge of hiring these agents, using both federal and municipal funds; to benchmark their efforts, we use the number of agents funded by the Federal government. Thus, our performance indicator is the ratio of ACE agents per municipality to the maximum number funded by the federal government, which varies substantially across Pernambuco. Treatment information was delivered in a manner similar to that of the field experiment, but vote intention was recorded immediately after information delivery. Because the outcome variable was measured in the same survey – rather than several weeks later, as in our panel study – one might expect larger treatment effects.

Despite the intense media coverage of the Zika outbreak, we find that providing information about the municipality's efforts to combat mosquito-borne illnesses has no detectable effect on intended vote for the incumbent mayor, regardless of whether the municipality was a good or poor performer on our metric.[24] These findings also apply to parents of young children or those planning to conceive in the next several years, a population that might be particularly concerned about the effects of the Zika virus on fetal development. However, we find strong reactions to negative information among respondents who know someone with a child affected by microcephaly or the Zika virus. For this group, the treatment lowers support for the incumbent by 37.7 percentage points

---

[24] Boas and Hidalgo (2019).

in poor performing municipalities. Hence, only among respondents with a personal connection to the negative consequences of Zika – for whom information about mosquito control should be particularly salient – do we observe any electoral sanctioning effect.

We find a similar result when examining voters' response to information about municipal school performance.[25] The second arm of the field experiment informed about changes in scores on the National Literacy Evaluation (*Avaliação Nacional de Alfabetização* or ANA) during the mayor's first term. Among all respondents, we find an unexpected result: voters tend to punish good municipal performance on the ANA and are generally indifferent to poor performance. However, this result masks considerable heterogeneity by whether the respondent has a child enrolled in a municipal school. Among parents of enrolled children, for whom the issue should be most salient, we find the expected relationship: voters punish poor performance and reward (or are indifferent to) good performance. As with anti-disease efforts, a personal connection to the policy in question appears to be a prerequisite for information about incumbent performance to change voting behavior.

9.6 CONCLUSION

Vertical accountability might seem to offer a recourse for institutions of horizontal accountability whose efforts to sanction officeholders are blocked by legal obstacles or political maneuvering. While executives may be able to thwart the constraints imposed by other government entities, in a democracy they are more vulnerable to the punishment imposed by voters. If institutions like Brazil's State Accounts Courts can communicate their decisions directly to the public, they can potentially induce citizens to act directly, voting against and possibly defeating corrupt or malfeasant incumbents. The strength of Brazil's anti-corruption norm – confirmed in multiple surveys, including our own – suggests that voters might indeed have the will to do so.

The results of our Metaketa project underscore the limits of this form of "roundabout horizontal accountability." While Brazilian voters condemn corruption and malfeasance in the abstract, they fail to take action in a real election when presented with the same sort of information

---

[25] Boas, Hidalgo and Toral (2017).

about their own mayor. We argue that a variety of other factors serve to constrain voting behavior, including attitudes towards local political dynasties and the greater salience of more tangible aspects of incumbent performance, such as job creation. Hence, our findings underscore that robust, direct horizontal accountability is the most promising way to combat corruption and malfeasance in Brazil.

Dilemmas and Challenges of Citizen Information Campaigns: Lessons from a Failed Experiment in India

Neelanjan Sircar and Simon Chauchard

10.1 INTRODUCTION

Between June 2014 and October 2015, we developed, designed, and implemented with our partner SUNAI the India component of EGAP's first Metaketa project in the state of Bihar. This chapter provides an account of our project and of its interruption after an incident in which two of the enumerators working on the project were unlawfully detained by political workers, and later by local policemen.

The incident took place in the field on the second day of treatment delivery in October 2015, as the two enumerators were delivering the main treatment in our study – information about the criminal charges faced by all candidates in a constituency. As a result, we do not have data allowing us to test, as initially planned, any of the hypotheses originally specified in our pre-analysis plan.

However, a postmortem such as the one we provide in this chapter is important for a number of reasons. The first one relates to the imperative of transparency inherent to the kind of research promoted by EGAP and by this inaugural Metaketa. Experiments and other forms of empirical research are commonly interrupted and/or fail.[1] Other (especially junior) researchers need to be aware of this general fact,[2] and of the causes that often lead to these failures.[3] Second, the fact that experiments fail in some contexts and not others has implications in terms of external validity: do some contexts or types of treatment (e.g., information on criminality) make treatment failures more likely? More generally,

[1] Karlan and Appel (2016).
[2] https://chrisblattman.com/2016/10/20/14743/
[3] Karlan and Appel (2016).

what does this incident tell us about information and accountability? And what can we conclude from a comparative project such as the Metaketa in light of missing data from one of the sites? Third, revisiting this failure allows us to evaluate what mistakes, if any, were made by the various players on the research team (especially ourselves), the extent to which our design and protocols could have better dealt with potential difficulties, and what we would do differently if we were to implement a similar project in North India today. Finally, this incident provides us with an opportunity to introspect on the tradeoffs that researchers have to make at the design stage between risks, quality/strength of the treatment, and feasibility, and how these tradeoffs might impact what claims one can make from the Metaketa.

In order to address these questions, the rest of this chapter is organized as follows. We first describe the rationale and the design of the study, as we had planned to run it. Second, we describe the context in which the project took place during the 2015 State Assembly elections. In Section 4, we narrate the chain of events that eventually led to the failure of the project. In this section we rely on interviews of key stakeholders as well as on our own notes to describe the incident that led to the premature interruption of the project. In Section 5, we discuss what the interruption of the project tells us about the link between information and accountability and what measures might have helped us avoid the costly incident that prematurely led to the interruption of our study. We also question whether these alternative measures would have allowed us to run a valuable and scientifically sound study. Since we conclude that a "safer" study may not have been possible, the online appendix presents a detailed theoretical framework to help researchers think about the management of risk in large field experiments. We outline the tradeoffs researchers are forced to make as they design studies and expose the way in which these tradeoffs impact the inferences that can be made from a comparative project such as a Metaketa.

10.2 THE EFFECT OF INFORMATION AND LOCAL INTERMEDIARIES ON VOTE CHOICE

Like other projects included in this volume, our research sought to assess the impact of information dissemination on the selection of political candidates by voters. In the Indian context, our focus was on information about the criminal records of candidates. Would dissemination of this information lead voters to choose candidates facing fewer criminal charges?[4]

While the Election Commission of India has made this data public and online for over a decade, and while both English-language and vernacular newspapers routinely report on these charges ahead of elections, the extent to which this information reaches the median voter – and in what form – remains unclear. Accordingly, the objective of our treatment was to expand on the work of the institution in charge of ensuring fairness in Indian elections and to further publicize already publicly accessible information.

Furthermore, the "second arm" of our project (see Chapter 2) was not only interested in the effect of information, but also in the identity of those delivering the information about politicians. For this, we varied in this arm the identity of the individuals directly providing information to voters, as described further in Section 10.2.2.

While our study might have been run in any other large Indian state, several important reasons led us to focus on the state of Bihar. The state first struck us as a relevant context in which to investigate the relationship between information and accountability. Bihar is often seen – along with the eastern part of the adjacent state of Uttar Pradesh – as a hotbed for "criminal politics" and corruption in the country.[5] According to Vaishnav (2017): 177, "on a percentage basis, Bihar sends the largest number of politicians facing pending criminal indictments to its state assembly of any state in India." The combination of these high levels of criminality within the political class with comparatively low levels of literacy and high levels of poverty among voters, both of which can be assumed to correlate with difficulty to access information, made Bihar particularly relevant to the Metaketa Initiative. Insofar as we assumed access to information to be more costly to the median voter in Bihar than in other states in which we could have run the study, a large-scale dissemination effort may be particularly beneficial in that context.

This belief was reinforced by the fact that several local civil society organizations – especially the Association for Democratic Reforms (ADR) – had in the past attempted to mount awareness campaigns that echoed our own efforts in this project. While no campaign had ever been run on such a scale in the state, early discussions with local civil

---

[4] Candidates are required to publicly declare all criminal cases (with corresponding penal code article) at the time of filing for candidacy.

[5] Vaishnav (2017).

society stakeholders suggested that a lack of resources (as opposed to a lack of will to publicize this data) had been the cause of this absence. A field experiment such as the one we designed allowed us to build on these efforts and to test what various types of informational interventions, and the various types of politically relevant individuals that may be the bearers of this information, can do to increase accountability against "criminal types."

Beyond these theoretical rationales, our decision to focus on Bihar also owed to practical and logistical concerns. For one, Bihar was one of only three large states to have elections scheduled during the window of time defined by this Metaketa round. It was also a state which both of us had recently visited on separate research projects, where we knew of reliable implementing partners and whose main language (Hindi) we could, to various extents, understand. None of this was true of the other large states that held elections in 2015–16. While Bihar was relevant to the topic outlined for this round, it should thus also be noted that we did not have much of a choice if we were to be part of the inaugural Metaketa.

10.2.1   Research Design: General Principles and Scope

As summarized by Figure 10.1 below, our design aimed to compare the attitudes of voters randomly assigned to three different experimental groups: a control group and two different interventions.

In the first intervention, a survey research team (provided by SUNAI, our Patna-based partner) was to provide information on criminality to voters. In the second intervention, we were to provide the same information but instead were to enlist locally influential individuals to disseminate the information. Details on the format, the scope, and the content of these interventions are discussed below.

To do this, all of our treatments were to take place at the polling booth level.[6]

When measuring reactions to these treatments, we were interested in two types of outcomes:

1.   Official polling-booth-level electoral results and polling-booth-level turn-out data;

---

[6] That is, our design was a cluster-randomized experiment, with the cluster defined as the polling booth.

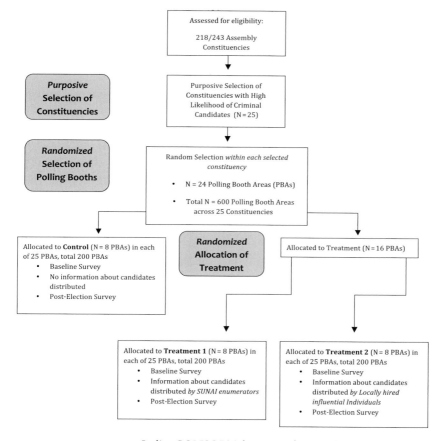

FIGURE 10.1 India: CONSORT diagram of research design

2. Voters' self-reported attitudes and preferences, as retrieved as part of a postelection survey.

In order to gather baseline data on prior beliefs and other covariates, as in several other Metaketa projects, and to increase the precision of treatment effect estimators, we had also started to run a baseline survey prior to our interventions and prior to the election.

There were, thus, three phases in this field experiment:

1. A baseline survey weeks before the election in which we were to survey twenty voters in each polling booth selected to be part of the experiment (including those assigned to the control condition);

2. An intervention phase (in two out of our three experimental groups);

3. A postelection survey in which we were to survey the same voters in each polling booth.

The 600 polling booths (200 in each of the three experimental groups) in which the study was to take place were stratified over twenty-five assembly constituencies across Bihar. In each polling booth, twenty randomly selected voters (as per the most recent voting list) were enlisted to be surveyed in the baseline and again in the postelection period.[7] Since only a small proportion of polling booths were treated in each targeted constituency, our experiment was extremely unlikely to affect the final result of the elections, in line with the principles of the Metaketa.

With our Bihar-based implementing partner, SUNAI, we prepared a list of "safe" constituencies in which the project would be feasible. The reasons to remove constituencies were varied – from poor accessibility and infrastructure to ongoing social conflicts and safety concerns. From the list of safe constituencies, we selected twenty-five assembly constituencies (ACs), and within each AC, twenty-four polling booths. While polling booths and voters within them were randomly selected,[8] constituencies were not.

Since our treatment was predicated on disseminating information about criminals, we did our best to maximize the probability of selecting ACs in which candidates facing criminal charges would be competitive. Unfortunately, since candidates are not known in India until two weeks prior to polling day, and since renomination rates of incumbents tend to be very low in India,[9] we had to rely on educated guesses. Using data on candidates in past elections assembled by the Association for Democratic Reforms, we compiled a list of candidates who faced serious criminal charges in previous state elections.[10] We found that constituencies in which competitive candidates (i.e., those finishing in the top two) had faced serious criminal charges were likely to see candidates with serious

---

[7] More detailed guidelines on the selection of voters within polling booths and on replacement rules are available in our study's original pre-analysis plan.

[8] Note that eight polling booths were selected for each of three treatment conditions (control, treatment 1, treatment 2) within each constituency.

[9] This was compounded by the formation of new pre-electoral alliances, which reduced the potential number of candidates from the major parties.

[10] ADR codes charges as "serious" based on the penal code under which the charges fall. These largely include violent crimes like murder.

criminal charges in subsequent elections. Thus, in order to select our constituencies, we selected every constituency (in which our partner deemed it was safe to work) where both competitive candidates were facing serious criminal charges in 2010. This yielded twenty-two constituencies. We then selected another eleven constituencies (enough to reach twenty-five, plus eight reserve constituencies) by selecting constituencies with the eleven highest vote shares for those facing serious criminal charges where the winner was also facing serious criminal charges. This was intended to lessen the chance that we would "lose" a constituency once the list of actual candidates was announced (only two weeks before the polls) because our treatments were not relevant there.

10.2.2   Interventions

In our two interventions (hereafter referred to as treatment 1 and treatment 2), we planned to disseminate publicly available information on pending criminal charges faced by each candidate running in the constituency. In each intervention, an average of two-thirds of the households in each selected polling booth area were to receive a flyer providing information on all of the candidates running in the relevant assembly constituency.[11] This flyer mentioned the number of criminal cases faced by all candidates who face criminal charges, as well as the specific charges (as per the Indian penal code) brought against these candidates.

In order to provide recipients of the flyer with a benchmark, each flyer provided information about the average number of criminal cases faced by candidates in other constituencies in the same subdivision of the state. Importantly, departing from the usual practice in existing studies on information and accountability, the enumerators delivering these prompts did not simply drop this material in front of the respondent's home. They were also tasked with explaining it to every household member they managed to meet.[12] Finally, the enumerators asked respondents to keep this prompt visible in their household up until the election.

This design allowed us to test not one but two definitions of "good news" and "bad news," as defined in the meta-preanalysis plan (MPAP).

---

[11]   The fact that this information was about all candidates, and hence did not target any specific candidate or party, helped ensure the nonpartisan nature of this study. This helped to reduce, in our opinion and in the opinion of our implementing partner, the potential for strong negative reactions among targeted voters or among candidates and their associates.

[12]   We had budgeted an average of six minutes per household towards this objective.

Voters may be sensitive to the extent of criminal charges among candidates in the constituency, in which case we expect those candidates displaying more criminality than the mean/median candidate in the constituency to be penalized by voters more in the elections. Alternatively, voters may only be concerned about whether a candidate is broadly a good or bad candidate with respect to his/her level of criminal behavior as compared to similar constituencies. In this case, voters would primarily respond to the regional benchmarks provided on the flyer.

In treatment 1, enumerators from SUNAI were to deliver this information. To the best of our knowledge, interventions have so far relied on such a delivery mechanism (i.e., using survey teams and/or NGO workers that rarely belong to the community to which voters themselves belong). While the identity of team members may be irrelevant if the treatment is constituted of materials anonymously delivered at voters' houses, this should matter in the context of a door-to-door campaign in which these enumerators are tasked with explaining the material and gaining voters' trust.

Accordingly, in treatment 2, our plan was to enroll locally recruited intermediaries and/or other locally influential citizens from each polling booth area in order to disseminate this same information. Successful civil society and political campaigns often conduct door-to-door activities in India, with parties and organizations usually enlisting a variety of locally influential notables, intermediaries, or "brokers" in order to carry a message (and promises, including promises in kind) to voters.[13]

Our design allowed us to identify these local intermediaries through our baseline survey, in which we asked people to name the three most important intermediaries in their polling booth area. Our implementing partner was then to contact the two most frequently named intermediaries in each polling booth area and provide them with an opportunity to work for us for a few weeks in the lead up to the election.[14] We would then have tabulated the names across all of the respondents in the polling booth area and selected two influential

---

[13] Chauchard (2018).

[14] In practice, we asked each respondent for three local (i.e., in the sampled or adjacent polling booth area) influential individuals as an answer to the following question: "In India, poor people often need help accessing state benefits and documentation. When people need help to access documents (for instance: aadhar card, BPL, and caste certificate) or to gain admission to a hospital in this/village/block/hamlet, who do they seek help from?"

individuals, attempting to hire the most named individuals and working down a list in descending order of popularity if these individuals refuse to work with us.

Similarly to SUNAI enumerators, these individuals would have conducted a door-to-door campaign during which they would have targeted two-thirds of the households in the polling booth area, subject to weekly unannounced monitoring from SUNAI.[15] To ensure that this amount of households was reached by the intervention and to ensure that the treatment was delivered properly, we planned to combine two monitoring strategies. We would first have our supervisors drop by unannounced in the polling booth area twice during the seven days which the intervention would take place. This visit would include an accounting of which households had been visited until that point (as well as a random check for a small percentage of households). Second, in order to incentivize these individuals, we were to reward them with a weekly wage of Rs. 2,500.[16]

10.2.3   Approval Process

After having reviewed a design document, P. K. Dash, then a deputy commissioner at the Election Commission of India (ECI), approved the broad principles of this design during a long and enthusiastic discussion with one of us (Chauchard) at the ECI's headquarters in Delhi on February 14, 2015. On that day, the deputy commissioner appeared eager to see the results of the study and warmly supported the research project, insisting that no authorization was needed, insofar as the information to be disseminated was public data that the ECI itself was trying to publicize before elections. This initially led the deputy commissioner to doubt the need for an authorization letter. After Chauchard insisted that such a

---

[15] Hired influencers were to attend a day-long meeting at the block level prior to the intervention, during which they would have received clear instructions about this target, and about the message to convey. The message conveyed would have included an instruction to display and keep the calendar/flyer in the home. To monitor the efforts of these locally hired intermediaries, we had planned to assign a SUNAI supervisor to monitor the work of these intermediaries in each polling booth. We would have also incentivized these intermediaries by measuring, in our postelection survey, the percentage of polling booth residents who were aware of the information contained on the flyers.

[16] Rs. 2,500 was chosen to ensure high take-up. Given incomes in rural Bihar, Rs. 2,500 (about US$38 at then-prevailing exchange rates) is an extremely strong incentive to participate for most individuals referred to as influential and to continue participating until the end of the intervention.

letter might serve us well in the field, he nonetheless agreed to produce such a letter.

On the following day, we received a document on ECI letterhead signed by Dash's principal secretary (S. K. Rudola)[17] stating that "data from affidavits can be used for your research purpose and also for the purpose of dissemination among the electors." A month later, we met officials at the Election Commission's office in Patna, presented the letter and similarly discussed the project after we had distributed design documents. They promised their full cooperation during the implementation of the project and detailed electoral data afterwards.

Both SUNAI and we repeatedly met with these officials over the next few months, mostly in order to obtain information and documents regarding the upcoming elections. No opposition to the project was voiced during any of these meetings in Patna. In parallel, SUNAI had established channels of communication with the main parties in the state, though it should be noted here that we refrained from presenting a detailed design including our prompts to political parties in Patna.[18]

10.2.4 Prompt in Treatment 1 and Treatment 2

Each voter targeted by either of our interventions (treatment 1 or treatment 2) was to receive a flyer containing information about the criminal charges faced by political candidates in her/his constituency.

In our design, respondents in both our treatment conditions were presented with information regarding a single topic: criminal charges filed against candidates. The flyer contained a general slogan in the header which read "the more honest your representative, the more work will be done for you."[19] It also contained information about the number of criminal cases of which each of the listed candidates actually facing criminal charges in the constituency were accused. Below this information, the flyer in each case mentioned that "this is more charges than x percent of candidates running in this election." At the bottom, a mention in bold suggested that "all other candidates running in this constituency

---

[17] It is not clear why Dash did not sign the letter himself. We do not think that this mattered down the line.

[18] This was at the insistence of the ECI, which argued that this was unnecessary in light of the public nature of the data we were to disseminate

[19] The word used in Hindi for "honest" was *imaandar*, which is typically used to denote an honest person in the sense of a morally upstanding character.

[i.e., THOSE NOT LISTED ON THIS SHEET] are NOT facing criminal charges." Finally, a mention at the bottom of the document explained that this is an independent, nonpartisan campaign sponsored by an American university and a Delhi-based think tank, and implemented by a Bihar-based partner (SUNAI). It also provided respondents with a local phone number from which they were able to obtain further information on the project should they want to do so.

10.2.5 Hypotheses

Our hypotheses were almost identical to the hypotheses outlined in the MPAP. For that reason, and since we have no test to run in light of the early interruption of the project, we do not reproduce them here (see Chapter 3). All necessary details are included in our study's pre-analysis plan, linked in the online appendix.

10.3 BIHAR POLITICS AND THE 2015 ELECTIONS

We implemented this research design ahead of the 2015 State Assembly elections. In order to provide some context for the following section (in which we detail the incident that led to the interruption of the project), we describe the climate in which the campaign took place and present the main contending forces.

Bihar, a state whose population is comparable in size to that of the Philippines (almost a hundred million), has for the past few decades exemplified changing trends in Indian politics, such as the rise of lower-caste politics (with the emergence of lower-caste parties such as the Rashtriya Janata Dal [RJD]), of communal politics (with the steady progress of a Hindu-majoritarian party such as the Bharatiya Janata Party [BJP]), and the so-called "criminalization of politics," with an ever growing number of parliamentarians and candidates facing serious criminal charges as they stand for election (Vaishnav, 2017).

Insofar as they constituted the first election in a major state since the triumph of the ruling party at the national level (the BJP), the Bihar 2015 elections had acquired national importance. The national importance of these elections was, in this context, heightened by the creation of an unprecedented coalition – a grand coalition, or *mahagathbandhan* – gathering previously opposed forces (the RJD, the Janata Dal (United) [JD(U)], and the Congress party) to take on the party of current Prime

Minister Narendra Modi, the BJP. While they had been clear rivals in
the past, the RJD and the JD(U) had opportunistically united after the
demise of the alliance between the BJP and the JD(U), and were later
joined by a weakened Congress party. These four parties and their leaders were the main focus of the race. Altogether, candidates fielded by one
or the other of these four parties received 231 of the state Assembly's 243
seats.

Importantly for our purposes, plenty of other, smaller political forces
competed in these elections. According to the records of the Election
commission, candidates from no fewer than 157 parties competed, in
addition to a large number of independent candidates, and an average
of 14.2 candidates ran in each constituency. While most of these parties received a minuscule portion of the vote, some of their candidates
had developed strongholds at the local level, and a very small number of
these actually won an election or came close to it.

High levels of violence or even "booth-capturing"[20] have in the past
marked electioneering in Bihar.[21] Both the records of the Election Commission and press sources however suggest that no major incidents
affected the tight schedule of the 2015 elections, either during the campaign period or on voting day. The Election Commission ordered very
few repolls, and remarkably few technological problems with voting
machines were officially reported. Altogether, this suggests that the campaign was relatively peaceful on the ground, and that the most obvious
forms of electoral malpractice had by and large disappeared by 2015, in
spite of the fact that the campaign had been heated in rhetorical terms.
Of course, this does not mean that all forms of electoral malpractice
or undue influence had disappeared, as observers denounced the role of
money, gifts, and electoral handouts in these elections,[22] as in most other
recent elections in India.[23]

This does not imply either that the candidates competing in these elections were flawless. Far from this, data assembled by the Association for
Democratic Reforms suggests that many candidates were facing crimi-

---

[20] In the Indian context, booth capturing means that members of a party or faction
forcefully occupy a polling booth and cast fake votes in the names of those registered as voters, and/or prevent voters of opposing factions from reaching the polling
booth.

[21] Quraishi (2014).

[22] See for instance: https://scroll.in/article/762967/booth-capturing-may-be-gone-but-cash
-flows-like-never-before-in-the-battle-for-bihar.

[23] Björkman (2014).

nal charges, including serious criminal charges in 2015: no fewer than 30 percent of candidates were charged in a criminal case, and 23 percent were charged in a serious criminal case (including charges of murder, attempted murder, rape, and kidnapping). These almost equally belonged to all parties, regardless of their electoral importance or the part of the state in which their strongholds were located.

Given that our sampling strategy was geared towards the selection of criminal candidates, this means that more than 30 percent of the candidates in the constituencies we had selected faced criminal charges (48 percent did), and hence would have been reported as such on our flyer. In Teghara, where the incident described in the next section happened, no fewer than four candidates (out of a total of seven) were listed on our flyers as facing criminal charges, including a candidate from one of the main parties (the BJP).

10.4　HOW THE PROJECT FAILED

On October 21, 2015, on the second day of treatment delivery (treatment delivery was planned to last over a month), field supervisors from SUNAI heard that two of the enumerators in charge of delivering the treatment were embroiled in a heated discussion with a group of men in a village of the Teghara constituency in Begusarai district. Earlier that morning, the two enumerators had attempted to distribute the treatment flyers to members of a randomly selected household in one of the polling booth areas of the village. Upon explaining the content of the flyer, they immediately faced the ire of the head of household, who asked for additional information as to the identity of the individuals behind this campaign.

Following the protocol they had been provided during the week-long training session a few weeks prior, the enumerators reiterated that they were employees of SUNAI, a Patna-based survey firm who had been contracted by two academics (one based in the US, one based in Delhi), and that the project had been cleared with various authorities in Patna, including the Election Commission. They also showed the copy of the official authorization letter that we had obtained from the Election Commission. Finally, in line with what they had been instructed to explain, they highlighted the fact that the campaign was not targeting any specific candidate or party (as a matter of fact, the flyer they had distributed listed criminal charges against no fewer than four of the seven candidates running in that constituency). They also explained several times that the campaign was implemented as part of a research project and that neither they nor the people employing them belonged to or were paid by one of the political forces competing in the elections.

None of this assuaged the concerns of the individual who had, by then, according to our enumerators, raised his voice, and accused the enumerators of attempting to ruin the reputation of one of the candidates whose name (and corresponding criminal charges) were mentioned on the flyer: the candidate from the Communist Party of India (CPI). It is useful here to describe the profile of this candidate. As mentioned in the affidavit he had submitted as he filed his candidacy a week before (from which our own flyer drew), the candidate faced no fewer than thirty-three charges across five different cases. This included charges related to attempted murder (article 307 of the Indian Penal Code), physical violence (article 337), concealment of stolen property (article 414), and voluntarily causing hurt by dangerous weapons or means (article 324). While the CPI is overall weak in Bihar (it won no seat and overall received 1.36 percent of the vote in the 2015 elections), it was relatively strong in Teghara, and it had chosen this local "strongman" as its candidate. In a relatively unlikely turn of events, we had randomly sampled the household of a close associate of that candidate. The man perceived the flyer, however legal it might have been, as a personal attack on the honor of his preferred candidate, and voiced this opinion in unequivocal terms. Insisting on the neutrality of the project and attempting to have a discussion with the individual soon became impossible, as a crowd gathered around. The arrival of a senior supervisor in the village did not improve the situation. Accordingly, it was quickly agreed upon by all parties that the team was to leave the village as soon as possible and to skip treatment delivery in that whole polling booth area.

At this point, the supervisor left on a motorcycle and the enumerators hitched a ride out of the village with a local vehicle in order to reach the main bus stand that would bring them back to the team's headquarters in Begusarai (there was no other way to leave the village). While they were waiting for the bus a few hours later, some ten kilometers away from the village, a group of men – some of whom had been present during the heated discussion earlier that morning – asked them to climb into a vehicle that brought them back to the village. There, they were sat in a house and physically prevented from leaving "until [their] bosses come to explain what is going on." While they were detained, they were not physically hurt or verbally abused, in part, it seems, because the men understood that these enumerators were only doing their job. During this detention, they were not prevented from using their cell phones, and made ample use of them, alerting both SUNAI supervisors at the block and district levels, as well as other enumerators working on the project throughout Bihar by posting messages and pictures on the messaging service "WhatsApp." As news of their detention spread, various supervisors and senior enumerators working in that part of the constituency made it to the village in an attempt to intercede with the group of men preventing the enumerators from leaving the village. These efforts did not succeed, and some of these team members were in turn prevented from leaving the building in which the enumerators were kept.

By the early afternoon we, along with the senior staff of SUNAI in Patna, were made aware of the developing situation. Pranav Chaudhary (the head of SUNAI) and his staff were in contact both with the group of men detaining the enumerators and with authorities at the district and at the state level (including members of the State Election Commission, Bihar). As it became clear that the enumerators were not going to be released until a face-to-face meeting was arranged, Chaudhary organized a car to take himself along with a member of the Election Commission and with members of the district administration to the village. When they reached the village at 9 pm (the village was more than four hours away from Patna, and the car faced rough evening traffic), the enumerators were by then detained at the local police station.

It remains unclear why the enumerators were moved from one location to the other; in particular, it remains unclear whether the candidate's associates willingly brought the men to the police station, or whether the police took control of the situation after having heard that an incident involving outsiders had happened. Regardless of what the answer to this question actually is, the policemen with whom Chaudhary talked voiced the same concerns as the candidate's own associates. While they agreed that they did not have any legal justification for the detention of the enumerators, they claimed that the reputation of that candidate had been affected, and perceived this as problematic, both legally and from a moral point of view. Upon meeting the delegation organized by Chaudhary, and after assurances were once more given that the enumerators would not come back to the constituency to campaign, local policemen agreed in a matter of minutes to free the enumerators.

While it is difficult to identify what so quickly led to this reassuring outcome, we may venture some hypotheses. The most likely possibility in our opinion is that local policemen had colluded with the candidate's associates all along, to extort the research team, to prevent the campaign from happening, or both. However, the impressive assemblage of local officials that Chaudhary had brought to the village (or reached on the phone throughout the day) had proved sufficient to pressure them into following the law, maybe because they feared that such connections could lead to blame from their (distant) superiors, either at the district level or in the state capital. A second, though not entirely impossible, hypothesis is that they genuinely were unaware of the law and of the already public nature of the data on criminal charges, and accordingly thought that they had nabbed individuals engaging in illegal forms of campaigning, a grave offense under the "model code of conduct" in place during Indian elections. Once this agreement between all parties was reached, all SUNAI staff left the village and returned to Patna. None of us have since heard from this group of men.

While the worst outcomes were avoided (in this case, arguably, physical harm to members of SUNAI staff), the events of that day led us to suspend the project. Even though we debated continuing the project (after revising our design), both we and the senior staff of SUNAI eventually came to the conclusion that it would be irresponsible to send another enumerator into the field after what had happened in Teghara.[24] We and SUNAI had been relatively surprised by the incident, having assumed greater respect for the Election Commission and for its orders than was obviously true in some pockets of the country. We also recognized that we had bad luck by randomly selecting the house of a close associate of one of the most controversial candidates across the state on the second day of treatment delivery.[25] But in IRB parlance, the risks in our view now clearly outweighed any potential benefit, the Teghara incident having caused us seriously to update our beliefs about potential dangers.[26]

This realization logically led us to end the project. It is however important to note that we would not have been able to carry on with the

---

[24] While we would undeniably have reached that conclusion, it did take us a few days to fully admit that the only right thing to do was to end a project that had been planned for over a year, at a relatively high cost. Meanwhile, all operations remained suspended.

[25] For what it is worth, no significant incident took place on Day 1. Besides, no incident took place in other locations on Day 1 or Day 2 (treatment delivery was interrupted across the state in the afternoon of Day 2).

[26] The risks of harm that IRBs usually consider are explicitly not to enumerators; rather, they focus on risks of harms to subjects. In line with Chapter 2, we thus implicitly contend that risks of harm should be extended and explicitly consider risks to enumerators and other staff. It is in this spirit that we reached this conclusion.

project (at least in its original design) after this incident, even if we had been oblivious enough to overlook security concerns to our staff. There are two reasons for this. First, our enumerators might have refused to work, or more likely in our view, they would have delivered the treatment extremely selectively. This is because all staff members had been informed of the developing incident in a matter of minutes and hours through social media, in many cases even before the SUNAI senior staff and we learned about it. This would have dramatically lowered the quality of treatment delivery and generated quality issues that no analysis would have been able to overcome.

Second, and most importantly, officials at the Election Commission refused to continue to support the project after the incident. Officials with the Patna office demanded that SUNAI stop treatment delivery the day following the incident. A few weeks later, as we were evaluating whether an alternative treatment delivery was feasible and if we could move the project to another state, the ECI reiterated the same demand in an order addressed to SUNAI, and additionally stated that we would not be allowed to survey voters close to election dates. Insofar as this reverted a previous authorization, and deliberately made the project impossible to carry out, the message was clear: we had lost the support of the authority without whom the project could not be carried out. Election Commission officials are notoriously overworked during elections, and their main objective is not to assist researchers, even if those researchers run a project that builds on their efforts. As such, although frustrating for us, the Commission's decision was understandable.

10.5 LESSONS FOR INFORMATION AND ACCOUNTABILITY EXPERIMENTS IN INDIA (AND ELSEWHERE)

What does this series of events tell us about researchers' ability to run information and accountability experiments in India, and about the likelihood that these experiments bring about promising change?

10.5.1 Can Researchers Distribute Information about Criminal Charges?

The first question to ask relates to our choice of informational treatment, i.e., information about criminal charges. One possibility is that the project was interrupted because the effect of the information distributed was conceivably bigger than it could have been, had we distributed other types of information, for instance information regarding politicians' performance in office. Shall we infer from this incident that the type of information distributed was too sensitive, and that information and accountability experiments should altogether refrain from distributing information about criminality to avoid a similar outcome?

A number of reasons lead us to think that the kind of information we distributed was not necessarily the problem, and that such information might still be distributed in future experiments. For one, all other politicians incriminated by our treatment in Teghara and in the other constituencies in which we had time to distribute the treatment did not react to it, or at least we did not hear about any such reaction.[27]

But, we also found it theoretically implausible that most candidates, at least those from the main parties, would have violently reacted against our information dissemination, even if we had had enough time to properly observe their reactions. We give three reasons why below.

The first is that recent social scientific research on North Indian voters' reactions to information about criminality does not suggest that this information would have had an effect large enough to dissuade voters from choosing candidates with criminal cases. A series of recent survey experiments suggest that voters do react negatively to news that candidates face criminal cases, but also that the effect of this information is much smaller than the effect of other considerations,[28] leading to the conclusion that voters often choose criminals in spite of the fact that they disapprove of criminality. Besides, Vaishnav (2017) argues that voters in polarized settings are likely to prefer candidates facing criminal charges. Overall, recent empirical research on Bihar hardly suggests that voters' reactions would have been strongly negative. Assuming political actors have a sense of this, it is not straightforward that they would feel compelled to react to our treatment and attempt to prevent its implementation. In that sense, it is possible to think that the reaction we faced in Teghara was not representative of the median voter, but rather of a close associate of a particularly controversial candidate.

The second is that such reactions would have tarnished the reputations of their authors and of their parties at the state, or even at the

---

[27] All would have very likely heard about it, either from their party leaders or from their supporters on the ground. This was true of candidates of both leading and smaller parties.

[28] Chauchard (2016).

national level. Since the race was largely followed in the Indian media, beyond Bihar, and since the stakes were high for the ruling party at the national level, we believe it is highly unlikely that a candidate from one of the main parties would have taken this kind of risk. While this does not solve the problem of smaller candidates, independents, and other actors less sensitive to reputational costs, this strikes us as an important nuance: if political actors from the main parties are unlikely to react violently to this type of treatment, it may be possible to create incentives for smaller candidates to react similarly. More importantly, this implies that better preparation on our side – for instance, better coordination ahead of elections with each candidate (including small candidates) – may have allowed us to distribute similar information and avoid incidents. Of course, this may have generated alternative design issues to which we return below, but it is nonetheless worth noting here.

Finally, accounts collected from enumerators suggest that the associates of the candidate who led to the interruption of the project would actually have opposed any form of negative campaigning (or at least, campaigning perceived as negative) by outsiders to their village. From what we can gather, their opposition did not only owe to the content of the flyers, but also to the identity of those distributing it. Survey practitioners, politicians, and researchers are well aware of the risks of sending outsiders to a village to campaign – regardless of what that campaign is. While this suggests that we did not adequately account for every possible risk, it does not necessarily suggest that the risks were specific to information about criminality. It is conceivable that the kind of information we provided increased these risks with some candidates, but it does not follow that this kind of information is squarely to blame. As mentioned below, a different design, better preparation on the institutional front, and other changes might have allowed us to distribute similar information.

10.5.2   Did We Pick the Wrong Setting?

Since the kind of information we distributed may not be squarely to blame, is it then that we chose the wrong setting?[29]

As noted above, Bihar is widely reputed across India for its high levels of criminality and lawlessness. We were and remain well aware of this.

---

[29] Though, as noted above, we did not have many options in this case, in light of practical and logistical constraints. Hence the term "choice" may not be quite appropriate.

While neither we nor anyone else among the dozens of Indian academics, politicians, civil society practitioners, and bureaucrats we talked to in the lead up to the project came near to predicting this outcome, our priors have changed and we have learned a lesson. However, we remain reluctant to blame Bihar or to imply that such an incident would not have happened elsewhere in India. This is because the mechanisms that led to the demise of our project are not specific to Bihar.

Our experience in Teghara generally highlights the fact that risks exist when the rule of law is weak. As mentioned above, the overwhelming majority of politicians incriminated by our treatment did not react, nor do we have evidence suggesting that they would have. But when the rule of law is weak, any reaction from candidates – however rare it might be – can have very costly consequences.

In India, as we suspect in a number of other countries in which Metaketa I took place, politicians eager to act against an information dissemination campaign would not mount a counter-campaign and engage with researchers' dissemination efforts in the marketplace of ideas. This is because they could much more easily encourage physical violence and intimidation, and/or manipulation of agents of the state. The incident that happened during our study is a case in point. In spite of the fact that we had received necessary authorizations by the time the campaign started, associates of a candidate deliberately engaged in violence and some agents of the state were very easily manipulated in the process. If and when interference with researchers' campaigns take this form, any incident is likely to be worrisome enough for researchers and their staff to prefer abandoning the implementation of their project. Though this may be obvious, here it is important to note that researchers in such contexts are (and should be) more risk-averse than political actors. Because of this disadvantage, information dissemination campaigns implemented in areas in which the rule of law is weak inherently risk interruption.

Furthermore, when the rule of law is weak and the mechanism of interference with the campaign does not take place in the marketplace of ideas, small actors can have a big effect. Had the Teghara candidate engaged with our campaign by mounting a campaign suggesting that the information on our flyer was false, or had he suggested to voters in a speech that these criminal charges would not prevent him from being a great representative, our study would not have been affected, especially so because that candidate appeared to have a very small following. The fact that his interference took another form instead led to the complete collapse of the study, for the reasons described above.

Finally, when the rule of law is weak, support from high-level authorities may by definition be insufficient, insofar as these authorities may not themselves command respect on the ground, at the very local level. The aforementioned reversal of the Election Commission is here a case in point: officials at higher levels were enthusiastic about the project until they realized – or until they could no longer hide the fact – that political actors on the ground did not respect their orders.

While Bihar probably would not rank among the Indian states with the highest levels of rule of law, it does not strike us as being extremely different from many other states in India, a country in which police forces have been generally described by one prominent observer as only having "provisional authority."[30]

If neither Bihar nor the kind of information we distributed is squarely to blame, what is? We believe the culprit to be some aspects of the design of our study and of our preparation ahead of treatment delivery.

10.5.3 How Could We Have Further Minimized Risks?

Before we outline the flaws of our project, it is worth noting that we took a rather extensive series of steps to minimize risks. Both districts and polling booths were chosen selectively, in collaboration with our implementing partner, in order to avoid what we predicted to be the most problematic booths; as is common with surveys, enumerators never traveled or provided the treatment alone; multiple channels of communication existed between each team and supervisors and between supervisors and the senior staff of our implementing partner, which allowed the incident to be reported, and dealt with, extremely quickly; and extensive security protocols were provided to enumerators, who generally followed them.

More drastic and restrictive measures would have been needed to ensure that the aforementioned incident was avoided. In light of what we now know, and in light of our greater risk-averseness, we now would probably prefer not to run a project similar to this one in India before we are able to:

1. Build a stronger and clearer partnership with the ECI (and other local authorities). How we could have achieved this or obtained the necessary guarantees remains unclear to us. We are, however, keenly

---

[30] Jauregui (2016).

reminded that seeking authorizations from these organizations did not equate to full support. ECI officials may never have committed more than they did. Nonetheless, we wish we had better assessed how committed the ECI really was to helping us implement the project. If we had a clearer sense that the institution's enthusiasm would crumble after a single incident, we would have refrained from launching our treatment.

2. Ensure that we sample safe areas, if need be at the expense of external validity. It is now clear to us that we should have skipped constituencies in which one or several small candidates were described as "strongmen" or had a reputation for lawlessness, regardless of whether these characters were "small" or independent candidates. From an introspective point of view, it is true that we did not spend enough time parsing through the names and the profiles of small candidates after these became known. This would have been expensive and hard to achieve in practice since candidates tend to be known at the last minute in India (two weeks before elections, when our treatment would have to be launched). It may not have been a completely unrealistic a task, if we had committed much of our resources to it. Even if we had invested in this task, it remains that learning about small candidates (there were fourteen candidates on average, per constituency, across Bihar in 2015) would have been very hard in a short time frame. Nonetheless, this might have allowed us to skip one or several districts in which obviously problematic characters ended up running, including Teghara, and hence to complete our project.

3. Upon having chosen constituencies in which our treatment was to be delivered, systematically hold a meeting with each candidate, warning candidates of the precise format and content of the intervention. More should have been done in a project of this type. While we did establish channels of communications with the main parties, we did not adequately address smaller players in the election. This incident suggests a need to inform all stakeholders mentioned in every treatment beforehand – in this case, candidates at the local level – including small and independent candidates, rather than party apparatuses in the state capital. It also suggests the need to inform these stakeholders by providing them with more detailed, concrete information about our treatments, e.g., by showing them a prompt before treatment delivery. This was mainly a function of time constraints in our case, as we had too little time between candidate nominations and treatment delivery. But there may have been alternative designs (a design focusing on fewer constituencies, for instance), in which we may have been able to allocate more time to such a task.

4. Refrain from sending outsiders to the village to deliver our treatment. This may have taken place in one of two ways. First, we may have replaced enumerators by insiders to the village or locally recruited enumerators. Second, though this may be seen as an extreme revision of our design, we may alternatively have refrained from sending any enumerators at all to deliver the treatment, for instance by changing the format of treatment delivery from a face-to-face interaction to a text/SMS or to a radio message. Had we proceeded in one of these ways, risks would have been severely reduced and data collection likely would have taken place as planned.

If we had to run a similar project in India today, we would definitely want to ensure that our design takes into account these four points.

10.5.4 Was a Safer Version of the Project Worth Running?

With this in mind, it does not necessarily follow that our decision process would be straightforward if we were presented with the opportunity to do this all over again. At the risk of sounding exceedingly pessimistic, this is simply because there may not exist in our view an experiment that is: 1) safe; 2) feasible from a practical standpoint; and 3) scientifically interesting in this context, once the constraints of the situation are properly factored in. Correcting our mistakes, while reducing risks, might lead us to come up with a less valuable experiment from a scientific point of view. Alternatively, it may lead us to develop a very inefficient, under-powered design, or frankly an unrealistic one, as the management of risks is directly correlated to the cost or to the complexity of a design.

As noted above, ensuring that we did not sample constituencies in which small, independent candidates with problematic reputations exist, might have been possible. However, this would have required that we deploy an impressive army of surveyors over a very short period of time in order to collect information about the reputation and the networks of each and every declared candidate. Assuming this had somehow been possible, this would have likely led us to allocate our resources differently, and probably to sample fewer constituencies altogether. This may have had problematic consequences in terms of statistical power and external validity. Worse, assuming we had successfully managed to exclude constituencies in which these problematic profiles were planning to contest, we would have obtained results based on a biased sample, making the interpretation of our results – and of the Metaketa – rather challenging.

Better informing candidates mentioned in the treatments, including small candidates from small parties, might also have been possible, even if accounting for every potential political actor (with an average of fourteen candidates per constituency) would have been a daunting task. This may not however have been desirable from a methodological point of view, as it raises an important question about what the optimal "strength" of a treatment should be. Such deliberation with local notables would have changed the nature and the strength of the treatment, insofar as incriminated politicians would have likely developed rebuttals to our flyer. Besides, such a design might have made the work of our teams of interviewers even riskier. Finally, this raises a host of practical questions relating to sampling and external validity: how would we proceed if some small candidates refused treatment delivery in their constituency upon hearing about it during said meeting? Would we then refrain from delivering the treatment altogether, leading to further bias and external validity issues?

Replacing enumerators by insiders to the village or locally recruited enumerators may be a solution. This is more or less what the second arm of our study proposed to do, and we note that no incident took place in the booth in which this treatment was implemented. But the little data we have suggest that we may have faced other issues with our second arm, namely, compliance issues on the part of "local" workers with whom neither SUNAI nor ourselves had a strong relationship. This again raises questions about what the optimal strength of a treatment should be and about the trade-offs between the quality of a design and the risks that are associated with it.

Operating without enumerators may be the most realistic solution from a budgetary point of view. We probably would want to proceed in this fashion if we were to attempt to run a similar project again in India. One way to do this may be to rely on text messages, as in the Uganda 2 study described in this volume (see Chapter 7). While there were serious practical hurdles to implementing such a strategy in our case (we would have had to collect numbers ourselves first, since no sampling frame existed), this could have been tried.[31] A text-based (SMS) treatment is not

---

[31] In our design, which included both a baseline and a post-poll survey, even this method of treatment delivery may not have been risk-free for our staff. Suppose, for instance,

something either of us was initially interested in implementing, insofar as this appeared to us to be a particularly weak treatment – i.e., one that few people effectively receive and even fewer effectively process. In light of some of the results presented in this volume and elsewhere, our priors have started to change on this point. But it remains, that such a treatment delivery raised major selection issues in rural Bihar as of 2015. Many household members may not own a mobile phone and rates of literacy remain low in rural Bihar; if combined, this suggested to us that we would reach a relatively low proportion of our targeted voters, and hence that we would be wasting our resources on a relatively weak treatment.

In light of these remarks, we believe that a "safe" version of our original project – that is, one taking into account the suggested revisions listed above – may not necessarily be worth running, at least as of today. Of course, all of this may change in the not-so-distant future as Bihar and India evolve, and all of this depends quite a bit on the kind of budgets that are made available to researchers. But everything else held constant, it is not clear to us that there is a meaningful, scientifically sound and safe study to be run at this point in this context on this topic, in light of these constraints.

More generally speaking, we believe our experience in Bihar highlights difficult tradeoffs researchers have to make between perceived risks and the scientific quality of a design. Accordingly, we believe the discussion that researchers need to have is a discussion about design choices in light of risks. In the online appendix, we set out a formal model of the decision process guiding researchers as they strive to balance risk, the scientific soundness of their design, and project feasibility in light of costs and time constraints.

that we collected cellphone numbers from our baseline survey before treatment delivery and subsequently used these numbers to send materials to our respondents as part of our treatment. To truly minimize risks, we would have had to ensure that our population of respondents did not subsequently identify the enumerators running the post-poll survey as the ones that recorded their phone numbers a few weeks before. This may be a risky bet.

PART III

CUMULATIVE LEARNING

11

Meta-Analysis

Thad Dunning, Clara Bicalho, Anirvan Chowdhury, Guy Grossman, Macartan Humphreys, Susan D. Hyde, Craig McIntosh, and Gareth Nellis

Do informational interventions shape electoral choices and thereby promote political accountability?

The chapters in Part II of this book provided answers to this question in particular contexts. The studies individually provide rich insights not only into the impact of interventions that were common to all studies, but also on the effects of alternative interventions that were specific to each one.

In this chapter, we assess the larger lessons that we can glean from our coordinated studies. As outlined in Chapter 3, all studies seek to test common hypotheses about the impact of harmonized informational interventions, using consistent measurements of outcome variables. Our preregistered analysis allows us to evaluate whether, pooling data from the set of studies in the initiative, information about politician performance led voters to alter their electoral behavior. It also informs a discussion about the conditions under which they did or did not do so.

We find that the overall effect of information is quite precisely estimated and not statistically distinguishable from zero. The analysis shows modest impacts of information on voters' knowledge of the information provided to them. However, the interventions did not appear to shape voters' evaluations of candidates, and, in particular, they did not discernibly influence vote choice. This slate of null results obtains in nearly all analyses for the individual country studies too.[1] Nor is there strong evidence of impact on voter turnout, though under some specifications

---

[1] As we discuss later, differences in operationalization and analysis of the common datasets result in minor differences between country-specific analyses in our meta-analysis and several results reported in Part II.

we find suggestive evidence that bad news may boost voter mobilization. Our results are robust to different analytic strategies and across a variety of modeling and dataset construction choices. The findings also suggest that the estimated effect in our missing study would have needed to be extremely large to alter our broader conclusions.[2] The size of our meta-analysis reduces the chances that null estimated effects stem from low statistical power, and the fact that our results are so consistent across the individual studies limits the possibility that our mostly null effects are due to idiosyncrasies in implementation or study design.

In the rest of this chapter, we first describe the prespecified approach that we use to analyze the pooled dataset. We then report our main findings, point out the consistency of results across studies, and report robustness checks. Next we consider several possible reasons for our null findings by testing the prespecified hypotheses. The most plausible reason for the null effects stems from the failure of the interventions to shape voters' perceptions of politicians; we do not find evidence, however, that this is due to partisan or ethnic attachments or other heuristic substitutes for information. It is critical to underscore the similarities of these interventions to previous treatments in the experimental research literature and to interventions for which donor organizations in the transparency space routinely advocate. Indeed, our interventions were crafted by researchers with substantial country-specific expertise, usually in collaboration with local NGOs. Our null results across wide array of contexts therefore provide an important baseline of evidence against which future studies can be weighed.

This chapter could be profitably read in conjunction with Chapter 3, which discusses the common interventions and our measurement of key variables, but it can be read as a standalone chapter as well.

11.1 PRIMARY ANALYSIS: AVERAGE EFFECTS ACROSS CASES

11.1.1 Hypotheses and Estimation

In previous chapters, we described the core theories of political accountability that motivate our focus on information and electoral behavior. As

---

[2] As described previously, a planned study on incumbent criminality in India did not take place due to implementation challenges (see Chapter 10).

outlined there, each of the informational interventions in our Metaketa focused on the performance of politicians or their parties. Thus, six studies provided information related to incumbents' legislative performance (Adida et al. in Benin), spending irregularities (Boas et al. in Brazil, Arias et al. in Mexico, and Buntaine et al. in Uganda 2), the caliber of public services in their jurisdictions (Lierl and Holmlund in Burkina Faso), and their policy positions and quality as candidates (Platas and Raffler in Uganda 1). In their common intervention arms, each of the studies sought to disseminate publicly available performance information that is directly attributable to an incumbent candidate or party; to provide this information privately to individuals within a month prior to an election; and to divulge performance information that is presumed to be relevant to voter welfare. In their second, complementary treatment arms, studies also independently varied the medium for information provision; the kind of information provided; or the scale of the information provision, for example, by providing information publicly to groups instead of privately to individual voters.[3]

We focus on meta-analysis of the common intervention arm in this chapter, as registered in our meta-preanalysis plan (MPAP).[4] Critically, each study was designed to allow measurement of the extent to which voters update their beliefs about the performance of the politicians positively or negatively in light of the information – and to allow measurement of the difference between prior beliefs and provided information. As described in Chapter 3, we expected effects to derive from *new* information rather than *any* information. Most teams gathered information on voter priors at baseline (in both treatment and control groups) with respect to the information that would be provided. Where possible, prior beliefs were gathered on the same scale as the information that was eventually provided to individuals assigned to the treatment groups. This allows us to identify voters who would have received positive or negative information, if assigned to the treatment group. Our empirical strategy therefore takes account of both the content of the information and prior beliefs.

Our core hypotheses for meta-analysis thus concern the impact of positive and negative information (or "good" and "bad" news, see

[3] Table 3.1 in Chapter 3 provides a summary.
[4] The MPAP appears in the Appendix.

Chapter 3) on vote choice, as well as turnout.[5] We preregistered two primary hypotheses related to electoral behavior:

- H1a: Positive information increases voter support for politicians.
- H1b: Negative information decreases voter support for politicians.

These hypotheses are straightforward, yet critical: as discussed in Chapter 3, they are necessary components of many models of electoral accountability. We also registered secondary hypotheses related to electoral participation:

- H2a: Good news increases voter turnout.
- H2b: Bad news decreases voter turnout.

We describe in Sections 11.1.2 and 11.4 other prespecified hypotheses about the impact of our informational interventions on intermediate outcomes, such as perceptions of candidate integrity and effort; the possibility that politicians would mount campaigns in response to negative information; and the conditional effects of information, depending for example on coethnic and partisan ties between citizens and politicians.

The most straightforward way to test our primary and secondary hypotheses across studies is to divide subjects into groups based on whether they would receive good or bad news if exposed to the treatment.[6] For each group, we randomly assign the information treatment to some respondents and not to others. Thus, we use random assignment to estimate the effect of information in the good news group and do the same for the bad news groups. These are subgroup effects, because the groups are defined according to subjects' prior beliefs as well as the provided information.

In one set of analyses, we estimate average treatment effects with simple differences of means, where comparisons between treatment and control groups (within each of the good and bad news subgroups) are unadjusted by covariates, other than fixed effects for treatment assignment blocks. There are tradeoffs involved in the use of covariates. Precision gains from covariate adjustment may be substantial; and transparent prespecification of the covariates used for adjustment removes,

---

[5] In this chapter, we use outcome data at the individual level. Only some studies collected aggregate data (e.g., on official electoral results), and we do not pool those analyses here. Some of the individual studies presented in Part II (e.g., the Arias et al. study in Mexico; see Chapter 5) do present analysis of aggregate data.

[6] See also Chapter 3.

in principle, the possibility of data mining and specification searches.[7] However, implementing covariate adjustment across projects is not trivial, in part because covariates must be gathered and measured in similar ways across studies. For example, we prespecified a list of fourteen covariates in our MPAP, but in the end project teams could only measure ten of these across all studies.[8] Unadjusted results have the advantage of simplicity, and it is easiest to hew closely to the prespecified analysis when covariates are not included.[9]

In another set of analyses, however, as prespecified in our MPAP, we estimate average treatment effects by fitting two regressions, one for the good news and one for the bad news group:[10]

$$E(Y_{ij}|i \in L^+) = \beta_0 + \beta_1 N_{ij}^+ + \beta_2 T_i + \beta_3 T_i N_{ij}^+ + \sum_{j=1}^{k}(v_k Z_i^k + \psi_k Z_i^k T_i) \quad (11.1)$$

and

$$E(Y_{ij}|i \in L^-) = \gamma_0 + \gamma_1 N_{ij}^- + \gamma_2 T_i + \gamma_3 T_i N_{ij}^- + \sum_{j=1}^{k}(v_k Z_i^k + \psi_k Z_i^k T_i). \quad (11.2)$$

Here, T_i is the treatment assignment variable: that is, $T_i = 1$ if respondent i is assigned to receive the informational treatment and zero otherwise. Also, N_{ij}^+ and N_{ij}^- are the gaps between priors and information in each group, standardized to have zero mean and unit variance in each group in each individual study. Thus, $N_{ij}^+ \equiv Q_j - P_{ij}$, given that $Q_j - P_{ij} > 0$, where Q_j is the provided information about politician j and P_{ij} is voter i's prior belief about politician j, on the dimension about which

---

[7] See Chapter 2. On covariate adjustment, see Freedman (2008a, b); Lin (2013).

[8] The covariates used in the results in this chapter include measures of N_{ij} (described in the following paragraph), age (M14), years of education (M17), wealth (M18), whether the respondent voted in the previous election (M20), whether the respondent voted for the incumbent in the previous election (M21), exposure to clientelism (M22), perception of the credibility of the information source (M24), baseline belief in secret ballot (M26), and whether the respondent perceived the election as free and fair (M27). Here, we give in parentheses the measure numbers used in the MPAP; see the book's Appendix.

[9] Moreover, in an experiment this large, the precision gains from covariate adjustment are often minimal; and unadjusted and covariate-adjusted estimated effects and standard errors differ little.

[10] While Equations 11.1 and 11.2 are convenient for estimation, our estimands are all defined under the Neyman potential outcomes model. In the Neyman model, potential outcomes under treatment or control are fixed for each respondent but are free to vary across respondents; see Splawa-Neyman, Dabrowska, and Speed (1990), Rubin (1978), and Holland (1986). The only random element in this model is the stochastic assignment to treatment or control.

information is provided. A voter i is in the good news group ($i \in L^+$) when performance exceeds her priors, or when performance information confirms positive priors: that is, $Q_j - P_{ij} > 0$, or $Q_j = P_{ij}$ and Q_j is greater than the median performance in the relevant locality. Otherwise, she is in the bad news group ($i \in L^-$). Furthermore, $Z_1, Z_2, \ldots, Z_k$ are prespecified covariates, also standardized with zero mean; the regressions include a full set of treatment-covariate interactions.[11] As prespecified, we impute missing values of covariates using the average value of the covariate in the smaller randomization block.[12]

Given the mean-centering of all variables, β_2 denotes the average treatment effect of information for all voters receiving good news; and γ_2 is the average treatment effect of information for all voters receiving bad news. When the dependent variable Y_{ij} measures support for the candidate or party about whom information is provided, then according to our primary hypotheses we expected $\beta_2 > 0$ and $\gamma_2 < 0$. We estimate Equations 11.1 and 11.2 by OLS, adding fixed effects for the blocks within which random assignment occurred (when appropriate).[13] This is akin to estimating a linear probability model, which we do for ease of interpretation of the coefficient estimates.[14] Following our MPAP, we also correct for multiple testing across pairs of regressions; for example, for the effect of good and bad news, in addition to the simple p-values reported for each regression, we calculate, using randomization inference, a p-value for the *pair* of regressions which is the probability that, under the sharp null hypothesis of no effect of exposure to information (good or bad) for any unit, *both* the estimated $\widehat{\beta_2}$ or $\widehat{\gamma_2}$ would be as large (in absolute value) as they are. Where appropriate, this joint p-value appears in tables reporting prespecified analyses in this chapter.

---

[11] See discussion in Lin (2013).

[12] Note that there are still some missing values after imputation, reflecting observations for which no data on a particular measure is available in the control-group block. Note also that our MPAP specified that we would report study-by-study F statistics for the hypothesis that all covariates are orthogonal to treatment, using the full set of baseline covariates described in that document. See individual studies in Part II and our online appendix for balance tests.

[13] Where treatment assignment is clustered, our analysis reflects that (i.e., model-based standard errors are clustered at the level of assignment). For instance, the unit of randomization in Adida et al.'s study of Benin (Chapter 4) was the rural village or equivalent urban quarter; in Arias et al.'s study of Mexico (Chapter 5), it was the precinct.

[14] Substantive results do not change if we instead use probit or logit models.

To test a secondary hypothesis that information effects are stronger when the gap between voters' prior beliefs about candidates and the information provided is larger, we combine data from the good and bad news groups and estimate more simply:

$$E(Y_{ij}) = \delta_0 + \delta_1(Q_j - P_{ij}) + \delta_2 T_i + \delta_3 T_i(Q_j - P_{ij}). \qquad (11.3)$$

In our MPAP, we expected $\delta_3 > 0$ but noted important caveats about this analysis. For example, our measures of $Q_j - P_{ij}$ are largely ordinal not interval; estimating a linear marginal effect of the gap may not be meaningful if the marginal effect is not in fact linear. Note critically that the experiments do not manipulate priors, and we lack an identification strategy that would allow us to make strong causal claims about the effects of such a gap.

Our meta-analysis demands conceptualization of the units to which our inference applies. In our primary approach, we draw inferences simply to the study group at hand: it is as if we have data from a single, large experiment, with treatment assignment blocked by country.[15] This approach involves minimal assumptions, compared to alternatives. For example, we do not conceive of the study group of subjects as a random sample from a larger population: the study sites (countries and locations within countries) are not random draws from a well-defined population of possible sites. To be sure, the meta-analysis implies that interventions and outcome measures are sufficiently comparable that an overall average treatment effect – say, the effect on vote choice of exposure to good news – is meaningful. Creating such comparability is one goal of our integration of studies, and the harmonization of measures of good and bad news across contexts makes an important contribution in that regard. In addition to this primary approach, we explore in Section 11.2 a secondary analysis using a Bayesian approach, in which realized effects are in fact conceived of as draws from a common population-level distribution of effects.

We also focus in the first instance on a particular estimand: the average of the study-specific effects, that is, the average of the average treatment effects in each study. This approach permits us to assess a single causal parameter across studies but also allows for natural investigation

---

[15] That is, units were grouped into blocks and random assignment was conducted separately within each block. In our analysis, blocking is in the first instance at the country level; but there is also blocking within countries, as a strategy for reducing the variance of treatment effect estimators.

of heterogeneous effects across study sites. To estimate this parameter, we weight by the inverse of the ratio of the country study group size to the pooled study group size, so that smaller studies are upweighted and larger studies are downweighted. This approach equalizes the contribution of each study to the overall estimate and prevents larger studies from being arbitrarily upweighted in our estimation of the average study-level effect of information. Alternatively, rather than the average study effect, we also take as our estimand the simple average treatment effect across the pooled study group of all respondents. In that case, we instead pool the data without weighting; this approach relies more heavily for the overall estimate on higher-powered studies. Our results are substantively similar with or without study-level weighting.

Our analysis closely follows our MPAP wherever possible. Unfortunately, some decisions were not specified with sufficient precision to guide our analysis fully. Many of these choices involve coding and sample selection issues in distinct studies that were prespecified neither in the MPAP nor in study-specific PAPs. We discuss these issues further in Section 11.3.3 and show the degree of robustness of our results to different analytic choices.

11.1.2   The Effect of Information on Electoral Support

How, then, does performance information affect electoral performance?

Figure 11.1 shows the average effects of the informational treatments on vote choice. The left panel shows estimated effects for the good news subgroup and the right panel shows estimates for the bad news subgroup.

As the top row of Figure 11.1 suggests, the overall effect of the informational treatments on vote choice is quite precisely estimated – and null. Across the 18,186 respondents in the study group for the unadjusted analysis (8,959 in the good news group and 9,227 in the bad news group), we see null estimated effects of information in both the good and bad news cases.[16] The results are stable across estimation strategies: we focus in the figure on a covariate-unadjusted treatment effect estimator that gives equal weight to the six studies and includes only fixed effects

---

[16] The number of observations in the regressions, however, is 13,577 in the good news group and 12,806 in the bad news group, as we include votes for LCV councilors as well as chairs in the Uganda 2 study; see Buntaine et al., Chapter 8. Thus, each respondent in the Uganda 2 study enters twice via outcomes for two offices, and we cluster the standard errors at the individual level. The Ns differ somewhat from the covariate-adjusted analysis presented in Table 11.1 due to missing values of covariates.

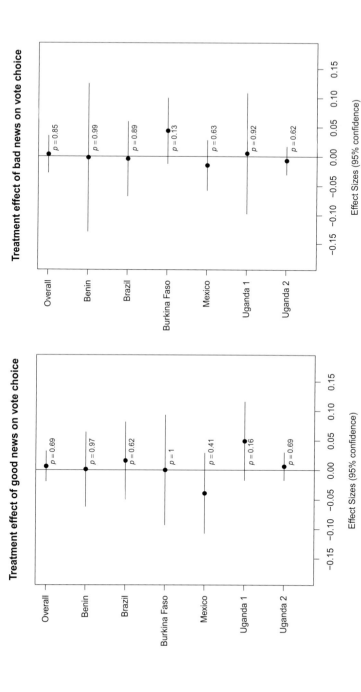

FIGURE 11.1 Meta-analysis: country-specific effects on vote choice. Estimated change in the proportion of voters who support an incumbent after receiving good news (left panel) or bad news (right panel) about the politician, compared to receiving no information. Weighted unadjusted estimates; results are similar for covariate-adjusted analysis (see Table 11.1 and online appendix). Horizontal lines show 95 percent confidence intervals for the estimated change. Entries under each estimate show *p*-values calculated by randomization inference. In all cases, the differences are close to zero and statistically insignificant.

for treatment assignment blocks; however, results are very similar without weighting, and with covariate adjustment as in Equations 11.1 and 11.2.[17] See Table 11.1 for a full covariate-adjusted analysis that includes the gap between information and priors (N_{ij}) and its interaction with treatment.

Figure 11.1 also shows results for each of the individual studies. As we discussed in Chapter 3, contextual differences across studies are important – and could, in principle, account for any differences in results across the settings in which our interventions were fielded. Consider, for example, that performance information was attributed alternately to candidates or to parties, depending on whether the electoral system makes one or the other type of cue more pertinent. In Mexico, mayoral term limits (with no immediate reelection of incumbent candidates) render information on the performance of individual candidates less relevant; in Burkina Faso, closed-list proportional representation (PR) similarly makes party cues more salient.[18] In other settings – such as Ugandan general elections or Indian state assembly elections – it could be feasible to use either party or candidate cues, as each candidate is associated with one party but also represents a single-member constituency, and those studies opted for information about candidates.[19] There are other distinctions across studies, for example, in the office of politicians (e.g., mayor or member of parliament), the type of performance information provided, and the medium for communicating the information.

Strikingly, despite these important distinctions, we in fact find negligible differences across studies in the effects of the informational treatments. As Figure 11.1 shows, not only is the overall meta-analysis result indistinguishable from zero – but the estimates for every single country, and for both good and bad news, are statistically insignificant as well. Note that for reasons discussed further below, these estimates may differ slightly from those presented in Part II – for example, because of differences in the analysis protocol that was prespecified for individual chapters and that prespecified for this meta-analysis. These differences are mostly minor, however, and the figure therefore provides a useful summary of findings in Part II of the book.

---

[17] See Section 11.3.3.

[18] See Arias et al. (Chapter 5) and Lierl and Holmlund (Chapter 8) for evidence on the relevance to voters of information about party performance.

[19] See Platas and Raffler's (Chapter 6) study of candidates for Ugandan Parliament, Buntaine et al.'s (Chapter 7) study of Ugandan district councilors and district council chairs, or Sircar and Chauchard's study of state assembly elections in the Indian state of Bihar (Chapter 10).

We also find null results overall with our main secondary outcome, voter turnout (Figure 11.2). In the good news case, although we find a statistically significant effect in one study (Uganda 1), the point estimate for the meta-analysis is almost exactly zero, whether or not we weight countries equally and whether or not we use covariate adjustment. The estimated effect of bad news on turnout, by contrast, is around 2 percentage points with an associated *p*-value of 0.18 and a combined *p*-value across the two turnout tests of 0.31, which is far from conventional levels for statistical significance. We note that though the estimate is not significant, it is the largest effect we estimate across the four main outcomes and that the estimates are positive in all studies (though close to 0 in two). Moreover, the effect is significant across five studies when Uganda 1 is dropped (this study elimination was not a preregistered analysis, however) and significant across all studies when an alternative coding of *N* for Uganda 1 is used, as we discuss in Section 11.3.3. Though clearly not robust, there is some suggestive evidence of a possible mobilization effect of bad news in which nonvoters turn out to vote for the opposition, an effect that contrasts with those found in Chong et al. (2015).[20]

Finally, to test the hypothesis that information effects are stronger when the gap between voters' prior beliefs about candidates and the information provided is larger, the final two columns of Table 11.1 present the results of estimating Equation 11.3 on the pooled data set (including both the good and bad news groups). Overall, the average causal effect of information is indistinguishable from zero – and we find no evidence that the magnitude of the impact depends on the gap between voters' prior beliefs and the provided information.

In sum, our findings offer no evidence, either in the aggregate or in individual studies, that our common informational interventions shaped vote choice. Not only is there no evidence for any effect overall, but there is almost no evidence for an effect using the prespecified meta-analysis in any of our six completed studies. There is some evidence of impact for our secondary outcome, voter turnout, though only for the bad news case and only in some specifications. The consistency of these results underscores the value of repeating similar studies across diverse settings: despite the heterogeneity across contexts and interventions, the effects of our informational interventions appear quite similar – and quite uniformly weak.

---

[20] See also Section 11.3.3.

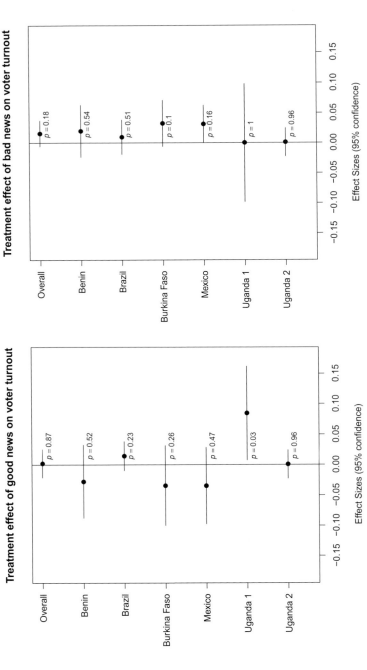

FIGURE 11.2 Meta-analysis: country-specific effects on turnout. Estimated change in the proportion of voters who turn out to vote after receiving good news (left panel) or bad news (right panel) about the politician, compared to receiving no information. Weighted unadjusted estimates; substantive results are similar for covariate-adjusted analysis (see Table 11.1 and online appendix). Horizontal lines show 95 percent confidence intervals for the estimated change. Entries under each estimate show *p*-values calculated by randomization inference.

TABLE 11.1 *Effect of information on vote choice and turnout*

	Vote Choice		Turnout		Vote Choice	Turnout
	Good News (1)	Bad News (2)	Good News (3)	Bad News (4)	Overall (5)	(6)
Treatment	0.0004 (0.015)	−0.003 (0.015)	0.002 (0.013)	0.018 (0.012)	0.003 (0.010)	0.017* (0.008)
N_{ij}	−0.017 (0.015)	−0.049*** (0.014)	−0.003 (0.014)	0.011 (0.013)	−0.050*** (0.012)	0.009 (0.011)
Treatment * N_{ij}	−0.010 (0.019)	−0.001 (0.019)	0.001 (0.019)	−0.0001 (0.015)	−0.002 (0.012)	−0.002 (0.011)
Control mean	0.356	0.398	0.843	0.835	0.369	0.837
RI p-value	0.981	0.866	0.892	0.167	0.813	0.062
Joint RI p-value	0.954		0.29			
Covariates	Yes	Yes	Yes	Yes	Yes	Yes
Observations	13,196	12,531	14,500	13,148	25,820	27,737
R^2	0.299	0.281	0.200	0.160	0.274	0.165

Note: Columns 1–4 estimate Equations 11.1 and 11.2, while columns 5–6 estimate Equation 11.3. "Vote choice" indicates support for the incumbent candidate or party. Standard errors are clustered at the level of treatment assignment. Pooled results exclude non-contested seats and include vote choice for LCV councilors as well as chairs in the Uganda 2 study (see Buntaine et al., Chapter 8). This means each respondent in the Uganda 2 study enters twice, and we cluster the standard errors at the individual level. We include randomization block fixed effects and a full set of covariate-treatment interactions. Control mean is the weighted and unadjusted average in the control group. * $p < 0.05$; *** $p < 0.001$

11.2 SECONDARY ANALYSIS: A BAYESIAN APPROACH

An alternative approach to meta-analysis takes as the target of inference a general parameter associated with a class of processes, rather than the average effect in a set of cases.[21] Here we implement such an analysis, similar to that prespecified in our MPAP as a secondary analysis.[22]

[21] We follow the approach used by Rubin (1981) and others in the analysis of the effects of training on student performance in eight schools; a general treatment of this example is given in Gelman et al. (2014, ch. 3); for an informal introduction to this approach, see https://tinyurl.com/eight-schools, and also the discussion in Chapter 2, Section 2.3.5.

[22] In the MPAP, we specified an analysis that assesses the distribution of effects based on the count of votes for the incumbent and the total number of voters. The analysis as specified, however, is at odds with the design, since it does not take account of the fact that the treatment was randomized within blocks. Accounting for this would require a

The key feature of the approach is that we assume that the treatment effect in a particular case, μ_j, is drawn from a population of treatment effects with mean μ and standard deviation τ. Note that there is no assumption of homogeneity across cases. If in fact there is large fundamental heterogeneity, then we should infer a large τ. Note also that "fundamental" heterogeneity here does not mean that common logics do not obtain across places; it is possible that heterogeneity arises because of other unmodeled features, such as characteristics of subjects or of polities. If modeled, the mean μ could be a function of these features, and we would expect lower values of τ. Given the lack of observed heterogeneity in effects, we do not pursue that approach.

The simplest analysis, which we present here, uses only the information provided above on the estimated effects and estimates of uncertainty (clustered standard errors) for each case, which we will call $\widehat{\mu}_j$ and σ_j. We place flat priors on μ and on τ (subject to a nonnegativity constraint), and the likelihood function uses the probability of observing the estimate for a given country $\widehat{\mu}_j$ given σ_j and parameter μ_j, where the probability of μ_j is itself a function of μ and τ:

$$\mu_j \sim N(\mu, \tau)$$

$$\widehat{\mu}_j \sim N(\mu_j, \sigma_j)$$

Note that this analysis treats the individual case estimates as if they were drawn from a common distribution. This is clearly a very strong assumption and requires at a minimum a conceptualization of the kinds of cases that form the population as well as an assumption that the selection of a case is not related to the size of its treatment effect. In addition the particular model assumes normality; this is also a substantive assumption, though not as fundamental as the assumption regarding case selection.

Bayesian analysis allows for estimation of the parameters of this model: μ, τ and μ_j, $j = 1, 2, \ldots 6$. The results are shown in Figure 11.3 for candidate support for the good news and bad news cases, and Figure 11.4 for turnout.

more complex multilevel structure with block and country effects; instead we elected to use a closely related model that is similar in spirit but that uses the study-level estimated effects as inputs.

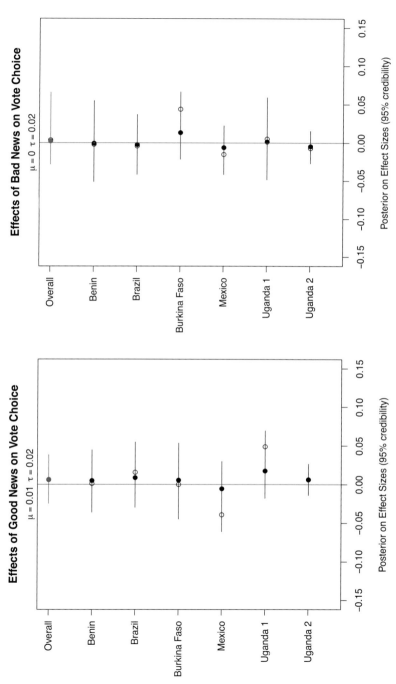

FIGURE 11.3 Bayesian meta-analysis: vote choice. The solid dots and lines show the estimates from the Bayesian model; the top row shows the overall meta-estimate of μ and τ. The white dots show the original frequentist estimates: in many cases shrinkage can be observed, especially in cases that have effects that are more imprecisely estimated.

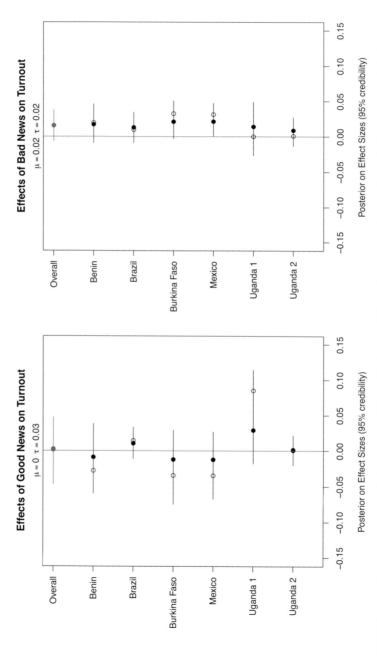

FIGURE 11.4 Bayesian meta-analysis: turnout. The solid dots and lines show the estimates from the Bayesian model; the top row shows the overall meta-estimate of μ and τ. The white dots show the original frequentist estimates: in many cases shrinkage can be observed, especially in cases that have effects that are more imprecisely estimated.

We see from these results that the estimated μ is very similar to the estimated average effect in our main frequentist analyses, in all cases very close to zero. We also estimate quite a low level of fundamental heterogeneity, which in general spans zero. Finally, as is typical in such models, we see that our individual estimates for cases are in general closer to our estimate of μ than the estimates generated by each case separately. Note that exceptional cases – for instance, the larger point estimates of good and bad news for the Uganda 1 and Burkina Faso studies, respectively – get substantially revised in this meta-analysis, reflecting the singularity of the results but also the fact that they are themselves measured with considerable uncertainty. Results of the meta-analysis for the bad news/turnout case suggest similarly weak effects as the primary frequentist analysis, with the credible interval for the posterior crossing zero.

To further probe the robustness of this result, we also conducted an analysis in which we sequentially leave out one study at a time and estimate μ and τ under this assumption. The analysis confirms that overall results differ little from those in Figures 11.3 and 11.4.

Overall, the Bayesian results support the conclusion of our frequentist analysis: effects of the common arm intervention are small, and quite uniformly small, across cases.

11.3 ROBUSTNESS AND RELIABILITY OF RESULTS

How robust are these null results? Several possible threats to the validity of our conclusions bear special scrutiny. In this section, we consider (1) the reliability of our outcome measures and (2) study-level attrition. We also assess (3) the robustness of the findings to different modeling and data analysis choices, focusing both on several deviations from the MPAP and divergent study-specific decisions about dataset construction. Finally, we evaluate (4) the statistical power of the meta-analysis.

11.3.1 Measurement of Outcome Variables

A first consideration involves our outcome data, in particular, the contrast between self-reported vote choice and aggregate official results. Our choice to focus on individual, self-reported voting and turnout as our primary outcomes reflects the exigencies – and perhaps the limitations – of our emphasis on cumulative learning: while we might have otherwise privileged official electoral results, such aggregate data cannot be gathered reliably in a symmetric way across all studies. We focus on an individual vote-choice variable because it can be gathered in every study; and we opted for dichotomous measurement (rather than a more sensitive graded measure of vote preference) to capture the outcome of real interest, which is the electoral performance of incumbents. We reflect further in our concluding chapter on the way in which coordination across studies required such choices and the tradeoffs involved. Here we note that biases in the self-reported data may certainly exist; see for instance the comparison of self-reported and official voting data in Adida et al. (Chapter 4) or Arias et al. (Chapter 5).

However, it is unlikely that reporting unreliability of the individual-level data explain our null results. After all, social desirability-type concerns might suggest that voters in the treatment group would differentially overreport vote choice for incumbents, at least in the good news group. This conjecture might lead us to falsely reject true null hypotheses – rather than fail to reject false nulls. We also draw from a number of studies that used secret-ballot measures of self-reported vote choice, and which found self-reported voting outcomes that substantially track official results; see, for example, Boas et el. (Chapter 9) on Brazil or Lierl and Holmlund (Chapter 6) on Burkina Faso. In these studies, estimated effects of information are also null. Finally, where studies can rely on official returns, for example, in estimating aggregate effects at the level of polling stations, we find results that are broadly consistent with those we report in this chapter.[23]

Turning to secondary outcomes, our study teams also measured individual-level turnout. To be sure, mean reported turnout is fairly high, at 85 percent in the pooled control group in Table 11.1. In principle, given the high level of self-reported turnout, ceiling effects could conceivably account for the weak impact of information, but nonetheless there appears to be room for movement. The high self-reported turnout may reflect social desirability bias. Yet we might expect this to operate symmetrically across the treatment and control groups, or, as with vote choice, to lead to overreporting of turnout among treated respondents, at least in the good news group. Thus, the bias would again run against the null findings.

---

[23] There are some differences, however. See e.g., studies of Benin and Mexico in Chapters 4 and 5.

11.3.2 The Missing India Study

Second, could study-level attrition account for our null overall results? One virtue of our pre-specification of studies and of integrated publication is that they make implementation failures – and missing studies – evident. This is an advantage from the point of view of transparency, as it counters an under-recognized file drawer problem in experimental research. Missing studies limit our ability to draw inferences to the whole study group. Our planned India study did not occur due to local political backlash, as Sircar and Chauchard (Chapter 10) describe. If politicians correctly anticipated large effects of our informational interventions in that context – and in consequence moved to block implementation of the study – this could indicate that treatment effects would have been larger in India, had the study occurred.[24]

To evaluate this question, we conduct a sensitivity analysis. We ask the following question: how big (in absolute value) would the estimated effect in India need to have been to produce a non-null estimated effect in the overall meta-analysis, given the findings of our other studies?

We can answer this question with some algebra. Let $\widehat{\mu}$ be the average estimated effect in the six realized studies, $\widehat{\theta}$ be the estimated effect in India had the study taken place, and $\widehat{\gamma}$ be the average effect we would have estimated had all seven studies taken place. Then,

$$\widehat{\gamma} = (6\widehat{\mu} + \widehat{\theta})/7, \tag{11.4}$$

and its estimated standard error is

$$\widehat{\sigma_{\widehat{\gamma}}} = \sqrt{36\widehat{\sigma_{\widehat{\mu}}}^2 + \widehat{\sigma_{\widehat{\theta}}}^2}/7, \tag{11.5}$$

where $\widehat{\sigma_{\widehat{\mu}}}^2$ is the estimated variance of $\widehat{\mu}$ and $\widehat{\sigma_{\widehat{\theta}}}^2$ is the estimated variance of $\widehat{\theta}$.[25] Then the t-statistic for the estimated average treatment effect

---

[24] Whether the dropping of the India study leads to bias in estimates of the overall treatment effect depends ultimately on unknowables. On the one hand, as Sircar and Chauchard (Chapter 10) detail, the planned India study did not occur due to logistical and implementation problems in one treatment village, which was somewhat atypical in that local politicians came from a small, independent party; Sircar and Chauchard had negotiated agreement to their study with all of the largest parties in Bihar, but not with that party. On the other hand, given the presence of this small party in other villages, it is also plausible that the exposure of any of those villages to treatment would also have resulted in study-level attrition; in other words, India could have dropped out of the study under almost any possible treatment assignment vector, limiting attrition bias. Such conjectures are ultimately unverifiable, making sensitivity analysis critical.

[25] This is because $\operatorname{Var}(\widehat{\gamma}) = \operatorname{Var}[\frac{6\widehat{\mu}+\widehat{\theta}}{7}] = \frac{36\operatorname{Var}(\widehat{\mu})+\operatorname{Var}(\widehat{\theta})}{49}$; we replace $\operatorname{Var}(\widehat{\gamma})$ with the estimate $\widehat{\operatorname{Var}}(\widehat{\gamma})$, and the square root is the standard error. This calculation assumes

across the seven studies would have been greater than 1.96 if and only if the estimated effect in India had satisfied the following inequality:[26]

$$\widehat{\theta} \geq 1.96\sqrt{36\widehat{\sigma_{\mu}}^2 + \widehat{\sigma_{\theta}}^2} - 6\widehat{\mu}. \qquad (11.6)$$

These calculations allow us to place bounds on how large the estimated treatment effect in India would have needed to be to produce a statistically significant result in the meta-analysis. First, assume an SE of 0.012 in India (i.e., 1.2 percentage points for the 0–1 vote choice variable); this is the smallest of the study-specific standard errors seen in our baseline specifications.[27] This implies that in the good news case with our primary outcome of vote choice, we would have needed an estimated average treatment effect of 0.172, or 17.2 percentage points, to see a significant effect in the seven-study meta-analysis. We can perform the same calculation inputting the largest country-specific standard error (0.065). Under this assumption, we would have needed an estimated average treatment effect of 0.212 – that is, 21.2 percentage points – for the seven-study meta-analysis to register a finding statistically distinguishable from zero.[28] These are enormous effects – an order of magnitude bigger than anything we see in other studies, including those, like Mexico, where we also see evidence of politician backlash to the treatment implementation (Section 11.4.2). Even in the case where we see the largest $\widehat{\mu}$ – in the bad news case with our secondary outcome, turnout – we calculate that we would have needed an estimated treatment effect in India of between 4.1 and 7.1 percentage points to see a significant effect in the overall estimate.[29]

In sum, it appears very likely that completion of the India study would not have altered our overall conclusions.

independence of the effect estimates across countries. We took many measures to ensure that results in one study would not affect others – for example, by blinding researchers to results in other studies until all studies had been completed.

[26] The *t*-statistic is given by $\widehat{\gamma}/\widehat{\sigma_{\gamma}} = 6\widehat{\mu} + \widehat{\theta}/\sqrt{36\widehat{\sigma_{\mu}}^2 + \widehat{\sigma_{\theta}}^2}$.

[27] See the online appendix. Note that this assumption is likely to be conservative, since the India study clustered treatment assignment at the polling station level. Considering only the common intervention arm and the control group, there were to be 400 polling stations with 20 citizen respondents in each polling station; see Chapter 10 and the India team's PAP.

[28] In this case, $\widehat{\mu} = 0.001$ and $\widehat{\sigma_{\mu}}^2 = (0.015)^2$. These values and the country-specific estimated standard errors can be extracted from the Shiny app we discuss later.

[29] We are grateful to Fredrik Sävje for his advice on this approach.

11.3.3 Deviations from Preregistered Analyses

Several features of our analysis were not clearly prespecified or were erroneously prespecified in the MPAP; our analysis also required a number of ex-post choices concerning individual studies. These omissions or errors lead to several deviations and extensions, which we itemize in Table 11.2. In this subsection, we assess the consequences of these analytic choices for our conclusions.

First, with the MPAP, we specified that we would cluster standard errors on politicians (j) but this was a mistake in our prespecification, as random assignment occurs within politicians; our analysis thus clusters standard errors at the level of treatment assignment in each study.[30] Second, while our MPAP is not entirely clear on this point, we intended to conduct hypothesis tests by randomization inference (RI), and we present RI-based p-values in all tables and figures and use them for our primary hypothesis tests.[31] Third, while our MPAP was silent on the procedure for weighting studies, we weight studies by the inverse of their sample size and also conduct unweighted analyses, as discussed previously.[32]

With respect to study-specific issues, several dataset construction and modeling choices were not fully prespecified, either by teams or in the MPAP; or in a small number cases, study teams prespecified different analytic choices than did the MPAP.[33] Because some decisions for the meta-analysis differ from those of the study teams, the country-specific results presented in this chapter do not perfectly align with those presented in the chapters of Part II. Our goal is to be transparent about the different approaches, allowing readers to see what distinctions may be driving different findings.

---

[30] If politicians were cluster-sampled at random in our designs, it might have made sense to cluster on politicians; see, for example, Abadie et al. (2017).

[31] Critically, our RI procedure follows the design of each study, including any clustering or blocking of randomization. Thus, we simulate the permutation distribution of estimators such as $\hat{\beta}$ or $\hat{\gamma}$ in Equations 11.1 and 11.2 under the strict null hypothesis of no unit-level effects, given the design of each study. See replication code for details.

[32] The MPAP was also silent on the issue of missing data on priors. In our primary analysis, we followed individual studies' approach to coding goodness of news in this case (denoted "P recoded when missing" in Figures 11.5 and 11.6 below). In alternate analyses, we code goodness of news as missing in all these cases (denoted "P dropped when missing" in those figures)

[33] We do not see this as problematic, as different studies can approach the same data in different ways, and sometimes even reach different substantive conclusions. Clear prespecification of the different approaches allows readers to see in a transparent way what distinctions may be driving different findings.

TABLE 11.2 *Deviations from MPAP and study PAPs in meta-analysis*

Registered Analysis in MPAP	Deviation	Rationale
Cluster standard errors on politician j	Cluster standard errors on the unit of treatment assignment	Registered analysis incorrect, since the target parameter is the effect for our study group of politicians
No specification of hypothesis testing by randomization inference (RI)	Report RI p-values in all tables and treat as primary tests	Ambiguity in MPAP; preference for design-based tests
No specification of study-level weighting	Results with equal study-level weighting (primary) as well as unweighted analysis (secondary)	Average study-level effect is important estimand; without weighting, studies with larger samples contribute more to estimate
For six hypothesis families, present joint RI p-values (see text) and tests employing false discovery rate (FDR) correction, in addition to nominal p-values	Present joint RI p-values and nominal p-values, but not FDR correction	For primary meta-analysis, all estimated effects insignificant at conventional levels
Prespecified hypotheses about intermediate outcomes and moderators, employing data from all studies; 14 baseline covariates to increase statistical precision	Most secondary hypothesis tests conducted on incomplete data; only 10 pretreatment covariates used for adjustment	Not all prespecified variables were gathered by all teams
Secondary Bayesian analysis that assesses the distribution of effects based on the count of votes for the incumbent and the total number of voters in each study	Employ approach proposed in Rubin (1981), using study level estimates and standard deviations as inputs	MPAP specification at odds with the design, since it does not take account of the fact that the treatment was randomized within blocks; accounting for this would require a more complex multilevel structure with block and country effects; we use a closely related model that is simpler in structure but similar in spirit

TABLE 11.2 *(continued)*

Mexico PAP

Procedure for estimating block-level priors using the control group	Primary meta-analysis ignores priors (Q only), although robustness checks use difference in individual-level posteriors and block-level priors	Baseline data could not be collected due to budget constraints; block-level priors measured on different scale from Q

Uganda 1 PAP

Definition of good news/bad news based on aggregating across six subdimensions; $N \neq 0$ when $P = Q$ within subdimension	Uganda 1 PAP's good news/bad news coding retained for primary meta-analysis, but robustness checks use a good/bad news coding where $N = 0$ when $P = Q$ within subdimension	MPAP unclear on how to handle definition of N for Uganda 1, although study PAP is clear

Uganda 2 PAP

No restrictions on study group: analysis of all sampled respondents	Restriction to contested constituencies	Electoral contestation is arguably a necessary condition for political accountability

TABLE 11.2 (*continued*)

Uganda 2 PAP (*continued*)

No stipulation of politician type for common-arm analysis in MPAP or study PAP	Inclusion of LCV chairs and councilors in main analysis, clustering standard errors on respondent, and including a fixed effect for councilors; chairs-only analysis examined in supplementary material	No consensus on what was intended thus err on side of inclusion
No stipulation of common arm treatment	Budget treatment treated as common arm	Recollection of intent by Uganda 2 team
No stipulation of level of office for common arm analysis	Meta-analysis focuses on LCV and ignores LCIII	Recollection of intent by Uganda 2 team
Unequal treatment assignment propensities inherent in multistage randomization not discussed	Meta-analysis implements inverse probability weights	Unweighted estimator yields a biased estimate of the average treatment effect

Burkina Faso PAP

Vote choice outcomes defined for those who did not intend to turn out to vote	Vote for incumbent (M_1) recoded as 0 if turnout (M_3) = 0	Follows M_1 coding in MPAP

These choices and deviations from study-specific PAPs are outlined in Table 11.2. First, in the Mexico study (Arias et al., Chapter 5), a baseline survey was prohibitively expensive; thus, rather than use individual-level prior perceptions of incumbent malfeasance as the measure of P, the authors estimate the randomization block-level average from questions in the endline survey, using only control-group respondents.[34] In addition, after gathering individual-level outcome data (e.g., vote-choice and turnout) in the control group, they show the treatment flyers to control-group respondents, and ask again about perceptions of malfeasance of the incumbent party. Finally, for their individual-level analysis, they use the change in perceptions from prior to posterior to operationalize good and bad news. From the perspective of the meta-analysis, however, this approach has several disadvantages. First, it is based on the updating of perceptions rather than the performance information (Q) itself. In addition, the measure of priors is necessarily defined at the randomization block level.[35] Finally, Q is measured on a different scale from the measurement of priors and posteriors. In our primary analysis, we therefore operationalize good and bad news in Mexico using the alternate approach discussed in Chapter 3, which is based on Q alone.[36]

Second, the Uganda 1 study (Platas and Raffler, Chapter 6) gathered data both on perceptions of incumbents and opposition candidates, as registered in their study PAP; in the meta-analysis, we use data only on incumbents, as prespecified in the MPAP. In addition, Uganda 1's prespecified definition of good news and bad news is based on calculating the difference between P and Q in each of six subdimensions (six types of information) and then aggregating across the differences for an overall definition N; within each subdimension, $N \neq 0$ when $P = Q$.[37] We use this approach for our primary meta-analysis (the MPAP did not

---

[34] See Arias et al.'s study in Chapter 5 for discussion of the assumptions necessary for this approach to recover the average priors in the treatment group; no within-block spillovers and inter-temporal stability of perceptions are the key elements, together with randomization of the treatment.

[35] Much of the analysis in Chapter 5 focuses on precinct-level analysis of official electoral returns, though the common measures of individual, self-reported vote choice and turnout measures (MPAP measures M1 and M3) are also analyzed.

[36] In more detail, we take as Q the difference between the two percentages presented on the flyer shown to the common-arm treatment group: that is, the percentage of unaccounted or misspent funds in the subject's municipality, minus the percentage in the other municipalities in the state governed by opposition parties. Following our MPAP's definition, we then define respondents as having received good news if they receive a below-median difference and bad news if they receive an above-median difference, where the median is defined for the sample of municipalities.

[37] See Chapter 6 for further explanation.

explicitly specify any different approach than this for Uganda 1). Yet we also conduct robustness checks with a good/bad news coding where $N = 0$ when $P = Q$ within subdimensions, which is arguably most consistent with the MPAP definition.

Third, the Uganda 2 study (Buntaine et al., Chapter 7) registered no exclusions of sampled constituencies; however, a portion of the seats were uncontested or redistricted, or candidates switched parties. The authors' analysis in Chapter 7 excludes non-contested elections and candidates who switched parties, effectively dropping a third of the study's observations. The study PAP is also unclear on the politician type (e.g., councilor or chair), the level of office (LCV or LCIII), and the identity of the common intervention arm (budget or public services treatment) for the primary analysis. There was no clear consensus on how to address these ex-post choices of the study team, but in the meta-analysis, we focus on the budget treatment and LCV chairs and councilors, in contested constituencies only. We discuss the consequences for results of these choices momentarily.[38]

Finally, two other differences between country-specific analyses in this Chapter 11 and those in Part II deserve further mention. The study in Brazil by Boas et al. (Chapter 9) uses a pre-specified Lasso routine to select covariates, while here we use those specified in the MPAP (that were gathered consistently across studies). The study in Burkina Faso by Lierl and Holmlund (Chapter 8) measured vote intention for those who did not intend to vote, but in the meta-analysis, vote choice for the incumbent was recoded as 0 for all those not intending to turn out to vote.

How sensitive are our findings to these deviations and discrepancies? To answer this question as comprehensively and succinctly as possible, we implement a specification curve analysis.[39] Thus, we first identified the set of decisions having to do with dataset construction and modeling that we took in the course of performing the meta-analysis, including centrally those in Table 11.2 as well as areas in which the MPAP proposed more than one strategy (for instance, inclusion or exclusion of covariates). We also include in our specification curve an unregistered "leave one out" analysis in which we calculate the overall meta-analysis estimate, excluding one study at a time. From this we

---

[38] In addition, the Uganda 2 PAP does not discuss the implications of unequal treatment assignment propensities inherent in the multistage randomization, which may lead an unweighted estimator to produce a biased estimate of the average treatment effect; the meta-analysis implements inverse probability weights to account for these unequal propensities.

[39] See Simonsohn, Simmons and Nelson (2015).

identify the exhaustive set of 18,886 possible specifications; for every possible specification, we estimate a statistical model.

Figures 11.5 and 11.6 plot estimates for the full set of models. For each plot, the horizontal axis depicts the estimated average treatment effect. The vertical axis lists the set of decisions. Decisions all come in pairs (e.g., unadjusted vs. covariate-adjusted analysis), with the exception of the leave-one-out analyses, which involves a set of seven options. Within the row associated with a particular decision, that decision is held fixed, and estimates from all other possible specifications – i.e., specifications

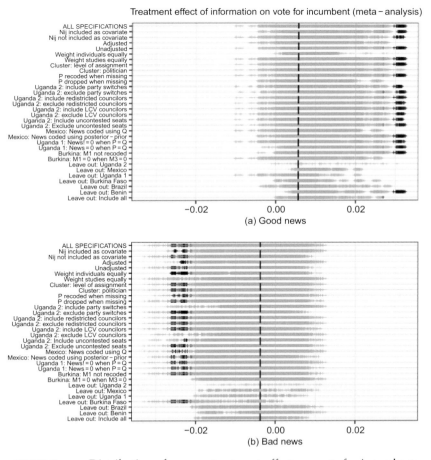

FIGURE 11.5 Distribution of average treatment effects on vote for incumbent for a given specification choice, varying all other choices. Darkened vertical lines show estimates for which $p < 0.05$. The dashed vertical line indicates average treatment effect reported in Table 11.1 following Equations 11.1 and 11.2.

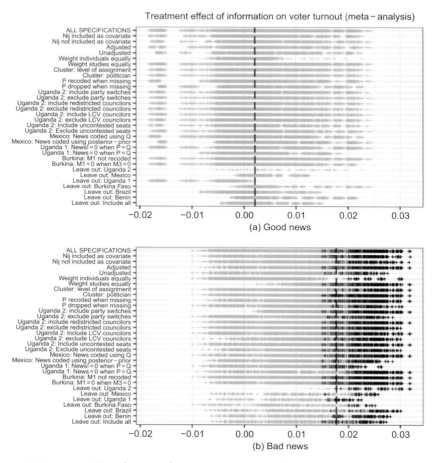

FIGURE 11.6 Distribution of average treatment effects on voter turnout for a given specification choice, varying all other choices. Darkened vertical lines show estimates for which $p < 0.05$. The dashed vertical line indicates average treatment effect reported in Table 11.1 following Equations 11.1 and 11.2.

based on all combinations of other decisions – are then presented. Thus each vertical dash in the body of the plot denotes a point estimate for a single model. We darken those estimates that are statistically significant at the 0.05 level.

The results are telling. For one of the plots–good news/turnout (Figure 11.6, Panel (a)) – we do not estimate a single statistically significant effect in the meta-analysis, underscoring the robustness of our overall null results in this case. For good news/vote choice (Figure 11.5, Panel (a)), significant effects do materialize in a small set of specifications, yet these only occur when all studies are weighted equally, when estimations are not covariate-adjusted, and when news in the Mexico study is coded using the difference in individual-level posteriors and block-level priors. For bad news/vote choice (Figure 11.5, Panel (b)), the treatment effect estimate is significant in 0.6 percent of specifications. These all occur in specifications which exclude the Burkina Faso study and which do not weight countries equally. They also all occur when we make certain specification choices related to the Uganda 2 study, in particular excluding candidates who switched parties, and analyzing support for both LCV councilors and chairs.

The results for bad news/turnout depicted in Figure 11.6, Panel (b) show the most evidence of impact, though even then in a minority (10.3 percent) of specifications. Here, we observe significant effects across a greater range of specifications, most notably when the Uganda 1 study is excluded from the analysis, or when that study PAP's definition of good and bad news is discarded in favor of the alternative discussed above, and when standard errors are clustered by politician. While we emphasize that the effect in our primary specification remains statistically insignificant, the specification curve provides suggestive evidence that disseminating bad news to voters about a sitting politician may spur them to turn out to vote. In other unregistered analyses, we also see hints that nonvoters exposed to bad news may turn out to vote against the incumbent; we cannot confidently reject the null of no effect, but there is suggestive evidence that bad news leads a small set of people that would otherwise not vote to turn out to vote for opposition candidates.[40] In sum, these results suggest the robustness of the null results in our meta-analysis.

Our meta-analytic results are therefore substantially stable across specifications. However, data analysis choices can have substantial consequences for specific studies.

The most substantial discrepancies arise in the Uganda 2 study of Buntaine et al. (Chapter 7). Their analysis in this book finds mixed effects across type of office, with significant effects of information on vote choice when analyzing support for LCV councilors, but null effects for LCV chairs as well as LCIII councilors or chairs (the LCIII results arise in connection with their public services treatment). Thus, there are null effects

---

[40] Our preregistered outcome equals 1 if a citizen votes for the incumbent and 0 if she votes for the opposition or does not turn out to vote; for the "vote against" analysis, the dependent variable equals 1 if a citizen votes for the opposition and 0 if she votes for the incumbent or does not turn out.

both for higher-profile officials about whom voters may already have substantial information (LCV chairs), and lower-profile officials about whom they may not (LCIII councilors and chairs). In other work, however, four of the five authors of Chapter 7 have emphasized the significant effect of their SMS intervention on LCV councilors, advancing the idea that the greater availability of information about LCV chairs may explain the null effects for that office.[41] Several choices around unregistered sample specifications are critical for this conclusion: in particular, the exclusion of constituencies where incumbents switched parties, as well as the separate analysis of councilors at the LCV level and the restriction of attention to the budget treatment. Differences in views on the defensibility of these decisions explain differences between results in the meta-analysis presented here and results published separately in Buntaine et al. (2018).

For the Mexico study, using the definition of good news in Chapter 5 but individual-level outcome data, we find no substantive difference in our meta-analysis results but, oddly, a strongly negative effect of good news for Mexico; this result is also reported and discussed in Chapter 5 and its online appendix. Using an alternate definition that subtracts the individual-level prior from an individual-level posterior, measured in both the treatment and the control groups, we do not find this negative effect.[42] Overall, the weak effects are substantially stable to the different ways of operationalizing good and bad news in the Arias et al. study. Finally, in the Uganda 1 study, while we focus on incumbents in the meta-analysis, Platas and Raffler (Chapter 6) find somewhat more evidence of effects when looking at the performance of opposition candidates in their "Meet the Candidates" debates, especially when restricting analysis to credible candidates who ended up winning a minimum percentage of the vote.

To allow further transparent assessment of the consequences of deviations and discrepancies, we constructed a Shiny app – a web interface that allows users to vary sample specification and modeling choices and assess how results change, for the meta-analysis or for individual studies.[43] The interface allows readers to specify the inclusion of covariates, to include

---

[41] See Buntaine et al. (2018).

[42] Using this individual-level measure of the difference between the posterior and the prior to define the good and bad news groups may also risk posttreatment bias; indeed, we find treatment assignment predicts the prior belief in both the good and bad news groups.

[43] See http://egap.org/content/metaketa-i-shiny-app.

or exclude specific studies, and to alter several other modeling and data construction choices, as well as access our replication data. We encourage readers to use this user-friendly interface themselves to investigate the sensitivity of both study-specific and overall results to these choices.

In conclusion, our results are remarkably consistent to different ways of operationalizing the good and bad news groups, different measures of the outcome variable, and different subgroups of the population. This is true both for the meta-analysis and, in the main, for particular studies. Regardless of the choices we discuss in this section, our results provide very little evidence of impact of the informational interventions.

11.3.4 Power Analysis

How informative a null result is depends in part on the design; a poorly "powered" design might be nearly guaranteed to deliver a null result, even if in truth there is a strong effect. Our confidence intervals tell us something about the credibility of our null results: points outside of the confidence intervals are effects that are inconsistent with the data (in the sense that if these were the true effects then it is unlikely we would get such low estimates). Our confidence intervals, especially for the primary outcome, are quite tight.

Even still, it is useful to know whether a null result was a forgone conclusion. We answer this question by conducting an ex-post power calculation. Calculating the power of our design is somewhat difficult since there are many blocks and clusters of unequal size, multiple assignment schemes – that are different in different studies – and complex estimation involving inverse propensity score weights, country weights, and clustered standard errors. Moreover, the average effects of interest are averages over heterogeneous effects that depend upon our specification of good news and bad news groups. Off-the-shelf power calculators are not able to deliver estimates of power for designs like this.

Nevertheless, power calculations are possible using a simulation approach, at least conditional on a model of the data-generating process. We implement this approach using the `DeclareDesign` package, in which we formally declare our data structure, our conjectured data generating process, our assignment schemes, our estimands, and our estimation strategy.[44] We then use Monte Carlo simulations to "run" the design many times and assess statistical power – that is, the fraction of

---

44 Blair et al. (2016).

runs in which we reject a false null hypothesis – conditional on different conjectures about the size of the true effect.[45]

We provide the full design code in supplementary materials, but the most important feature involves the specification of a data-generating process.[46] For the power analysis, we assume that an individual in block b and cluster c will vote for the incumbent with probability p_{bc}^o, where p_{bc}^o is drawn from a distribution centered on the observed *block level* share supporting the incumbent in the control group, with a variance that produces an intra-cluster correlation coefficient (conditional on block, b) approximately equal to the observed correlation in that group.

For any stipulated effect δ we assume that individuals support the incumbent in the treatment condition with probability p_{bc}^1:

$$p_{bc}^1 = \phi \left(\phi^{-1}(p_{bc}^o) + \delta N_i \right) \qquad (11.7)$$

where ϕ is the standard normal density and ϕ^{-1} its inverse. The approach here then assumes that treatment induces a constant effect (conditional on the value of N_i) on a latent support variable that determines the propensity to support the incumbent. For instance, for $\delta = 1$ an individual that supports an incumbent with probability $p^o = 0.5$ in control and for whom $N_i = 1$, would support the incumbent with probability 0.84 in treatment (i.e., $\phi(0 + 1)$). In practice, a probit-type approach is employed, in which an individual has a normally distributed shock e_i and votes for the incumbent if e_i falls below $\phi^{-1}(p')$ for condition t; this ensures that in realizations individuals with positive effects have non-negative changes in their votes. Note that for any specified δ, different individuals have heterogeneous effects that depend upon the propensity in their control condition and their own value of N_i. Given all these different propensities across all individuals, the estimand of interest is the average difference in voting propensity, across studies, for individuals in treatment and control. To calculate power, we consider a range of possible δs and for each one calculate the implied estimand and the probability

---

[45] We note that a bonus of this approach is that we can check that our estimates are unbiased, given our design. This is a nontrivial question since the estimation strategy had to be tailored to match different assignment strategies used in different sites. Moreover, unbiasedness is not guaranteed given heterogeneous cluster sizes in some studies (Imai et al., 2009). The results from the "diagnosis" of this design suggest no bias concerns.

[46] The DeclareDesign code is available along with our replication data at https://github.com/egap/metaketa-i; for the code, see the "/ch11_meta-analysis/fig_MDE_with_controls.Rmd" file.

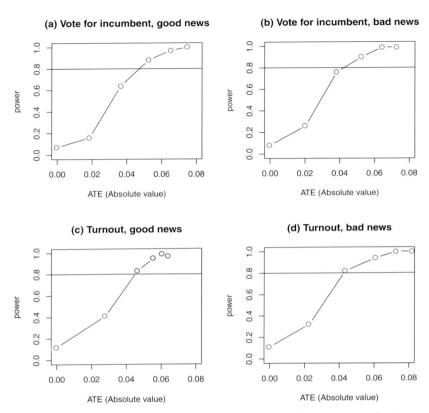

FIGURE 11.7 Power analysis of minimal detectable effects, computed using Monte Carlo simulation. The horizontal axis varies the conjectured average treatment effect, while the vertical axis shows statistical power: the probability of rejecting the null hypothesis at $\alpha = 0.05$.

that our estimate of that estimand will be statistically significant. Results are presented in Figure 11.7 below.

We see that power for different average effects depends on the outcomes of interest. For the electoral support outcomes, we hit 80 percent power for average treatment effects of around 5 percentage points; for the turnout quantities, we would hit power of 80 percent with effects of around 4 percentage points. In other words, to register a statistically significant result on our primary outcome in 80 percent of repeated hypothetical experiments, the interventions would have had to have changed the vote choice of five out of every 100 voters. Together with the tightness of our observed confidence intervals, we see these results as evidence that null results were not forgone conclusions.

11.4 MAKING SENSE OF THE NULL FINDINGS

What explains the weak effect of information on voter behavior in our pooled data?

Figure 3.1 in Chapter 3 outlined a causal chain through which informational interventions might shape vote choice, and ultimately political accountability.[47] According to this framework, existing information must be disseminated, and it must be received and understood by voters. Those voters in turn must update their perceptions or beliefs in response to the new information. This updating must then produce changes in their voting behavior, ultimately leading them to sanction poorly performing politicians or reward well performing ones. As discussed in Chapter 3, this is the route through which adverse selection – the choosing of "bad politician types" – can be reduced and thus political accountability can be improved.

However, there are numerous ways such a causal chain can break down. In this section, we use our pooled data to assess the various possibilities, focusing especially on the hypotheses about intermediate outcomes registered in our MPAP. We use observational and experimentally induced variation to evaluate both what may be driving the overall null effect and what alternative forms of information dissemination might have had stronger effects than those we found. We note that while we endeavored to measure all of the variables registered in the MPAP in a symmetric and consistent fashion across studies, this was not always possible, or it did not always take place. In our analyses below, we therefore pool results for a particular intermediate outcome or conditioning variable using only the countries for which data on the relevant indicator were gathered.

11.4.1 Voter Updating

Manipulation check. In each of our studies, third-party information on politician or party performance existed; and it was successfully disseminated by researchers or the third-party organizations with whom they partnered, in the sense that the flyers, SMS messages, videos, and other experimental stimuli were in fact deployed and directed to voters in the treatment groups. It is possible, however, that treated respondents did not absorb the information to which they were exposed. For example, they

---

[47] See also Lieberman, Posner, and Tsai (2014) and Kumar, Post, and Ray (2017).

may have failed to read the flyer or text message they were sent. Table 11.3 assesses this possibility, using a dichotomous manipulation check coded as one if the respondent correctly answered a question about the disseminated information at endline, and zero otherwise.[48]

Overall, treated respondents were 7.2 percentage points more likely to correctly recall the substance of the information than respondents in the control group. The magnitude of this difference is quite small, however, and is driven by the Mexico and Uganda 1 studies.[49] We also conduct what is in principle a more sensitive analysis in which we assess the impact of treatment assignment on the difference between posterior knowledge and prior beliefs about politician performance, in the good and bad news cases (Table 11.4). Unfortunately, we can only conduct this test on a subset of the cases, and these are the cases with the weakest manipulation checks in the analysis of correct recall; yet, we find some further evidence in the bad news case that treatment leads to convergence of priors and posteriors.

Simple failure to absorb the information – or to "receive" it, in the language of the causal chain in Chapter 3, Table 3.1 – does not therefore fully explain the null results. That said, it is surprising not to see stronger evidence on the manipulation check. Some of the cross-study contrast on this score could be due to dissemination technology; for example, the SMS messages deployed by Uganda 2 can be a difficult way to convey nuanced messages.[50] Note that elsewhere four of the authors of the Uganda 2 study present evidence of a significant effect of information in a simple t-test, though per Table 11.4 there is no such evidence when properly controlling for randomization blocks.[51] Yet Table 11.3 shows null effects even for studies in which respondents were presented

---

[48] The manipulation check was not preregistered.
[49] Two caveats deserve mention. First, for Mexico, we assess in Table 11.3 the effects of treatment assignment on an indicator variable for correct recall about the type of information conveyed by the flyer (rather than the substance of the information), and answers to this question may thus not be clearly interpretable for respondents in the control group. We therefore also explored whether assignment to the treatment made respondents significantly more likely to remember receiving such a flyer; we find that it did, with 6 percent of the control group and 32 percent of the treatment group stating that they remember the flyer, a highly statistically significant difference. Second, we note that the manipulation check does not show up as significant for Brazil in Table 11.3; yet using their preregistered block-by-treatment interactions in Chapter 9, Boas et al. do show significant effects of treatment on knowledge of whether accounts were accepted or rejected.
[50] Fafchamps and Minten (2012); Aker, Collier, and Vicente (2017).
[51] Buntaine et al. (2018), Supplementary Information.

TABLE 11.3 *Manipulation check: Effect of treatment on correct recollection, pooling good and bad news [unregistered analysis]*

	Correct Recollection					
	Overall (1)	Benin (2)	Brazil (3)	Mexico (4)	Uganda 1 (5)	Uganda 2 (6)
Treatment	0.072***	0.050	0.038	0.149***	0.119***	−0.0001
	(0.015)	(0.059)	(0.021)	(0.015)	(0.035)	(0.008)
Covariates	No	No	No	No	No	No
Observations	16,173	897	1,677	2,089	750	10,760
R^2	0.320	0.276	0.378	0.137	0.035	0.205

Notes: The table reports results on manipulation checks across studies, using recollection or accuracy tests at endline that were specific to the content of each study's interventions (MPAP measure M30). The dependent variable, correct recollection, is dichotomized in each study using the following measures: Benin: whether correctly recalled the relative performance of incumbent in plenary and committee work; Brazil: whether correctly recalled whether municipal account was accepted or rejected; Mexico: identification of content of the flyer; Uganda 1: index consisting of knowledge of MP responsibilities, MP priorities for constituency, and identities of contesting candidates. Individuals with an index equal to or greater than 1.5 on a 0–3 scale were coded as correct recalls; Uganda 2: whether correctly recalled relative financial accountability relative to other districts. We include randomization block fixed effects. Standard errors are clustered at the level of treatment assignment. *** $p < 0.001$.

with information in easy-to-understand graphical form.[52] This difficulty appears a critical practical challenge for organizations that would like to increase political accountability through informational interventions.

Perceptions. Even if there is some evidence that overall and across studies, information was communicated and a portion of voters received it, this does not imply that their perceptions changed as a result of it.[53] We registered two hypotheses about beliefs concerning politician characteristics that we thought might change through the provision of performance information (the numbering here, as elsewhere, follows our MPAP):

- H3: Positive (negative) information increases (decreases) voter beliefs in candidate integrity.

[52] Consider, for example, the case of the Brazil study, which distributes audit information very similar to Ferraz and Finan (2008), albeit via direct delivery at the individual level rather than the dissemination at the municipal level via community radio featured in that study.
[53] See step 4 in the chain in Chapter 3, Figure 3.1.

TABLE 11.4 *Manipulation check: Absolute difference between posterior and prior beliefs for pooled good and bad news [unregistered analysis]*

	Absolute difference between posterior and prior beliefs			
	Overall (1)	Benin (2)	Brazil (3)	Uganda 2 (4)
Treatment	0.006 (0.025)	0.063 (0.089)	−0.003 (0.022)	−0.023 (0.023)
Covariates	No	No	No	No
Observations	12,704	389	1,677	10,638
R²	0.241	0.176	0.358	0.111

Notes: The table reports differences between beliefs about politician performance after (MPAP measure M30) and prior to treatment (MPAP measure M9). Posterior beliefs are measured using recollection tests at endline specific to the content of each study's intervention. Burkina Faso is excluded because their recollection measure was collected among treated subjects only. Mexico is excluded from results because the study does not contain pretreatment measures of subjects beliefs. Uganda 1 is not included because the M30 measure is an aggregate measure of subjects' political knowledge and cannot be directly compared with the scale used for measuring priors. We include randomization block fixed effects. Standard errors are clustered at the level of treatment assignment.

- H4: Positive (negative) information increases (decreases) voter beliefs that candidate is hardworking.

Table 11.5 reports results for our pooled measures of politicians' integrity and effort, respectively. We measure perceptions of incumbents' integrity and effort using similar questions across studies.[54]

We find no evidence that the interventions shape these perceptions and beliefs. Estimates are statistically indistinguishable from zero in both the good and bad news groups, as well as in the whole study group. We also show in the online appendix that information does not in the aggregate change the importance that respondents attach to different policy priorities, such as community and personal benefits, politician efficiency and integrity, or ethnic or partisan identity. Note that there

---

[54] Sample question on MPAP measure M5 of candidate effort: "In your opinion, does [incumbent] make much more, a little more, a little less, or much less effort to get things done than other deputies in this [Department]?" Sample question from MPAP measure M6 of candidate integrity/honesty: "How surprised would you be to hear from a credible source about corruption involving your [MP/Mayor/Councilor]? Would you say you would be (1) Very surprised (2) Somewhat surprised (3) Not too surprised (4) Not surprised at all."

TABLE 11.5 *Effect of information on perception of importance of politician effort and honesty*

	Effort		Dishonesty	
	Good News (1)	Bad News (2)	Good News (3)	Bad News (4)
Treatment effect	−0.014	−0.051	−0.053	0.099
	(0.046)	(0.051)	(0.047)	(0.098)
Control mean	2.449	2.7	2.755	2.724
RI p-value	0.788	0.474	0.356	0.754
Joint RI p-value		0.5		0.282
Covariates	No	No	No	No
Observations	7,039	5,963	7,278	6,755
R^2	0.253	0.294	0.300	0.231

Note: The table reports the effect of the treatment on voters' perception of how hard-working (MPAP measure M5) and dishonest (MPAP measure M6) the incumbent politician is. We pool Benin, Burkina Faso, Uganda 1, and Uganda 2 in columns (1) and (2), and Benin, Burkina Faso, Mexico, and Uganda 2 in columns (3) and (4). MPAP measures M5 (effort) and M6 (dishonesty). Regressions include randomization block fixed effects; standard errors are clustered at the level of treatment assignment.

is considerable scope for learning, as we showed in Chapter 3, in that correlations between our aggregate measures of priors (P) and politician quality (Q) are present but also modest; prior beliefs, however, are linked to perceptions of other candidate characteristics and to vote choice. Yet, here we find no overall impact of the information on perceptions of politicians' characteristics, at least on these dimensions. We consider later, in our discussion of heterogeneous effects, possible reasons for the finding that voters on average absorbed the information and yet posteriors over candidates on the dimension of the information did not budge. For instance, we consider there the question of whether voters filter the information through partisan lenses.

This evidence suggests a critical point at which the information–accountability causal chain may have broken down in our studies. Without shaping perceptions of politician performance attributes such as honesty and effort, it is difficult to see how these interventions could induce important changes in voter's electoral choices.

Source credibility. On average, the disseminated information therefore did not cause voters to update their perceptions of candidate effort and honesty. Why not? One possibility is that the information was not provided by a credible source. Of course, perceptions of source credibility

TABLE 11.6 *Effect of information and source credibility on evaluation of politician effort and honesty [unregistered analysis]*

	Dependent variable:			
	Effort		Dishonesty	
	Good News (1)	Bad News (2)	Good News (3)	Bad News (4)
Treatment	−0.034	−0.088	−0.037	0.210
	(0.079)	(0.090)	(0.085)	(0.202)
Credible Source	−0.051	−0.010	−0.022	0.125
	(0.079)	(0.081)	(0.064)	(0.100)
Treatment × Credible Source	0.033	0.070	0.010	−0.197
	(0.095)	(0.105)	(0.093)	(0.205)
Control mean	2.451	2.703	2.75	2.679
RI *p*-values	0.728	0.518	0.708	0.861
Joint RI *p*-value	0.482		0.614	
Covariates	No	No	No	No
Observations	6,436	5,406	6,483	5,844
R^2	0.261	0.293	0.329	0.256

Note: The table reports the effects of information and the credibility of the information source on voter's perception of how hard-working (MPAP measure M5) and dishonest (MPAP measure M6) the incumbent politician is. We pool Benin, Burkina Faso, Uganda 1, and Uganda 2 in columns (1) and (2), and Benin, Burkina Faso, Mexico, and Uganda 2 in columns (3) and (4). Regressions include randomization block fixed effects; standard errors are clustered at the level of treatment assignment.

could vary both across studies and for different individuals in the same study. We measured perceptions of the credibility of different possible sources of information.[55] We can thus code whether the information source deemed most credible by a particular respondent was in fact the source of the information to which she was exposed (or would have been exposed, if in control) in the study in which she was included.

Table 11.6 presents an exploratory analysis, which we emphasize was not preregistered; our goal in presenting it is to assess whether source

[55] The sample question for M24 in the MPAP reads as follows: "Suppose that you received information about a politician, for example, information about how he or she had performed in office. Which of the following sources would you trust the most [second most; third most] for that information? [READ OPTIONS]: (a) Local politician; (b) Flyer or pamphlet from an NGO; (c) A person conducting a survey; (d) An influential member of your community; (e) In a debate between candidates; (f) Other."

TABLE 11.7 *Relationship between evaluation of politician effort and honesty with vote choice [unregistered analysis]*

| | Incumbent vote choice | | | |
| | Good news | | Bad news | |
	(1)	(2)	(3)	(4)
Effort	0.052***		0.066***	
	(0.006)		(0.006)	
Dishonesty		−0.054***		−0.026***
		(0.005)		(0.005)
Covariates	No	No	No	No
Observations	11,040	11,452	10,190	10,943
R²	0.229	0.217	0.282	0.266

Note: The table reports the effects of information and the credibility of the information source on voter's perception of how hard-working (MPAP measure M5) and dishonest (MPAP measure M6) the incumbent politician is. We pool Benin, Burkina Faso, Uganda 1, and Uganda 2 in columns (1) and (3), and Benin, Burkina Faso, Mexico, and Uganda 2 in columns (2) and (4). Results exclude non-contested seats and include vote choice for LCV councilors as well as chairs in the Uganda 2 study. Regressions include randomization block fixed effects; standard errors are clustered at the level of treatment assignment.

credibility and the treatment interact, looking at perceptions of effort and integrity as outcomes. We find no evidence here that the credibility of the information source interacts with treatment, however. That is, at least as measured here, information does not lead to significantly more updating when the respondent has at baseline deemed its source to be credible.[56]

Association of perceptions and electoral support. Given the lack of apparent connection between the informational treatments and perceptions of politician effort and honesty, it is also useful to assess how those perceptions in turn correlate with vote choice. We emphasize that such an analysis does not shed any light on the causal effect of those perceptions on electoral support; nor does it tell us whether any influence of information on perceptions would in turn lead to an impact on vote choice. Nonetheless, it is interesting to see that in the unregistered analysis in Table 11.7, there is a strong significant association between perception of the incumbents' effort and honesty

---

[56] See previous note.

as measured at baseline and voters' subsequent electoral support for the incumbent.

The evidence thus far supports the idea that the breakdown in the information and accountability chain occurred both at the level of reception and especially the perception of the information. Thus, one major failure of the causal chain in Figure 3.1 is at steps 3 and 4: voters received and assimilated the information, but only substantially so in two studies; and in most cases, the disseminated information did not cause them to update their perceptions of candidate effort and honesty. Observational evidence suggests that had perceptions been altered, vote choice might have been influenced as well. It is difficult thus far to say why the interventions had little impact on respondents' updating, but we return to that question later.

11.4.2 Politician Response

We registered another hypothesis that may bear on the connections between information and accountability along the causal chain. Perhaps politicians respond to negative information by altering their campaign strategies. Politicians have a menu of options to counterbalance "bad" information: they can divert more time to campaigning in treatment areas, they can increase vote buying, and they can counteract negative impacts of the information by undermining the credibility of the information source.[57] At the extreme, they may attempt to stop the dissemination efforts altogether. This possibility suggests a more complicated causal chain, with more feedback between nodes, than contemplated by Figure 3.1.

We preregistered this hypothesis as:

- H5: Politicians mount campaigns to respond to negative information.

Indeed, we see substantial evidence that politicians were not passive and in some cases indeed attempted to derail information dissemination efforts. Sircar and Chaucard (Chapter 10), for example, describe how the actions of representatives of a small party in Bihar, India imperiled the safety of some of their enumerators and ultimately led to the termination of their fieldwork. Arias et al. (Chapter 5) describe similar episodes

---

[57] See Cruz, Keefer, and, Labonne (2016), Humphreys and Weinstein (2013).

in several municipalities in Mexico. There, incidents included not only potential threats to enumerator safety but also the fabrication by political actors of fake fliers, which were designed to mimic those distributed by the research team's NGO partner but which, unlike the real fliers, provided explicitly partisan negative information. These episodes did not, however, lead to the cancellation of the project in the Mexican case. On the other hand, see also Platas and Raffler (Chapter 6) on politicians' positive reaction to their interventions in Uganda, and Buntaine et al. (Chapter 7) on how the method of dissemination (e.g., SMS) can affect politicians' ability to counteract negative information.

We can assess quantitative evidence for backlash to some extent as well. Research teams in the Benin and Mexico projects asked treatment and control group respondents a question similar to the following: "In the week before the election did you hear of [incumbent candidate] or someone from their party making statements about [the dimension of information provided to treated groups]?"[58] As prespecified, we account for the clustered nature of treatment assignment when comparing treated and control respondents – and the presumably clustered nature of politicians' response, in targeting treated areas. As Table 11.8 shows, treatment had a substantial and statistically significant effect, elevating "yes" responses to the question about incumbent statements by 7 percentage points overall, with significant effects individually in the Mexico study (but not Benin). Following H5, we focus only the bad news case.

Yet, can such politician response explain our null effects? Probably not, for several reasons. First, it appears unlikely that this backlash occurred as systematically as would be required to counteract a true effect of the information interventions on voters. In Mexico, for example, we find quantitatively that treatment did provoke politicians' backlash, and have qualitative evidence on attempts to prevent our intervention in a handful of municipalities.[59] However, while the presence of backlash by politicians was positively correlated with the amount of malfeasance reported in the fliers, it was not correlated with whether voters interpreted the information as good or bad news. In other words, the response

---

[58] Measure M8 in our MPAP. The question was not included in the Brazil, Burkina Faso, or Uganda 2 instruments; and the India study did not complete an endline survey. We have data on this question for Uganda 1, but treatment is assigned at the individual level, complicating the assessment of politician backlash – which is presumably targeted at particular areas and which would therefore affect both treatment and control individuals in those areas.

[59] This is parallel to the situation in India, where one village caused the problems that led to the stopping of implementation.

TABLE 11.8 *Effect of bad news on politician backlash*

	Politician response / backlash		
	Overall (1)	Benin (2)	Mexico (3)
Treatment effect	0.069* (0.028)	0.068 (0.057)	0.070*** (0.010)
Control mean	0.108	0.068	0.146
RI *p*-value	0.082	0.435	0
Covariates	No	No	No
Observations	2,052	702	1,350
R^2	0.623	0.504	0.848

Note: The table reports on whether the treatment led to the incumbent party or candidate campaigning on dimensions of the disseminated information (MPAP measure M8). Backlash was measured for studies with clustered assignment. Regressions include randomization block fixed effects; standard errors are clustered at the level of treatment assignment.
* $p < 0.05$;*** $p < 0.001$

of politicians did not take into account voters' prior beliefs. Also, such a hypothesis would also not be consistent with the null effect of good news we find even in those settings where backlash did not occur. Finally, we estimate null effects even in those contexts, like Benin, where we have no qualitative or quantitative evidence of politician backlash.

A more plausible hypothesis may therefore be that interventions providing positive or negative performance information in fact have little impact on voters – yet politicians often believe that they will. In many contexts, politicians misjudge the preferences and behaviors of their constituents, and they may therefore misjudge the impact of information about their performance on voters.[60] Politicians may also tend to react because they are risk averse, especially given the high cost of campaigning, and especially where levels of political competition are relatively high. As we noted in Chapter 3, our interventions focus on the selection mechanism: they are targeted at voters, whose sanctioning is key in many models of political accountability. They were not designed, however, to address the moral hazard (politician) dimension. Relatedly, the timing of the interventions may be important: given that information is

---

[60] See, for instance, Broockman and Skovron (2018) on the extent to which politicians misjudge voter ideology, or Rosenzweig (2017) on the extent to which they overestimate the efficacy of electoral violence.

delivered within one month of an election, is there sufficient time for the information to become part of the larger campaign debate? One worry in delivering information in this short window is that it gives the incumbent time to punch back, but may not allow challengers to respond and reinforce the information.[61] Differences in timing of the intervention relative to the election could conceivably underlie the different findings of the well-known Ferraz and Finan study – which found very large impacts of publicizing corruption allegations in Brazil, but in the year before an election – and the findings reported by Boas et al. (Chapter 9).[62] As we discuss in the conclusion to this chapter and the conclusion of the book, such hypotheses generated by our findings are interesting and should be explored in greater depth in future research.

11.4.3 Learning from Variation

In the Metaketa approach, in addition to accumulating evidence on the average effects of our interventions across studies, we aim to learn from variation in effects across respondents, contexts, and interventions. We therefore test prespecified hypotheses that treatment effects vary as a function of two types of moderators: (a) characteristics of the respondents; (b) variation in contexts and features of interventions.[63] In addition, the Metaketa approach offers an additional advantage: we can test hypotheses about heterogeneous effects developed inductively in one of the studies described in Part II on out-of-sample data from the remaining studies.

We emphasize that a causal interpretation of such heterogeneous effects within and across studies is not justified by design: the experiments cannot manipulate the conditioning covariates, and we lack an identification strategy that would allow us to make strong causal claims about the effects of these variables. Nonetheless, comparing and contrasting effects across different subgroups can give important hints about mechanisms that may explain our findings. Understanding such variation may also shed light on the voter types for whom effects are strongest; with such

---

[61] See, for example, Grossman and Michelitch (2018) on the importance of the timing of information campaigns to the options available for politicians' responses.

[62] Ferraz and Finan (2008).

[63] In the next section, we consider experimentally induced variation in alternative treatment arms.

evidence, we could also assess whether those types are relatively rare in our population, possibly explaining our overall null effect. Learning from variation may allow us further to assess possible breakdowns along the causal chain from information to accountability. Table 11.9 describes our registered hypotheses about the heterogeneous impacts of our treatments and summarizes our results.

Substitution effects. First, we conceptualized several hypotheses that involve coethnicity, partisanship, and clientelism as substitution effects, in the sense that ethnicity or partisanship could provide heuristic substitutes for information. These hypotheses relate closely to steps 3, 4, and 5 in Figure 3.1 in Chapter 3. Thus, we hypothesized that information effects would be more positive for voters that do not share the incumbent's ethnic identity (H6 in the MPAP), have weaker partisan identities (H7), and have not received clientelistic benefits (H8).[64] We employ a dichotomous, subjective measure of coethnicity.[65] For partisanship, we measure attachment to the incumbent's party.[66] And to investigate the potential moderating effect of clientelism, we measure perceptions that the incumbent engages in clientelism.[67]

We find little evidence that the strength of the treatment varies as predicted by our hypotheses (Table 11.10). Interestingly, coethnicity is

---

[64] While we expected that information would operate on vote choice in part by reducing the weight voters place on ethnicity, copartisanship, and clientelistic relations, we expected overall that information would have more positive effects for voters that do not share ethnic, partisan, or clientelist ties with candidates.

[65] Specifically, enumerators posed the question: "Thinking of the [incumbent politician], would you say that you [come from the same community/share the same ethnic group/share the same race] as this candidate?" Note that we do not have this measure for Mexico or Burkina Faso since researchers did not judge ethnicity to be a salient dimension of political identity in these settings.

[66] These are modeled on sample question for M19, from the MPAP: "On this scale of one to seven, where seven means you are very attached to [INCUMBENT'S PARTY], and one means you are not very attached to [INCUMBENT'S PARTY], what degree of attachment do you feel for [INCUMBENT'S PARTY]?"

[67] We use responses to the following question, implemented with minor variations across all of our study sites: "How likely is it that the incumbent, or someone from their party, will offer something, like food, or a gift, or money, in return for votes in the upcoming election." Here, responses are recorded on a four-point scale ranging from "not at all likely" to "very likely." It should be borne in mind that the question does not ask respondents to say whether they personally have benefited (or expect to benefit) from a handout from the incumbent; it captures respondents' beliefs about how likely the incumbent is to engage in clientelistic mobilization and corrupt vote-buying practices more generally.

TABLE 11.9 *Additional hypotheses and results*

MPAP hypothesis	Prediction	Moderator measure	News subgroup	Evidence for interaction
Substitution effects: Ethnicity, partisanship, or clientelist relations could provide heuristic substitutes for information				
H6: Non-coethnics	Good news effects more positive for incumbent's non-coethnics	M15	Good	No (Table 11.10)
H6: Non-coethnics	Bad news effects more negative for incumbent's non-coethnics	M15	Bad	No (Table 11.10)
H7: Partisanship	Good news effects more positive for voters with weaker partisan identities	M19	Good	No (Table 11.10)
H7: Partisanship	Bad news effects more negative for voters with weaker partisan identities	M19	Bad	No (Table 11.10)
H8: Clientelism	Good news effects more positive for voters who have not received clientelistic benefits	M22	Good	No (Table 11.10)
H8: Clientelism	Bad news effects more negative for voters who have not received clientelistic benefits	M22	Bad	No (Table 11.10)
Context-specific heterogeneity: Information will have greater impact among voters with less exposure to information in the pretreatment period, and in competitive, free and fair elections				
H9: Informational environment	Good news effects are more positive in low information environments	M11	Good	No (Table 11.11)
H9: Informational environment	Bad news effects are more negative in low information environments	M11	Bad	No (Table 11.11)

H10: Competitive elections	Good news effects are more positive where electoral competition is greater	M25	Good	No (Table 11.12)
H10: Competitive elections	Bad news effects are more negative where electoral competition is greater	M25	Bad	No (Table 11.12)
H11: Free and fair elections	Good news effects are more positive where elections are believed to be free and fair	M26/M27	Good	No (Table 11.11)
H11: Free and fair elections	Bad news effects are more negative where elections are believed to be free and fair	M26/M27	Bad	No (Table 11.11)
Intervention-specific heterogeneity				
H12: Information content	Information effects – both positive and negative – are stronger when the gap between voters' prior beliefs about candidates and the information provided is larger	N_{ij}	All	No (Table 11.13)
H13: Information welfare salient	Good news effects are more positive the more the information relates directly to individual welfare	M23	Good	No (Table 11.13)
H13: Information welfare salient	Bad news effects are more negative the more the information relates directly to individual welfare	M23	Bad	No (Table 11.13)
H14: Credible source	Good news effects are more positive the more reliable and credible is the information source	M24	Good	No (Table 11.13)
H14: Credible source	Bad news effects are more negative the more reliable and credible is the information source	M24	Bad	No (Table 11.13)
Covariate-treatment interactions in Equations 11.1 and 11.2	Demographics			No (Online Appendix Tables G9 and G10)

not strongly associated with vote choice in these data.[68] Copartisanship, however, is significantly associated in these regressions with a nearly 20 percentage point increase in the probability of voting for the candidate, an association that may help to validate the measures.[69] Yet, neither for coethnicity, copartisanship, nor clientelism do we find any evidence of a significant interaction. We note one ambiguity of measurement for copartisanship, which is that our common indicator actually measures strength of attachment to the incumbent, rather than the overall strength of partisan identities. It is possible that a voter who is not very attached to the incumbent's party has strong attachments to another party, or no partisan attachment at all. However, H7 would still predict different effects on average for those who are attached to the incumbent's party and those who are not, since the latter group plausibly includes both opposition partisans and nonpartisans or swing voters. In the supplementary analysis (not reported), we present additional exploratory specifications to test H7, for example, a quadratic specification and one in which we present treatment effects at each level of scales measuring partisan attachment to the incumbent (rather than dichotomizing copartisanship as we do in this chapter). As in Table 11.10, we see essentially no evidence that the treatment effect varies with the partisan attachment to the incumbent.

Context-specific heterogeneity. Second, we considered variation in effects that may be due to the context in which interventions were delivered. We expected information to have greater impact in contexts where information was less readily available at baseline (H9 in the MPAP and Table 11.9). To operationalize a test at the individual (as opposed to system) level, we asked respondents to state how certain they were about their priors regarding politicians' performance or background; our assumption is that voters are uncertain about their priors when they have worse access to information, making this a reasonable proxy. We also hypothesized that voters will be more attentive to information – and

---

[68] This may be due in part to the inclusion of a case, Brazil, in which per the MPAP coethnicity was not expected to be highly salient for vote choice (Bueno and Dunning, 2017). The lack of association may also be due to lack of within-district or within-village variation in coethnic relations between voters and politicians, especially in the studies in Africa. (We use fixed effects for randomization blocks such as districts or villages in these regressions.)

[69] Our measure of clientelism, meanwhile, has a negative and significant association with vote choice; though the sign appears odd at first glance, it may reflect the way in which the question was asked, as discussed momentarily.

TABLE 11.10 *Effect of moderators on incumbent vote choice*

	Incumbent vote choice					
	Good news	Bad news	Good news	Bad news	Good news	Bad news
	(1)	(2)	(3)	(4)	(5)	(6)
Treatment	0.018	0.0004	−0.0001	0.013	0.001	0.004
	(0.015)	(0.022)	(0.025)	(0.021)	(0.014)	(0.016)
Coethnicity	−0.022	0.0003				
	(0.029)	(0.041)				
Treatment × Coethnicity	0.058	−0.042				
	(0.033)	(0.049)				
Copartisanship			0.216***	0.289***		
			(0.032)	(0.028)		
Treatment × Copartisanship			0.001	0.004		
			(0.038)	(0.036)		
Clientelism					−0.041***	−0.044***
					(0.009)	(0.011)
Treatment × Clientelism					0.013	0.006
					(0.012)	(0.015)
Control mean	0.365	0.442	0.36	0.397	0.359	0.383
RI *p*-values	0.276	0.988	0.998	0.564	0.936	0.84
Joint RI *p*-value	0.618		0.829		0.876	
Covariates	No	No	No	No	No	No
Observations	11,502	10,320	11,688	10,999	13,246	12,288
R²	0.268	0.230	0.276	0.289	0.279	0.259

Note: The table reports results of the treatment on three prespecified moderators – coethnicity (MPAP measure M19) and indulging in clientelistic practices (MPAP measure M22) – on incumbent vote choice. The following cases are included in each regression: Co-ethnicity – Benin, Brazil, Uganda 1, Uganda 2; Co-partisanship – Benin, Brazil, Mexico, Uganda 1, Uganda 2; Clientelism – Benin, Burkina Faso, Brazil, Mexico, Uganda 1, Uganda 2. Pooled results exclude non-contested seats and include vote choice for LCV councilors as well as chairs in the Uganda 2 study. Regressions include randomization block fixed effects; standard errors are clustered at the level of treatment assignment. $p < 0.001$

more willing to devote time and cognitive resources to processing it – in environments where electoral competition is great, and thus their vote is more likely to be pivotal in swaying the final result (H10).[70] We measure competition using administrative data.[71] Finally, if voters suspect that their vote will not count – perhaps because they expect politicians to stuff ballot boxes or doctor vote totals – or if they believe their vote choices will be observable to an incumbent who may punish them for voting the "wrong" way, then information interventions may fall flat. To gain empirical traction on this hypothesis about electoral fraud (H11), survey teams posed two questions to respondents. First, enumerators asked how likely it is that "powerful people can find out how you vote, even though there is supposed to be a secret ballot in this country." Second, voters were asked whether the counting of votes in the forthcoming election is likely to be free and fair. We interact these ordinal measures – available for individuals – with the treatment indicator and look for evidence of a significant interactive effect.

For these context-specific hypotheses, we again find little evidence of such heterogeneity. For tests on H9 and H11, the six coefficients on the interaction terms are very small in magnitude and statistically insignificant at conventional levels (Table 11.11). We test H10 with another set of regressions. Because our measures of electoral competitiveness vary at the block level, and our regressions include block fixed effects, we split the samples at the median level of electoral competition and run our block fixed effects regressions. Here, too, we find no evidence for this kind of context-specific heterogeneity driving our results (Table 11.12).

Intervention-specific heterogeneity. Third, we prespecified three hypotheses about heterogeneity related to features of the interventions themselves – and voters' attitudes towards them. For one, information effects, both positive and negative, may be stronger when the gap between

---

[70] Counterarguments also suggest themselves: electorally competitive environments might already be flooded with information – as parties, journalists, and civil society groups typically focus more attention on those races. This could attenuate the effects of any additional news, of the kind delivered by our interventions.

[71] In countries using simple plurality voting, competitiveness is calculated at the constituency level and is given as one minus the margin of victory for the winning candidate – over the runner up – in the most recent election. For countries using proportional representation, the calculation is more involved, and is performed at the party or candidate level, depending on whether the system employed is closed list or open list, respectively. The full description is provided in the MPAP, measure M25; see the Appendix.

TABLE 11.11 *Effect of information and context heterogenity on incumbent vote choice*

	Incumbent vote choice					
	Good news	Bad news	Good news	Bad news	Good news	Bad news
	(1)	(2)	(3)	(4)	(5)	(6)
Treatment	-0.062	-0.011	0.015	-0.005	-0.034	0.021
	(0.055)	(0.054)	(0.024)	(0.030)	(0.035)	(0.033)
Certainty	-0.015	0.021				
	(0.017)	(0.018)				
Treatment × Certainty	0.032	-0.003				
	(0.024)	(0.024)				
Secret ballot			-0.001	0.010		
			(0.008)	(0.010)		
Treatment × Secret ballot			-0.005	0.005		
			(0.010)	(0.011)		
Free, fair election					-0.003	0.009
					(0.009)	(0.010)
Treatment × Free, fair election					0.013	-0.005
					(0.011)	(0.011)
Control mean	0.362	0.412	0.383	0.357	0.351	0.386
RI *p*-values	0.296	0.856	0.559	0.889	0.348	0.524
Joint RI *p*-value	0.417		0.688		0.26	
Covariates	No	No	No	No	No	No
Observations	10,993	9,622	13,419	12,589	13,199	12,490
R^2	0.328	0.267	0.258	0.235	0.256	0.240

Note: The table reports results of whether the treatment had different effects depending on voters' certainty about their priors (MPAP measure M11), and their perceptions about the secrecy of their ballot (MPAP measure M26) and how free and fair the election was (MPAP measure M27). Pooled results exclude non-contested seats and include vote choice for LCV councilors as well as chairs in the Uganda 2 study. Regressions include randomization block fixed effects; standard errors are clustered at the level of treatment assignment.

TABLE 11.12 *Effect of information and electoral competition on vote choice*

	Incumbent vote choice			
	Low competition		High competition	
	Good news (1)	Bad news (2)	Good news (3)	Bad news (4)
Treatment	0.009	−0.043	0.004	0.015
	(0.022)	(0.031)	(0.030)	(0.037)
Control mean	0.342	0.414	0.392	0.294
RI *p*-values	0.692	0.272	0.912	0.757
Covariates	No	No	No	No
Observations	1,450	1,433	1,113	1,307
R²	0.221	0.231	0.240	0.128

Note: The table reports results of whether the treatment had different effects in constituencies with low or high levels of electoral competition (MPAP measure M25). We pool Benin, Brazil, Mexico, and Uganda 1. Regressions include randomization block fixed effects; standard errors are clustered at the level of treatment assignment.

voters' prior beliefs about candidates and the information provided is larger (H12). For another, we hypothesized that informational effects are stronger when information relates more directly to individual welfare, and thus the more relevant or salient the information is (H13). For instance, in deciding how to cast their vote, some citizens may care little about how often incumbents attend legislative committee meetings, believing instead that a politician's diligence in attending to constituency work is the more important yardstick of performance. Similarly, some citizens may worry deeply about the corruption in public administration, whereas other may view this as a secondary concern. At baseline, the Metaketa teams presented respondents with a list of activities in which their local incumbent politician(s) might regularly be involved. Respondents had to describe which of these activities they would most like to receive information about. We generate a dichotomous variable indicating whether or not the activities that were the subject of the actual intervention – activities that differ across studies – matched the activity described by the respondent as being the one they were most interested in. Finally, we posited that informational effects might be stronger the more reliable and credible is the information source (H14). Whereas we previously analyzed how source credibility interacts with treatment to affect perceptions of effort and honesty (Table 11.6), here we use the same measures of source credibility to assess interactive impacts on vote choice itself.[72]

We report the results of heterogeneous effects analyses employing these three measures in Table 11.13. In making inferences, we look to see whether the interaction between the treatment indicator and these moderating variables enters the regression as statistically significant. In fact, none of them does. The data reveal no signs that gaps in prior beliefs, information salience, or source credibility moderate the effects of the treatment.

Heterogeneity by demographics. Finally, we use the Metaketa structure to test hypotheses derived inductively from one case on data from the rest of the studies. In Benin, Adida et al. (Chapter 4) find evidence of stronger effects among younger and poorer voters.[73] In Mexico, Arias et al. (Chapter 5) find that treatments mattered more in high-competition as well as in low-information environments (the latter measured as places where voters were more knowledgeable about politics or had higher levels of media consumption); in the Uganda 1 study, Platas and Raffler (Chapter 7) find that good news mattered among those who thought debates were a credible source of information and among those who expected favors from the politician if he or she were elected. Some of these findings have been assessed previously in this chapter using pooled data; and not all of these hypotheses are testable in the pooled meta-analysis, given the smaller number of covariates for which data were collected. However, several of them are. Thus, having been derived inductively in those cases, hypotheses about these subgroup effects can then be tested on the whole dataset.

In Tables G9 and G10 of the online appendix, we present the results of estimating full interaction models, showing the estimated coefficients on interactions between treatment and covariates as well as the constituent terms. Note that some of the covariates were assessed previously in this chapter but here we present the full regression as specified our MPAP. The first column shows the estimates for the pooled metadata (it includes both LCV chairs and councilors in the Uganda 2 study). The other columns

---

[72] Note that the India study of Sircar and Chauchard (Chapter 10), which was not implemented, planned an evaluation of H14 through experimental manipulation of the identity of the messenger as the alternative treatment arm.

[73] They also find evidence, for their alternative arms, that effects were strongest among those who received the worst news; see Chapter 4 for discussion.

TABLE 11.13 *Effect of information and intervention-specific heterogeneity on vote choice*

	Incumbent vote choice					
	Good news	Bad news	Good news	Bad news	Good news	Bad news
	(1)	(2)	(3)	(4)	(5)	(6)
Treatment	0.001	−0.010	0.025	−0.022	−0.017	−0.013
	(0.016)	(0.016)	(0.024)	(0.036)	(0.021)	(0.023)
N_{ij}	−0.027	−0.053***				
	(0.016)	(0.014)				
Treatment × N_{ij}	−0.006	−0.006				
	(0.020)	(0.019)				
Information salient			−0.016	−0.041		
			(0.029)	(0.035)		
Treatment × Information salient			−0.015	0.053		
			(0.034)	(0.042)		
Credible source					−0.007	0.005
					(0.028)	(0.027)
Treatment × Credible source					0.036	0.020
					(0.030)	(0.031)
Control mean	0.356	0.398	0.355	0.435	0.363	0.385
RI p-values	0.955	0.596	0.314	0.62	0.438	0.646
Joint RI p-value	0.783		0.235		0.352	
Covariates	No	No	No	No	No	No
Observations	13,274	12,563	12,343	10,587	12,354	11,407
R^2	0.275	0.249	0.265	0.221	0.260	0.240

Note: The table reports results of the effect of information and (a) the gap between priors and information (MPAP measure M_{23}) and (c) credibility of information source on voters' decision to vote for the incumbent. Columns 1, 3, 4 and 6 pool observations from all studies while Columns 2 and 5 pool Benin, Brazil, Uganda 1 and Uganda 2. Results exclude non-contested seats and include vote choice for LCV councilors as well as chairs in the Uganda 2 study. Regressions include randomization block fixed effects; standard errors are clustered at the level of treatment assignment. *** $p < 0.001$

then show country-specific regressions. We only include covariates that were measured in comparable ways across all studies. As with our previous analysis of the gap between priors and information, here we see some associations between the covariates and votes for the incumbent candidate/party about whom information was provided. For example, wealth and previous support for the incumbent are positively and significantly associated with incumbent vote choice; so, interestingly, is exposure to clientelism, but also the belief that the vote is secret and elections are free and fair. These associations are not the focus of our conditional hypotheses, however; rather, we seek to assess the heterogeneity of treatment effects across values of these covariates.

However, as indicated by the general lack of significance of the interaction terms, we find little evidence, at least per the linear interaction model, that treatment effects vary conditional on these covariates. We do see some evidence in particular countries. The Metaketa approach provides a very useful way to test subgroup effects derived from one country on a wider dataset, but in this case we see little evidence of such heterogeneity.

In sum, we gain little insight from the analyses in this section that effects vary according to the subgroup characteristics we have examined. From one perspective, the uniformity of our subgroup results is therefore disappointing. From another perspective, however, the findings in this section only underscore – in a uniform and quite powerful way – that the common interventions had very little impact on voter behavior. These findings therefore add confidence in the robustness of the null effects of interventions – a critical finding in light of the fact that our treatments echo those in the previous experimental literature as well as interventions for which donor and transparency organizations routinely advocate.

11.5 LOOKING FORWARD: DOES PUBLIC INFORMATION BOOST INFORMATIONAL EFFECTS?

The structure of the Metaketa was also intended to allow assessment of alternative interventions that might prove more effective than the common intervention arm. Thus, we sought to explore divergent effects within studies, especially from experimentally induced variation in the delivery of treatments. In particular, we forecast that comparisons between the common and alternate intervention arms within each study might provide insights into the conditions under which information was more or less effective.

The studies in Part II of this book report intriguing evidence in this regard. For example, Adida et al. (Chapter 4) suggest that treatment works when it is combined with (1) a civics message educating people about the welfare importance of legislative productivity; and (2) the information is widely disseminated in lots of villages in a constituency. Platas and Raffler (Chapter 7) find that publicly screened videos increased political knowledge and slightly but discernibly affected vote choice in Uganda. And Boas et al. (Chapter 9) used the second arm of their field experiment to inform voters about municipal-level changes in scores on the National Literacy Evaluation during the mayor's first term. Among parents of children enrolled in school, for whom the issue should be most salient, they find that voters punish poor performance and reward (or are indifferent to) good performance. They conclude that a personal connection to the policy in question may be a prerequisite for information about incumbent performance to change voting behavior.

Such hypotheses are interesting and promising, and should be tested systematically. While we cannot evaluate all of them in this Metaketa, we fortuitously had three projects with similar alternative arms, in which information was provided to voters in a public rather than private fashion. As underscored by the pre-analysis plans for those projects, the hypothesis was that the provision of information in a public rather than private setting would generate common knowledge of the intervention and foment greater collective action – and therefore evidence a greater impact on vote choice. We also registered this hypothesis in the MPAP as H15: Informational effects are stronger when information is provided in public settings.[74]

We pool data from the three projects with public treatment arms to assess this hypothesis. Tables 11.14 and 11.15 report the pooled effect as well as the effect in each country, for the good and bad news cases respectively. Here, we regress vote choice for the incumbent on an indicator for the private information condition and an indicator for the

---

[74] We cannot fully assess one remaining hypothesis in the MPAP systematically: H16: Informational effects are not driven by Hawthorne effects. We discussed the possibility of randomizing the content of consent forms but did not implement this across the studies; in part, our commitment to informed consent in all cases limited our capacity to estimate its effect through comparison to randomized control groups that did not receive the consent request.

TABLE 11.14 *Private vs. public information: Effect of good news on incumbent vote choice*

	Incumbent vote choice, good news			
	Overall (1)	Benin (2)	Mexico (3)	Uganda 1 (4)
Private information	−0.008	0.012	−0.029	0.008
	(0.023)	(0.044)	(0.043)	(0.027)
Public information	0.055*	0.146**	−0.002	0.019
	(0.022)	(0.047)	(0.041)	(0.023)
Control mean	0.356	0.439	0.498	0.186
F-test *p*-value	0.018	0.006	0.598	0.708
Covariates	No	No	No	No
Observations	2,962	776	784	1,402
R^2	0.192	0.189	0.088	0.068

Note: The table reports results of the effect of good news about the incumbent on vote choice, depending on whether voters received this information in private or public settings. We pool Benin, Mexico, and Uganda 1. Regressions include randomization block fixed effects and standard errors are clustered at the level of treatment assignment. * $p < 0.05$; ** $p < 0.01$;

public information condition. As anticipated by the analysis in this chapter, we estimate a null effect on the private condition – but a large and statistically significant effect of the informational treatment in the public condition, for the good news case. This is driven by an extremely large effect in Benin. However, we find null effects of public information in the bad news strata. This tentative evidence on the effects of publicly delivered information may connect to a literature emphasizing the impact of information delivered through the media.[75] These initial findings may point to promising grounds for future systematic study – perhaps a Metaketa in which public delivery constitutes the common intervention arm.

11.6 CONCLUSION

Our meta-analysis suggests that informational interventions, at least of the kind we have considered in this research project, are not an effective way of shaping voter behavior. Pooling data from six of seven planned

[75] See citations in Chapter 3.

TABLE 11.15 *Private vs. public information: Effect of bad news on incumbent vote choice*

	Incumbent vote choice, bad news			
	Overall (1)	Benin (2)	Mexico (3)	Uganda 1 (4)
Private information	−0.027	−0.012	−0.036	−0.035
	(0.030)	(0.074)	(0.030)	(0.042)
Public information	0.009	0.006	0.015	0.009
	(0.026)	(0.069)	(0.032)	(0.032)
Control mean	0.441	0.535	0.383	0.426
F-test *p*-value	0.018	0.006	0.598	0.708
Covariates	No	No	No	No
Observations	2,909	601	1,309	999
R^2	0.178	0.241	0.102	0.153

Note: The table reports results of the effect of bad news about the incumbent on vote choice, depending on whether voters received this information in private or public settings. We pool Benin, Mexico, and Uganda 1. Regressions include randomization block fixed effects and standard errors are clustered at the level of treatment assignment.

experimental studies on the effect of information on politicians' performance, we find no evidence of impact on vote choice. There is some evidence of an effect on electoral participation, though only for the bad news case, and the result appears only in some specifications. Our results are also strikingly consistent across the six independent studies: using our meta-analysis procedure, we find that no individual experiment shows significant impacts of voter information interventions conducted shortly before the election, in the common arms of our study. Neither the directionality of the information shock (good versus bad news) nor the magnitude of the shock (difference from priors) generates changes in voters' choices.

Importantly, these interventions induced no measurable change in voters' beliefs. While perceptions may be important drivers of voting behavior, none of the types of intervention studied here appeared meaningfully to impact those views in our studies. In addition, none of the forms of heterogeneity to which we precommitted are present in the data; and subgroup effects reported by individual studies do not manifest themselves as general meta-results.

Given these findings, a reader might suspect that these particular informational treatments are simply not strong or salient enough to shape behavior. This might owe to the mode of delivery, timing, or content of the information. We would not dispute this interpretation. We would again point out, however, that the informational interventions in our studies were designed by country experts often in collaboration with local NGOs; and several are quite similar to others in the previous literature that have exhibited apparently strong effects on electoral behavior.[76] We find systematically weak effects across a range of coordinated studies. This underscores the value of the Metaketa approach: the initiative produces systematic evidence that addresses problems of study scarcity, study heterogeneity, and publication bias that appear to beset many research literatures.

What, then, do we learn from this meta-result that is different from what could be gleaned from any individual study? First, of course, there is the issue of power: any individual study if powered normally has a 20 percent chance of failing to find a result that is actually there, while our meta-study has a much lower probability of Type II error than most of our individual studies. By replicating a non-result in six contexts, we can conclude with a degree of statistical certainty that would not otherwise be possible. There is also an important point about implementation to be made. When looking at any single study, there is always the question as to whether implementation on the ground was problematic and thus the research may have failed to test the hypothesis adequately. The aggregation of six studies, none of which had major obvious problems of this kind, makes it much less likely that our lack of results arises from such implementation challenges. The lack of meta-impacts even on perceptions of politician performance suggests a set of important foundational questions for future research: how performance in specific dimensions is incorporated into an overall perception of politician quality, and the way that the credibility of the information source may alter the degree of updating.

Stepping back, these results speak to the comparative impact of transparency-promotion interventions more broadly. As discussed in Chapter 3, our studies all sought to manipulate only the selection margin of voter choice. Fielded immediately before elections, they were not intended to induce an incentive effect on politician behavior. However,

---

[76] See also Chapter 3.

because the most obvious mechanism generating pressure on politicians to respond is precisely the effectiveness of information on the selection margin, our non-result should imply that politicians have no reason to respond to such interventions at all. In this case these programs would similarly not have generated an improvement in politician moral hazard even if they had been introduced further before the election. Of course, the fact that in two of our studies politicians attempted to end or undermine the intervention suggests that in some cases they did in fact perceive it as a threat, and introduces the possibility that we have lost from the study precisely those circumstances under which the information would have been most important. Normatively, politicians should have the opportunity to respond to information and defend themselves against particular charges of malfeasance or ineptitude.[77] Yet, the fact that they may do so is of more than academic concern, given that real-world implementers would face similarly heterogeneous opposition to implementation by political leaders. The implication is that informational interventions can only be easily conducted in contexts where they will be ineffective. In this sense, our findings provide important information to donor collaboratives, policymakers and project implementers. In light of the optimism among such organizations about using informational campaigns to boost transparency and accountability, our core results provide a cautionary tale about the effectiveness of simple – but frequently utilized – interventions targeted at voters.

At the same time, our results do point to interesting alternative conditions under which informational interventions may have more impact – in particular, our pooled findings on the public intervention arms. These and other results that are idiosyncratic to studies reported in Part II, should be assessed systematically, perhaps in future Metaketas. To justify the case for extending this model to other areas, however, it is imperative to have more evidence on the usefulness of the approach itself. It is to this topic that we turn in the next chapter.

---

[77] For example, criminal charges, while officially recognized, may be politically motivated (India), or politicians' lack of effort in some areas – say, shirking their legislative responsibilities in Benin – may be more than compensated for by efforts in other areas.

12

Learning about Cumulative Learning: An Experiment with Policy Practitioners

Gareth Nellis, Thad Dunning, Guy Grossman,
Macartan Humphreys, Susan D. Hyde, Craig
McIntosh, and Catlan Reardon

12.1 INTRODUCTION

At the heart of the Metaketa initiative is the idea that multiple, coordinated studies allow for stronger inferences about the effect of a treatment or program than standard approaches to research. The previous chapters have shown the model in action. We assessed whether increasing the amount of information available to citizens just before an election causes them to be more likely to turn out to vote, to sanction underperforming incumbents, and to reward high achievers. The studies, both individually and in aggregation, uncover little evidence that informational interventions of this kind influence voter behavior.

In this chapter, we put the Metaketa concept itself to the test.[1] Taking a sample of the intended consumers of the Metaketa's findings as subjects, we investigate (a) whether coordinated research can alter policymakers' beliefs about an intervention's effectiveness, as well as improve their ability to make out-of-sample predictions; and (b) whether results from multiple coordinated research projects have stronger effects than the results of individual, "standalone" studies in this regard.

To date, these questions have mostly escaped systematic investigation. This is somewhat ironic. Champions of experimental methods routinely criticize traditional, nonexperimental impact evaluations for making overly confident claims. However, they have levied this charge without demonstrating that experimental evidence is capable of changing beliefs or decisions on the ground.

[1] Special thanks to Richard Sedlmayr, who was central to conceptualizing this study and encouraged us to do it.

375

It seems natural to expect that providing policymakers with the best available evidence will lead them to reach better decisions. Yet there are reasons to be skeptical. For one thing, studies rarely speak in perfect unison. Findings can differ across studies owing to contextual factors and sampling variability, both of which complicate the task of drawing general policy lessons. Even when evidence is unambiguous, decision-makers often appear reluctant to change ongoing policies or programs. Reviewing the case literature on how policy is formulated, Weiss and colleagues conclude that "most studies seem to be used in selective bits, reinterpreted to fit existing preferences or ignored."[2] There is a need for a controlled yet realistic test of these issues. The six Metaketa I studies offer a good opportunity to undertake such a test. The topic they address is policy-relevant: information and transparency interventions are a main-stay of democracy promotion efforts worldwide. The study designs are closely congruent with one another, facilitating side-by-side comparison of the findings. Perhaps most importantly, the studies show little hetero-geneity: all suggest that the treatment in question has little or no effect. Admittedly, we did not know these results when we planned the evalua-tion presented in this chapter. Still, the fact that they are near-identical is fortuitous. We can cleanly identify the additional effect of a meta-analysis compared to an individual study, holding constant the substantive con-clusions furnished by the evidence. Few existing sets of studies meet these criteria.

We integrated a field experiment into a one-day "evidence summit" held in Washington, D.C. Our research subjects were mostly mid-level and senior policymakers and practitioners active in the capital. They included both federal government employees, as well as individuals working at think tanks and not-for-profit organizations. The sample, therefore, comprises exactly the types of people that policy-focused political scientists seek to reach and persuade.

We randomly varied the order in which event attendees were exposed to different presentations of the Metaketa results, in addition to a placebo condition and a non-Metaketa study on the same topic-area. By tak-ing frequent measurements of outcomes, the design allows us to assess whether access to a larger dose of coordinated studies affects beliefs and out-of-sample prediction accuracy. It also sheds light on a variety of other hypotheses about cumulative learning, which we now develop.

---

[2] Weiss et al. (2008): 33.

12.2 EXPECTATIONS

12.2.1 Existing Evidence

Before describing our experiment, we review the state of knowledge on three questions: Is external validity possible in the social sciences? Are policymakers responsive to evidence? And if so, what role might additional evidence play in shaping beliefs about the effects of a policy or program?

For our experiment to generate meaningful results, external validity must be attainable. In common usage, studies are said to lack external validity when the manner or environment in which they were performed is unrepresentative of a larger set of cases. But simple statistical theory suggests that the problem may run deeper. To make inferences about a population of interest, we typically investigate a sample of cases drawn randomly from that population.[3] Yet studies designed to estimate causal effects are rarely – if ever – chosen in this manner. Without random sampling, generalizing from one context to another may be a tenuous exercise. This is especially true for interventions whose effects are heterogeneous – moderated heavily by external factors, or changeable over time.[4]

A sizable body of work has sought to measure whether external validity obtains. On balance, the empirical record is quite optimistic. There are a number of cases of successful extrapolations from studies to broader populations. For example, DellaVigna and Pope (2017) show that academic experts guess the results of online behavioral experiments with remarkable accuracy. Tetlock and Gardner (2016) identify "super-forecasters" who consistently predict national security and foreign policy outcomes on the basis of very limited information. Strikingly, in betting markets, both experts and nonexperts are able to forecast at high rates whether experimental studies in psychology and economics will replicate (Dreber et al., 2015; Camerer et al., 2016).[5]

---

[3] Since the expected value of this sample average is known to equal the population average, extrapolating outside of the sample is trivial in this case.

[4] Thinking formally, prediction could still be possible, even in the absence of randomly sampled studies if, for example, there are informative beliefs about the sampling process.

[5] To be sure, some interventions have been shown to succeed in one place only to fail when tried elsewhere (Grossman, Humphreys, and Sacramone-Lutz, 2019). For further examples on both sides of this debate, see Banerjee and Duflo (2009): 160–61.

Our experiment provides a further test of the viability of out-of-sample prediction, and thus of external validity writ large. It diverges from existing literature, however, which mostly elicits forecasts about the results of laboratory studies. By contrast, we measure and verify predictions about a corpus of field experiments conducted in five different countries worldwide. Ex ante, this represents a much harder test.

Next, our experiment speaks to the issue of whether policymakers internalize the lessons from rigorous evaluations. The literature highlights several pathologies. Policymakers may process research in "directional" (i.e., biased) ways. Individuals frequently discount evidence that contradicts prior judgments, and over-weight confirming evidence (Molden and Higgins, 2012; Nyhan and Reifler, 2015; Baekgaard et al., 2017). Institutional constraints might also pose a hurdle in this regard. NGOs or government agencies that have sunk significant resources or political capital into backing particular interventions may be unwilling to change course, no matter what the evidence says. Similarly, evidence might be sought out, but only selectively – to legitimate decisions that have already been taken (Patton, 2015). There is a danger that policymakers fixate on studies demonstrating large, significant results, without paying attention to replicability or context specificity. It is possible, too, that the skills needed to properly decipher and interpret statistical evidence are in short supply. Policymakers, mindful of questionable research practices, might reasonably distrust much of the evidence being produced. In short, policymakers could well predict how evaluations will play out, but still not have that information affect their beliefs and decision-making.

While these arguments are plausible, hard evidence about elite behavior is scant. Most of what we know about the policymaking process comes from qualitative research. Our experiment enables us to test systematically whether a relevant sample of active policymakers suffer from consistency bias, recency bias, and the overweighting of statistically significant research findings. We can also measure the magnitude of updating over different types of beliefs.

The forgoing discussion addresses whether policymakers are responsive to evidence at all. A final question is whether exposure to additional evidence on a given topic will affect how policymakers update their beliefs. In a recent paper, Vivalt and Coville (2017) propose a simple learning model in which policymakers have to decide between two programs: one whose impact is certain, and another whose impact is uncertain. Policymakers seek to maximize program effects. A research study provides a signal about the effectiveness of the uncertain program, and policymakers update beliefs in response to the information. The marginal benefit of carrying out an extra study is the probability that its evidence will be pivotal in determining which program the policymaker selects, multiplied by the anticipated gains from choosing that program instead of the other one. Simulations, as well as real data on policymakers' priors, suggest that studies are rarely pivotal in practice. Studies matter more for updating when there is less evidence available, and when there is greater initial uncertainty about a program's impact.[6]

While important, these results only employ data on policymakers' priors; actual updating in response to new information is not observed. Moreover, an assumption behind the model is that policymakers are rational Bayesians – something that may or may not be true. Our study can help plug both these evidentiary gaps.

12.2.2 Hypotheses

Prior to implementing the experiment we registered six hypotheses about how the Metaketa evidence might influence policymakers. Our hypotheses focused on the effects of learning about (a) an individual Metaketa study; (b) a meta-analysis of the Metaketa studies; and (c) an external study, conducted outside the Metaketa project but focused on the same questions and employing a credible research design. We purposively excluded one single study from the meta-analysis. Predictions were then made about this omitted "unseen" study.

Our first two hypotheses relate to the changes in predictions we expected over time owing to exposure to all types of evidence:

- H1: Subjects will be more accurate in forecasting the results of an unseen study at endline compared to baseline, having been exposed to all types of presentations (a nonexperimental comparison).
- H2: Subjects will be more confident in their forecasts regarding the results of an unseen study at endline compared to baseline (a nonexperimental comparison).

---

[6] Beynon et al. (2012) conduct an experiment on the impact of policy briefs, a commonly used tool for disseminating evidence to policymakers. Overall, the study indicates that policy briefs summarizing research in a simplified format do little to shift perceptions about what kinds of interventions work, although policymakers with flat priors do update somewhat.

Three hypotheses relate to the separate effects of these three sources
of information:

- H3: Subjects exposed to an individual study will be more likely
  to make a correct prediction about the result of the unseen study
  than subjects exposed to the placebo information (an experimental
  comparison).
- H4: Subjects exposed to the external study will be more likely to
  make a correct prediction about the result of the unseen study than
  subjects exposed to the placebo (an experimental comparison).
- H5: Subjects exposed to the (leave-one-out) meta-analysis will
  be more likely to make a correct prediction about the result of
  the unseen study than subjects exposed to the placebo, or to an
  individual Metaketa study, or to the external study (experimental
  comparisons).

The final hypothesis centers on decision-making about the use of
programming funds:

- H6: Subjects exposed to the meta-analysis will reduce the percentage of funds allocated to the voter information intervention
  compared to subjects exposed to the placebo, or to an individual Metaketa study, or to the external study (experimental
  comparisons).

12.3   DESIGN

To test these hypotheses, we conducted a field experiment with policymakers and program officers based in the Washington D.C. area, and
working in the fields of governance and democracy promotion. The
experiment was embedded within a one-day "evidence summit," billed as
an opportunity for interested parties to learn the results of the Metaketa I
initiative. The event lasted approximately four hours. The setting for the
experiment was naturalistic insofar as seminars, workshops, and one-day
conferences occur regularly in the US capital.

  On entering the event space, subjects were asked to provide informed
consent and were handed a manila envelope.[7] They were asked to hold
on to their assigned envelope for the rest of the day. Paper-clipped to the

---

[7] The experimental protocol was approved by the Institutional Review Board at the
University of California, Berkeley, under case number 2017-04-9779.

front was a list of instructions and an entry survey. Subjects completed the entry survey, but were told not to open the envelope until instructed to do so.

Participants then gathered in the main auditorium. Here, we introduced the EGAP network and the Metaketa research model. We went on to provide key background information on Metaketa I: its common research question, the intervention, operational definitions of "good" and "bad" news, and the harmonized outcome measures. Next, each of the six Metaketa I teams that had completed their studies delivered a short (five minute) presentation describing the country in which their experiment was fielded, the type of information delivered to citizens, its mode of delivery, the politicians about whom information had been provided, and the study's sample size. Importantly, none of the presentations mentioned any study results.

After the teams had finished speaking, we briefed the audience on the upcoming experimental part of the event. We told subjects that they could now open their envelopes, which contained three items: results-free summaries of each Metaketa study; a personalized itinerary telling the participant which room to go and when; and five identical outcome sheets stapled together in a bundle. All five sheets elicited predictions and beliefs about one of the six Metaketa studies. (We refer to this as the subject's "unseen" study, since they did not get to learn its actual results until after the experiment had concluded.)

The logistical directions were straightforward. Subjects were to go to the four rooms indicated on their personalized schedule at the prescribed times, and to complete an outcome sheet immediately after hearing each presentation. To avoid spillovers, we emphasized the importance of not conferring with other attendees while the experiment was in progress. We said that participants should fill in the top-most outcome sheet in their packets before leaving the auditorium, providing us with pretreatment predictions and beliefs.

Once these preliminaries were over, participants moved to a nearby block of classrooms. The classrooms were numbered one through eight, corresponding to the room numbers given on the participants' schedules.

12.3.1 Treatments

The experiment consisted of four rounds. Subjects were exposed to four types of presentations – one presentation per round – in an order that varied randomly by individual.

The four presentation types were as follows:

1. **Single (Individual Metaketa study).** Participants were exposed to the results of one of the six completed Metaketa I studies.
2. **Meta (Leave-one-out meta-analysis).** In preparation for the event, we generated all six possible versions of the Metaketa meta-analysis that had one of the six studies omitted. Participants were exposed only to the version of the meta-analysis that did not include their unseen study.
3. **Ext (External study).** We presented every participant with the results of a non-Metaketa study: Ferraz and Finan's "Exposing Corrupt Politicians: The Effect of Brazil's Publicly Released Audits on Electoral Outcomes."[8] This influential paper, like Metaketa I, addresses how the availability of information impacts electoral behavior. Unlike the Metaketa studies, however, Ferraz and Finan report large, statistically significant effects. In particular, they find that the release of corruption audits in Brazil significantly depressed the vote share of incumbent mayors, notably in places where the audits unearthed a greater than median number of infractions (akin to the Metaketa's "bad news" condition). Unlike the Metaketa studies, they do not investigate the effects of information on voter turnout.
4. **Placebo (Placebo condition).** This consisted of a presentation about the forthcoming Metaketa II, III, and IV initiatives. It was uninformative about the results of Metaketa I.

In total, there were fourteen unique presentations: six individual studies, six meta-analyses, the external study, and the placebo. Because multiple presenters were involved, it was important to standardize the presentations as much as possible. All results derived from parsimonious analyses without covariate adjustment.[9]

---

[8] Ferraz and Finan (2008).

[9] However, fixed effects for blocks used in the randomization were included in the models. The presentation slides are given in the online appendix (as examples) and in the replication materials (in full). The meta-analysis presentations were based on an early version of the meta-analysis which contained a coding error for the Burkina Faso study. Specifically, the codings of good and bad news were mistakenly reversed in the presented findings that involved this study. However, it is important to highlight that the estimated effects remain null – both in the meta-analysis and in the Burkina Faso study results – before and after we fixed this mistake.

They were presented as simple bar plots showing average outcomes in treatment and control groups. To make style and structure as uniform as possible, presenters rehearsed their talks jointly in advance of the event. We allowed respondents to ask clarifying questions at the end of each presentation. However, they were not permitted to discuss comparisons across the studies.

12.3.2 Outcomes

Over the course of the experiment – at baseline, and at the conclusion of each round – participants filled in five outcome sheets.[10] These were deposited in bins as participants exited each room. The sheets contained six questions.

For the first set of questions, participants were asked to guess what was the estimated effect of the bad news information on turnout and vote choice in the unseen study they had been assigned. They could circle one of three options: positive and statistically significant; negative and statistically significant; or no statistically significant effect.[11] Two additional questions instructed participants to state, using a three-point scale, how confident they felt about the predictions they had given.

The sheet's remaining questions probed beliefs about the effectiveness of the intervention. Focusing still on the unseen study, one question asked whether participants thought that receiving the bad news information would have made voters more or less likely to vote for the incumbent politician or party, regardless of whether they expected the study to have found statistically significant effects.

The final question sought to capture broader beliefs about the intervention's worth. We asked participants to imagine that an organization had put them in charge of a program to improve political accountability in developing democracies. They had $1 million to spend on three

---

[10] A unique subject ID tied outcome sheets to participants. Participants were required to fill out the same prediction sheet five times. Participants were instructed that they were free to change their answers or keep them the same across rounds, as they saw fit.

[11] To help participants, the sheet included a short primer on statistical significance. It was explained as follows: "The difference between measured outcomes in treatment and control groups is said to be statistically significant when such a difference is highly unlikely to be due to random chance alone. On the other hand, a difference is said to be not statistically significant when it is quite possible that it is due to chance." We also clarified the meaning of a "positive" and "negative" effect in relation to the specific outcomes.

ongoing initiatives. Their job was to allocate the funds in the most cost-effective manner. The three initiatives were:

- Providing information to voters about politician performance in the run-up to an election;
- Giving special training to politicians and bureaucrats that tries to help them better perform their duties;
- Funding nonpartisan observers to monitor upcoming elections and check for irregularities.

The original outcome sheet is given in the online appendix. The six dependent variables, which are based directly on the questions given on this sheet, are then as follows:

1. **Vote (Est.).** Whether or not the respondent correctly predicted vote choice for the unseen study (based on outcome sheet, question 3).
2. **Vote (Cert.).** Respondent's confidence in the vote choice prediction (based on question 4).
3. **Turnout (Est.).** Whether or not the respondent correctly predicted turnout for the unseen study (based on question 1).
4. **Turnout (Cert.).** Respondent's confidence in the turnout prediction (based on question 2).
5. **Vote (Real).** Absolute scale-point difference, squared, between the response given, and the "null" option on the scale – i.e., "Neither more nor less likely" (based on question 5).[12]
6. **Allocation.** Proportion of funds allocated to the voter information intervention (based on question 6).

12.3.3 Randomization

The basic idea behind our experimental set up is to expose each subject to all four types of presentation – Single, Meta, External, and Placebo – in a randomized order, and to randomly assign each subject an "unseen" study, about which they declare five sets of predictions over the course of the event. Note that there are six versions of the leave-one-out meta-analysis presentation and six single study presentations. For the design,

---

[12] Consider, for example, a respondent who answered "Much more likely" to question 5. Their outcome value would be recorded as 4, since the answer they provided is two scale points away from "Neither more nor less likely," and $2^2 = 4$. Meanwhile, a respondent who answered "Somewhat less likely" would have an outcome value of 1.

the specific meta-analysis and single study to be viewed is randomly chosen for each participant. This ensures that our findings do not pick up
beliefs about – or idiosyncratic features of – any one particular study
or context. We stipulate a given subject's unseen study to be the one
excluded from his or her assigned meta-analysis (e.g., for a subject
assigned the meta-analysis without Benin, her unseen study is Benin).
The randomization is constrained so that an individual's assigned single
study cannot be the same as her unseen study. A key virtue of the randomization is that it safeguards against order or period effects biasing
our results.

Concretely, the randomization procedure is implemented in three
steps.

First, the fourteen unique presentations are randomly assigned to
rooms and time slots. This is a restricted randomization in which, for
logistical reasons, the Uganda 1 and Mexico single studies are randomly
assigned to different time slots in room 1. Then the other four studies are
assigned randomly to rooms 2 and 3 in rounds 1 and 2. The resulting
pattern of assignments to slots and rooms is repeated for rounds 3 and 4.
The same pattern is then replicated for the leave-one-out meta-analysis:
the six presentations are allocated to three rooms across four rounds,
with each meta-analysis appearing twice. With the external study and
the placebo allocated to rooms 7 and 8 for all rounds, this step results in
a full timetable indicating what is presented in each of eight rooms over
four rounds (see Table 12.1).

Second, conditional on the room assignments, 192 treatment profiles
are identified. Each profile is a sequence of four rooms to visit across the
four rounds. These profiles form the exhaustive set of profiles in which
each contains one single country study, one meta-analysis, one placebo,
and one external study viewing.[13]

In the final stage, an ordering of profiles is preassigned to subjects 1
through n (where n is the total number of subjects), ordered as they register. Randomization ensures that the specific treatment profiles assigned

---

[13] To see where 192 comes from, label the first three single studies shown A, B, and C, and
the second three D, E, F. Note that a subject viewing single study A could view a meta-
analysis excluding study B and C in one of two orders (i.e., in rounds 1–3 or 3–1) and
could view a meta-analysis excluding study D, E, or F in four ways (i.e., 1–2, 1–4, 3–2,
3–4). Given the same possibilities for any other study there are $6 * (2 * 2 + 3 * 4) = 96$
position combinations for the single study and the leave-one-out meta-analysis to take.
With the positions of these two studies fixed, the placebo could either precede or follow
the external study. This produces $96 * 2 = 192$ combinations.

TABLE 12.1 *Room allocations in each round of the experiment. Country names refer to single studies. Study names preceded by "w/o" refer to meta-analyses with that one study left out.*

	Round 1	Round 2	Round 3	Round 4
Room 1	Uganda 1	Mexico	Uganda 1	Mexico
Room 2	Brazil	Uganda 2	Brazil	Uganda 2
Room 3	Burkina Faso	Benin	Burkina Faso	Benin
Room 4	Meta w/o Uganda 1	Meta w/o Mexico	Meta w/o Uganda 1	Meta w/o Mexico
Room 5	Meta w/o Brazil	Meta w/o Uganda 2	Meta w/o Brazil	Meta w/o Uganda 2
Room 6	Meta w/o Burkina Faso	Meta w/o Benin	Meta w/o Burkina Faso	Meta w/o Benin
Room 7	External Study	External Study	External Study	External Study
Room 8	Placebo	Placebo	Placebo	Placebo

are unrelated to subjects' time of registration. We use blocked random assignment of subjects (blocking across treatments) to guarantee that the number of subjects across all rooms is the same in round 1. Were there to be 192 subjects, perfect balance would be maintained in all rounds. With fewer than 192, balance is maintained in the first round but lost thereafter (although it is maintained in expectation). In practice many fewer than 192 subjects attended.

The randomization code is provided as an R script in the online appendix.

12.3.4 Sample

We employ a convenience sample of policymakers based in Washington, D.C. EGAP staff, in conjunction with EGAP's membership, compiled a list of 284 possible attendees. We targeted individuals working in international development, democracy promotion, and governance. Subjects were recruited via email, sent out three weeks before the event. 124 individuals confirmed attendance, while fifty-five invitees participated in the experiment.

Sample characteristics are summarized in Online Appendix Table H1. Most attendees were active policy practitioners. Just over half worked in not-for-profit organizations, and 21 percent were government employees.

TABLE 12.2 *Distribution of subjects' priors –
as reported in the entry survey – on the effects
of providing voters with bad news on turnout
and voting for the incumbent*

Expectation	Turnout	Vote
Much less likely	0.02	0.07
Somewhat less likely	0.43	0.72
No difference	0.33	0.09
Somewhat more likely	0.2	0.11
Much more likely	0.02	0

Proportions in cells may not sum to 1 due to rounding.

(Six participants were academics.) 54 percent of subjects are male. 71 percent hold either mid-level or senior-level positions within their organizations. The sample was highly educated: 82 percent held either a master's degree or doctorate. Moreover, 60 percent indicated that they were either "somewhat proficient" or "very proficient" in statistics, and 70 percent reported having worked on impact or policy evaluations in the past. In short, the sample largely consisted of individuals familiar with quantitative research methods, making them well equipped to engage with the results of the Metaketa.

We also gathered data on subjects' prior beliefs about the effects of "bad news" information on voting behavior – framed in the abstract, and not in relation to the specific Metaketa studies. The distribution of these priors is shown in Table 12.2. Interestingly, most participants believe that information matters for turnout propensity, although there is disagreement on the direction of the effect, with the plurality expecting that bad news depresses turnout (consistent with the findings of Chong et al., 2015). 78 percent believe that bad news makes voters less likely to vote for incumbents, but most expected these effects to be modest. About one in twelve expected strong effects on vote choice and a small share expected positive effects (consistent perhaps with Vaishnav, 2017).

12.3.5 Estimation Strategy

We carry out two kinds of analysis: (a) causal estimates of the impact of exposure to one type of presentation versus another; (b) nonexperimental, before/after comparisons of participants' predictions and beliefs about the unseen study. For the experimental analyses, we estimate average causal effects within each pairwise combination of the four aggregated treatment categories – thus six possible pairwise comparisons in all.

Because policymakers are a hard-to-reach population, we anticipated a small sample size. To maximize statistical power, each experimental comparison uses one data point from every subject. Doing this requires a more involved statistical analysis.

For ease of exposition, suppose the four main treatment categories (i.e., presentation types) have the initials A, B, C, and D, and suppose our interest lies in comparing the effect of viewing A instead of B.

We classify participants into one of three strata, depending on the randomized schedule they were assigned:

- **Stratum 1.** Round 1 responses by participants exposed to either A or B in Round 1;
- **Stratum 2.** Round 2 responses by participants exposed to either A or B in Round 2, and who were not exposed to either A or B in Round 1;
- **Stratum 3.** Round 3 responses from participants exposed to either A or B in Round 3, and who were not exposed to either A or B in either Round 1 or Round 2.

Conditional on stratum, the probability of being in condition A or B is 50 percent, and so simple fixed effects analysis is sufficient to take account of differences across strata. The estimating equation is as follows:

$$Y_i = \kappa + \delta Treatment_i + \theta_s + \epsilon_i \qquad (12.1)$$

where κ is a constant, and θ are the fixed effects for strata s. We want to know δ, the estimated average treatment effect associated with outcome Y of exposure to A rather than B.

For the nonexperimental analyses, we restrict the estimation sample to responses provided in the baseline and endline surveys only, yielding two observations per participant. We then run first-differences OLS regressions of the following form:

$$Y_{i,t} = \alpha + \beta Endline_i + \gamma_i + \epsilon_{i,t} \qquad (12.2)$$

Here, $Y_{i,t}$ stands in for one of our six dependent variables; i indexes participants; t indexes time, where $t = \{baseline, endline\}$; γ_i are subject fixed effects; α is a constant; and $\epsilon_{i,t}$ is the error term. The parameter of interest is β: the within-subject estimated difference for a given Y across outcomes measured in the baseline and endline surveys.

12.4 RESULTS

We now discuss the results of the experiment, which we estimate following the specifications in equation (12.2).

12.4.1 Effects of Exposure to Presentation Types

The study's main findings are plotted in Figure 12.1. The paired comparisons being made in each row are listed on the vertical axis. The dot and whiskers plots visualize the estimated average treatment effects and their associated confidence intervals. Each column summarizes effect estimates for one of our six dependent variables.

The first row of Figure 12.1 presents the strongest experimental contrast: the differences in responses for subjects exposed to the meta-analysis (of five out of six Metaketa studies, with the subject's unseen study left out) compared to the external study. Recall that all versions of the meta-analysis report null effects, whereas the external study shows negative, statistically significant effects of bad news on vote choice. Given these divergent findings, we expect the gap in our experimental outcomes – in terms of predictions and beliefs about the intervention – to be widest when juxtaposing these two groups.

This is what we find. Looking at the prediction tasks, Figure 12.1, row 1 demonstrates large differences in the expected direction for both vote choice (column 1) and turnout (column 3). Note that these are dichotomous outcome measures taking one when the respondent's prediction aligns with the result reported in the unseen study, and zero otherwise. Viewing the meta-analysis instead of the external study significantly increases the likelihood that respondents correctly forecast the results of the unseen study.

The effects on confidence in these predictions (Figure 12.1, row 1, columns 2 and 4) are less pronounced and not statistically significant. This makes some sense. In principle, both the external study and the meta-analysis could increase participants' certainty about their predictions relative to baseline. Still, the coefficients are positively signed, suggesting that the meta-analysis produces greater gains in certainty than exposure to the external study. Since the meta-analysis

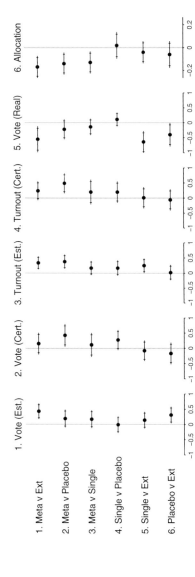

FIGURE 12.1 Causal effects of exposure to presentation types, and 95 percent confidence intervals (ticks denote 90 percent confidence intervals). The experimental comparisons being made are shown by row. For each paired comparison, the first listed item is the treatment condition, and the second item is the comparison condition. The six dependent variables, listed by column, are as follows: (col. 1) whether or not respondent correctly predicted vote choice in the unseen study; (col. 2) respondent's confidence in vote choice prediction; (col. 3) whether or not respondent correctly predicted turnout in the unseen study; (col. 4) respondent's confidence in turnout prediction; (col. 5) beliefs about intervention's "real" effectiveness; (col. 6) proportion of funds allocated to the voter information intervention. N is 46–49 for each analysis.

was the more informative about the unseen study, this chimes with expectations.

We also see sizeable effects in Figure 12.1, row 1 for beliefs about the intervention's effectiveness (column 5). Interpreting the column 5 coefficients requires some care. Responses to the original survey question were given on a five-point ordinal scale, asking how likely it is that the intervention affected vote choice. For the purposes of the analysis, responses are re-coded so as to create a measure of the absolute scale-point difference, squared, from what the Metaketa suggests is the best answer to this question (i.e., no effect). A negatively signed coefficient thus indicates a shrinking of this distance, with respondents moving towards what the six studies point to as the intervention's impact; a positive value indicates that participants' beliefs are moving away from the conclusion of the studies. In row 1, column 5, we see that exposure to the meta-analysis induced significant movement towards the Metaketa's null result, when compared to those who viewed the external study.

There are very substantial differences in Figure 12.1, row 1 on decisions about how to allocate expenditures (column 6). The exercise was to divide a fixed amount of money ($1 million) between three democracy promotion schemes. The dependent variable used in column 6 is the fraction of total funds allocated to "Providing information to voters about politician performance in the run up to an election," in other words, the Metaketa intervention. The statistically significant negative effect on allocation decisions in row 1, column 6 corresponds to a 17 percent drop in allocations when the meta-analysis is seen, as opposed to the external study. Policymakers' willingness to transfer funds away from the intervention is reassuring in view of the strong meta-analysis evidence that providing information to voters is ineffectual.

It is important to highlight that the effects displayed in Figure 12.1, row 1 are relative effects. They could be driven by the negative impacts of the meta-analysis on beliefs about the intervention's effectiveness, the positive impacts of the external study, or both simultaneously. By looking at a larger set of experimental comparisons, we can unpack which of these effects predominates.

The other analyses displayed in Figure 12.1 help to decompose these results. We next compare the effects of the meta-analysis against the placebo, and the placebo against the external study. Focusing on the predictions about vote choice (column 1), we observe that the effects of the meta-analysis and the external study push in opposite directions. Exposure to the meta-analysis boosts predictive accuracy relative to the placebo (row 2, column 1). Exposure to the placebo boosts accuracy relative to the external study (row 6, column 1), which of course indicates that the external study is leading respondents to mispredict the results of the unseen study at higher rates. Interestingly, the effects of the external study on the vote choice prediction in row 6, column 1 turn out to be larger in absolute magnitude than the effects of the meta-analysis (row 2). Put simply, the external study moved predictions more than the meta-analysis.

The picture is reversed for the turnout predictions in Figure 12.1, column 3. The estimates here suggest that the difference in prediction accuracy between groups exposed to the meta-analysis and the external study (in row 1) are attributable wholly to the effects of the meta-analysis. (To see this, contrast the significant, positive effect in row 2, column 3, with the null effect in row 6, column 3.) Since the external study did not analyze turnout at all, the noneffect in row 6, column 3 is both unsurprising and logical.

The differences in effects on beliefs about intervention effectiveness and allocations are split between effects driven by the meta-analysis and effects produced by the external study. Again, we use the placebo as a benchmark. The meta-analysis gives rise to a bigger change in allocation decisions than the external study (contrast Figure 12.1, rows 2 and 6 in column 6). But the external study more strongly alters beliefs about the "real" effects of the intervention (row 2 versus row 6 in column 5).

What of the differences in the effects of single Metaketa studies compared to the meta-analysis? This is an important comparison for validating the Metaketa approach. The initiative is built on the notion that multiple, coordinated field experiments provide a stronger basis for assessing a program's impact than individual studies performed and published in isolation. Our hope, therefore, is that policymakers update more after viewing a meta-analysis than an individual Metaketa study.

The data lend only partial support. Two sets of comparisons in Figure 12.1 are illuminating. First, scanning across columns, it is noteworthy that the effect of the meta-analysis compared to the placebo (row 2, significant for four of six outcomes) is much stronger than the effect of single studies compared to the placebo (row 4, null for all outcomes). On this barometer, subjects appear to assign substantially more weight to the meta-analysis.

However, the second, more exacting test is the head-to-head comparison between the meta-analysis and the single study presented in Figure 12.1, row 3. Qualitatively, the effects for outcomes in this row are positive in columns 1–4, and negative in columns 5–6. This is as we hypothesized; it is consistent with respondents placing extra weight on the meta-analysis over and above the single study. But in only one case does a coefficient in row 3 rise to the level of statistical significance – the one for allocation decisions in column 6.

Perhaps surprisingly, the differences in effects of the single Metaketa study versus the external study are large in two cases: the turnout prediction (Figure 12.1, row 5, column 3) and beliefs about program effectiveness (row 5, column 5). The direction of these two effects shows that participants are putting more credence in the single Metaketa study – appropriately so, given the task at hand.[14]

In general, the causal results show considerable responsiveness to information. They reveal sophistication in extracting information from distal studies, with greater weight placed on more relevant studies. Encouragingly, we do not see evidence that policymakers are captivated by studies that demonstrate large, significant effects. Perhaps the most disappointing result from the Metaketa point of view is that the differences in effects of single Metaketa studies versus multiple studies – though substantively large – are not significant in all specifications.

12.4.2   Baseline/Endline Comparisons (Nonexperimental)

The experimental analyses just discussed examine the effects of the different treatments relative to one another. By the end of the final round of the experiment, all participants had seen all treatments. We now explore the net impact of exposure to the full collection of presentations.

Figure 12.2 presents the average within-subject differences in outcomes across baseline and endline surveys. We urge caution in attaching a causal interpretation to these over-time estimates. Period effects – for example, growing fatigue or frustration on the part of subjects – could

---

[14] There is a proviso regarding the analyses in Figure 12.1. Two of the experimental contrasts in Figure 12.1 – Single versus Placebo (row 4) and Single versus Ext (row 5) – employ observations from subjects already exposed to the meta-analysis. In similar fashion, another two contrasts – Meta versus Placebo (row 2) and Meta versus Ext (row 1) – employ outcomes from subjects already exposed to a single Metaketa study. This unavoidable feature of the randomization is not a source of bias, but it may lead to attenuated treatment effects. In Figure H1 in the online appendix, we rerun the analysis, excluding subjects already exposed to these pieces of information. The effects appear somewhat stronger, as expected.

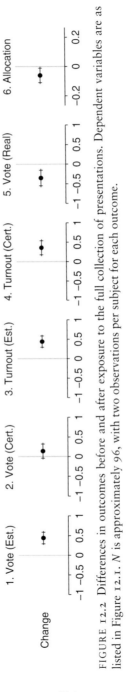

FIGURE 12.2 Differences in outcomes before and after exposure to the full collection of presentations. Dependent variables are as listed in Figure 12.1. N is approximately 96, with two observations per subject for each outcome.

conceivably drive patterns seen in the data.[15] That said, the experiment lasted only eighty minutes, making the inter-temporal changes more compelling.

We start by considering the results for study predictions. In Figure 12.2, we see a large uptick in predictive accuracy for both vote choice (column 1) and turnout (column 3). At baseline, 27 percent of respondents believed that the bad news treatment would have no statistically significant effect on vote choice; by endline, that figure had risen to 71 percent. The corresponding numbers for turnout are 44 percent and 88 percent, respectively. Viewing the four presentations in their entirety was associated with improved ability to make out-of-sample predictions.

Did participants' confidence in these forecasts go up as the experiment proceeded? Only modestly so, according to the self-reports (Figure 12.2, columns 2 and 4). Confidence was already low at baseline: on a three-point scale ranging from zero (low) to two (high), average confidence stood at just 0.97 (for vote choice) and 0.83 (for turnout) prior to the presentation of study results. By endline, these averages had moved up by 0.14 and 0.36 scale-points, respectively. Only the confidence increase for the turnout prediction is statistically significant. Subjects appear to be cognizant of difficulties in guessing how the results of any particular study might turn out.

Does participation in the event shape beliefs about the "real" impact of the intervention? Column 5 of Figure 12.2 suggests that participants were somewhat persuaded that the bad news information would have negligible impacts on voter behavior: the distance-squared index drops by a statistically significant amount. In a directional sense, therefore, respondents' expectations about the real-world impact of the intervention track how they are updating over the study results, with both sets of beliefs converging on the null.

A different perspective on this result can be gleaned by inspecting the raw, untransformed responses to the survey question used to construct the column 5 dependent variable. Strikingly, most respondents at endline – 61 percent – continued to report that voters presented with the bad

---

[15] For instance, one could imagine that fatigue or frustration might have led participants to offer an increasing number of neutral responses to the survey questions as the event progressed. This would be problematic in our application, since what we code as being the "correct" response to questions is usually the neutral one.

news information would be "Somewhat less likely" to vote for the incumbent politician. Only 32 percent said that the information would make voters "Neither more nor less likely" to back the incumbent – although this represented a large increase relative to the 10 percent who gave that answer at baseline. Learning about the Metaketa results swayed some participants at the event. But it was not enough to convince the majority that the intervention was ineffective.

Finally, we examine respondents' decisions about how to divide funds (Figure 12.2, column 6). The temporal change in this variable, although negative as expected, is arguably modest in size. There is a six percentage point reduction in the share of funds assigned to voter information programming at endline compared to baseline – a marginally significant difference. This substantively minor shift is perhaps surprising in view of the volume of Metaketa evidence showing the intervention to be inconsequential for voter behavior.

Why might this be the case? It could be that policymakers held fast to the idea that the intervention might be effective under certain conditions – in contexts where Metaketa studies had not been conducted. Another explanation is that policymakers thought that tweaks to the intervention itself might enhance its effects. More worrying is the possibility that policymakers, after hearing a slew of null results, negatively updated about the ability of studies to detect actually existing effects. We have some empirical traction on this issue. Respondents were asked in both the entry survey and at endline, "How valuable do you think randomized controlled trials are for identifying a program's effects in the real world?" At the start of the event, the mean response-score to this question – recorded on a five-point value scale, with 5 denoting "very valuable" – was 3.85; by endline, this figure had barely changed, standing at 3.70. Fortunately, therefore, exposure to the Metaketa null results does not seem to have heightened misgivings about the value of experimental evidence.

To sum up, we see quite dramatic increases in predictive accuracy as the experiment progressed. Beliefs about the potency of the intervention also moved, but to a lesser extent, with hypothetical allocations to the voter information program dropping only slightly. Although more participants thought that the intervention's true impact in the unseen study was essentially zero, most continued to believe at endline that the intervention would have an effect in the unseen studies, despite the raft of Metaketa evidence to the contrary.

12.5 ARE POLICYMAKERS BAYESIANS?

We see strong evidence for updating in the expected directions. But is this updating "optimal"? The standard approach to rational updating is to use Bayes' rule. One starts with a prior belief about a hypothesis and then updates in a specific way, given new data.[16]

Without a strong handle on individuals' beliefs about the probability of data under the hypothesis – for example, here the probability that study B would find effects if the excluded study A were to exhibit effects – and a good understanding of priors, assessing conformity with Bayes' rule is difficult. Nevertheless, one testable implication can be exploited. According to Bayes' rule, the order in which data is presented should not affect conclusions. A subject seeing the meta-analysis first and the results from Ferraz and Finan (2008) later should ultimately form the same view as a subject seeing Ferraz and Finan first and the meta-analysis later. We can check this prediction against patterns in the data. Specifically, we can examine the differences across treatment groups based on what information subjects received first (differences that should be large) compared to the differences across groups defined by what they received last (differences that should be negligible). In simple terms, by the end of the experiment, everyone had been exposed to the same information. If Bayesian updating is in force, therefore, all participants should converge on (roughly) the same posterior.

Table 12.3 reports empirical tests. We regress outcomes about beliefs in "real" effects (columns 1–3) and fund allocations (columns 4–6) on indicators for exposure to various presentation types. The excluded category is the external study condition. Columns 1 and 4 show the effects of round 1 treatment assignment on round 1 outcomes; columns 2 and 5 show the effects of round 4 treatment assignment on round 4 outcomes; and columns 3 and 6 show the effects of round 1 treatment assignment on round 4 outcomes.

If policymakers suffer from recency bias – heeding only the most recent information they came into contact with – then we should observe significant effects in columns 2 and 5 of Table 12.3; put otherwise, participants' round 4 (endline) responses should be influenced heavily by

---

[16] Specifically let $p(H)$ denote the prior about hypothesis H, let the belief about the likelihood of seeing the data that is seen under the hypothesis be given by $p(D|H)$, and the probability of seeing that data under any hypothesis by $p(D)$. One then updates using the rule: $p(H|D) = p(D|H)p(H)/p(D)$.

TABLE 12.3 *Treatment effects in individual rounds. T refers to treatment assignment for a given round, while R refers to outcomes in that round. Thus "T1 on R4" is the estimated effect of round 1 treatment assignment on round 4 outcomes.*

	Vote (Real)			Allocation		
	T1 on R1 (1)	T4 on R4 (2)	T1 on R4 (3)	T1 on R1 (4)	T4 on R4 (5)	T1 on R4 (6)
Meta analysis	−0.879***	−0.194	−0.164	−0.195***	0.008	−0.100
	(0.295)	(0.202)	(0.204)	(0.067)	(0.093)	(0.083)
Placebo	−0.645**	0.159	−0.300	−0.112	−0.085	−0.149*
	(0.309)	(0.191)	(0.209)	(0.070)	(0.088)	(0.085)
Single study	−0.795**	−0.179	0.018	−0.087	−0.108	−0.099
	(0.295)	(0.180)	(0.204)	(0.067)	(0.083)	(0.083)
Constant	1.545***	0.750***	0.800***	0.445***	0.367***	0.390***
	(0.213)	(0.132)	(0.148)	(0.048)	(0.061)	(0.060)
Observations	45	46	42	45	46	42
Adjusted R^2	0.149	0.031	0.005	0.113	−0.006	0.006

Note: $^*p < 0.1$; $^{**}p < 0.05$; $^{***}p < 0.01$

their treatment assignment in round 4. Meanwhile, if consistency bias is at work, then effects should be concentrated in columns 3 and 6: respondents' answers at endline should be decided first and foremost by the information they viewed at the very start of the experiment. If respondents are Bayesians, however, we should see effects in columns 1 and 4 only: assignment should shape beliefs in round 1, but by the conclusion of round 4 – at which point, all subjects have received the same bundle of information – there should be no discernable difference according to round 4 treatment assignment.

It is the Bayesian hypothesis that receives most support in Table 12.3. The round 1 treatment effects account for 15 percent of the variation in the effectiveness outcome in column 1, and 11 percent of the variation in the allocations outcome in column 4. Other columns, meanwhile, demonstrate no evidence of either recency bias or consistency bias. We show the results for the remaining dependent variables in Table H2 in the online appendix.

12.6   CONCLUSION

In recent years, social and political sciences have undergone both a "micro-revolution" and a "credibility revolution" (Laitin and Reich,

2017, Angrist and Pischke, 2010). Advances in method and substance have dramatically expanded the scope for research findings to have tangible impacts. A central goal of the Metaketa initiative is to generate evidence that incites policy change. Yet its success in this endeavor hinges critically on how policymakers respond to coordinated research – a question on which existing literature is mostly silent.

Using a field experiment, we show that multiple, coordinated studies aid learning in a sample of active policy practitioners. Exposure to a meta-analysis (of five of the six Metaketa studies) improves out-of-sample prediction accuracy. It also changes beliefs about the effects of interventions, as well as stated preferences over resource allocation. The effects of the meta-analysis are strongest when the comparison group is presented with an "external," non-Metaketa study – one that shows results contradicting the Metaketa's. We also see effects of the meta-analysis relative to a placebo. Both of these findings help vindicate the Metaketa model. Somewhat tempering them, however, is the fact that inferences from the meta-analysis are not significantly stronger than inferences from a single Metaketa study, in most models.

Impressively, the kinds of biases often associated with learning are not visible here. Participants do not place additional weight on "positive," non-null results. Also, they do not appear to suffer from recency or consistency bias, emerging instead as rational Bayesians.

Overall the results speak to the ability of coordinated research to inform policy, and to influence out-of-sample beliefs in an "evidence-accurate" manner. More broadly, the results provide evidence of external validity, despite the fact that the set of studies implemented was in no sense a random sample from a larger population.

We began this chapter by underscoring an irony: proponents of rigorous impact evaluation have failed to demonstrate its value as a tool for affecting policy. We are open to a similar sort of critique. Our finding of external validity may itself not generalize. This could be true in two ways. First, our case is an easy one for learning. The results from the Metaketa are uniformly null. Thus the question at stake was simply how quickly participants would come to realize that the information interventions were ineffective wherever they were attempted. The inferential challenge is likely to be much more acute in the presence of heterogeneity (Vivalt, 2016). Second, the results derive from a convenience sample – albeit a highly relevant one for our application. Even still, we believe that the chapter shows at a minimum an important proof of concept:

the external validity of a study – that is, the utility of a study for making inferences to unseen cases – is not simple a problem to worry about, it is a quantity that can be empirically assessed. Policymakers can learn across studies even when these are not randomly sampled from a population, and their learning can improve both their accuracy and their confidence.

PART IV

CONCLUSION

13

Challenges and Opportunities

Thad Dunning, Guy Grossman, Macartan
Humphreys, Susan D. Hyde, Craig McIntosh, and
Gareth Nellis

Drawing on results from this inaugural project of the Metaketa Initiative, we have presented in this book the individual and joint findings from six field experiments on information and political accountability, an analysis of a "failed" field experiment that was part of the initiative but could not be implemented, and an evaluation of how practitioners process and utilize cumulative evidence relative to single studies. Substantively, the book's conclusions raise serious questions about the ease with which common types of interventions aimed at increasing the availability of credible information necessarily change voter behavior such that electoral accountability improves. Methodologically, the volume also introduces the Metaketa approach to coordinating field experimental research with the goal of knowledge accumulation. The project's steering committee, composed of five of this volume's editors, have worked together since 2013 to design the Metaketa model, select and fund the participating studies, oversee their coordination and implementation, and bring the findings from the studies into a joint framework for meta-analysis. The authors of the individual studies contributed substantially to the refinement of the model and the substantive focus of the project, providing significant expertise and delivering outstanding research products. We wish to underscore the considerable effort and intellectual contributions of each of the thirty-one participating researchers.

Throughout the process, we sought to adhere to high standards for transparency in research, and aimed to address barriers to knowledge accumulation associated with study sparsity, study heterogeneity, and selective reporting, as defined in the introduction. The integrated analysis and joint publication were planned in advance, indicating that the results presented in this book sidestepped many of the problems that are known to generate biases in bodies of published research. Yet, unforeseen difficulties and limitations also became apparent in the course of the project.

This concluding chapter thus briefly summarizes our central findings, discusses implications of these findings for future research on information and electoral accountability, and details lessons learned – which may be relevant to future research efforts aimed at improving knowledge accumulation across studies in the social sciences.

13.1 SUMMARY OF FINDINGS

The aggregate empirical findings presented in this book are clear. The common informational interventions included in all six studies had little effect on voters' choices or behavior, neither in the aggregate nor in individual studies. Given the multiplicity of contexts, the variation in the exact nature of information provided, the heterogeneity in the degree to which voters were already aware of politicians' performance, and the power provided by the joint analysis, the null findings provide credible evidence against the effectiveness of simple – but very common – types of informational interventions that seek to increase electoral accountability.

The noneffect of the treatment is remarkably stable across many characteristics of individual voters and across many settings. For instance, overall, there is little evidence in our studies that copartisan or coethnic attachments between voters and politicians moderate the impact of the informational treatments.

Why did voters not respond to information in ways predicted by many models of political accountability? This remains subject to some debate. Although there is some evidence that some voters absorbed the substance of the information, this induced no statistically significant change in perceptions about politicians' honesty or effort, breaking a link in the causal chain presented in Chapter 3. Put simply, the informational interventions did little to shape voters' beliefs, and thus did not shape behavior. We found some suggestive evidence of impact when information is publicly provided and can therefore serve as a coordinating device for voters.

Additionally, we presented evidence that the Metaketa model can lead to improvements in cumulative learning. We conducted a separate randomized controlled trial to evaluate whether aggregate evidence from this Metaketa is more persuasive to practitioners, policymakers, and researchers than are individual studies; and whether it leads to better understanding and prediction of results in new contexts, thus boosting the external usefulness of our evidence. We showed that exposure to the results of our meta-analysis boosted the ability of practitioners to make accurate predictions about an additional study. Moreover, we found some corroboration that integrated evidence changed beliefs and enhanced prediction accuracy to a greater extent than single studies. These experimental findings complement other evidence in the book and suggest that the Metaketa approach can improve cumulative learning.

13.2 SUBSTANTIVE IMPLICATIONS OF THE NULL FINDINGS

Given the contemporary debate over the role of information (and disinformation) in driving voter behavior, this book's findings are timely. In many respects, the null result is surprising. A large theoretical literature in political science and economics uses electoral models that are built fundamentally on the idea that voters can and will sanction politicians at the ballot box based in part on how well politicians perform in office. Decades of focus on promoting a free and competitive press in developing countries is predicated on the driving role that transparency and objective, factual information is supposed to play in supporting a democratic electoral process in which electoral accountability can operate. Yet, many developed democracies are facing a crisis of confidence in objective evaluation of politician performance as more populist, identity-driven political orientations have emerged. A proliferation of nontraditional media outlets raise fundamental questions about the credibility of political reporting and have introduced skepticism about the ability of factual information to shift electoral behavior.

This book suggests that our current understanding of how to induce electoral accountability is limited, and information alone – at least of the kind discussed in this book – is likely insufficient. Null findings of the type presented here are rarely published, yet they are critically important in the real-world practice of development and democracy promotion. Although any experienced practitioner is well aware that not every program works exactly as intended, null results are seldom the focus of program evaluations, and the development community in general has well-documented difficulty in learning from its mistakes.[1]

Our results, however, certainly should not be taken to indicate that politician performance, or the broader informational environment

---

[1] Easterly (2002).

around elections, is unimportant. Our findings do not speak readily to the importance of independent media, for example, or to the broader question of availability of information in a political system: they speak centrally to the impact of promulgating available but not widely disseminated information. Important next steps for researchers and practitioners include careful attention to what types of interventions may be more successful in delivering information that is likely to be absorbed by voters in a way that affects their political behavior. Several of the Metaketa studies included in Part II have provided suggestive evidence that informing voters can be important for specific types of voters, or when the information is combined with other elements – such as voter education campaigns— or when the knowledge is disseminated publicly. In this context, a key takeaway from this book is that making constituents more informed about their electoral choices, by providing them individually with information on a single topic in the run up to an election, does not necessarily change their electoral behavior. It may have important effects on specific subpopulations; it may need to be provided in public settings; or it may need to be a long-term strategy tied to targeted candidate recruitment, civic education, engagement with civil society, or to the strengthening of a free and independent media. Future work should more directly investigate how voters process new political information, and the implications of variables like the timing of information dissemination, the delivery mechanism, the intensity of the treatment, the combination of voter information campaigns with other interventions, and other ways in which information can be made salient. In particular, scholars should pay close attention to the conditions under which voter beliefs about politicians are updated in a manner that is relevant to their electoral behavior.

13.3 REFLECTING ON THE CUMULATIVE LEARNING INITIATIVE

Returning to the Metaketa Initiative as a whole, and the research model that we developed, we now turn to a discussion of lessons learned. This project began with a relatively ambitious goal of figuring out a way to fund and promote field experimental research that would lead to greater knowledge accumulation. Although the model worked reasonably well in this inaugural effort, we highlight six important challenges we faced and offer reflections on possible future directions.

The challenge of defining a common research question. In a cumulative learning exercise, where should the research question come from? We adopted a fairly "bottom-up" approach, in the sense that we were centrally interested in identifying questions about which sufficient numbers of highly skilled researchers would be interested in conducting studies. For Metaketa I, we created a two-stage process. First, we requested short Expressions of Interest (EOIs) from the broader research community for studies proposing interventions that could increase effective citizen engagement in the electoral process. We then used these researcher-generated EOIs to define potential clusters around specific research questions, eventually selecting what we felt to be the most promising cluster. This step required some difficult judgment calls about how much we could reasonably ask teams to modify their proposals from what they had initially described. We then issued a Request for Proposals (RFP) focused on the question that had sufficient researcher interest and enough high-quality proposals. The RFP process was opened to the full research community (not limited to EOI submissions, nor to EGAP members) in order to maximize participation. Upon reviewing the RFPs, we asked seven teams to revise and resubmit their proposals and began the challenging task of bringing their studies in line with one another.

In hindsight, an alternative would have been a more "top-down" process. It may be possible to identify a pressing question with both scholarly and policy significance, develop a general theoretical structure, locate a population of cases, sample those cases across dimensions of theoretical importance, and then launch an RFP with sufficient lead time to allow participants to forge new partnerships with the Metaketa in mind. Indeed, under such a model, it may be possible to accept new studies into a Metaketa on a continuous basis if they meet a set of specified criteria.

Future Metaketas could prioritize questions about which views were divided regarding the likely results, or perhaps those for which one or a few studies had produced exciting but unreplicated positive findings. In addition, it may be useful to include both researchers and practitioners in the definition of the question, as that may be most likely to produce research that has both practical and theoretical importance.

The challenge of aligning researchers' incentives. Within the social sciences, it is well documented that researchers' incentives to replicate are low, and publishing studies that are "mere" replications is difficult to do and rarely rewarded professionally. Moreover, motivations to repeat studies may decline with each additional replication. We faced this issue centrally, as our initiative aimed not to replicate a single study once but was instead oriented towards the creation of multiple similar studies. The problem we confronted can be seen in terms of the decentralization of credit for replication of previous studies, and diminishing marginal returns for replications.

We worried that weak incentives to replicate would deter top researchers from participating. As described in detail in Chapter 2, the steering committee discussed numerous models for motivating researcher participation. The decision to ask teams to submit two treatment arms (one common and one alternative to the common treatment arm) and a factorial design was, we think, critical.[2] The fact that our approach allowed researchers room to preserve unique material for separate publications while creating simultaneous replication of the common treatment arm was an essential element in securing buy-in from multiple independent research teams.

An alternative model might involve greater centralization of credit for a group of replications. For example, one might fund a single research unit or organization to coordinate centrally and carry out their own simultaneous replications of a field experiment or randomized evaluation.[3] This is because the credit associated with such a large contribution would be concentrated rather than diffuse. However, although selecting a single grantee who would carry out multiple studies would solve many incentive (and coordination) problems, there are also many benefits from bringing a large number of diverse, outstanding scholars into a research agenda. Our approach may also be more generally workable given the decentralization of scholarly research; the Metaketa model may be more scalable across many researchers and across time than a more centralized approach would be.

There is another way in which career objectives of individual researchers may not always align with the Metaketa Initiative's objectives. Despite our efforts to ensure best practices of reporting results transparently within this volume, we recognize that the broader environment for publishing research continues to impose real pressures on scholars to emphasize non-null findings in their articles and research reports. Without a sea change in this broader adverse environment, we

---

[2] This was relatively straightforward to implement as a grant-making model, though the ability to build factorial designs may have been greater in our project (involving, for example, individual level data) than it might be in future Metaketas.

[3] This was the case in the six-country study on BRAC's Targeting the Ultra-Poor program; see Banerjee et al. (2015).

worry about the publication prospects for single studies reporting null effects. This is an endemic problem that a single project such as ours cannot, on its own, hope to solve; yet an accumulation of Metaketas may provide an impetus for transforming this reality.

The challenge and value of joint publication and results blind analysis. This integrated publication was accepted under contract through "results blind" review, meaning that the press and its reviewers were willing to agree to publish the book before knowing the results of the studies. We believe that joint publication along with results blind review has two major advantages. First, it is clearly an effective way to guard against publication bias. If papers are accepted prior to their results being known, the full distribution of completed study results will ultimately be part of the literature, which might otherwise comprise only studies with statistically significant or surprising results. And second, it permits a more comprehensive evaluation of the overall universe of efforts in any intervention space, even allowing for the publication of failed projects, should they occur.

Of course, opportunities for results blind review are not under researcher control; its value is still a subject of ongoing debate in social science. There may be a perception among journal editors that null results are a nonevent in terms of reader interest, and that the drive to publish studies that will generate buzz and become highly cited is simply too strongly in conflict with the epistemic requirement to publish high-quality studies whatever their findings. Editors may recognize the need at a systemic level, but may not want to volunteer their own particular journal to this endeavor. Joint publication helps overcome this problem because the results of a coordinated study are themselves sufficiently interesting and important that agreeing to results blind publication likely becomes more palatable to publishers. An alternative possibility would be a broader disciplinary shift towards valuing the evidence presented in chapters of integrated books such as this one, rather than valuing standalone journal articles to the extent that many scholars currently do. We hope that integrated publications can provide an effective way of guaranteeing that single-study null results find their way into the published record.

We note also the value of pre-analysis plans for meta-analysis, which are a key innovative feature of the Metaketa approach. Individual study PAPs have now become relatively common; similarly, many new efforts at conducting replications or systematic reviews involve registering PAPs. What distinguishes the type of meta-analysis plan (MPAP) for coordinated research that we filed for this project is that it can provide a rigorous environment in which researchers can theorize as to the relationships between studies before the study-level effects are already known – which clearly differs from the preregistration of collective hypotheses for a systematic review conducted after all the individual study results are already known. Each study in the coordinated project can, in turn, preregister the ways in which heterogeneity (both internal and relative to other studies) is expected to play out in the meta-environment.

The challenge of harmonizing interventions. A significant challenge involved assessing how much coordination between interventions was necessary, and how uniform the treatments needed to be in order to contribute to a preplanned meta-analysis. In theory, it may sound straightforward to implement the same field experiment in multiple countries. In practice, however, many factors can lead to variation in the interventions. To some extent, interventions around elections across contexts are necessarily different, as electoral politics can be so distinctive between countries that the same type of information in two contexts may mean substantively different things to voters. The same type of information may simply not be available or relevant in all countries, the same sorts of delivery mechanisms may not be used in the same way in different contexts, etc. In fact, as we note in Chapter 3, there are multiple dimensions along which the studies in this project vary, for example, with regards to the type of politicians studied and the substance of the information.

Although we expect that some will view this variation as a weakness, we see advantages to it. Given the myriad details that can define an informational intervention, ensuring exact uniformity across all interventions could make for a precise but very narrow set of findings. Indeed we could end up producing results that would never be relevant in any other context. More positively, if the goal is to assess a general claim of broad interest, then some variation in the form of intervention is both entirely consistent with real-world programmatic interventions that occur in multiple countries, and potentially desirable as long as the interventions tap into the same theoretical logic and outcome measures can be analyzed in the same framework. Fundamentally, it is the logic and the underlying theory we seek to test, not a very precisely defined identical intervention, which may be impossible across contexts in many substantive areas.[4]

---

4 This may be especially true in the realm of governance interventions, as opposed to, say, micro-finance; see Chapter 2.

In our case, because the results ended up being consistent across studies, some diversity in treatments resulted in greater confidence that the null finding is valid. Had the results been more varied, the interpretation would have been more challenging, as variations in details of interventions could then become candidates for explaining variation in outcomes. In the next item, we explore inferential strategies Metaketas could adopt in that case.

We would also point to a difficulty we faced throughout this Metaketa that is especially pronounced in the effort to harmonize informational interventions specifically. Even under the simplest homogeneity assumptions, voters will respond to what is learned from these interventions, not what is said; and, therefore, the heterogeneity arising from different priors is baked into the treatment effects that can be recovered from this type of study. Further, the specific types of information that are available, salient, but not broadly known will differ dramatically from context to context. Hence, even when one desires to impart a homogeneous informational shock in different political contexts, both the message and the messenger must necessarily vary. Again, because our studies returned such consistent null effects, this variation does not appear central to the interpretation of the results at hand, but moving forward, this is likely to remain a critically important issue for similar interventions.

The challenge of determining the right number of studies. If the goal is cumulative learning, and funding were unlimited, how many studies would one ideally want to include in a Metaketa? Answering this question first presumes defining what is a study. If seven field experiments were conducted by a single entity, as described in point 2, would this count as seven studies or one? At the other extreme, might a randomization block within one RCT count as its own mini-experiment? These questions highlight that the key issue concerns the degree of heterogeneity and the extent of statistical power more than the number of studies per se.

Nonetheless, in the Metaketa approach of funding multiple independent teams of scholars to pursue harmonized research strategies in different countries and contexts, an important practical question relates to the number of such teams – or, for shorthand, studies – to fund. While we knew that six or seven studies was a lot better than one, we worried that we simply had too few studies to be able to make claims at the cross-study level. Interestingly, however, as the results from the India sensitivity analysis, as well as the leave-one-out Bayesian analyses (both described in Chapter 11) show, the homogeneity of results was such that our results would likely not have been affected by adding an additional study. More broadly, the answer to this question, of course, depends on what sort of knowledge one wants to accumulate and the degree of variation across cases.

Ideally, with sufficient evidence, closely coordinated studies would begin to answer questions about the conditions under which specific interventions are likely to work or the cost effectiveness of interventions. It is clear that context is an important determinant of the effectiveness of many interventions, and the "how many studies" question may be best answered in concert with a debate about what components of context are thought to be most critical and whether they vary within specific country settings. It may be possible for studies to be designed such that the study N is larger than the number of grants issued, if, for example, the relevant study units are defined subnationally and participating teams can contribute multiple research clusters.

The fact that each of our studies returns a null result in the meta-analysis of vote choice suggests that further investigation of the heterogeneity in the results is not likely to be particularly fruitful, and indeed, overall, our data show very few subgroup impacts in the pooled analysis. In this sense we are "lucky" in that we are not faced with the thorny problem of untangling why some groups experience larger effects than others. It is nonetheless worth discussing how Metaketas or collective learning endeavors in general might grapple with these issues.

One perspective on this problem is to consider that the differences between and within studies (i.e., the sources of heterogeneity) can be defined at different levels: for instance, we have discussed heterogeneity at the individual level, treatment level, and election or context level.[5] Had we found substantial individual level heterogeneity in responses to the treatment, and had the treatment effects varied significantly between studies, we could then have used the pooled data to analyze various possible explanations for the cross-country differences in outcomes. For individual level covariates, we would have a large number of degrees of freedom and could make very clear statements about the role of context, even with a small number of studies.

However, for differences between studies at the treatment, election, or country level, we are fundamentally constrained, and have too few

---

[5] See Chapter 11.

studies to consider multiple dimensions of heterogeneity simultaneously. Indeed, given the loss of the India study we cannot, in fact, simultaneously test all seven treatment and election level dimensions of heterogeneity presented in our MPAP. Hence, for these aggregated sources of heterogeneity, we recommend that future cumulative learning exercises consider preregistering a very few specific sources of study or country level heterogeneity in an effort to increase the credibility of such analyses.

In terms of increasing the total number of studies in the meta-analysis, we were ultimately limited by available funding. However, looking forward, one can imagine that the N in this meta-analysis could also increase over time. Future field experimental studies on information and political accountability could borrow the common elements of this Metaketa, include these as the central alternative hypothesis, and then test the Metaketa I common treatment arm against another innovative treatment arm and/or more systematically design their studies to detect heterogeneous treatment effects. If the research agenda progressed such that this happened many times, a large number of studies could aggregate over time, with ongoing contributions of new data into the meta-analysis. More broadly, such an approach could be a fruitful way to implement more decentralized versions of the Metaketa model, in which a core team lays out strategies in advance and criteria for inclusion (including, perhaps, reporting of details on case selection and a requirement to sign on prior to project implementation) and future research teams opt in when undertaking a relevant project.

This last point raises further questions that are worth considering. The description seems to reflect an idealized version of the way the accumulation of knowledge is supposed to work in ordinary scholarly reality. Yet, we have argued that this model has not worked well in practice. Without the grant funding provided by the Metaketa and without the centralization of effort in the form of a steering committee (a kind of Politburo!), what will motivate researchers to engage in such decentralized replication? What are the conditions under which such an approach can become self-sustaining? While such questions are difficult to answer, the scale of Metaketas may increase future researcher interest in the set of interventions included in them. Metaketas can create a new and integrated evidence base against which researchers may be motivated to compare alternative interventions explicitly; the model of combining replication and innovation within particular studies could therefore become more widespread. We hope that this kind of initiative can increase researchers' interest in embedding similar interventions in their own studies and thereby allow a type of researcher-driven cumulative learning to take place.

The coordination challenge among diverse research teams. There are significant tradeoffs between the benefits of researcher agency and the benefits of centralized control. To allow researcher independence and agency, we elected to avoid dictating a precise set of hypotheses, outcome measures, and estimation strategies prior to the EOI and RFP calls. The teams were deeply involved in the design of the overall project from the very first stages including identification of the cross-study hypotheses and estimation strategies.

Given the broad range of researchers involved, there were also extensive efforts to coordinate the work of teams. Despite these efforts, there were still important differences between the studies. We noted above that we believe that there are some advantages to heterogeneity between studies; but we should also note that we had little control over some dimensions of variation. A more top-down approach might have been able to determine, in a more systematic way, both the selection of cases and the dimensions along which they vary. In particular, the capacity to pursue theoretically motivated case selection could be an important departure and improvement for future Metaketas.

We also point out that, despite significant coordination, implementation varied in some unexpected ways: not all agreed measures were collected in all studies and, ex post, there was reasonable disagreement in some instances about the interpretation of analysis plans or on when deviations from analysis plans were justifiable. In some cases, these differences may produce differences between the conclusions from this volume and conclusions that can be drawn from individual studies. Again, such issues might not arise with a more centralized approach.

On the other hand, there were clear upsides to having multiple broad teams of motivated scholars involved in this initiative. Bringing the teams together for several coordination meetings was extremely valuable for developing agreed upon best practices for design, measurement, and implementation; the joint authorship of the MPAP was useful for individual teams in writing their own PAPs; the collective discussions on ethical concerns allowed a wide variety of views to be aired and gave space for solutions that enjoyed broad buy-in. We note the significant advantages that our project seemed to offer to younger scholars: many of the PIs on the initiative were advanced graduate students or early career professors at the time the projects were launched, and the Metaketa offered extensive opportunities for learning, mentoring, and network-building.[6] In all, for this Metaketa, we felt that the coordination and deliberation among many scholars strengthened the initiative, though it was not without its challenges. We do not expect that this will invariably be true for future projects of this form.

13.4 WHAT'S NEXT?

Thirty-one scholars pooled their efforts to see what happens when you subject a simple proposition to what we believe are the most demanding standards of theory testing in social scientific research. Using experimental variation, we sought to avoid inferential biases and to make claims based on fresh data. Preregistering individual and collective research output helped guard against instincts to redefine tests in light of patterns observed in the data. Sharing our data and submitting to third-party replication limited risks of human error. Working with common designs in multiple sites meant trading off claims for individual innovation for a chance to contribute to a broader analysis; doing so allowed us to treat contextual variation as a feature that might possibly enhance the generality of claims that can be made collectively, rather than as grounds to protect a study from questioning when it produces contrary findings. For all that, the null substantive findings will seem, to some audiences, disappointing. This most simple of hypotheses, that providing voters with new information about the performance of a candidate makes them change their behavior, garners little support.

We take our findings as motivation for both more modesty and greater ambition. The lesson for modesty is to focus combined efforts on establishing simple conjectures about political processes, which can serve as building blocks for more nuanced theories. It is hard to have faith in complex propositions when the most basic logics do not pan out. The lesson for ambition is to focus first on higher-dosage interventions for which null results – should they arise – will be still more striking and positive results will give us a more solid foundation for future work.

---

[6] See the contribution of participants to the discussion in Dunning et al. (2018) for further reflections on this topic.

This Metaketa proposed an approach to creating empirical knowledge that substantially addresses problems of study scarcity and heterogeneity as well as selective reporting. We hope that the payoff is apparent not only in this substantive application but through the accumulation of results from future projects that adopt this model.

Appendix: Meta-Pre-Analysis Plan (MPAP)

Political Information and Electoral Choices: A Pre-Meta-Analysis Plan*

Thad Dunning[#8] Guy Grossman[#8] Macartan Humphreys[#8] Susan D. Hyde[#8] Craig McIntosh[#8] Claire Adida[#1] Eric Arias[#2] Taylor Boas[#4] Mark Buntaine[#7] Sarah Bush[#7] Simon Chauchard[#3] Jessica Gottlieb[#1] F. Daniel Hidalgo[#4] Marcus E. Holmlund[#5] Ryan Jablonski[#7] Eric Kramon[#1] Horacio Larreguy[#2] Malte Lierl[#5] Gwyneth McClendon[#1] John Marshall,[#2] Dan Nielson[#7] Melina Platas Izama[#6] Pablo Querubin[#2] Pia Raffler[#6] Neelanjan Sircar[#3].

ABSTRACT

We describe our plan for a meta analysis of a collection of seven studies on the impact of information on voting behavior in developing countries. The seven studies are being conducted simultaneously by seven separate research teams under a single "Metaketa" grant round administered by EGAP and University of California, Berkeley's Center on the Politics of Development. This analysis plan has been produced before launch of any of the seven projects and provides the analysis for the joint assessment of results from the studies. Individual studies have separate pre-analysis plans with greater detail, registered prior to the launch of each study.

* This meta-preanalysis plan was registered on the EGAP registry on March 9, 2015 (see https://egap.org/registration/736). It is reproduced here as registered, with some minor spelling errors corrected.

** Author annotations are: #1 Benin study, #2 Mexico study, #3 India study, #4 Brazil study, #5 Burkina Faso study, #6 Uganda 1 study, #7 Uganda 2 study, #8 the Metaketa committee. We have many people to thank for generous thoughts and comments on this project including Jaclyn Leaver, Abigail Long, Betsy Paluck, Ryan Moore, Ana de la O, Don Green, Richard Sedlmayr, and participants at EGAP 13. The Metaketa is funded by an anonymous donor.

Contents

Contents

1 INTRODUCTION

In this document we describe the research and analysis strategy for an EGAP "Metaketa" on information and accountability. Metaketas are integrated research programs in which multiple teams of researchers work on coordinated projects in parallel to generate generalizable answers to major questions of scholarly and policy importance. The core pillars of the Metaketa approach are:

1.   **Major themes:** Metaketas focus on major questions of scholarly and policy relevance with a focus on consolidation of knowledge rather than on innovation.
2.   **Strong designs:** all studies employ randomized interventions to identify causal effects.
3.   **Collaboration and competition:** teams work on parallel coordinated projects and collaborate on design and on both measurement and estimation strategies in order to allow for informed comparisons across study contexts.
4.   **Comparable interventions and measures:** differences in findings should be attributable primarily to contextual factors and not to differences in research design or measurement.
5.   **Analytic transparency:** all studies share a commitment to analytic transparency including design registration, open and replicable data and materials, and third-party analysis prior to publication.
6.   **Formal synthesis:** aggregation of results of the studies is achieved though pre-specified meta-analysis and via integrated publication platform to avoid publication bias.

The Information and Accountability Metaketa was launched in Fall 2013 and will run until Spring 2018. Its key objective is to implement a series of integrated experimental projects that assess the role of information in promoting political accountability in developing countries. This Metaketa is being administered by the Center on the Politics of Development at the University of California, Berkeley. This first registration document (dated: March 9, 2015) has been posted publicly to the EGAP registry prior to the administration of treatment in any of seven projects taking part in this Metaketa.

2 INTERVENTIONS AND MOTIVATION

Civil society groups and social scientists commonly emphasize the need for high quality public information on the performance of politicians as an informed electorate is at the heart of liberal theories of democratic practice (Fearon, 1999). The extent to which performance information in effect make a difference in institutionally weak environments is, however, an open question. Specifically when does such information lead to the rewarding of good performance candidates at the polls and when are voting decisions dominated by nonperformance criteria such as ethnic ties and clientelistic relations?

The studies in this project address the above questions by examining a set of interventions that provide subjects with information about key actions of incumbent political representatives. We assess the effects of providing this information on vote choice and turnout, given prior information available to voters.

2.1 Primary Intervention Arm

Each of the seven projects has at least two treatment arms. The first arm is an informational intervention focused explicitly on the performance of politicians. While the specific political office (e.g., mayor or member of parliament), the type of performance information provided, and the medium for communicating the information vary somewhat across studies, the interventions are designed to be as similar as possible to each other; they are also similar to several previous informational interventions in research on political accountability (e.g., Banerjee et al. (2011); Humphreys and Weinstein (2012); Chong et al. (2015)). Most importantly, each intervention is designed to allow voters to update their beliefs about the performance of the politicians positively or negatively in light of the information. The extent to which such updating actually takes place will play a key role in comparing the impact of the performance information across contexts.

A very brief description of the primary informational treatment, Tl, in each study is included in Table 1. We summarize the interventions here; for more details, see the pre-analysis plans for each individual study.

- In **Benin**, researchers provide information to respondents on indices of **legislative performance** of deputies in the National Assembly. Videos featuring bar graphs highlight the performance of the legislator responsible for each commune and present this information relative to other legislators in the department (a local average) and the country (national average).
- In **Mexico**, researchers provide information in advance of municipal elections on **corruption** (measured as the share of total resources

TABLE 1 *Primary Informational Intervention Across Projects*

Project	Title	PIs	Information on...	Method
Benin	Can Common Knowledge Improve Common Goods?	Adida, Gottlieb, Kramon, & McClendon	Legislative performance of **deputies in the National Assembly**	Legislator performance info provided publicly or privately & a civics message
Mexico	Common Knowledge, Relative Performance & Political Accountability	Larreguy, Querubin, Arias, & Marshall	Corruption & the misuse of public funds by **local government officials**	Leaflets distr. door-to-door complemented w/cars with loudspeakers drawing attention to the provided leaflets
India	Using Local Networks to Increase Accountability	Chauchard & Sircar	Financial crimes by **members of the state assembly**	Door-to-door campaigns vs. public rallies
Brazil	Accountability & Incumbent Performance in the Brazilian Northeast	Hidalgo, Boas, & Melo	Performance gathered from audit reports of **the local government**	Report cards & an oral message
Burkina Faso	Citizens at the Council	Lierl & Holmlund	Service delivery by the **municipal government**	Scorecard & participation in local council meetings
Uganda I	Information & Accountability in Primary & General Elections	Raffler & Platas Izama	Service delivery by the **local government**	Recorded candidate statements viewed publicly & privately
Uganda II	Repairing Information Underload	Nielson, Buntaine, Bush, Pickering & Jablonski	Service delivery by the **local government**	Information sent by SMS to randomly sampled households.

that are used in an unauthorized manner) or on **misuse of public funds** (the share of resources that have benefited non-poor individuals from funds that are explicitly earmarked to poor constituents).

- In **India**, researchers provide information on **criminal backgrounds of candidates** in state assembly races. Publicly available information, culled from India's Election Commission, will be disseminated in a door-to-door campaign across 18 randomly selected polling booths within 25 electoral constituencies in the Indian state of Bihar.

- In **Brazil**, researchers will distribute information about general government **corruption** in mayoral races. In partnership with the Accounts Court in the northeastern state of Pernambuco, the research team will provide voters with information on incumbent malfeasance via report cards and oral communication, drawing on publicly available data from annual auditing reports.

- In **Burkina Faso**, researchers provide information on the performance of municipal governments with respect to national targets for public service delivery. After pilot tests, it will be determined whether this information will be presented in the form of relative performance rankings of the municipalities within a region, or in the form of scores that indicate a municipality's performance relative to normative targets.

- In **Uganda (study 1)**, researchers provide information on **service delivery in Parliamentary constituencies** using scorecards.

- In **Uganda (study 2)**, researchers will use text-messaging (SMS) to provide information on **service delivery** in district government races. Specifically the researchers will disseminate information on local government budget allocations, as well as comparative quality of public services (roads, water supply, and solid waste).

2.2 Secondary Intervention Arm

The studies include second arms that test conditions under which the provision of information might be more or less effective. As part of the second arm, studies assess the effects of variation in the *message content* (absolute or relative information), the *type of messenger* (surveyor vs. community elites), and *delivery method* (providing information collectively vs. individually to groups of voters). Many studies compare a *public* treatment which may generate *common knowledge*

of the intervention to a private baseline. We refer to these secondary
interventions as T2:

- In **Benin**, researchers use a 2 × 2 factorial design plus pure control. One dimension of the factorial design concerns whether the
  information is provided in a *public* or *private* fashion. In the public condition, the informational video will be screened in a public
  location; a random sample of villagers will be invited to the film
  screening. In the private condition, the same video will be shown
  to randomly sampled individual in households in one-to-one interactions. The other dimension crosses the presence or absence of
  a *civics message* highlighting the implications of poor legislator
  performance for voter welfare.

- In **Mexico**, researchers use a 2 × 2 factorial design plus control.
  Similarly to the Benin study, one treatment group will receive information about municipal-level corruption and misuse of funds only
  privately (via fliers) whereas another will receive this information
  in a public manner (using cars with megaphones). The other cross-
  cutting dimension concerns whether or not citizens also receive
  benchmark information about the state average.

- In **India**, this study examines the causal effect of the information "messenger" In one treatment group, surveyors will distribute
  a flyer and summarize the information included in the flyer in
  face-to-face interactions. In the second treatment group, locally
  influential individuals will be contracted to disseminate the exact
  same information in a similar manner.

- The **Brazil** study explores the effect of varying the saliency of
  the information communicated to voters. Specifically, for the alternative arm, the researchers will provide information on mayoral
  compliance with a highly salient crop insurance program, which
  allows testing for the importance of providing information on
  policies directly relevant to voters' lives.

- In **Burkina Faso**, the alternative arm includes a personal invitation
  to a municipal council meeting. Here first-hand experience with
  the municipal decision process is expected to make the political
  information disseminated as part of the main (common) arm more
  salient to citizens.

- In **Uganda** (**study 1**), researchers will provide information via
  screenings of structured debates of parliamentary candidates. The
  researchers plan to exploit an additional source of variation: intra-

vs. inter-party competition (i.e., primaries of the ruling party vs. general election). The idea is to explore whether performance information is more likely to have a bite in primary settings when the impact of partisanship on vote choice is minimized.

- In **Uganda (study 2)**, researchers will vary the saturation of the level of information.

Because treatments in the second arm differ across studies by design, we will not conduct pooled analysis or formal comparison of the effects of many of these treatments. However, our final report and publications will present estimates of the effects of the second arm in each study, both in absolute terms and relative to the first arm in each project. In addition, we will compare the pooled effects of *private* vs. *public* treatments, as a way to assess whether the generation of common knowledge may strengthen the effects of informational interventions. These analyses may provide important hypotheses for further studies to assess rigorously, for example, through Metaketas in which promising secondary arms in our set of studies are tested as primary (common) arms.

2.3 Additional Variations

We inform respondents in surveys (including those assigned to control groups) that they may be provided with information on candidate quality, and we seek consent to participate. While this enhances subject autonomy, it also risks creating Hawthorne-type biases. To assess this possibility, a set of studies will also employ a variation, T3, that randomly varies the consent script among control units (though consent for measurement is sought in all cases).

3 HYPOTHESES

We now lay out six *families* of hypotheses which will be tested across the seven studies.

3.1 Primary Hypotheses

We have two closely related primary hypotheses:

H1a   Positive information increases voter support for politicians (subgroup effect).

H1b   Negative information decreases voter support for politicians (subgroup effect).

We define positive information, i.e., "good news" and negative information i.e., "bad news" in Section 5.1.

3.2   Hypotheses on Secondary Outcomes

A secondary hypotheses relates to overall participation. Theoretical work suggests that greater information should increase turnout, whether it is good or bad; yet recent experimental evidence finds that information that highlights corruption may reduce engagement with electoral processes. We state distinct hypotheses on turnout as a function of information content though we highlight that our interest is in estimating the relation, whether it is positive, or negative, or context dependent.

H2a   Bad news decreases voter turnout.
H2b   Good news increases voter turnout.

3.3   Hypotheses on Intermediate Outcomes

We also focus on first-stage relations between treatment and intermediate outcomes. These outcomes could be conceived of as *mediators* that link treatments to our primary and secondary outcomes (vote choice and turnout). However, it is possible not only that beliefs shape behaviors but also that behaviors shape beliefs. We thus do not take a strong position on whether these outcomes are necessarily channels through which treatment affects our primary and secondary outcomes. We also analyze mechanisms by conducting implicit mediation analysis (Gerber and Green 2012), in which we use the variation in treatments across primary and secondary interventions within studies (see H13–H15).

H3   Positive (negative) information increases (decreases) voter beliefs in candidate integrity.
H4   Positive (negative) information increases (decreases) voter beliefs that candidate is hardworking.
H5   Politicians mount campaigns to respond to negative information.

3.4 Hypotheses on Substitution Effects

We expect that information will operate on vote choice in part by reducing the weight voters place on ethnicity, co-partisanship, and clientelistic relations. Thus for example we expect good news to reduce the bias for voting against non-coethnic outgroup candidates and bad news to reduce the bias for voting for coethnic candidates. However, even though information may reduce the weight voters place on these relations, we expect that information has more positive effects for voters that do not share ethnic, partisan, or clientelist ties with candidates.

H6   Information effects are more positive for voters that do not share *ethnic identities.*[1]

H7   Information effects are more positive for voters with weaker *partisan identities.*

H8   Information effects are more positive for voters who have not received *clientelistic* benefits from any candidate.

While substitution effects and other heterogeneous effects are important, we note that a causal interpretation of these heterogeneous effects is not justified by the experimental design. We do not manipulate the conditioning covariates in our experiments, and we lack an identification strategy that would allow us to make strong causal claims about the effects of these variables.

3.5 Context-Specific Heterogeneous Effects

H6–H8, though related to a logic of mechanisms, are analyzed here in terms of heterogeneous effects. Two other sets of heterogeneous effects are also examined. The first set relates to the electoral environment and reflects expectations that new information will have a bigger impact in informationally poor environments and in settings where votes count – i.e., where fraud is low and chances of votes making a difference are greater.

H9   Informational effects are stronger in informationally weak environments.

H10   Informational effects are stronger in more competitive elections.

---

[1] This hypothesis is not relevant for all projects, e.g., Mexico and Brazil; see measurement section.

H11   Informational effects are stronger in settings in which elections are believed to be free and fair.

3.6   Intervention-Specific Heterogeneous Effects

A final set of heterogeneous effects analyses relate to the design of the interventions, which differ in part across study, though some of the differences may also have local granularity.

H12   Information effects – both positive and negative – are stronger when the gap between voters' prior beliefs about candidates and the information provided is larger.

H13   Informational effects are stronger the more the information relates directly to individual welfare.

H14   Informational effects are stronger the more reliable and credible is the information *source*.

H15   Informational effects are stronger when information is provided in *public settings*.

H16   Informational effects are not driven by Hawthorne effects.

4   MEASUREMENT

4.1   Outcome Measures

This section outlines core measures that are common to all project teams. Most project teams will measure additional outcomes as specified in individual pre-analysis plans.

4.1.1   *Vote Choice*

M1   VOTECHOICE. The primary outcome is *individual level vote choice*. The measure takes a value of 1 if the constituent voted for the *incumbent* (or the incumbent's party when no incumbent is up for reelection) and 0 if she did not (whether or not she actually voted). Teams may ask the question about vote choice in different ways, seeking to maximize reliability of the measure in each context (sample question below). All teams asking the question in face-to-face will ask sampled respondents to place a vote in a ballot box.

- When possible the measurement of vote choice should take place before official results are announced.
- This should take place in private when possible.

- Only the researcher has an ability to connect between a code on the envelope and the identity of respondents.

When PIs collect individual-level vote choice remotely via telephone or USSD/SMS, the following principles apply:

- Data collection needs to take place before official results are announced.
- Respondents should be contacted by automated voice system or USSD with random question order and random response choice to prevent sample-level reconstruction of the data.
- PIs need positive consent in the case where they cannot guarantee encryption of messages /voice response. Encryption is dependent on particular mobile service networks.

Sample question:

- For which [candidate/party] did you vote for [MP/ Mayor/Councilor] in the most recent [type of election] elections.

M2   OFFICIALVOTE. Official vote choice data. Whenever possible, teams will assemble *polling station-level vote choice* outcomes using official electoral commission data.

4.1.2 *Turnout*

M3   TURNOUT.: Teams that measure individual-level treatment effects will measure individual turnout. Measures will be employed in the following order:

(a) Use individual-level turnout data from the official electoral commission, where available.

(b) Use direct survey responses, even as surveys tend to inflate turnout due to social desirability bias. Confirmations such as ink marks should be sought whenever possible.

M4   GROUPTURNOUT: Teams that measure group-level treatment effects will measure turnout at the level used for randomization when possible.

(a) First best is using official electoral commission data at the polling station level (or other level, if randomization is at that level), if possible.

(b) Second best is to use the share of sampled respondents that have voted. The key here is to go back to villages/municipalities/localities immediately after the election and ask to verify vote through official marking (in ID, ink, etc.)

4.1.3 *Intermediate Outcomes*

These intermediate outcomes are likely to be affected by treatments and can offer insight into the mechanisms at play – and thus may be mediators. All studies will measure a core set of beliefs about attributes of incumbents, specified below. Project teams may, however, measure additional mediators as specified in individual pre-analysis plans.

M5   EFFORT.: Evaluation of the extent to which a politician is hardworking/provides effort.

– In your opinion, does [INCUMBENT] make much more, a little more, a little less or much less effort to get things done than other deputies in this [Department]?

M6   HONESTY.: Evaluation of the extent to which a politician is honest.

– How surprised would you be to hear from a credible source about corruption involving your [MP/Mayor/Councilor]? Would you say you would be (1) Very surprised (2) Somewhat surprised (3) Not too surprised (4) Not surprised at all

M7   CRITERIA. Did the respondent change the criteria they used to evaluate candidate? (endline)

– What was most important to you when deciding which [candidate/party] to support in the [Type] election? [Enumerator codes each of the following elements of answers; may be asked as a closed-ended question if necessary, e.g., for Uganda 2 survey]:

1. Identity (ethnicity; group representation)
2. Personal benefits targeted at voter or their family
3. Local benefits
4. National or policy contributions
5. How hardworking the politician is (effort)
6. Character of politician (integrity)
7. Endorsements by others (leaders; family members).

M8   BACKLASH. Did politicians respond to information provided at cluster level? Cluster average of: (endline)

– In the week before the election did you hear of [incumbent] or someone from their party making

statements about [dimension of information
provided to treated groups]?

4.2 Priors on Treatment Information

M9   PRIORS (P) All groups will gather information on voter priors at baseline (in both treatment and control groups) with respect to the information that will be provided.[2] Where possible, this will be gathered on the same scale as the information that will eventually be provided.

Example from Benin: Consider [NAME OF REP], does she/he participate in plenary sessions of the National Assembly much more, a little more, a little less or much less than other deputies in this Department? (1) Much more; (2) A little more; (3) A little less; (4) Much less.

M10   GOODNEWS. An indicator of "good news" is generated based on M9 and the information provided to treatment groups (see Section 5.1).

M11   CERTAIN. A measure of how certain voters are about their prior opinions in M9:

- How certain are you about your response to this question? (1) Very certain; (2) Certain; (3) Not certain; (4) Very uncertain.

M12   CLUSTERPRIORS. Group priors are given by the cluster level of average priors as measured by M9.

4.3 Controls and Moderators

Moderators are contextual factors that are not affected by the treatments, but that might be responsible for heterogeneous treatment effects. A core set of measures will be harmonized across studies. Project teams might measure additional controls and moderators as specified in individual pre-analysis plans.

4.3.1 Individual-Level Items

M13   GENDER (baseline).

[2] One project team (Mexico) will not conduct a baseline survey due to prohibitive costs. This team will instead gather aggregate information at the precinct level (the level of treatment assignment) on priors in the control group at endline.

M14   AGE (baseline): year of birth

M15   COETHNIC (baseline):

- Thinking of the [candidate for MP/Mayor/ Councilor], would you say that [you come from the same community/share the same ethnic group/share the same race] as this candidate?

This is a subjective measure of co-ethnicity.[3] Teams may wish to develop additional study-specific measures appropriate to each context.

M16   COGENDER. Whether the individual is of the same gender as the candidate *about which information will be provided to the treatment group(s)* (baseline)

M17   EDUCATION: number of years of education (baseline)

M18   WEALTH (baseline)

- In general, how do you rate your living conditions compared to those of other [Brazilians/Mexicans/ Indians/Beninois/Burkinabés/Ugandans]? Would you say they are much worse, worse, the same, better, or much better?

M19   PARTISAN (baseline).

- On this scale of one to seven, where seven means you are very attached to [*INCUMBENT'S PARTY*], and one means you are not very attached to [*INCUMBENT'S PARTY*], what degree of attachment do you feel for [*INCUMBENt'S PARTY*]?

M20   VOTED (baseline):

- Did you vote in the last [...] elections?

M21   SUPPORTED (baseline)

- Did you support the incumbent in the last [...] elections?

M22   CLIENTELISM (baseline)

- How likely is it that the incumbent, or someone from their party, will offer something, like food, or a gift, or money, in return for votes in the upcoming election (1) Not at all likely (2) Not very likely (3) Somewhat likely (4) Very likely

---

[3] More objective measures of co-ethnicity are challenging to develop in all study contexts, especially in Mexico and Brazil.

4.3.2 *Treatment-Level Items*

M23   SALIENT (baseline): Measure of the extent to which information *provided in the primary treatment arm* relates to welfare (baseline).

> I am going to read you a list of activities in which your [REP] could be involved. Suppose you could receive information about one of these things. I'd like to ask you to tell me about which of these activities you would most like to receive information:
>
> (a) How well the politician performs his/her duties in the [national legislature], for example, attendance in plenary sessions and council or committee meetings
> (b) Whether the politician has been engaged in corruption
> (c) Whether the politician has been accused of committing a crime
> (d) Whether the politician is effective at delivering services and bringing benefits to this community
>
> ...Now, thinking of the previous question, please tell me a second activity about which you would like to receive information about your [MP/Mayor/Councilor] [read three options not previously chosen]
>
> ...Now, thinking of the previous question, please tell me a third activity about which you would like to receive information about your [MP/Mayor/Councilor] [read two options not previously chosen]

M24   SOURCE. Credibility of the information source:

> Suppose that you received information about a politician, for example, information about how he or she had performed in office. Which of the following sources would you trust the most [second most; third most] for that information? [READ OPTIONS]:
>
> (a) Local politician
> (b) Flyer or pamphlet from an NGO
> (c) A person conducting a survey

  (d) An influential member of your community
  (e) In a debate between candidates
  (f) Other

4.3.3 *Election (Race) Level Features*

M25   COMPETITIVENESS. This measure will vary across systems.
  - For candidates elected through single-member/first-past-the-post elections, this is 1 minus the margin of victory of the incumbent l-(vote share - vote share of runner up) (historical data from the electoral commission).
  - For proportional representation (closed list) systems, a candidate ranked in position k of a party that received m seats out of n, is accorded competitiveness score of $1 - (1 + m - k)/n$. Thus individuals positioned 1,2,3 in a party that received 3 out of 7 seats have competitiveness scores 4/7, 5/7, 6/7 respectively.
  - For proportional representation (open list) systems, this is the difference in raw votes of the incumbent and the vote share of the candidate who received the largest number of votes and did not receive a seat

A general measure of free and fairness will be made by averaging standardized versions of the following two measures:

M26   SECRETABLLOT: Voter confidence in the secret ballot (baseline)
  - How likely do you think it is that powerful people can find out how you vote, even though there is supposed to be a secret ballot in this country?
    (1) Not at all likely (2) Not very likely
    (3) Somewhat likely (4) Very likely
M27   FREEANDFAIR: Voter beliefs that the election will be free and fair in constituency (baseline)
  - How likely do you think it is that the counting of votes in this election will be fair (1) Not at all likely (2) Not very likely (3) Somewhat likely (4) Very likely

4.3.4 *Country-level Data*

M28   FREEPRESS. Freedom House measure of freedom of the press
M29   DEMOC. Polity measure of democratic strength

4.3.5 *Manipulation Checks*

Manipulation checks data is also gathered which can be used to assess whether treatment groups absorbed the treatment (i.e., did the individual understand the information?); whether control groups learned more about representatives between baseline and the election; and whether there was informational spillovers between treated and control units.

M30   CHECK At endline, data should be gathered from treatment and control groups about the performance of representatives using the same approach as used for Measure M9.[4]

5   ANALYSIS DETAILS

In this section we describe the primary empirical strategy that will be used to test the above set of hypotheses across studies.

The most straightforward way to combine results across the seven studies pools units into one large study group and estimates treatment effects, as one would do in a large experiment in which treatment assignment is blocked. For this analysis we proceed as if blocking is implemented at the country level.

From one perspective, this approach involves weak assumptions. The study group in the large experiment is not conceived as a random sample from a larger population. This follows from the design of the studies: in most of the seven projects, individuals in the study groups are not themselves random samples, and the study sites (countries and locations within countries) are also not random draws from a well defined population of possible sites. From another perspective, pooling does imply that we can treat interventions and outcome measures as sufficiently comparable that an overall average treatment effect (say, the effect on vote choice of exposure to "good news") is meaningful. Creating such comparability is the goal of the Metaketa initiative, but in practice the information that is provided in different projects differs quite substantially, even when focusing explicitly the primary information arm. We account for this heterogeneity partially by formally examining the effects of heterogeneity in our analysis.

---

[4] Here we recognize that voters could have absorbed the information and yet posteriors over candidates on the dimension of the information may not have budged – perhaps because voters filter the information through partisan lenses.

5.1 Main Analysis

Since expected effects derive from *new* information rather than *any* information, the core estimates need to take account of both the content of the information and prior beliefs.

Let P_{ij} denote the prior beliefs of voter i regarding some politically relevant attribute of politician j and let Q_j denote the information provided to the treatment group about politician j on that attribute, *measured on the same scale*. Let $\hat{Q}_j$ denote the median value of Q_j in a polity (or, for teams using local comparison groups, the median in the relevant comparison group).

Define L^+ as the set of treatment subjects for whom $Q_j > P_{ij}$ or $Q_j = P_{ij}$ and $Q_j \geq \hat{Q}_j$. These are subjects that receive good news – either the information provided exceeds priors or the information confirms positive priors. Let L^- denote the remaining subjects. Let N_{ij}^+ denote the difference $Q_j - P_{ij}$, defined for all subjects in L^+ and standardized by the mean and standard deviation of $Q_j - P_{ij}$ in the L^+ group in each country (or relevant locality). N_{ij}^+ is therefore a standardized measure of "good news" with mean o and standard deviation of 1. Let N_{ij}^- denote the same quantity but for all subjects receiving bad news.

Then the two core estimating equations are:

$$E(Y_{ij}|i \in L^+) = \beta_0 + \beta_1 N_{ij}^+ + \beta_2 T_i + \beta_3 T_i N_{ij}^+ + \sum_{j=1}^{k}(\nu_k Z_i^k + \psi_k Z_i^k T_i)$$

(1)

$$E(Y_{ij}|i \in L^-) = \gamma_0 + \gamma_1 N_{ij}^- + \gamma_2 T_i + \gamma_3 T_i N_{ij}^- + \sum_{j=1}^{k}(\nu_k Z_i^k + \psi_k Z_i^k T_i)$$

(2)

where $Z_1, Z_2, \ldots, Z_k$ are prespecified covariates, also standardized to have a o mean.

Here β_2 is the *average treatment effect* of information for all voters receiving good news; γ_2 is the *average treatment effect* of information for all voters receiving bad news. Recall that according to H1a and H1b we expect $\beta_2 > 0$ and $\gamma_2 < 0$. Note that models 1 and 2 assume that potential outcomes (e.g., vote choice or turnout after good news, bad news, or no news) are fixed and may differ from individual to individual; the only random element in the above models is assignment to the treatment condition T_i (given priors, which by definition are determined before treatment assignment).

In addition to reporting these as our primary results we will report the results for the analogous specification without covariates. We will also report the mean value of Y_{ij} by treatment condition for both sets of individuals (those in L^+ and those in L^-), i.e., without conditioning on N_{ij}^+ or N_{ij}^-.

Estimation is conducted using OLS, clustering standard errors on politicians (j) and adding fixed effects for constituencies. If treatment assignment is blocked within projects, and treatment assignment probabilities vary across blocks, analysis will account for the blocking, e.g., by the weighting of block-specific effects (or fixed effects for blocks when appropriate). For analysis of aggregate data with clustered assignment, variables are aggregated to their cluster means (where cluster is the level of treatment assignment) or standard errors are clustered at this level. If no uniform weights are used, inverse propensity weights will be employed.

5.2 Analysis of Heterogeneous Effects

Following from the main estimating equations, for a covariate X_{ij} the heterogeneous effect of positive and negative information will be estimated through interaction analysis. Note that we again do not pool since we expect heterogeneous effects to work differently for good news and bad news, as is the case if a covariate is associated with stronger or weaker effects.

$$E(Y_{ij}|i \in L^+) = \beta_0 + \beta_1 N_{ij}^+ + \beta_2 T_i + \beta_3 T_i N_{ij}^+ + \beta_4 X_i + \beta_5 T_i X_i$$
$$+ \sum_{j=1}^{k}(\nu_k Z_i^k + \psi_k Z_i^k T_i) \tag{3}$$

$$E(Y_{ij}|i \in L^-) = \gamma_0 + \gamma_1 N_{ij}^- + \gamma_2 T_i + \gamma_3 T_i N_{ij}^- + \gamma_4 X_i + \gamma_5 T_i X_i$$
$$+ \sum_{j=1}^{k}(\nu_k Z_i^k + \psi_k Z_i^k T_i) \tag{4}$$

Where X is the variable of interest (which we assume is not included in the set of other covariates Z). The heterogeneous effects of the impact of positive information, for average news levels, are given by β_5 and the heterogeneous effects of negative information are given by γ_5. Note that we do not include a triple interaction between T, X and N^+/N^- in these analyses.

For H12 we can combine data and estimate more simply:

$$E(Y_{ij}) = \delta_0 + \delta_1(Q_j - P_{ij}) + \delta_2 T_i + \delta_3 T_i(Q_j - P_{ij}) \qquad (5)$$

Under H12 we expect $\delta_3 > 0$. Note that our measures of $Q_j - P_{ij}$ are largely ordinal not interval; and estimating a linear marginal effect of the gap may not be meaningful if the marginal effect is not in fact linear. Perhaps more importantly, we do not manipulate priors in our experiments, and we lack an identification strategy that would allow us to make strong causal claims about the effects of such a gap. Such caveats should be born in mind, yet we believe it is valuable to assess H12 with the tools at our disposal.

The mapping between hypotheses (Section 3) and measures (Section 4) is outlined in Table 2. Where CONTROLS are:

- for individual level specifications: {M14, M15, M16, M17, M18, M19, M20, M21, M22, M26, M27}
- for cluster level specifications: averages of {M15, M17, M18, M19, M20, M21, M22, M26, M27}

5.3   Adjustment for Multiple Comparisons

We handle multiple comparisons concerns in two ways.

First note that most tests are conducted using pairs of analyses – e.g., the (positive) effect of good news on voting and the (negative) effect of bad news. For each of these pairs of analyses, in addition to the simple *p*-values reported for each regression, we will calculate a *p*-value for the *pair* of regressions which will be given by the probability that *both* the coefficients would be as large (in absolute value) as they are under the sharp null of no effect of exposure to information (good or bad) for any unit.[5]

Second, for each of our six families of hypothesis, we will present tests using both nominal *p*-values and tests that employ a false discovery rate (FDR) correction to control the Type-1 error rate.[6] We will control the FDR at level 0.05. Thus, for a given randomization with m (null)

---

[5] We calculate this *p*-value using randomization inference. Let $f(b)$ denote a bivariate distribution of coefficients b_1, b_2 generated under the sharp null, and let $b^* = (b_1^*, b_2^*)$ denote the estimated coefficients. Then the *p*-value of interest is given by $\int \mathbb{1}(\min(|b^*|) \geq \min(|b|)) \times \mathbb{1}(\max(|b|) \geq \max(|b^*|)) f(b) db$, where $\mathbb{1}$ is an indicator function.

[6] See Benjamini and Hochberg (1995).

TABLE 2 *Specifications, Hypotheses and Measures*

Family	#	Abbreviated Hypothesis	Y	X	Interact'n	Controls	Subset	Spec'n
Primary	H1a	Good news effects	M1	T1		✚	M10=1	Eq1
(1)	H1b	Bad news effects	M1	T1		✚	M10=0	Eq2
Secondary	H2a	Turnout (Good news)	M3	T1		✚	M10=1	Eq1
(2)	H2b	Turnout (Bad news)	M3	T1		✚	M10=0	Eq2
	H4	Candidate effort	M5	T1		✓	M10=1	Eq1
	H4	Candidate effort	M5	T1		✓	M10=0	Eq2
Mediators	H3	Candidate integrity	M6	T1		✓	M10=1	Eq1
(3)	H3	Candidate integrity	M6	T1		✓	M10=0	Eq2
	H5	Candidate responses	M8	T1		✓	M10=0	Eq2
Substitution	H6	Non coethnics	M1	T1	M15	✓	M10=1	Eq3
(4)	H6	Non coethnics	M1	T1	M15	✓	M10=0	Eq4
	H7	Partisanship	M1	T1	M19	✓	M10=1	Eq3
	H7	Partisanship	M1	T1	M19	✓	M10=0	Eq4
	H8	Clientelism	M1	T1	M22	✓	M10=1	Eq3
	H8	Clientelism	M1	T1	M22	✓	M10=0	Eq4
Context	H9	Informational environment	M1	T1	M11	✓	M10=1	Eq3
(5)	H9	Informational environment	M1	T1	M11	✓	M10=0	Eq4
	H10	Competitive elections	M1	T1	M25	✓	M10=1	Eq3
	H10	Competitive elections	M1	T1	M25	✓	M10=0	Eq4
	H11	Free and fair elections	M1	T1	M26+M27	✓	M10=1	Eq3
	H11	Free and fair elections	M1	T1	M26+M27	✓	M10=0	Eq4

(Continued)

TABLE 2 (*continued*)

Family	#	Abbreviated Hypothesis	Y	X	Interact'n	Controls	Subset	Spec'n
Design (6)	H12	Information content	M1	T1		✓	All	Eq5
	H13	Information welfare relevant	M1	T1	M23	✓	M10=1	Eq3
	H13	Information welfare relevant	M1	T1	M23	✓	M10=0	Eq4
	H14	Credible Information	M1	T1	M24	✓	M10=1	Eq3
	H14	Credible Information	M1	T1	M24	✓	M10=0	Eq4
	H15	Public Channels	M1	T1	T2	✓	M10=1	Eq3
	H15	Public Channels	M1	T1	T2	✓	M10=0	Eq4
	H16	Hawthorne	M1	T1	T3	✓	M10=1	Eq3
	H16	Hawthorne	M1	T1	T3	✓	M10=0	Eq4

Here, ✓ indicates that we will present results with and without controls; see Sections 5.1 and 5.3.

hypotheses and m associated p-values, we order the realized nominal p-values from smallest to largest, $p_{(1)} \leq p_{(2)} \leq \cdots \leq p_{(m)}$. Let

$$k \text{ be the largest } i \text{ for which } p_{(i)} \leq \frac{i}{m} 0.05.$$

Then, we reject all $H_{(i)}$ for $i = 1, 2, \ldots, k$, where $H_{(i)}$ is the null hypothesis corresponding to $p_{(i)}$. Note that FDR corrections will be implemented using the estimated p-values from pairs of tests. Thus for example if in a family there are three pairs of tests, then the FDR correction will be applied using three p-values, one extracted from each pair.

We consider as families of tests those outlined in Table 2. For example, for the primary hypotheses and outcomes, we consider good news effects and bad news effects on vote choice (with and without controls); for the primary hypotheses and secondary outcomes, we consider good news and bad news effects on turnout (with and without controls).

5.4 Contingencies

5.4.1 *Non-Compliance*
Studies will analyze subjects according to their treatment assignation under the intended design, and the primary analysis will ignore non-compliance or failure to treat due to logistical mishaps.

5.4.2 *Attrition*
If there is attrition for entire blocks containing four or more treatment and control units (e.g., if entire studies fail to complete or if regions within countries become inaccessible) these blocks will be dropped from analysis without adjustment unless there is substantive reason to believe the attrition is due to treatment status.

Studies will test for two forms of attrition. First, are levels of attrition different across treatment and control groups? Second, are the *correlates of attrition* differential between the treatment and control? The former test will be conducted by comparing mean attrition in treatment and control groups, and reporting t-test statistics. The second test will be conducted regressing an attrition indicator on the interactions of treatment and the core baseline control measures specified above and reporting the F-statistic for all of the interacted variables.

Data from studies that find no evidence for problematic attrition from these two tests will be analyzed ignoring attrition.

If differential attrition is detected, Lee bounding techniques will be used to provide estimates of the magnitude of bias that could have resulted from differential attrition, from problematic studies, as well as testing whether the core findings of the study are robust to the observed rate of differential attrition.

5.4.3 *Missing Data on Control Variables*
If there is missing data on control variables, missing data will be imputed using block mean values for the lowest block for which data is available.

6 ADDITIONAL (SECONDARY) ANALYSIS

In addition to the core analyses described above we will undertake a set of secondary analyses.

6.1 Randomization Checks and Balance Tests

Using the full set of baseline covariates described in this document we will report study-by-study F statistics for the hypothesis that all covariates are orthogonal to treatment. In addition we will report balance for all covariates in terms of the country-specific standard deviation of these covariates.

6.2 Disaggregated Analyses

In addition to the core metanalysis described here we will present the same analyses but conducted on all of the individual studies separately.

6.3 Controls

Versions of the core tests described in Table 3 but without the use of any covariates will also be reported.

6.4 Possible Additional Analysis of Official Data

For many studies official data on turnout and voting at the group level may become available. At this stage the granularity of this data is not known and, pending other official data, there is uncertainty about the polling station level dosage of interventions administered by the different studies. Official data has the advantage of being free of reporting biases (at least when elections are free and fair), but has the disadvantage of providing a noisy measure in cases with low dosage.

The decision to include polling station areas for analysis using official data will be made as follows. Polling stations will be ordered, $1, 2, \ldots, k, \ldots, n$ in terms of treatment intensity (share of registered voters exposed to treatment T_1) within each study (separately for the good news and bad news groups). Then, for each k the power to identify an effect as large as the estimated effect from the individual level analysis will be assessed, given an analysis including areas with density as large as k or greater. The largest group of polling station areas that collectively yield power of 50% or more will be included in this analysis. Note that with low dosages this set may be empty.

For any included sets the analysis will assess the effect of treatment as follows:

Define D_h as the share of cluster h (polling station area) individuals that *would* get treated if the unit were in treatment (dosage). Let $\overline{D}$ denote the (country specific) mean of D. Let $D' = D - \overline{D}$ denote D normalized to have a o mean. Then conditional on the polling station receiving good news (based on average values of $Q_i - P_{ij}$) estimate:

$$y_h = \beta_0 + \beta_1 N_j^+ + \beta_2 T_h + \beta_3 T_h N_h^+ + \beta_4 T_h D_h' + \beta_5 D_h'$$

$$+ \sum_{j=1}^{k} (\nu_k Z_i^k + \psi_k Z_i^k T_i) + \epsilon_h \qquad (6)$$

where y_h is the vote share for the incumbent, T_h is the treatment status of the cluster, N_j^+ is the cluster average of N_{ij}^+, normalized again to have o mean across clusters, the Z variables are cluster level controls, and ϵ_h is an error term. Here β_2 is the estimated treatment effect for a unit with average dosage. $\beta_1/\overline{D}$ is the estimated *individual level treatment effect* (under the assumption of no spillovers), generated from the polling station level data.

The analogous expression holds for bad news poling station areas.

In implementing this analysis we are conscious of the risk of ecological biases since the good news assessment is defined based on a group average but treatment effects may be derived by different individuals. As robustness check we plan to supplement this analysis with the same analysis but not conditioning on Q only and not P_{ij}. Good news areas for that analysis will be areas with performance equal to or above the median.

6.5   Bayesian Hierarchical Analysis Model

A second analysis will employ Bayesian, multilevel meta-analysis techniques to allow for learning across cases and probe the sources of variation across cases. This approach requires stronger assumptions than the primary analysis but allows one to reassess the most likely estimates for each case in light of learning from other cases.

The simplest approach, drawing on a canonical model described in Gelman et al. (2013) (p 424) is of the following form.

Say there are n_{1j} treated units and n_{oj} control units in study j. Let m_{1j} and m_{oj} denote the number of votes for the incumbent among treated and control units in study j respectively.

Then the data model is:

$$m_{ij} \sim \text{Bin}(n_{ij}, p_{ij}) \text{ for } i \in \{0, 1\} \tag{7}$$

This captures simply the idea that the number of votes in favor of the incumbent is a draw from a binomial distribution with a given number of voters and a given probability of supporting the incumbent in each arm of each study. Working on the logit scale we define parameters:

$$\beta_{1j} = \frac{1}{2}(\text{logit}(p_{1j}) + \text{logit}(p_{oj})) \tag{8}$$

$$\beta_{2j} = \text{logit}(p_{1j}) - \text{logit}(p_{oj}) \tag{9}$$

These correspond to the average support for the incumbent and the treatment effect of the informational intervention, respectively. We are interested especially in β_{2j} which corresponds to the average treatment effect in each study, on the log-odds scale.

Our priors on the collection of pairs (β_{1j}, β_{2j}) is given by a product of bivariate normal distributions with parameters α and Λ:

$$p(\beta|\alpha, \Lambda) = \prod_{j=1}^{7} N \left(\begin{pmatrix} \beta_{1j} \\ \beta_{2j} \end{pmatrix} \Big| \begin{pmatrix} \alpha_1 \\ \alpha_2 \end{pmatrix} \Lambda \right) \tag{10}$$

Here α_2 is of particular interest corresponding to the population analogue of β_{2j}.

For hyperpriors we assume uninformative uniform priors over $\alpha_1, \alpha_2, \Lambda_{11}, \Lambda_{22}$ and the correlation $\Lambda_{12}/(\Lambda_{11}\Lambda_{22})^{\frac{1}{2}}$.

The quantities we extract are the treatment effects for each study (with credibility intervals) as well as the posteriors on α_1, α_2.

In addition to this simple model we will report results from a second hierarchical logistic model that allows for systematic individual and study level variation in the same manner assumed in the core specification but allowing country level covariates to enter at the country level and cluster and individual level covariates enter at those levels. As with the core model, inverse propensity weights are included when non-uniform assignment propensities are employed. Again from this model study level average treatment effects will be estimated along with population parameters.

6.6 Exploratory Analysis

In addition to the core tests described above, the analysis will engage in more exploratory analyses to assess how treatments altered the decisions voters took (using measure M7) as well as the comparability of effects across sites. For the latter analysis the country level treatment effects will be compared in light of the effects of treatment on mediators – that is, we will seek to report the shift in voting outcomes for units of treatment *scaled* in terms of the effects of treatment on mediators.

6.7 Learning about Learning

One of the key tests of the usefulness of the Metaketa Initiative is the extent to which the research and the policy communities learn from the aggregation of the coordinated studies. At the end of this Metaketa, we will gather a set of policymakers and academics, randomly divide them into samples, provide a briefing on the design of all studies, and then elicit prior beliefs about the effects of all studies. For treatment samples, we provide each with results from a random set of five of the studies, and incentivize them to provide updated expectations of results from the remaining studies. Some treatment samples will be encouraged (or required) to use predictive models while others will rely on subjective assessment and subject-matter knowledge. From this we expect to learn how results from some studies affect general beliefs, whether they make beliefs more accurate and how subjective inferences across studies fares relative to out-of-sample assessments of fitted models. The full analysis strategy for this component will be developed at a later stage.

7 ETHICS

All projects in the Metaketa will abide by a common set of principles above and beyond minimal requirements (i.e., securing formal IRB approvals, avoiding conflicts of interest, and ensuring all interventions do not violate local laws):

- The egap principles on research transparency http://egap.org/resources/egap-statement-of-principles/
- Protect staff: Do not put research staff in harm's way.
- Informed consent: Subjects that are individual exposed to treatments will know that information they receive is provided as part of a research project. Core project data will be publicly available in primary languages at http://egap.org/research/metaketa/
- Partnership with local civil society or governmental actors to ensure appropriateness of information.
- Non-partisan interventions: Only non-partisan information will be provided where by non-partisan we mean that (1) it is coming from a non-partisan source; (2) it reveals information about performance of incumbents (candidates) regardless of their party.
- Approval from the relevant electoral commission when appropriate.

The studies in general will not seek consent from individual politicians even though these may be affected by the interventions. The principle is that any information provided is information that exists in the political system that voters can choose to act upon or not and that this information is provided with consent, in a non-partisan way, without deception, and in cooperation with local groups, where appropriate.

8 CAVEATS

We are conscious of a number of limitations of this research design which will be relevant for interpretation of some results. Most important are:

1. Although we are in the good position of being able to assess comparable interventions in multiple sites, these sites are not themselves random draws from a population of sites. They reflect case level features such as the timing of elections and the feasibility of doing research as well as research team features such as researcher connections to these sites.
2. Although the information that is provided in different areas share many features they also differ in systematic ways (see discussion above).

3. Although there is reasonable statistical power in individual studies and in pooled analyses; power is weak for assessing some heterogeneous effects, especially those operating at the country level.

4. By design, with information provided to voters and treatment status not assigned at the politician level or made known to politicians, the effects estimated are partial equilibrium effects.

5. Although we gather data on the information available to voters prior to administration of treatment (in all studies with a baseline survey), we do not know what information voters receive between baseline and the vote. Thus estimates should be interpreted as intent-to-treat estimates even when treatment is delivered to all treatment units (and only those). Manipulation checks can be used to assess the extent to which treated and control units change beliefs between baseline and endline.

REFERENCES

Banerjee, Abhijit V., Selvan Kumar, Rohini Pande and Felix Su. 2010. "Do Informed Voters Make Better Choices? Experimental Evidence from Urban India." *Mimeo*.

Benjamini, Yoav and Yosef Hochberg. 1995. "Controlling the false discovery rate: a practical and powerful approach to multiple testing." *Journal of the Royal Statistical Society. Series B (Methodological)* pp. 289–300.

Chong, Alberto, Ana L. De La O, Dean Karlan and Leonard Wantchekon. 2015. "Does corruption information inspire the fight or quash the hope? A field experiment in Mexico on voter turnout, choice, and party identification." *The Journal of Politics* 77(1):55–71.

Fearon, James D. 1999. Electoral Accountability and the Control of Politicians: Selecting Good Types versus Sanctioning Poor Performance. In *Democracy, accountability, and representation*, ed. Adam Przeworski, Susan C. Stokes and Bernard Manin. Cambridge: Cambridge University Press, pp. 55–97.

Gelman, Andrew, John B. Carlin, Hal S. Stern and Donald B. Rubin. 2013. *Bayesian Data Analysis*. 3 ed. Chapman and Hall.

Humphreys, Macartan and Jeremy M. Weinstein. 2012. "Policing Politicians: Citizen Empowerment and Political Accountability in Uganda." *Working Paper*.

Bibliography

Abadie, Alberto, Susan Athey, Guido W. Imbens, and Jeffrey Wooldridge. 2017. "When should you adjust standard errors for clustering?" National Bureau of Economic Research Working Paper # 24003.

Acemoglu, Daron. 2010. "Theory, general equilibrium, and political economy in development economics." *Journal of Economic Perspectives* 24(3): 17–32.

Achen, Christopher H. and Larry M. Bartels. 2016. *Democracy for Realists: Why Elections Do Not Produce Responsive Government*. Princeton, NJ: Princeton University Press.

Adida, Claire L. 2015. "Do African voters favor coethnics? Evidence from a survey experiment in Benin." *Journal of Experimental Political Science* 2(1): 1–11.

Adida, Claire L., Jessica Gottlieb, Eric Kramon, and Gwyneth McClendon. 2017a. "Breaking the clientelistic voting equilibrium: The joint importance of salience and information." AidData Working Paper # 48.

Adida, Claire L., Jessica Gottlieb, Eric Kramon, and Gwyneth McClendon. 2017b. "Reducing or reinforcing in-group preferences? An experiment on information and coethnic voting." *Quarterly Journal of Political Science* 12(4): 437–477.

Afrobarometer. 2015. "Afrobarometer Data Round VI, Uganda." Digitized dataset, available from http://afrobarometer.org/countries/uganda-0.

Aker, Jenny C., Paul Collier, and Pedro C. Vicente. 2017. "Is information power? Using mobile phones and free newspapers during an election in Mozambique." *Review of Economics and Statistics* 99(2): 185–200.

Angrist, Joshua D. and Jörn-Steffen Pischke. 2010. "The credibility revolution in empirical economics: How better research design is taking the con out of econometrics." *Journal of Economic Perspectives* 24(2): 3–30.

Arias, Eric. 2018. "How does media influence social norms? Experimental evidence on the role of common knowledge." *Political Science Research and Methods*. Advance online publication.

Arias, Eric, Horacio Larreguy, John Marshall, and Pablo Querubín. 2018. "Priors Rule: When do malfeasance revelations help or hurt incumbent parties?" National Bureau of Economic Research Working Paper # 24888.

Arias, Eric, Horacio Larreguy, John Marshall, and Pablo Querubín. 2019. "When does information increase electoral accountability? Lessons from a field experiment in Mexico." In *Information, Accountability, and Cumulative Learning: Lessons from Metaketa I*, ed. Thad Dunning, Guy Grossman, Macartan Humphreys, Susan D. Hyde, Craig McIntosh and Gareth Nellis. Cambridge: Cambridge University Press (Chapter 5, this volume).

Aronow, Peter M. and Cyrus Samii. 2016. "Does regression produce representative estimates of causal effects?" *American Journal of Political Science* 60(1): 250–267.

Auditoría Superior de la Federación. 2014. "Informe del Resultado de la Fiscalización Superior de la Cuenta Pública 2012." Audit Summary Report.

Avenburg, Alejandro. 2016. "Corruption and Electoral Accountability in Brazil." PhD Dissertation, Boston, MA: Boston University, Department of Political Science.

Baekgaard, Martin, Julian Christensen, Casper Mondrup Dahlmann, Asbjørn Mathiasen, and Niels Bjørn Grund Petersen. 2017. "The role of evidence in politics: Motivated reasoning and persuasion among politicians." *British Journal of Political Science*. Advance online publication.

Bainomugisha, Arthur et al. 2015. "Local government councils scorecard assessment 2014/2015." ACODE Policy Research Paper # 70-UG.

Banégas, Richard. 2003. *La Démocratie à Pas de Caméléon: Transition et Imaginaires Politiques au Bénin*. Paris: Karthala Editions.

Banerjee, Abhijit, Dean Karlan, and Jonathan Zinman. 2015. "Six randomized evaluations of microcredit: Introduction and further steps." *American Economic Journal: Applied Economics* 7(1): 1–21.

Banerjee, Abhijit and Esther Duflo. 2009. "The experimental approach to development economics." *Annual Review of Economics* 1(1): 151–178.

Banerjee, Abhijit, Esther Duflo, Nathanael Goldberg et al. 2015. "A multifaceted program causes lasting progress for the very poor: Evidence from six countries." *Science* 348(6236): 772–788.

Banerjee, Abhijit, Selvan Kumar, Rohini Pande, and Felix Su. 2011. "Do informed voters make better choices? Experimental evidence from urban India." Unpublished manuscript, Cambridge, MA: Massachusetts Institute of Technology.

Barro, Robert J. 1973. "The control of politicians: An economic model." *Public Choice* 14(1): 19–42.

Bauhr, Monika and Marcia Grimes. 2014. "Indignation or resignation: The implications of transparency for societal accountability." *Governance* 27(2): 291–320.

Benoit, William L., Glenn J. Hansen, and Rebecca M. Verser. 2003. "A meta-analysis of the effects of viewing US presidential debates." *Communication Monographs* 70(4): 335–350.

Berge, Lars Ivar Oppedal, Kjetil Bjorvatn, Kartika Sari Juniwaty, and Bertil Tungodden. 2012. "Business training in Tanzania: From research-driven experiment to local implementation." *Journal of African Economies* 21(5): 808–827.

Besley, Timothy. 2005. "Political selection." *Journal of Economic Perspectives* 19(3): 43–60.

Besley, Timothy and Andrea Prat. 2006. "Handcuffs for the grabbing hand? The role of the media in political accountability." *American Economic Review* 96(3): 720–736.

Besley, Timothy and Robin Burgess. 2002. "The political economy of government responsiveness: Theory and evidence from India." *Quarterly Journal of Economics* 117(4): 1415–1451.

Beynon, Penelope, Christelle Chapoy, Marie Gaarder, and Edoardo Masset. 2012. *What Difference Does a Policy Brief Make?* Institute of Development Studies, International Initiative for Impact Evaluation, and the Norwegian Agency for Development Cooperation.

Bidwell, Kelly, Katherine E. Casey, and Rachel Glennerster. 2015. "Debates: Voter and political response to political communication in Sierra Leone." Stanford University Graduate School of Business Research Paper # 15-50.

Björkman, Lisa. 2014. "'You can't buy a vote': Meanings of money in a Mumbai election." *American Ethnologist* 41(4): 617–634.

Bjuremalm, Helena, Alberto Fernandez Gibaja, and Jorge Valladares Molleda. 2014. *Democratic Accountability in Service Delivery: A Practical Guide to Identify Improvements through Assessments.* Stockholm: International Institute for Democracy and Electoral Assistance.

Blair, Graeme, Jasper Cooper, Alexander Coppock and Macartan Humphreys. 2016. *DeclareDesign* Version 0.3. Computer software, retrievable from https://declaredesign.org/.

Blair, Graeme, Jasper Cooper, Alexander, Coppock and Macartan Humphreys. 2019. "Declaring and diagnosing research designs." *American Political Science Review.* Advance online publication.

Boas, Taylor C., Daniel Hidalgo, and Guillermo Toral. 2017. "Evaluating students and politicians: Test scores and electoral accountability in Brazil." Unpublished manuscript, Boston, MA: Boston University.

Boas, Taylor C. and F. Daniel Hidalgo. 2011. "Controlling the airwaves: Incumbency advantage and community radio in Brazil." *American Journal of Political Science* 55(4): 869–885.

Boas, Taylor C. and F. Daniel Hidalgo. 2019. "Electoral incentives to combat mosquito-borne illnesses: Experimental evidence from Brazil." *World Development* 113: 89–99.

Boas, Taylor C., F. Daniel Hidalgo, and Marcus André Melo. 2019. "Norms versus action: Why voters fail to sanction malfeasance in Brazil." *American Journal of Political Science* 63(2): 385–400.

Bobonis, Gustavo J., Luis R. Cámara Fuertes, and Rainer Schwabe. 2016. "Monitoring corruptible politicians." *American Economic Review* 106(8): 2371–2405.

Bold, T., Kimenyi, M., Mwabu, G., and Sandefur, J. et al. 2018. "Experimental evidence on scaling up education reforms in Kenya." *Journal of Public Economics* 168: 1–20.

Botero, Sandra, Rodrigo Castro Cornejo, Laura Gamboa, Nara Pavao, and David W. Nickerson. 2015. "Says who? An experiment on allegations of corruption and credibility of sources." *Political Research Quarterly* 68(3): 493–504.

Broockman, David E. and Christopher Skovron. 2018. "Bias in perceptions of public opinion among American political elites." *American Political Science Review.* 112(3): 542–563.

Broockman, David E. and Donald P. Green. 2014. "Do online advertisements increase political candidates' name recognition or favorability? Evidence from randomized field experiments." *Political Behavior* 36(2): 263–289.

Brubaker, Jennifer and Gary Hanson. 2009. "The effect of Fox News and CNN's postdebate commentator analysis on viewers' perceptions of presidential candidate performance." *Southern Communication Journal* 74(4): 339–351.

Brunetti, Aymo and Beatrice Weder. 2003. "A free press is bad news for corruption." *Journal of Public Economics* 87(7): 1801–1824.

Bueno, Natalia and Thad Dunning. 2017. "Race, resources, and representation: Evidence from Brazilian politicians." *World Politics* 69(2): 327–365.

Buntaine, Mark T., Ryan Jablonski, Daniel L. Nielson, and Paula M. Pickering. 2018. "SMS texts on corruption help Ugandan voters hold elected councillors accountable at the polls." *Proceedings of the National Academy of Sciences.* 115(26): 6668–6673.

Bush, Sarah Sunn, Aaron Erlich, Lauren Prather, and Yael Zeira. 2016. "The effects of authoritarian iconography: An experimental test." *Comparative Political Studies* 49(3): 1704–1738.

Caldeira, Emilie, Martial Foucault, and Grégoire Rota-Graziosi. 2015. "Decentralization in Africa and the nature of local governments' competition: evidence from Benin." *International Tax and Public Finance* 22(6): 1048–1076.

Camerer, Colin F., Anna Dreber, Eskil Forsell et al. 2016. "Evaluating replicability of laboratory experiments in economics." *Science* 351(6280): 1433–1436.

Campbell, Donald T. and Julian C. Stanley. 1966. "Experimental and quasi-experimental designs for research." In *Handbook of Research on Teaching*, ed. N. Gage, Chicago, IL: Rand McNally, pp. 171–246.

Carlson, Elizabeth. 2015. "Ethnic voting and accountability in Africa: A choice experiment in Uganda." *World Politics* 67(02): 353–385.

Cartwright, Nancy and Jeremy Hardie. 2012. *Evidence-Based Policy: A Practical Guide to Doing It Better.* Oxford: Oxford University Press.

Chang, Eric C. C., Miriam A. Golden, and Seth J. Hill. 2010. "Legislative malfeasance and political accountability." *World Politics* 62(2): 177–220.

Chauchard, Simon. 2016. "Unpacking ethnic preferences: Theory and micro-level evidence from North India." *Comparative Political Studies* 49(2): 253–284.

Chauchard, Simon. 2018. "Electoral handouts in Mumbai elections: The cost of political competition." *Asian Survey* 58(2): 341–364.

Chong, Alberto, Ana L. De La O, Dean Karlan, and Leonard Wantchekon. 2015. "Does corruption information inspire the fight or quash the hope? A field experiment in Mexico on voter turnout, choice, and party identification." *Journal of Politics* 77(1): 55–71.

Chong, Dennis and James N. Druckman. 2010. "Dynamic public opinion: Communication effects over time." *American Political Science Review* 104(4): 663–680.

Chwe, Michael. 1998. "Culture, circles, and commercials: publicity, common knowledge, and social coordination." *Rationality and Society* 10(1): 47–75.

Cleary, Matthew R. 2007. "Electoral competition, participation, and government responsiveness in Mexico." *American Journal of Political Science* 51(2): 283–299.

Clemens, Michael A. 2017. "The meaning of failed replications: A review and proposal." *Journal of Economic Surveys* 31(1): 326–342.

Collord, Michaela. 2016. "From the electoral battleground to the parliamentary arena: Understanding intra-elite bargaining in Uganda's National Resistance Movement." *Journal of Eastern African Studies* 10(4): 639–659.

Cox, Gary W. 1997. *Making Votes Count: Strategic Coordination in the World's Electoral Systems*. Cambridge: Cambridge University Press.

Croke, Kevin. 2012. *What Does Dar Make of Education? Parents' Knowledge, Opinions and Actions in Dar es Salaam*. Dar es Salaam: Twaweza.

Cruz, Cesi and Christina J. Schneider. 2017. "Foreign aid and undeserved credit claiming." *American Journal of Political Science* 61(2): 396–408.

Cruz, Cesi, Philip Keefer, and Julien Labonne. 2016. "Incumbent advantage, voter information and vote buying." Inter-American Development Bank Working Paper # IDB-WP-711.

Dahl, Robert Alan. 1973. *Polyarchy: Participation and Opposition*. New Haven, CT: Yale University Press.

Dahl, Robert Alan. 1989. *Democracy and Its Critics*. New Haven, CT: Yale University Press.

De Figueiredo, Miguel, F. Daniel Hidalgo, and Yuri Kasahara. 2011. "When do voters punish corrupt politicians? Experimental evidence from Brazil." Unpublished manuscript, Cambridge, MA: Massachusetts Institute of Technology.

De Rooij, Eline A. Donald P. Green, and Alan S. Gerber. 2009. "Field experiments on political behavior and collective action." *Annual Review of Political Science* 12: 389–395.

Deaton, Angus. 2010. "Instruments, randomization, and learning about development." *Journal of Economic Literature* 48(2): 424–455.

Deaton, Angus and Nancy Cartwright. 2017. "Understanding and misunderstanding randomized controlled trials." *Social Science & Medicine* 210: 2–21.

Decalo, S. 1976. *Historical Dictionary of Dahomey (People's Republic of Benin)*. Metuchen, NJ: Scarecrow Press.

DellaVigna, S. and E. Kaplan. 2007. "The Fox News effect: Media bias and voting." *Quarterly Journal of Economics* 122(3): 187–234.

DellaVigna, Stefano and Devin Pope. 2017. "What motivates effort? Evidence and expert forecasts." *Review of Economic Studies* 85(2): 1029–1069.

Dowd, Robert A. and Michael Driessen. 2008. "Ethnically dominated party systems and the quality of democracy: Evidence from Sub-Saharan Africa." Afrobarometer Working Paper # 92.

Dreber, Anna, Thomas Pfeiffer, Johan Almenberg et al. 2015. "Using prediction markets to estimate the reproducibility of scientific research." *Proceedings of the National Academy of Sciences* 112(50): 15343–15347.

Druckman, James N., Donald P. Green, James H. Kuklinski, and Arthur Lupia. 2006. "The growth and development of experimental research in political science." *American Political Science Review* 100(4): 627–635.

Dunning, Thad. 2012. *Natural Experiments in the Social Sciences: A Design-Based Approach*. Cambridge: Cambridge University Press.

Dunning, Thad. 2016. "Transparency, replication, and cumulative learning: What experiments alone cannot achieve." *Annual Review of Political Science* 19: 541–563.

Dunning, Thad, Guy Grossman, Macartan Humphreys, Susan D. Hyde, and Craig McIntosh. 2018. "Reflections on challenges in cumulative learning from the Metaketa Initiative." *Political Economist* 14(1): 4–9.

Dunning, Thad, Guy Grossman, Macartan Humphreys et al. 2015. "Political information and electoral choices: A pre-meta-analysis plan." EGAP Experimental Design Registry, retrievable from http://egap.org/registration/736.

Dunning, Thad, Guy Grossman, Macartan Humphreys, Susan Hyde, Craig McIntosh, Gareth Nellis, Claire L. Adida, Eric Arias, Clara Bicalho, Taylor C. Boas, Mark T. Buntaine, Simon Chauchard, Anirvan Chowdhury, Jessica Gottlieb, F. Daniel Hidalgo, Marcus Holmlund, Ryan Jablonski, Eric Kramon, Horacio Larreguy, Malte Lierl, John Marshall, Gwyneth McClendon, Marcus A. Melo, Daniel L. Nielson, Paula M. Pickering, Melina R. Platas, Pablo Querubín, Pia Raffler, and Neelanjan Sircar. 2019. "Voter information campaigns and political accountability: Cumulative findings from a preregistered meta-analysis of coordinated trials." Forthcoming, *Science Advances*.

Dunning, Thad and Susan D. Hyde. 2014. "Replicate it! A proposal to improve the study of political accountability." Blog entry, *Monkey Cage, Washington Post*, May 6, 2014.

Easterly, William. 2002. "The cartel of good intentions: The problem of bureaucracy in foreign aid." *Journal of Policy Reform* 5(4): 223–250.

Eggers, Andrew. 2014. "Partisanship and electoral accountability: Evidence from the UK expenses scandal." *Quarterly Journal of Political Science* 9(4): 441482.

Enikolopov, Ruben, Maria Petrova, and Ekaterina Zhuravskaya. 2011. "Media and political persuasion: Evidence from Russia." *American Economic Review* 101(7): 3253–3285.

Fafchamps, Marcel and Bart Minten. 2012. "Impact of SMS-based agricultural information on Indian farmers." *World Bank Economic Review* 26(3): 383–414.

Falleti, Tulia G. 2010. *Decentralization and Subnational Politics in Latin America*. Cambridge: Cambridge University Press.

Fang, Albert, Grant Gordon, and Macartan Humphreys. 2015. "Does registration reduce publication bias? Evidence from medical sciences." Unpublished manuscript, New York, NY: Columbia University.

Fearon, James D. 1999. "Electoral accountability and the control of politicians: Selecting good types versus sanctioning poor performance." In *Democracy, Accountability and Representation*, ed. Adam Przeworski, Susan C. Stokes, and Bernard Manin. Cambridge: Cambridge University Press, pp. 55–97.

Ferejohn, John. 1986. "Incumbent performance and electoral control." *Public Choice* 50(1): 5–25.

Ferraz, Claudio and Frederico Finan. 2008. "Exposing corrupt politicians: The effects of Brazil's publicly released audits on electoral outcomes." *Quarterly Journal of Economics* 123(2): 703–745.

Ferree, Karen, Danielle Jung, Robert Dowd, and Clark Gibson. 2015. "Election ink and turnout in a fragile democracy." Unpublished manuscript, San Diego, CA: University of California, San Diego.

Findley, Michael G., Nathan M. Jensen, Edmund J. Malesky, and Thomas B. Pepinsky. 2016. "Can results-free review reduce publication bias? The results and implications of a pilot study." *Comparative Political Studies* 49(13): 1667–1703.

Fisman, Raymond, Florian Schulz, and Vikrant Vig. 2014. "The private returns to public office." *Journal of Political Economy* 122(4): 806–862.

Fossett, Katelyn. 2014. "How the Venezuelan government made the media into its most powerful ally." *Foreign Policy*. Online publication.

Franco, Annie, Neil Malhotra, and Gabor Simonovits. 2014. "Publication bias in the social sciences: Unlocking the file drawer." *Science* 345(6203): 1502–1505.

Gazibo, Mamoudou. 2012. "Beyond electoral democracy: Foreign aid and the challenge of deepening democracy in Benin." *World Institute for Development Economics Research Working Paper # 2012/33*.

Gelman, Andrew. 2013. "Preregistration of studies and mock reports." *Political Analysis* 21(1): 40–41.

Gelman, Andrew, John B. Carlin, Hal S. Stern, and Donald B. Rubin. 2014. *Bayesian Data Analysis*. Online: Chapman & Hall/CRC Texts in Statistical Science.

Gerber, Alan and Neil Malhotra. 2008. "Do statistical reporting standards affect what is published? Publication bias in two leading political science journals." *Quarterly Journal of Political Science* 3(3): 313–326.

Gerber, Alan S. and Donald P. Green. 2012. *Field Experiments: Design, Analysis, and Interpretation*. New York, NY: WW Norton.

Gerber, Alan S., Donald P. Green, and David Nickerson. 2001. "Testing for publication bias in political science." *Political Analysis* 9(4): 385–392.

Gerber, Alan S., James G. Gimpel, Donald P. Green, and Daron R. Shaw. 2011. "How large and long-lasting are the persuasive effects of televised campaign ads? Results from a randomized field experiment." *American Political Science Review* 105(1): 135–150.

Gherghina, Sergiu and Alexia Katsanidou. 2013. "Data availability in political science journals." *European Political Science* 12: 333–349.

Gottlieb, Jessica. 2016. "Greater expectations: A field experiment to improve accountability in Mali." *American Journal of Political Science* 60(1): 143–157.

Green, Donald P. and Alan S. Gerber. 2015. *Get out the Vote: How to Increase Voter Turnout*. Washington, DC: Brookings Institution.

Green, Donald P., Shang E. Ha, and John G., Bullock. 2010. "Enough already about 'black box' experiments: Studying mediation is more difficult than most scholars suppose." *Annals of the American Academy of Political and Social Science* 628(1): 200–208.

Green, Elliott. 2015. "Decentralization and development in contemporary Uganda." *Regional & Federal Studies* 25(5): 491–508.

Grossman, Guy and Janet I. Lewis. 2014. "Administrative unit proliferation." *American Political Science Review* 108(1): 196–217.

Grossman, Guy and Kristin Michelitch. 2018. "Information dissemination, competitive pressure, and politician performance between elections: A field experiment in Uganda." *American Political Science Review* 112(2): 280–301.

Grossman, Guy, Macartan Humphreys, and Gabriella Sacramone-Lutz. 2019. "Information technology and political engagement: Mixed evidence from Uganda." *Journal of Politics*. Advance online publication.

Guiteras, Raymond P. and Ahmed Mushfiq Mobarak. 2015. "Does development aid undermine political accountability? Leader and constituent responses to a large-scale intervention." National Bureau of Economic Research Working Paper # 21434.

Hacker, Kenneth L. 2004. "Using cognitive measurement for analysis of candidate images." In *Presidential Candidate Images*, ed. Kenneth L. Hacker. Boulder, CO: Rowman & Littlefield, pp. 211–230.

Hamermesh, Daniel S. 2007. "Replication in economics." *Canadian Journal of Economics* 40(3): 715–733.

Harris, J. Andrew and Daniel N. Posner. 2017. "(Under what conditions) do politicians reward their supporters? Evidence from Kenya's Constituencies Development Fund." Unpublished manuscript, Los Angeles, CA: University of California, Los Angeles.

Henrich, Joseph Patrick, Robert Boyd, Samuel Bowles, Colin Camerer, Ernst Fehr, and Herbert Gintis. 2004. *Foundations of Human Sociality: Economic Experiments and Ethnographic Evidence from Fifteen Small-Scale Societies*. Oxford: Oxford University Press.

Hidalgo, F. Daniel, Júlio Canello, and Renato Lima de Oliveira. 2016. "Can politicians police themselves? Natural experimental evidence From Brazil's audit courts." *Comparative Political Studies* 49(13): 1739–1773.

Hobolt, Sara B. and James Tilley. 2014. "Who's in charge? How voters attribute responsibility in the European Union." *Comparative Political Studies* 47(6): 795–819.

Hobolt, Sara B., James Tilley, and Jill Wittrock. 2015. "Listening to the government: How information shapes responsibility attributions." *Comparative Political Studies* 35(1): 153–174.

Holland, Paul W. 1986. "Statistics and causal inference." *Journal of the American Statistical Association* 81(396): 945–960.

Hollyer, James R., B. Peter Rosendorff, and James Raymond Vreeland. 2011. "Democracy and transparency." *Journal of Politics* 73(4): 1191–1205.

Humphreys, M., R. Sanchez, de la Sierra, and P. van der Windt. 2013. "Fishing, commitment, and communication: A proposal for comprehensive nonbinding research registration." *Political Analysis* 21(1): 1–20.

Humphreys, Macartan and Jeremy M. Weinstein. 2009. "Field experiments and the political economy of development." *Annual Review of Political Science* 12: 367–378.

Humphreys, Macartan and Jeremy M. Weinstein. 2013. "Policing politicians: Citizen empowerment and political accountability in Uganda." Unpublished manuscript, New York, NY: Columbia University.

Hutchings, Vincent L. and Ashley E. Jardina. 2009. "Experiments on racial priming in political campaigns." *Annual Review of Political Science* 12: 397–402.

Hyde, Susan D. 2015. "Experiments in international relations: Lab, survey, and field." *Annual Review of Political Science* 18: 403–424.

Imai, Kosuke, Gary King, and Clayton Nall. 2009. "The essential role of pair matching in cluster-randomized experiments, with application to the Mexican universal health insurance evaluation." *Statistical Science* 24(1): 29–53.

Jauregui, Beatrice. 2016. *Provisional Authority: Police, Order, and Security in India.* Chicago, IL: University of Chicago Press.

Kalla, Joshua L. and David E. Broockman. 2017. "The minimal persuasive effects of campaign contact in general elections: Evidence from 49 field experiments." *American Political Science Review* 112(1): 148–166.

Karlan, Dean and Jacob Appel. 2016. *Failing in the Field: What We Can Learn When Field Research Goes Wrong.* Princeton, NJ: Princeton University Press.

Kasara, Kimuli. 2007. "Tax me if you can: Ethnic geography, democracy, and the taxation of agriculture in Africa." *American Political Science Review* 101(1): 159–172.

Keefer, Philip and Stuti Khemani. 2012. "Do informed citizens receive more... or pay more? The impact of radio on the government distribution of public health benefits." World Bank Policy Research Working Paper # 5952.

Kendall, Chad, Tommaso Nannicini, and Francesco Trebbi. 2015. "How do voters respond to information? Evidence from a randomized campaign." *American Economic Review* 105(1): 322–53.

King, Gary. 1995. "Replication, replication." *PS: Political Science & Politics* 28(3): 444–452.

Klašnja, Marko. 2015. "Corruption and the incumbency disadvantage: Theory and evidence." *Journal of Politics* 77(4): 928–942.

Klašnja, Marko and Joshua A. Tucker. 2013. "The economy, corruption, and the vote: Evidence from experiments in Sweden and Moldova." *Electoral Studies* 32(3): 536–543.

Klein, Joshua R. and Aaron Roodman. 2005. "Blind analysis in nuclear and particle physics." *Annual Review of Nuclear and Particle Science* 55(1): 141–163.

Kosack, Stephen and Archon Fung. 2014. "Does transparency improve governance?" *Annual Review of Political Science* 17: 65–87.

Koter, Dominika. 2013. "King makers: Local leaders and ethnic politics in Africa." *World Politics* 65(02): 187–232.

Kumar, Tanu, Alison E. Post, and Isha Ray. 2017. "Flows, leaks and blockages in informational interventions: A field experimental study of Bangalore's water sector." *World Development* 106: 149–160.

Lagunes, Paul and Oscar Pocasangre. 2019. "Dynamic transparency: An audit of Mexico's Freedom of Information Act." *Public Administration* 97: 162–176.

Laitin, David D. 2013. "Fisheries management." *Political Analysis* 21(1): 42–47.

Laitin, David D. and Rob Reich. 2017. "Trust, transparency, and replication in political science." *PS: Political Science & Politics* 50(1): 172–175.

Langston, Joy. 2003. "Rising from the ashes? Reorganizing and unifying the PRI's state party organizations after electoral defeat." *Comparative Political Studies* 36(3): 293–318.

Larreguy, Horacio A., John Marshall, and Jr. Snyder, James M. 2016. "Publicizing malfeasance: How local media facilitates electoral sanctioning of mayors in Mexico." National Bureau of Economic Research Working Paper # 20697.

Larson, Jennifer M. and Janet I. Lewis. 2017. "Ethnic networks." *American Journal of Political Science* 61(2): 350–364.

Lassen, David. 2015. "The effect of information on voter turnout: Evidence from a natural experiment." *American Journal of Political Science* 49(1): 103–118.

Lenz, Gabriel S. 2012. *Follow the Leader? How Voters Respond to Politicians' Policies and Performance*. Chicago, IL: University of Chicago Press.

Levitsky, Steven and Lucan A. Way. 2010. *Competitive Authoritarianism: Hybrid Regimes after the Cold War*. Cambridge: Cambridge University Press.

Lieberman, Evan S., Daniel N. Posner, and Lily L. Tsai. 2014. "Does information lead to more active citizenship? Evidence from an education intervention in rural Kenya." *World Development* 60: 69–83.

Lierl, Malte and Marcus Holmlund. 2016. "Pre-analysis plan: Citizens at the council, phase 1." AEA Social Science Registry, retrievable from www.socialscienceregistry.org/trials/1283.

Lierl, Malte and Marcus Holmlund. 2017. "Why information campaigns fail to increase electoral accountability: Could ambiguity aversion play a role?" Unpublished manuscript, Washington, DC: World Bank.

Lin, Winston. 2013. "Agnostic notes on regression adjustments to experimental data: Reexamining Freedman's critique." *Annals of Applied Statistics* 7(1): 295–318.

Loko, Edouard. 2007. *Boni Yayi: "L'Intrus" Qui Connaissait la Maison*. Cotonou: Tunde.

Mahieu, Sylvie and Serdar Yilmaz. 2010. "Local government discretion and accountability in Burkina Faso." *Public Administration and Development* 30(5): 329–344.

Malesky, Edmund, Paul Schuler, and Anh Tran. 2012. "The adverse effects of sunshine: A field experiment on legislative transparency in an authoritarian assembly." *American Political Science Review* 106(4): 762–786.

McCullough, Bruce D., Kerry Anne McGeary, and Teresa D, Harrison. 2006. "Lessons from the JMCB Archive." *Journal of Money, Credit, and Banking* 38(4): 1093–1107.

McDermott, Rose. 2002. "Experimental methods in political science." *Annual Review of Political Science* 5(1): 31–61.

Melo, Marcus André, Carlos Pereira, and Carlos Mauricio Figueiredo. 2009. "Political and institutional checks on corruption." *Comparative Political Studies* 42(9): 1217–1244.

Molden, Daniel C. and E, Tory Higgins. 2012. "Motivated thinking." In *Oxford Handbook of Thinking and Reasoning*, ed. Keith James Holyoak and Robert G. Morrison. Oxford: Oxford University Press, p. 390.

Monogan III, James E. 2013. "A case for registering studies of political outcomes: An application in the 2010 House elections." *Political Analysis* 21(1): 21–37.

Morton, Rebecca B., and Kenneth C. Williams. 2010. *Experimental Political Science and the Study of Causality: From Nature to the Lab*. Cambridge: Cambridge University Press.

Murphy, Charlie. 2004. "The politician and the judge: Accountability in government." *American Economic Review* 94(4): 1034–1054.

Natamba, Edward F., Lillian Muyomba-Tamale, Eugene Ssemakula, Enock Nimpammya, and Immaculate Asiimirwe. 2010. "Local government councils performance and the quality of service delivery in Uganda: Ntungamo district council score-card 2008/9." ACODE Policy Research Paper # 39.

Ndegwa, Stephen N. and Brian Levy. 2004. "The politics of decentralization in Africa: A comparative analysis." In *Building State Capacity in Africa: New Approaches, Emerging Lessons*, ed. Brian Levy and Sahr John Kpundeh. Washington, DC: World Bank, pp. 283–322.

Novaes, Lucas M. 2018. "Disloyal brokers and weak parties." *American Journal of Political Science* 62(1): 84–98.

Nyhan, Brendan and Jason Reifler. 2015. "The effect of fact-checking on elites: A field experiment on US state legislators." *American Journal of Political Science* 59(3): 628–640.

Olson, Mancur. 1965. *Logic of Collective Action: Public Goods and the Theory of Groups*. Cambridge, MA: Harvard University Press.

Paiva, Natalia and Juliana Sakai. 2014. Quem São os Conselheiros dos Tribunais de Contas. Technical report: Transparência Brasil.

Palfrey, Thomas R. 2009. "Laboratory experiments in political economy." *Annual Review of Political Science* 12: 379–388.

Paluck, Elizabeth Levy and Donald P. Green. 2009. "Deference, dissent, and dispute resolution: An experimental intervention using mass media to change norms and behavior in Rwanda." *American Political Science Review* 103(4): 622–644.

Patton, Michael Quinn. 2015. "Misuse: The shadow side of use." In *Evaluation Use and Decision-Making in Society: A Tribute to Marvin C. Alkin*, ed. Christina A. Christie and Anne Vo. Charlotte, NC: Information Age Publishing, pp. 131–148.

Persson, Torsten and Guido Enrico Tabellini. 2002. *Political Economics: Explaining Economic Policy*. Cambridge, MA: MIT Press.

Peters, John G. and Susan Welch. 1980. "The effects of charges of corruption on voting behavior in congressional elections." *American Political Science Review* 74(3): 697–708.

Pew Research Center. 2015. "Cell phones in Africa: Communication lifeline." Online publication, available at www.pewglobal.org/2015/04/15/cell-phones-in-africa-communication-lifeline.

Pitkin, Hanna F. 1967. *The Concept of Representation*. Berkeley, CA: University of California Press.

Platas, Melina and Pia Raffler. 2017. "Meet the Candidates: Information and accountability in primaries and general elections." Unpublished manuscript, Cambridge, MA: Harvard University.

Platas, Melina and Pia Raffler. 2019. "Candidate videos and vote choice in Ugandan parliamentary elections." In *Metaketa I: Information, Accountability, and Cumulative Learning*, ed. Thad Dunning, Guy Grossman, Macartan Humphreys, Susan D. Hyde, Craig McIntosh, and Gareth Nellis. Cambridge: Cambridge University Press (Chapter 6, this volume).

Prat, Andrea. 2005. "The wrong kind of transparency." *American Economic Review* 95(3): 862–877.

Przeworski, Adam, Susan C. Stokes, and Bernard Manin. 1999. *Democracy, Accountability, and Representation*. Cambridge: Cambridge University Press.

Quraishi, Shahabuddin Yaqoob. 2014. *An Undocumented Wonder: The Great Indian Election*. New Delhi: Rupa Publications.

Raffler, Pia. 2017. "Does political oversight of the bureaucracy increase accountability? Field experimental evidence from an electoral autocracy." Unpublished manuscript, New Haven, CT: Yale University.

Redlawsk, David P. 2002. "Hot cognition or cool consideration? Testing the effects of motivated reasoning on political decision making." *Journal of Politics* 64(4): 1021–1044.

Reed, Steven R. 1994. "Democracy and the personal vote: A cautionary tale from Japan." *Electoral Studies* 13(1): 17–28.

Reinikka, Ritva and Jakob Svensson. 2005. "Fighting corruption to improve schooling: Evidence from a newspaper campaign in Uganda." *Journal of the European Economic Association* 3(2–3): 259–267.

Reinikka, Ritva and Jakob Svensson. 2011. "The power of information in public services: Evidence from education in Uganda." *Journal of Public Economics* 95(7): 956–966.

Republic of Uganda, Office of the Auditor General. 2014. *Annual Report of the Auditor General for the Year Ended 30th June 2014 (Local Authorities)*. Kampala: Office of the Auditor General.

Rogoff, Kenneth. 1990. "Equilibrium political budget cycles." *American Economic Review* 80(1): 21–36.

Rosenzweig, Steven C. 2017. "Dangerous disconnect: Voter backlash, elite misperception, and the costs of violence as an electoral tactic." Unpublished manuscript, Boston, MA: Boston University.

Rubin, Donald B. 1978. "Bayesian inference for causal effects: The role of randomization." *Annals of Statistics* 6(1): 34–58.

Rubin, Donald B. 1981. "Estimation in parallel randomized experiments." *Journal of Educational Statistics* 6(4): 377–401.

Rueda, Miguel R. 2017. "Small aggregates, big manipulation: Vote buying enforcement and collective monitoring." *American Journal of Political Science* 61(1): 163–177.

Sartori, Giovanni. 1970. "Concept misformation in comparative politics." *American Political Science Review* 64(4): 1033–1053.

Schill, Dan and Rita Kirk. 2014. "Courting the swing voter: Real time insights into the 2008 and 2012 US presidential debates." *American Behavioral Scientist* 58(4): 536–555.

Sen, Amartya. 2001. *Development as Freedom*. Oxford: Oxford University Press.

Simonsohn, Uri, Joseph P. Simmons, and Leif D. Nelson. 2015. "Specification curve: Descriptive and inferential statistics on all reasonable specifications." Unpublished manuscript, Philadelphia, PA: University of Pennsylvania.

Simonsohn, Uri, Leif D. Nelson, and Joseph P. Simmons. 2014. "P-curve: A key to the file-drawer." *Journal of Experimental Psychology: General* 143(2): 534.

Sircar, Neelanjan and Simon Chauchard. 2019. "Dilemmas and challenges of citizen information campaigns: Lessons from a failed experiment in India." In *Metaketa I: Information, Accountability, and Cumulative Learning*, ed. Thad Dunning, Guy Grossman, Macartan Humphreys, Susan D. Hyde, Craig McIntosh, and Gareth Nellis. Cambridge: Cambridge University Press (Chapter 10, this volume) .

Speck, Bruno W. 2011. "Auditing institutions." In *Corruption and Democracy in Brazil: The Struggle for Accountability*, ed. Timothy J. Power and Matthew M. Taylor. Notre Dame, IN: University of Notre Dame Press, pp. 127–161.

Splawa-Neyman, Jerzy, D. M. Dabrowska, and T. P. Speed. 1990. "On the application of probability theory to agricultural experiments. Essay on principles. Section 9." *Statistical Science* 5(4): 465–472.

Stohl, Cynthia, Michael Stohl, and Paul M. Leonardi. 2008. "Elite corruption and politics in Uganda." *Commonwealth & Comparative Politics* 46(2): 117–194.

Stokes, Susan C. 2005. "Perverse accountability: A formal model of machine politics with evidence from Argentina." *American Political Science Review* 99(3): 315–325.

Stokes, Susan C., Thad Dunning, Marcelo Nazareno, and Valeria Brusco. 2013. *Brokers, Voters, and Clientelism: The Puzzle of Distributive Politics*. Cambridge: Cambridge University Press.

Strömberg, David. 2004. "Radio's impact on public spending." *Quarterly Journal of Economics* 119(1): 189–221.

Tavits, Margit. 2007. "Clarity of responsibility and corruption." *American Journal of Political Science* 51(1): 218–229.

Tetlock, Philip E. and Dan Gardner. 2016. *Superforecasting: The Art and Science of Prediction*. New York, NY: Random House.

Teune, Henry and Adam Przeworski. 1970. *The Logic of Comparative Social Inquiry*. New York, NY: Wiley-Interscience.

Tripp, Aili Mari. 2010. *Museveni's Uganda: Paradoxes of Power in a Hybrid Regime*. Boulder, CO: Lynne Rienner.

Vaishnav, Milan. 2017. *When Crime Pays: Money and Muscle in Indian Politics*. New Haven, CT: Yale University Press.

Vera Rojas, Sofía Beatriz. 2017. "The heterogeneous effects of corruption: Experimental evidence from Peru." Unpublished manuscript, Pittsburgh, PA: University of Pittsburgh.

Vivalt, Eva. 2016. "How much can we generalize from impact evaluations?" Unpublished manuscript, Berkeley, CA: University of Berkeley.

Vivalt, Eva and Aidan Coville. 2017. "How do policymakers update?" Unpublished manuscript, Berkeley, CA: University of California, Berkeley.

Wantchekon, Leonard. 2003. "Clientelism and voting behavior: Evidence from a field experiment in Benin." *World Politics* 55(3): 399–422.

Weiss, Carol H., Erin Murphy-Graham, Anthony Petrosino, and Allison G. Gandhi. 2008. "The fairy godmother – and her warts: Making the dream of evidence-based policy come true." *American Journal of Evaluation* 29(1): 29–47.

Weitz-Shapiro, Rebecca and Matthew S. Winters. 2017. "Can citizens discern? Information credibility, political sophistication, and the punishment of corruption in Brazil." *Journal of Politics* 79(1): 60–74.

Welch, Susan and John R. Hibbing. 1997. "The effects of charges of corruption on voting behavior in congressional elections, 1982–1990." *The Journal of Politics* 59(1): 226–239.

Wellenstein, Anna, Angélica Núñez, and Luis Andrés. 2006. "Social infrastructure: Fondo de Aportaciones para la Infraestructura Social (FAIS)." In *Decentralized Service Delivery for the Poor, Volume II: Background Papers*, Mexico City: World Bank pp. 167–222.

Wilkins, Sam. 2016. "Who pays for pakalast? The NRM's peripheral patronage in rural Uganda." *Journal of Eastern African Studies* 10(4): 619–638.

Winters, Matthew S. and Rebecca Weitz-Shapiro. 2013. "Lacking information or condoning corruption: When do voters support corrupt politicians?" *Comparative Politics* 45(4): 418–436.

Winters, Matthew S. and Rebecca Weitz-Shapiro. 2016. "Who's in charge here? Direct and indirect accusations and voter punishment of corruption." *Political Research Quarterly* 69(2): 207–219.

World Bank. 2010. *Uganda public expenditure review: Strengthening the Effectiveness of the Public Investment Program in Uganda*. Washington, DC: World Bank.

Zaller, John. 1992. *The Nature and Origins of Mass Opinion*. Cambridge: Cambridge University Press.

Index

Elisabeth J. Wood, *Forging Democracy from Below: Insurgent Transitions in South Africa and El Salvador*

Elisabeth J. Wood, *Insurgent Collective Action and Civil War in El Salvador*

Deborah J. Yashar, *Homicidal Ecologies: Illicit Economies and Complicit States in Latin America*

Daniel Ziblatt, *Conservative Parties and the Birth of Democracy*